D0829390

THE TRASHING OF MARGARET MEAD

STUDIES IN AMERICAN
THOUGHT AND CULTURE

Series Editor

Paul S. Boyer

The Trashing of Margaret Mead

Anatomy of

an Anthropological Controversy

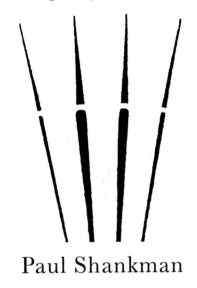

Paul Shankman

THE UNIVERSITY OF WISCONSIN PRESS

The University of Wisconsin Press
1930 Monroe Street, 3rd Floor
Madison, Wisconsin 53711-2059

uwpress.wisc.edu

3 Henrietta Street

London WC2E 8LU, England

Copyright © 2009
The Board of Regents of the University of Wisconsin System
All rights reserved. No part of this publication may be reproduced, stored in a retrieval system, or transmitted, in any format or by any means, digital, electronic, mechanical, photocopying, recording, or otherwise, or conveyed via the Internet or a Web site without written permission of the University of Wisconsin Press, except in the case of brief quotations embedded in critical articles and reviews.

1   3   5   4   2

Printed in the United States of America

Library of Congress Cataloging-in-Publication Data
Shankman, Paul.
The trashing of Margaret Mead: anatomy of an anthropological controversy /
Paul Shankman.
    p.   cm.—(Studies in American thought and culture)
Includes bibliographical references and index.
ISBN 978-0-299-23454-6 (pbk.: alk. paper)
ISBN 978-0-299-23453-9 (e-book)
1. Mead, Margaret, 1901–1978.   2. Freeman, Derek.
3. Ethnology—Methodology.   4. Ethnology—Samoan Islands.
I. Title.   II. Series: Studies in American thought and culture.
GN671.S2S53   2009
306.092—dc22
2009008197

To

SOL SHANKMAN

and to

SALLY and MICHAEL

CONTENTS

PART 5: **The Broader Issues**

ILLUSTRATIONS

FOREWORD

On August 30, 1850, Dr. John White Webster, a lecturer in chemistry at Harvard Medical School, was hanged for murder. The victim was his colleague Dr. George Parkman, a wealthy and socially prominent professor at the medical school from whom Webster had borrowed a large sum of money. After killing Parkman, the jury found, Webster had dismembered his body, burned parts of it in an oven in his laboratory, and disposed of the remnants in a privy. The deed was discovered by a suspicious Harvard janitor, who tunneled into the brick casing of the privy.

Fortunately, most disputes among academics do not end in grisly murder, but they can certainly generate intense passions. Paul Shankman's fascinating book tells of one such dispute that attracted major media coverage even though one party had been dead for five years. In fact, *The Trashing of Margaret Mead* represents an important contribution to American intellectual history for a number of reasons. At the most immediate level, Shankman has brilliantly re-created a bitter controversy that shook the field of cultural anthropology and roused broad public attention in the 1980s. Margaret Mead was not only one of America's leading anthropologists of the twentieth century but also a prominent public intellectual who played a role in U.S. cultural discourse for decades. Her classic work *Coming of Age in Samoa* (1928) brought her to public attention when she was still in her twenties, and she remained a formidable figure on the national stage until her death in 1978. She lectured at Columbia and other universities, served on government commissions, held a curatorial post at the American Museum of Natural History, wrote or edited nearly forty books, some directed to scholars and others to general readers, published hundreds of essays in the popular press, and gave endless interviews to journalists seeking her opinion on myriad subjects.

Thus, it was major news in 1983, five years after her death, when Derek Freeman, a New Zealand–born anthropologist, published *Margaret Mead and*

Samoa: The Making and Unmaking of an Anthropological Myth, a slashing attack criticizing Mead's near-iconic study as deeply flawed if not deliberately distorted to promote ideas that had as much to do with her own views on sex and with American culture of the 1920s as with adolescence in Polynesia.

Issued under the prestigious imprint of Harvard University Press, Freeman's critique not only became a cause célèbre among anthropologists but also elicited heated responses well beyond academia. While some criticized Freeman for the personal and *ad feminam* nature of his attack (and for not publishing his long-gestated work while Mead was still alive and able to defend herself), others welcomed what they saw as a salutary corrective to the inflated reputation of a media guru whose iconoclastic views on sexuality, marriage, child rearing, and other topics many had deplored as dangerously radical. Paul Shankman's balanced and judicious account is the definitive history of a memorable scholarly controversy that exposed sharp divisions among anthropologists and raised basic issues of research methodology and academic integrity in the social sciences.

\ | | /

The Trashing of Margaret Mead has still broader resonances, however, and these make it a particularly appropriate addition to the Studies in American Thought and Culture series. Indeed, it illuminates many interesting facets of American academic life and popular culture, including the role of the public intellectual. From academics of earlier eras like the sociologist William Graham Sumner, the psychologist William James, the physicist Albert Einstein, and the theologian Reinhold Niebuhr to more contemporary figures such as the economist John Kenneth Galbraith, the chemist Linus Pauling, the astronomer Carl Sagan, the historian Arthur Schlesinger, Jr., and the economist Paul Krugman, a few academics in each generation have gained wide visibility as media figures and commentators on issues of public interest—issues sometimes well beyond their area of expertise. Margaret Mead's career and the Mead-Freeman episode, Shankman makes clear, shed light on this phenomenon.

While documenting how Mead, a quintessential public intellectual, both reflected and shaped the ideological debates of her day, Shankman also suggests the capricious nature of celebrity culture in a media age when, as Andy Warhol famously put it, everyone can hope for fifteen minutes of fame. In attacking a figure of Mead's fame, even posthumously, Derek Freeman himself—in his mid-sixties and unknown outside his narrow geographic and academic sphere—gained a short-lived celebrity beyond anything he had ever experienced—a celebrity that he clearly craved and savored.

But Shankman also leaves no doubt that Margaret Mead's enduring popularity with the general public considerably outran her standing with her professional peers. This, again, illuminates a more general phenomenon: the frequent disparity between public intellectuals' popular appeal and their stature within their academic fields. Carl Sagan's public reputation as the charismatic host of public TV's *Cosmos* series far outpaced his repute as an astronomer. Linus Pauling's peace activism and enthusiasm for vitamin C as a cure for many human ills did little to enhance his standing with his fellow chemists.

As all this suggests, Shankman opens a window on the complex relationship between the world of scholarship and the world of the popular media. Freeman's attack on Mead invited media exploitation, as much of the press downplayed the methodological issues to focus on the titillating subject matter and the colorful personalities involved. Nevertheless, thanks to this controversy, many nonacademics did encounter, albeit in simplified form, serious issues relating to social science research and the nature of scholarly discourse that otherwise would have attracted little notice outside a narrow circle of specialists.

The Trashing of Margaret Mead sheds light, too, on the fraught encounter of Western anthropologists and other scholars in the social sciences and the humanities with colonized or premodern societies. In Shankman's explication of the controversy's origins, the Samoans on whom both Mead and Freeman built their careers emerge as vigorous actors in their own right, determined to set right what many took to be misleading representations of their culture. Anyone engaged with the emerging field of postcolonial studies will find much of interest in this work.

\ | | /

Finally, Shankman highlights aspects of academic life often obscured by idealized or depersonalized studies of the history of ideas. His candid examination of the personalities, human interactions, and career trajectories of Mead and Freeman makes clear the degree to which ambition, jealousy, resentment, personal quirks, intimate relationships, and idiosyncrasies of all kinds—what Isaiah Berlin called "the crooked timber of humanity"—all play a part in what can easily be misperceived as the rarefied and genteel world of scholarly publication and professional advancement.

Indeed, Shankman's dissection of this controversy contributes to our understanding of phenomena familiar to all academics yet rarely given the systematic attention they deserve. Examples abound. In the 1950s several American historians attacked a classic in the field, *An Economic Interpretation of the Constitution of the United States* (1913), the best-known work of the recently deceased historian Charles A. Beard, as ideologically driven and methodologically shoddy.[1] While these posthumous attacks involved significant historiographical issues, a full understanding of them also requires attention to the way reputations are built (and torn down) in academia and to the larger cultural context, both the reformist Progressive era that shaped Beard's seminal work and the conservative, consensus-minded climate of the 1950s that subtly or not so subtly influenced his critics.

In *The Double Helix: A Personal Account of the Discovery of the Structure of DNA* (1968), the molecular biologist James D. Watson candidly discussed the academic rivalries that helped propel the groundbreaking research for which he, Francis Crick, and Maurice Wilkins won a Nobel Prize in 1962. Even the Parkman murder case, mentioned above, generated controversy nearly 150 years later when the popular historian and media personality Simon Schama offered a partially fictionalized account of it in his 1991 book *Dead Certainties: Unwarranted Speculations.* In mixing his own reconstruction of events, conversations, and motivations with known historical fact, some reviewers complained, Schama had violated a basic credo of historians and obscured the bright line between history and fiction.

In the most bitter academic dispute of recent years, the Cornell professor Martin Bernal faced intense criticism for his work *Black Athena: The Afroasiatic Roots of Classical Civilization,* which argued for the Egyptian origins of Greek civilization and dismissed earlier Eurocentric theories as tainted by racist and colonialist biases. Like the Mead-Freeman controversy, the debate touched off by Bernal's book spilled beyond academia and transcended technical discussions of evidence to reveal deep ideological fault lines between Bernal's supporters and his critics. While Bernal had roots on the Left as the son of the British scientist and committed Communist J. D. Bernal, his fiercest opponent, the Wellesley classicist Mary Lefkowitz, was a prominent conservative activist in America's late-twentieth-century culture wars. (She also, as Shankman notes, became peripherally involved in the Mead-Freeman controversy.) While battling Bernal in *Not out of Africa: How Afrocentrism Became an Excuse to Teach Myth as History* (1997) and other polemical works, Lefkowitz also became embroiled in a dispute with a colleague in Wellesley's Africana studies department that eventually involved a lawsuit.[2]

In summary, Paul Shankman's wonderfully readable account of a memorable academic donnybrook, important in its own right, also contributes to our understanding of differing approaches to social science research, the paradoxes and pitfalls of academic celebrity in a media age, the relation of social scientists to their human subjects, and—not least—the sometimes unedifying inner history of academic discourse. I am delighted to welcome *The Trashing of Margaret Mead* to the Studies in American Thought and Culture series.

PAUL S. BOYER

Series editor, Studies in American Thought and Culture

Merle Curti Professor of History Emeritus, University of Wisconsin

ACKNOWLEDGMENTS

The Mead-Freeman controversy has been raging for more than twenty-five years, and many people—anthropologists, scholars in a variety of disciplines, Samoans, journalists, commentators, political figures, filmmakers, and others—have discussed, written, and argued about it. I have incorporated many of their ideas and data into my own scholarship. Without their work this book would not have been possible, yet acknowledging their contributions and expressing my appreciation do not imply that they would approve of or agree with my analysis and conclusions. The controversy encompasses a broad spectrum of opinion, and responsibility for the book's content is, alas, mine alone. Nevertheless, I want to thank a number of individuals, however briefly and inadequately, for their assistance and support.

There are four scholars who have been deeply involved in the controversy and who have been especially helpful in a variety of ways. James Côté, Martin Orans, Hiram Caton, and Lowell Holmes have all authored or edited books on the controversy, and Côté, Orans, and Caton read earlier versions of my manuscript and made valuable suggestions. Tracy Ehlers provided excellent early criticism of the manuscript. Roger Sanjek, Bradd Shore, Richard Shweder, Mary Catherine Bateson, Dennis McGilvray, Nancy McDowell, Reevan Dolgoy, Andrew Weissman, Dean Birkenkamp, and Jake Page also read earlier versions of the manuscript, and I want to thank each of them for offering thoughtful advice and encouragement.

Derek Freeman spent many hours with me in conversation in Canberra in 1984 and later recommended that I visit the Derek Freeman Papers in the Mandeville Special Collections Library at the Geisel Library of the University of California at San Diego. Freeman and his archive provided valuable information for the book. I also appreciate the assistance of Steve Coy and other staff members at the Special Collections Library.

Over the years a number of other colleagues and scholars have contributed to my understanding of Samoa and the controversy. They include Sharon Tiffany, Tim O'Meara, Thomas Bargatsky, Cluny Macpherson and La'avasa Macpherson, Serge Tcherkézoff, Unasa L. F. Va'a, Paul Cox, Patricia Francis, Margaret Caffrey, Mel Ember and Carole Ember, Penelope Schoeffel, Jeannette Mageo, Alessandro Duranti, Richard Feinberg, Peter Hempenstall, Mac Marshall, Jacob Love, Ben Finney, Niko Besnier, Grant McCall, Glenn Petersen, Virginia Yans, Ray Scupin, Ward Goodenough, Jane Goodall, Paula Brown Glick, Kathy Creeley, Jerry Meehl, Richard Goodman, Karla Rolff, Richard Warner, and Ben Kobashigawa. In addition to these individuals, the annual meetings of the Association for Social Anthropology in Oceania often served as a valuable forum for the exchange of ideas about the controversy.

My colleagues and former colleagues in the Department of Anthropology at the University of Colorado–Boulder have been very supportive, including Jack Kelso, Donna Goldstein, Charlie Piot and Anne Allison, Ilisa Barbash and Lucien Taylor, Carla Jones, and Carole McGranahan. My graduate students— Paulette Foss, James Dubendorf, and Tracy McNulty—provided valuable research assistance. And other former students—Anne Bolin, Evelyn Christian, Walter DiMantova, Wynne Maggi, Brion Morrisette, William Lukas, and Sarah Cook-Scalise—deserve recognition as well. In addition, generations of undergraduates in my course on the South Pacific have shared their ideas about the controversy in their papers, and I would like to extend my thanks to them.

Many Samoans have contributed to my knowledge of the islands and have been extremely generous with their time and understanding. I owe them a special debt of gratitude. In chapter 9 I discuss Samoan responses to the controversy, particularly those in published form. However, it should be apparent that I am not speaking on behalf of Samoans; they are more than capable of speaking for themselves. And I am expressing my appreciation to them collectively because they may not wish to be implicated in the controversy on an individual basis. Our conversations about Mead and their lives were informal and private rather than being part of a research project on the controversy, and they took place before I anticipated writing this book. In fact, much of my fieldwork in Samoa was conducted in the 1960s and 1970s, well before the controversy began.

During the publication process Gwen Walker and Paul S. Boyer at the University of Wisconsin Press have been extremely supportive. An A. Kayden Research Award from the University of Colorado–Boulder provided funding for permissions. In Boulder my editor, Marie Boyko, brought the loose ends of the writing process together and made this book possible.

My long-suffering family, Sally and Michael, have endured the writing of this book, and I'm sure that they as well as my many relatives and friends are relieved now that the process is complete. Finally, a special note of appreciation is owed to Pete Lillydahl, Pat Moran, Norm Aarestad, and the Epling family.

Note to Readers

For Samoan words I have used the orthography in Bradd Shore's *Sala'ilua: A Samoan Mystery*. Samoa refers to a group of islands that is culturally unified but politically divided into two separate entities: American Samoa and Western Samoa (or Samoa). American Samoa is a subgroup of islands that has been an American territory since 1900. This is where Margaret Mead did her fieldwork. Western Samoa, a separate subgroup of islands, was a German colony during the early part of the twentieth century until World War I, when it came under New Zealand colonial rule. In 1962 Western Samoa became the first independent country in the South Pacific. In 1997 the country was renamed Samoa. Derek Freeman did most of his work in Western Samoa or, as I sometimes refer to it in this book, Samoa or independent Samoa.

THE TRASHING OF MARGARET MEAD

Introduction

SHE WAS THE MOST FAMOUS anthropologist of the twentieth century. At the time of her death in 1978 Margaret Mead was America's first woman of science and among the three best-known women in the nation.[1] For many people, she was the embodiment of anthropology itself. As a successful professional woman Mead was also a heroine and role model for many younger women. *Time* magazine called her "Mother to the World."[2] As a public intellectual she spoke about sex and the family, on behalf of civil rights, for the environment, and against war. Her opinions on almost any contemporary issue were sought so frequently that it became a cliché to ask, "What would Margaret Mead say?" Easily recognizable with her cape and walking staff, she was considered an icon and an oracle.

During her fifty years in public life Mead wrote a number of popular books on topics of great public interest, including *Coming of Age in Samoa,* the book that inaugurated her career and remained her best-known work. Other popular books included *Male and Female; Culture and Commitment,* about young Americans and the "generation gap"; and *A Rap on Race,* with author James Baldwin, on race relations in the United States. She lectured tirelessly, networked broadly, served in many organizations and professional associations, and received many honors. Mead was the president of the American Anthropological Association and of the American Association for the Advancement of Science. She appeared on television and radio. And for sixteen years, between 1962 and 1978, she wrote a column for *Redbook,* a magazine read by millions of women each month.

Mead's most famous words are still cited today:

> Never doubt that a small group of thoughtful, committed citizens can change the world.® Indeed, it is the only thing that ever has.[3]

Whether displayed publicly on an antiwar T-shirt worn in San Francisco on the eve of the Iraq War in 2003 or held privately as an "idea to live by," these words resonated with large numbers of people.[4] No wonder people wanted to know what Margaret Mead would say.

If someone asked her opinion, she usually gave it, often acting as a social critic. When testifying in the 1960s before a congressional committee on marijuana use, Mead chastised adults for lecturing young people about the evils of marijuana while at the same time smoking cigarettes and consuming alcohol themselves.[5] She could casually stroll down the dinosaur hall near her office at the American Museum of Natural History in New York and engagingly discuss the implications of dinosaur extinctions for the future of the planet.[6] Mead consciously shaped much of her career around public issues, putting anthropology and herself on the map. She popularized the discipline in a way no one has before or since.

Mead was so well known that, for many Americans and others as well, her name and face were instantly recognizable. While she was still alive she had her own character in the first stage version of the musical *Hair*. After her death she appeared on a U.S. postage stamp. In 2001, the *Wall Street Journal* used a large photographic portrait of Mead in a prominent quarter-page ad about its online news service; her name appeared in tiny print, just in case someone had forgotten who she was.

Schools were named after her; so was a crater on the planet Venus. A recent book by Esther Newton humorously titled *Margaret Mead Made Me Gay* had little to do with Mead but nevertheless caught people's attention with its association of Mead and sex. An article in the *Nation* by Micaela di Leonardo titled "Margaret Mead vs. Tony Soprano" also traded on her name recognition, just as author Nicholas von Hoffman and cartoonist Garry Trudeau had decades earlier in their satirical book on Samoa, *Tales from the Margaret Mead Taproom*.

Mead touched many lives directly and indirectly. She even taught a future president of the United States. While she was a visiting professor at Yale in the 1960s, young George W. Bush enrolled in her popular undergraduate anthropology course and received one of the highest grades of his college career.[7] Apparently, though, Mead and anthropology had little influence on Bush, receiving no mention in his autobiography.

Of course, Mead was an anthropologist first, and anthropologists remember her because of her lasting contributions to the discipline. Within a span of fourteen years, between 1925 and 1939, Mead made five field trips to the South Pacific, studied eight different cultures, and published popular and professional works on most of them. After Samoa she went on to study the Manus off the coast of New Guinea, four cultures in New Guinea, the Balinese, and the Omaha of North America. While her works on these cultures are not particularly important for anthropology today, they became part of the foundation on which anthropologists built. No other American anthropologist—past or present—engaged in as much fieldwork in as many different cultures and produced as many works in as little time. And this was just the first part of her long career.

Mead was an innovator in her choice of research topics and methodologies. She was among the first anthropologists to focus on childhood, adolescence, and gender; today anthropologists approach these more wisely because of her work. She also learned to be a better fieldworker as a result of her own experiences. After Samoa, for example, Mead brought teams of male and female anthropologists to the field rather than single individuals, and she improved systematic data collection and analysis. She was among the first to use still photography and film as research tools in the field. And she applied her anthropological knowledge to the problems of contemporary life. Mead was a pioneer and a truly original scholar. Her fieldwork, theories, and methods have been criticized and continue to be reevaluated, as they should be. But this does not diminish her professional accomplishments.

Mead's most important role, however, was in the public sphere. As anthropology's ambassador to the world Mead was remembered in many ways. After her death she was awarded the Medal of Freedom by President Jimmy Carter.[8] The award noted: "Margaret Mead was both a student of civilization and an exemplar of it. To a public of millions, she brought the central insight of cultural anthropology: that varying cultural patterns express an underlying human unity. She mastered her discipline, but she also transcended it. Intrepid, independent, plain spoken, fearless, she remains a model for the young and a teacher from whom all may learn."

This was Mead's legacy, a record of accomplishment and influence rarely achieved by any individual. But all of this was about to change. Not long after her death an onslaught of criticism would commence that would call into question her very reputation.

The Controversy Begins

On January 31, 1983, the Monday morning headline in the *New York Times* announced the Super Bowl victory of the Washington Redskins over the Miami Dolphins. Other headlines were more mundane. Near the bottom of the front page, though, was a story with the intriguing title "New Samoa Book Challenges Margaret Mead's Conclusions." It would set off a firestorm of academic and public controversy lasting more than a quarter of a century.

Times science writer Edwin McDowell began the story as follows: "Two months before its official publication date, a book maintaining that the late

Derek Freeman, February 1, 1983, at his home in Australia. Photo by Glen McDonald. Courtesy of the *Canberra Times*.

anthropologist Margaret Mead seriously misrepresented the culture and character of Samoa has ignited heated discussion within the behavioral sciences."[9] McDowell was reporting on a prepublication copy of anthropologist Derek Freeman's new book, *Margaret Mead and Samoa: The Making and Unmaking of an Anthropological Myth*, a critical analysis of Mead's best seller, *Coming of Age in Samoa*. McDowell had seen the title on a list of future publications by Harvard University Press, thought it might be interesting, and requested a copy. After reading it, he sensed that it might make a good story.[10] And he was right.

Freeman's book was in part about how Samoa was puritanical and sexually restrictive rather than sexually permissive, as Mead described it. According to Freeman, Samoa was not a tropical paradise with islanders engaging in casual sex under the palms; instead, it was a repressive culture riddled with conflict, aggression, and rape. In contrast to Mead's portrayal of a relatively conflict-free adolescence, Freeman contended that Samoan adolescence was a time of storm and stress.

Freeman's book was also about the nature-nurture debate and whether Mead's emphasis on culture, as opposed to biology, was warranted. The nature-nurture debate had been a central part of Mead's argument in *Coming of*

Margaret Mead during her Samoan fieldwork, 1925–26. Library of Congress, Margaret Mead Papers, Box P25, folder 7. Courtesy of the Institute for Intercultural Studies, Inc., New York.

Age in Samoa.[11] She had noted that while puberty was a universal biological process, it did not lead inevitably to a period of adolescent turmoil in Samoa, as it had in America. For Mead, this demonstrated the importance of culture in shaping human behavior. For Freeman, however, adolescence in Samoa *was* difficult, just as he believed it was everywhere. He thus criticized Mead for being an "absolute" cultural determinist and for ignoring biology completely.[12]

In the early 1980s the nature-nurture debate was of great interest because it was one of the issues in the emerging "culture wars," with conservative American social commentators weighing in on the side of "nature" and criticizing those like Mead who were on the side of "culture."

Yet Samoa and the nature-nurture debate were not what attracted most readers' attention to the *Times* story. *Coming of Age in Samoa,* published fifty-five years earlier in 1928, had established Mead's reputation and was an important part of her legacy as America's best-known anthropologist. If Mead was fundamentally wrong about Samoa, then her reputation would suffer. Freeman's critique had the potential to tarnish if not severely damage Mead, and not merely as an anthropologist but as a public figure, a feminist, and a liberal. This was news.

Mead had died five years earlier, in 1978. There would be no debate between Margaret Mead and Derek Freeman. However, controversy began immediately, because *Margaret Mead and Samoa: The Making and Unmaking of an Anthropological Myth* was an attempt to unmake one of anthropology's almost mythical figures—Mead herself. The story in the *Times* became the opening salvo in the longest and most acrimonious controversy in the history of cultural anthropology. A virtual avalanche of media coverage followed.

The Critic

On the day the *Times* ran the story Derek Freeman was at his home in Canberra, where he had retired the previous year as professor of anthropology at the Australian National University. The *Times* article had suddenly given him recognition and exposure unprecedented in his professional career. As Freeman remembered, it was a day when "all hell broke loose."[13] He had been a somewhat obscure academic, best known among anthropologists for his professional work on the Iban, a tribal culture in Borneo. He had written very little on Samoa, although he had spent a great deal of time in the islands and knew a great deal about Samoan culture. Now that expertise would find an attentive audience.

Yet *Margaret Mead and Samoa* was not simply a scholarly accomplishment for Freeman. It was the culmination of decades of research and single-minded effort. The day that Freeman's book burst onto the public scene was a day that Freeman had anticipated for much of his life. Of that moment he wrote in his personal diary: "Now the matchless deed's achieved: determined, dared, and done."[14] It was for him a long-awaited, well-deserved moment of personal triumph.

The moment did not last very long, though. A barrage of criticism from anthropologists and others quickly followed.[15] To his critics, Freeman's portrait of Samoa, Mead, and anthropology seemed monochromatic. His evidence seemed selectively chosen, even cherry-picked. Freeman neglected information that did not fit his arguments, including information that he himself had gathered. Nor did his book provide a proper context for understanding Mead's work, the influence of *Coming of Age in Samoa,* or the nature-nurture debate. Furthermore, Freeman seemed to have more interest in confrontation than in the collaborative search for scientific knowledge.

Freeman, however, was not deterred by his critics. In the coming months and years the controversy would confirm for Freeman his own increasingly significant place in the history of ideas. In his words, he had "staggered the establishment."[16] There would be public appearances, more research, more allegedly damning evidence, and more publications. With each new version of his critique of Mead, Freeman's rhetoric escalated. Over the next eighteen years Mead's alleged "mistake" about the nature of Samoan adolescence would become the "hoaxing" of a naive, inexperienced young Mead by Samoan women. According to Freeman, Mead was unaware that Samoan women had told her innocent lies about their private lives that she sincerely believed and then published as the truth in a best-selling book.[17]

In Freeman's view Mead was not simply duped but "grossly hoaxed" by her own inexperience and by the preconceptions that she brought to Samoa. She thus became an unwitting accomplice in her own misunderstanding of Samoa. According to Freeman, Mead then "completely misinformed and misled the entire anthropological establishment," which had anointed *Coming of Age in Samoa* a sacred text.[18] Indeed, Freeman's second book on the controversy, *The Fateful Hoaxing of Margaret Mead* (1999), attempted to document exactly how she was misled by Samoans. He declared:

> We are here dealing with one of the most spectacular events of the intellectual history of the 20th century. Margaret Mead, as we know, was grossly hoaxed by her Samoan informants, and Mead in her turn, by convincing others of the "genuineness" of her account of Samoa, completely misinformed and misled virtually the entire anthropological establishment, as well as the intelligentsia at large. . . . That a Polynesian prank should have produced such a result in centers of higher learning throughout the Western world is deeply comic. But behind the comedy there is a chastening reality. It is now apparent that for decade after decade in countless textbooks, and in university and college lecture rooms throughout the Western world, students were misinformed about an issue of fundamental

importance, by professors placing credence in Mead's conclusion of 1928 who had themselves become cognitively deluded. Never can giggly fibs have had such far-reaching consequences in the groves of academe.[19]

Freeman saw himself as going beyond the mere refutation of *Coming of Age in Samoa* to a condemnation of the entire "Mead paradigm," or view of culture, a paradigm that he believed had held American anthropology back for more than half a century and had misled the whole world. The "Mead paradigm" was allegedly antibiological, antievolutionary, antiscientific, and culturally deterministic.[20] Freeman was committed to first sounding the alarm and then putting an end to what he saw as an intellectual disaster. For him, *Margaret Mead and Samoa* was not simply a necessary corrective to a "famous but flawed" scholar's work, as academic works often are. Freeman envisioned something much more profound, with his own work at the cutting edge of a new paradigm for a new millennium. He would conclude both of his books on Mead with an almost identical intellectual call to arms: "The time is now conspicuously due, in both anthropology and biology, for a synthesis in which there will be, in the study of human behavior, recognition of the radical importance of both the genetic and exogenetic and their interaction, both in the past history of the human species and our problematic future."[21]

As the controversy continued Freeman no longer cast himself as a critic of Mead but rather as a self-styled "heretic" in pursuit of the truth against the conventional wisdom of his own discipline. The title of the second edition of *Margaret Mead and Samoa,* published in Australia in 1996, became *Margaret Mead and the Heretic,* with Freeman sharing equal billing with Mead. In that same year one of Australia's leading playwrights, David Williamson, wrote a play called *Heretic* in which Freeman was the main character. Pursuing truth and reason, he was pitted against Mead, now in a secondary role, and the allegedly antiscientific establishment that had supported her.

As if to underscore the apocalyptic differences that Freeman perceived between Mead and himself, he published two articles titled "Paradigms in Collision."[22] The controversy was no longer primarily about Samoa, Mead, Freeman, or even the struggle for the soul of anthropology but about two diametrically opposed visions of humanity vying for global supremacy with world historical consequences. By the time of Freeman's death in 2001 it seemed to him that the controversy had confirmed his place in a new intellectual pantheon as well as Mead's demise. He was a heretic, a prophet whose time had come and whose work was vindicated; she had been a "holy woman" and household word who would now be consigned to the trash bin of history. For Freeman this was heady stuff. Everything was on the line.

The Mead-Freeman controversy thus involved a host of issues: Mead's Samoan fieldwork, *Coming of Age in Samoa* itself, the nature of Samoan culture, the nature-nurture debate, the credibility of anthropology, and Freeman's own contribution to paradigms of knowledge. For Freeman, these issues were seamlessly linked together with Mead's reputation. For him, Margaret Mead's Samoan scholarship was an intellectual "scandal" of momentous importance.[23] And he would press his case against her relentlessly.

Trashing Margaret Mead

Whatever the scholarly issues in the controversy, they would ultimately be linked to a public custody battle over Mead's legacy. And in the public arena Freeman was having considerable success in damaging her reputation. Within the scholarly community of anthropology, though, or at least American anthropology, *Margaret Mead and Samoa* was not well received. As we shall see, Freeman's work was sharply criticized by a variety of anthropologists and other scholars on a number of issues. Nor was Freeman able to found a new paradigm or acquire the intellectual following for which he had hoped. Yet Mead was a public figure, indeed a celebrity, and in the realm of public opinion Freeman's critique has been very harmful. Many intelligent people outside anthropology endorsed and embraced Freeman's views. Equally unsettling was that, among people who read or heard about the controversy, they remembered only, and often vaguely, that Mead *was* criticized in the media. On the basis of such imperfect knowledge, they believed that somehow she must have been wrong about Samoa. Her fame was now suspect.

When I mention Mead in lectures or casual conversations with people inside and outside of academia, they often ask, "Wasn't there some guy who showed that Mead was wrong?" or "Hasn't her work been largely discredited?" They do not remember Freeman by name or the specifics of his critique. However, they do remember that the critique appeared again and again in the media. Perhaps they remember that there was controversy over Freeman's claims. They may not believe Freeman entirely, but he raised the *question* of Mead's credibility. His argument, repeated often enough, has led people to wonder whether Mead's reputation was genuinely deserved, and, as a result, they have often abandoned the high regard in which they previously held her. Like Freeman, they might also question the integrity of anthropology as well.

Freeman's argument was authoritative, compelling, and easy to grasp, yet he presented a misleading and often inaccurate account of Mead's work, her influence, and the state of anthropology as well as a misleading portrait of Samoa. There is now a large body of criticism of Freeman's work from a number of perspectives in which Mead, Samoa, and anthropology appear in a very differ-ent light than they do in Freeman's work. Indeed, the immense significance that Freeman gave his critique looks like "much ado about nothing" to many of his critics.[24] So what was wrong with it?

Although some critics have agreed with Freeman on a number of narrow descriptive points about Samoa, they have disagreed with him on his broader portrayal of Mead and the trashing of her reputation. Mead was a resourceful and energetic ethnographer, not the naive and incompetent fieldworker that Freeman suggested. She spoke the language with some degree of fluency and worked closely with Samoan adolescent girls. There is no compelling evidence that she was "hoaxed." Mead's Samoan research is not immune from criticism, but such criticism should be based on a careful reading of the entire record, in-cluding her important professional monograph on Samoa, *Social Organization of Manu'a,* a source Freeman neglected.

Perhaps the most significant flaw in Freeman's critique was his caricature of Mead and the influence of *Coming of Age.* While her book did have great popu-lar appeal, it was not considered an important ethnographic or theoretical con-tribution within anthropology. There was, in fact, no "Mead paradigm" that anthropologists worshiped and against which Freeman could tilt. Mead was not an "absolute" cultural determinist; she recognized the importance of biology and evolution throughout her career. Freeman was able to advance his argu-ment only by very selective use of information, including the creative use of partial quotations and the strategic omission of relevant data at crucial junc-tures in his argument. The remarkable scenario that he envisioned—in which a young female anthropologist came back from her first field trip in the 1920s, wrote a popular book, transformed an academic discipline, and founded a major theoretical paradigm that framed the mindset of anthropology for decades—was a great notion but not reliable history. If there was a reigning "Mead paradigm," anthropologists and historians have yet to discover it.

Freeman constructed a "just so" story about Mead and a parallel story about himself. Just as he could not see *Coming of Age* for what it was, Freeman could not see his critique of Mead as a modest contribution to our knowledge of another culture. In his eyes his work was both revelatory and revolutionary. Just before his death in 2001 Freeman stated that his first book on Mead was "a truly historic event, that book of '83. It's the great turning point in anthropol-ogy."[25] By this time, though, Freeman's own assessment of his contribution was wearing thin with his colleagues. His attempt to tarnish Mead's reputation no longer enhanced his own.

This perspective on the controversy raises a series of questions: How was the controversy launched in the first place? How did it unfold in the media?

What were the real issues? How did Freeman become credible to the general public? Why did anthropologists for the most part find his critique of limited value, and why were their voices largely unheard? What did Samoans think of all of this? Will there be a final word, and, if so, who will have it? Can Mead's reputation be salvaged, or will Freeman prevail? These questions lead us into the story of the controversy.

Inside the Controversy: Down and Dirty

The public face of the controversy appeared first in the print media and on network television, well before the age of the Internet, and as cable TV was becoming popular. Freeman's book became news because it questioned Mead's reputation and was therefore "controversial." Controversy sold newspapers and magazines. It drew television viewers. But Freeman's book was not the only story of the period. There were other stories in 1983, the third year of the Reagan era, including news about the deepening cold war with the Soviet Union and the threat of nuclear confrontation, the bombing of Marine headquarters in Lebanon that killed 161 Americans, prolonged conflicts in Central America, and the American invasion of Grenada. In this context, there were diminishing returns to covering an anthropological controversy that the media had neither the expertise nor the resources to referee. So Margaret Mead and her critic would be relegated to the journalistic back burner. Within anthropology, though, the controversy had just begun. It would be dissected in professional journals and books, discussed at professional conferences, and gossiped about in private conversations and letters.

The controversy was fought not only in public but under the table as well. It was ugly, nasty, and dirty. In some respects it was more an intellectual smackdown than an academic debate. I was one of Freeman's numerous critics in the controversy. In fact, in a letter written in 1997 Freeman declared that I had become one of his major adversaries, a dubious achievement that I shared with three other academic critics: Lowell Holmes, James Côté, and Martin Orans.[26] Privately, Freeman referred to us as "the Four Horsemen of the Apocalypse" and promised to "vanquish" us. For him, this was a battle of epic proportions.[27] There could be no common ground.

Of course, many academic controversies have a personal dimension; that is, in part, what makes them interesting. Yet this controversy was particularly nasty. Behind the scenes Freeman was not content to simply criticize Mead and those who did not endorse his work, whom he labeled "crackpots."[28] Freeman personally threatened to sue people in court and destroy their careers. In correspondence with his critics he would accuse them of having "flagrantly monkeyed" with evidence, of misinforming readers with "scandalously inaccurate" claims, and of engaging in "ideologically-inspired postmodernist polemic."[29] Just as Freeman attacked the reputation of Margaret Mead and not simply the factual issues in the controversy, so he attacked his critics. As he stated in one interview, "You cannot convince lunatics. You know that. They are loonies. These crazy people that are around . . . do you think I can persuade the Pope or a rabbi? No, not a hope. They are in deep error, and they're happy in their error, and they can remain in their error."[30]

In print Freeman was only slightly more polite. His publications on the controversy were often filled with personal commentary designed to undermine an author's credibility. As an example, in 2001 a small Australian journal published Freeman's response to a very brief piece that I had written for the same journal.[31] In the space of three pages Freeman labeled me "a dyed in the wool Meadophile," "a zealot," "a grand master of obfuscation," "intellectually dishonest," and one of the "genuine zealots who can be expected to take their mistaken views to the grave." In addition, he noted that my work was "richly deceptive," "outright fabrication," and "a clear instance of intellectual dishonesty."[32] Although this is only part of the invective that Freeman used, gratuitous personal insult was integral to his style of argument. Freeman's rhetoric was used with gusto against virtually everyone with whom he disagreed. He was a virtuoso of the personal epithet who was energized by controversy. Bold assertions and condemnation of his critics with great moral certainty underlined the gravity of Freeman's mission.

When editors declined to publish his work, Freeman harassed them with a flood of letters demanding that his views be printed. Some editors published Freeman just to get him off their backs, while others held their ground. Michael Shermer, editor of the popular journal *Skeptic*, was deluged with correspondence from Freeman, filling almost half a filing cabinet drawer, over an article written about the controversy; Freeman demanded space for a reply. Since Shermer had already published an earlier article by Freeman, he denied his persistent requests.

Kendrick Frazier, editor of the *Skeptical Inquirer*, was also swamped by faxes from Freeman, sometimes daily, belittling Frazier and his organization for publishing articles critical of Freeman's work. Freeman demanded space for a reply, threatened litigation, and asked for an apology. In 1998 Frazier wrote to Freeman:

> We publish serious evaluations of claims and intellectual controversies within science and outside of science all the time. That is what we do. We try very much to be fair, and we offer space both to readers and aggrieved parties for response. I have done that.

In closing, I again lament your name calling and your personal attacks upon our authors. I don't find that befitting the factual intellectual arguments you say you have on your side.[33]

But Freeman did not relent. He continued to inundate Frazier and board members of the magazine with mail for another year and a half until he was provided space for a reply. In accepting his piece, Frazier's letter to Freeman concluded: "I cannot end without expressing my regret at your behavior: perhaps you don't even realize it, but you harass, intimidate, threaten, bully, invoke authority, use personal characterizations, and attempt to get people in trouble with their colleagues. Then you wonder why people try to ignore you. I am sure you are a fine scholar and perhaps even a nice person, but unfortunately I find these tactics quite unscholarly indeed."[34]

Freeman and Mead: Nothing Personal?

Although Freeman openly expressed animosity toward his critics, he maintained there was nothing personal in his critique of Mead. Anticipating that he might be accused of a personal attack, Freeman emphasized that there was nothing in his critique of her work directed at Mead herself. In his first book Freeman professed concern only with the scientific import of her Samoan research "and not with any aspect of her ideas of activities that lies beyond the ambit of her writings on Samoa."[35] He noted that he had met with Mead at Australian National University in 1964 and informed her of his critique in a long conversation. According to Freeman, they disagreed but were professional. They corresponded afterward, and Mead stated that, even if there was disagreement, it was the research itself that mattered.[36] Freeman represented himself as a gentleman and a scholar, an artful pose that, as we shall see in chapter 4, was not in accord with his actual behavior.

While Freeman trumpeted his "high regard" for Mead's achievements, he did not mention her many contributions in his books or interviews.[37] Indeed, her fifty-year career after Samoa was of little interest to Freeman except insofar as it reinforced his critique of her early work. When shown passages in *Coming of Age* that demonstrated Mead's interest in the interaction of biology and culture, Freeman insisted that she was nevertheless an "absolute" cultural determinist.[38] When read passages from Mead's later work demonstrating her interest in evolution, Freeman dismissed them as "totally irrelevant" because he was only interested in correcting her alleged "errors" in *Coming of Age in Samoa*.[39]

In his writing about Mead, Freeman subtly attempted to establish his superiority and authority while undermining hers. In *Margaret Mead and Samoa* he repeatedly referred to her as "Miss Mead," a literary convention from the early twentieth century that was gradually abandoned.[40] Although historically appropriate, the use of "Miss Mead" left the impression among some contemporary readers that she was not a full-fledged professional when she went to Samoa. In fact, she had completed her Ph.D. dissertation. And in his examination of Mead's motives and research methods, Freeman's language bordered on the personal. For example, in *Margaret Mead and Samoa* he referred to the "beguiling conceit" of early American anthropologists such as Mead and her mentors, Franz Boas and Ruth Benedict.[41] When asked if he considered this a personal slight rather than a professional comment, Freeman confidently replied that his phrasing could not possibly have been personal since no single individual was referred to; rather, according to Freeman, *"all"* of these scholars were guilty of "beguiling conceit."[42]

In his second book Freeman argued that, contrary to critics who viewed his portrait of Mead as a personal attack, he had actually salvaged Mead's reputation from certain ruin. After contriving to demonstrate that Mead was "fatefully hoaxed" by her own inexperience and preconceptions, Freeman stated that, although Mead was misled by Samoans, she did not *deliberately* mislead her readers. She was simply unaware that the hoaxing ever took place.[43] Freeman therefore acquitted Mead of being an outright fraud by arguing that she was merely a foolish young woman who never understood the nature of her error.

In private conversations and interviews Freeman was more candid about his view of Mead. In his conversations with me he dropped any pretense of his "high regard" for her and made no secret of his disdain. He disparaged Mead openly and often, berating her personally as well as professionally, including his allegation that Mead had an affair with a Samoan; that, for Freeman, confirmed her questionable moral character.[44] With other colleagues he had been critical of Mead since at least the late 1940s, stating to some of them that he was going to ruin her reputation. As anthropologist Robin Fox, a colleague of Freeman, remembered, Freeman "seemed to have a special place in hell reserved for Margaret Mead, for reasons not at all clear at that time."[45]

In the public relations campaign that helped drive the Mead-Freeman controversy Freeman explicitly connected his critique of Mead's Samoan research to the fate of her reputation. He linked the two in such a way that it seemed axiomatic that if his critique was accurate, then Mead's reputation was doomed. This was of great significance to Freeman, who stated that he "may have written a book that will create the greatest denouement in the history of anthropology so far, not excepting Piltdown Man!" He believed that his "matchless deed" would cause Mead's reputation to diminish at the rate of a "falling body" (32 feet per second squared), a prediction that Freeman made two years before his first book on Mead appeared in print.[46] This was personal, not merely academic.

Freeman was so convinced of the cogency of his critique that he did not think it would be necessary for others to closely reread Mead's Samoan work or her fifty years of research and publication after Samoa. There would certainly be no need to carefully evaluate Freeman's claims and evidence because, he asserted, he had already checked and rechecked his findings to such an extent that they would meet the highest standards of evidence in a court of law. Freeman proclaimed: "We can demonstrate conclusively as in a court of law that her formulations are in error. . . . The evidence that I have presented is final, it's devastating."[47] The use of a legal metaphor is worth noting because Mead and Freeman were not in a court of law. Mead was not on trial. She was dead. Yet Freeman seemed to believe that he was prosecuting a case against her rather than simply providing an academic review of her work. In one sense he was correct. There was a court of public opinion, and in this court Freeman was having considerable success in making his case.

What This Book Is About

The Mead-Freeman controversy unfolded within this highly charged and very personal context. As one of the participants in the controversy, I have written and spoken about it since its inception in 1983, and Freeman and I have presented our respective positions in print.[48] My own views about the controversy have been influenced by these experiences, and I will share some of them later in the book as well as offering a more conventional account of the controversy and the issues. While this book is not a purely academic endeavor, it is also not idle gossip posing as scholarship. Some of the book is based on personal experience, and some of it presents Freeman and Mead in an all-too-human light. It is difficult, if not impossible, to understand the genesis and development of the controversy without understanding the people involved, especially Derek Freeman. As Robin Fox commented, the controversy "would have never happened without Derek's particular personality meshing with the cultural clashes of the time."[49]

This book is the story of the controversy as it was conducted publicly and as it developed privately—the story of the assault on Mead's reputation. The book is intended for a general audience as well as an academic one because Margaret Mead was at least as important to the public as to her anthropological colleagues. Of course, many anthropologists are all too familiar with the controversy. But most anthropologists and the public have not heard this story, and this book may help in understanding the players, the layers, the issues, how the controversy was waged, and what was at stake. Because the book is for the public as well as for academics, many of the names, references, and additional information that would normally be in the body of an academic book can be found in the chapter notes at the end of the book. For anthropologists and other scholars, this may be an inconvenience, but for a more general audience readability may be enhanced.

The book is organized into five parts: the development of the controversy, the two protagonists in the controversy, Samoa, and the broader issues in play. Part 1 begins with a discussion of how the controversy developed in the popular media. Parts 2 and 3 take an extended look at Derek Freeman and Margaret Mead and how their own lives were sometimes reflected in their work. Part 3 also reviews Mead's fieldwork in Samoa and the context in which Mead wrote *Coming of Age,* that is, how Americans in the late 1920s interpreted her words about sex and Samoa. What was her audience thinking? Part 4 is about specific issues concerning sexual conduct in Samoa. Beginning with a review of how Samoans saw the controversy, these chapters discuss how complex sexual conduct can be, changing over time even within a single culture. Part 5 analyzes in detail Freeman's assertion that Mead was "hoaxed" by Samoan women who told Mead innocent lies that she then published as the "truth" in *Coming of Age in Samoa.* It also examines Freeman's more general belief that his work and Mead's represent "paradigms in collision." Finally, the book concludes with some of my own views of the controversy and its significance for anthropology, the general public, and the reputation of Margaret Mead.

My argument is certainly more sympathetic to Mead than to Freeman. Yet one of the misconceptions about the controversy is that there are only two sides to it. There are other voices, including Samoan voices. There are shades of gray. There are unanswered questions, and there are pieces of the controversy that do not always fit together as they should. This is a complex story, and I have tried to provide enough detail not only to tell the story clearly but to give readers a sense of how it unfolded.

To summarize briefly, Margaret Mead was a highly visible and easily recognizable target. At first glance, Freeman's critique seemed formidable and authoritative. Much of the media, a number of intelligent individuals, and at least some of the public were readily persuaded of the validity of Freeman's critique of Mead and did not look further. Different audiences found Freeman's critique useful for different reasons. American conservatives embraced Freeman as one of their own because they believed that people like Mead were responsible for the moral decline of the country. Sociobiologists and later evolutionary psychologists found Freeman's critique of Mead helpful in advancing their scientific agenda about human nature. While Freeman's views differed from those of some of his supporters at the outset of the controversy, he came to appreciate their shared interest and encouraged their criticism of Mead.

Many academics and most American anthropologists remained skeptical of Freeman's critique. Over time relatively obscure scholars working in the academic trenches effectively questioned Freeman's argument, but their voices went largely unheard in the media. These scholars, mostly anthropologists, were well qualified to do the research but limited in their ability to reach the public. The media were able to reach the public initially but were not well equipped to pursue the controversy in its many dimensions. As time passed, the media moved on to other stories, other personalities, and other controversies.

Although Mead's personality and motives were scrutinized by Freeman, both the media and professional anthropologists have been less interested and more reluctant to consider Freeman's motives and personality. Nevertheless, they are important to the controversy and a story within a story. While the factual issues in the controversy can be examined separately and without reference to the anthropologists involved, understanding the development of the controversy and its consequences for Mead's reputation (and Freeman's as well) cannot be separated from his personality and motives.[50] This is why the first part of the book spends considerable time on the message and the messenger— Freeman's critique of Mead and the man himself.

Ultimately, this book tries to extricate Mead's reputation from the quicksand of controversy. This should have been a relatively easy task, but twenty-five years of bad publicity have been difficult to overcome. Mead was not a saint or a holy woman. She was a human being who was fully aware that she had been, in her words, "publicly discussed, lambasted, and lampooned."[51] Her work in general and her Samoan work in particular have never been free from criticism. In fact, many American anthropologists have been ambivalent about her scholarship. Nevertheless, despite the flaws of *Coming of Age in Samoa,* she contributed much to our knowledge of Samoa and other cultures and gave so much to anthropology and the world at large that she deserves to be remembered for her many positive contributions. Freeman, although intellectually gifted and very knowledgeable, was no hero. Despite his contributions to revising the ethnographic record on Samoa, he seriously compromised this effort by attempting to trash Mead's reputation.

PART 1

The Controversy and the Media

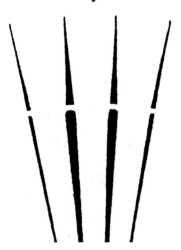

\ 1 /

The Controversy in the Media

A CLICHÉ HAS IT THAT journalists write the first version of a story. Other professionals then follow up with more thorough and perhaps more accurate versions. Yet for the general public, a journalist's version may not simply provide the first version they read or hear about; it may be the *only* version. There are so many stories and so little time to learn more about each one of them. How much attention can we pay to a single story? And if the story is a good story, a story that we *want* to believe, does it really matter if it is true?

This is how the Mead-Freeman controversy began. It was a good story. Suspicion stalks fame, and because some famous individuals, including prominent scientists, have turned out to be wrong or even fraudulent, Margaret Mead might well become suspect. Freeman's critique had the appeal of an exposé, putting the controversy on the public's radar. He would have the first word, and Mead's defenders would have to play catch-up. Freeman seemed to have understood that the more provocative the argument, the more memorable the headlines, the more attention the controversy would draw, and the more difficult it would be for critics to overcome his initial message and its momentum. Public curiosity is more likely to respond to exaggerated claims than to straightforward explanation and boring details, and Freeman provided a sense of high drama that his critics did not.

In considering the controversy from a marketing point of view, the media's decision to make it a major news story must have been easy. Mead was highly visible, Freeman's critique seemed believable, Harvard University Press was publishing the book, and Freeman's credentials as a scholar were impeccable. Add to this mix the intoxicating subject of sex in the romantic South Seas, and the story must have seemed irresistible. It would certainly be entertaining.

The reputable *New York Times* covered the story first, two months before the book was published.[1] Following front-page coverage in the *Times*, wire services carried the story around the globe. Provocative headlines highlighted the brewing drama with titles like "Mead Theories about Samoa Are Challenged"

(*Washington Post*, February 3, 1983), "Bursting the South Sea Bubble: An Anthropologist Attacks Margaret Mead's Research in Samoa" (*Time*, February 14, 1983), "Trouble in Paradise" (*Washington Post*, April 3, 1983), "Samoa: A Paradise Lost" (*New York Times Magazine*, April 24, 1983), "Tropical Storm: New Book Debunking Margaret Mead Dispels Tranquility in Samoa" (*Wall Street Journal*, April 14, 1983), and "Angry Storm over the South Seas of Margaret Mead" (*Smithsonian*, April 1983). Most major newsmagazines and newspapers had similar headlines.

Then there were the op-eds. And here the controversy, nominally about an academic subject, became political. Conservative columnist William Rusher wrote that not only was Mead wrong about Samoa but that in the name of science she had encouraged the loosening of moral constraints, condoned "free love" in America, and contributed to the moral decay of a nation.[2] Liberal columnist Ellen Goodman wrote that Freeman's book was akin to intellectual grave robbery and that when all was said and done, Freeman was not the brave man he pretended to be, seeking truth at all costs. Goodman surmised that Freeman sensed that people would enjoy watching the famous fall from their pedestals, especially a well-known woman like Mead. And Freeman's work was "full of the muckraker's delight in portraying Mead as a fraud, and more than a little patronizing."[3] Goodman also noted that as more academics weighed in on the controversy, Freeman's certainties about Samoa looked less convincing.

The controversy appeared on the editorial pages of newspapers as well. The *Wall Street Journal*, the nation's premier business paper, commented on July 25, 1983, "It now appears that she [Mead] was bamboozling readers with her tales of sexual permissiveness in Samoa." And an editorial in the *Denver Post* on February 15, 1983, titled "Anthropological Crisis" stated that as a result of the controversy "the real loser may be anthropology's reputation as a science. If its methods haven't made quantum jumps forward since Mead's day, the whole discipline might find a better home in creative literature."

This Just In . . .

News organizations quickly developed lists of experts, apart from Freeman, who could be called for their opinions about Freeman's critique. But because Freeman's book was not yet available, these experts could not provide "expert" opinions. For example, as the story broke, a *Los Angeles Times* science writer called me for my opinion.[4] Although I had worked in Samoa and knew the broad outlines of Freeman's argument, I told the reporter that I hadn't read the book because it had not been published yet and this made the playing field uneven. We agreed that both reporters and anthropologists were in an awkward position. Because the anthropological "jury" was still out—indeed, it had not yet been convened—it was difficult to provide useful information. Everyone had to rely on the media's representation of Freeman's critique rather than the book itself. So William Rusher's op-ed, cited earlier, was based on a report of what Freeman said. (Ellen Goodman's column, in contrast, came out only after she had read the book and *Coming of Age in Samoa*.)

In this sense, the way the controversy developed was unusual. Most academic controversies begin (and end) in professional journals, never emerging from their academic cocoons. Experts, having read articles in these journals, know the data and arguments. Should a controversy then appear in the media, they can knowledgeably respond. But Freeman's book was provided to the media before his argument appeared in academic journals. Although some experts knew of Freeman's antipathy to Mead and perhaps the general contours of his argument, the book came as a surprise to almost everyone. The story was also time-sensitive for the media. Newspapers and magazines could not wait for weeks or months for experts to get their hands on the book and read it, or they would be scooped by competitors working on the same story. To cover the controversy as breaking news, they had to tell the story immediately. So reporters who had not read the book were asking questions of experts who had not read the book.

Both reporters and experts did their best, and some articles in the newspapers and news magazines, which were under the most immediate time constraints to get the story out, were surprisingly good. But they would not be as thorough as the professional books and articles on the controversy that were published months, years, and even decades later. News cycles and academic research cycles are very different. Academics have the luxury of doing research over extended periods of time, but the great advantage of thoroughness in the academic research cycle cannot offset the immediacy of the news cycle. As a result, the large academic literature on the Mead-Freeman controversy gradually published over the next two and a half decades received very little media attention. Remaining within academia and outside the public's view, these publications would arrive long after the newsworthiness of the story had peaked.

Anthropologists and journalists have different goals and work in different environments. Anthropologists, like other academicians, choose their research topics and are expected to be experts, spending years conducting research in the field, archives, and/or libraries. Unlike most journalists, academics have advanced degrees and hold university posts; they typically specialize on a few narrow topics over the course of their academic careers rather than being generalists, as journalists often are. Furthermore, there are few deadlines for academics. They have time to develop complex arguments over many years as they write lengthy articles, book chapters, and books. In contrast, newspaper jour-nalists are assigned stories, operate under strict deadlines and word limits, are closely scrutinized by layers of editors, must use "sound bites" to capture the at-tention of a mass audience, and must be ready to move on to the next assign-ment. Journalists also have limited space to get across the essence of a major story with little opportunity for follow-up; Edwin McDowell's front-page story on the controversy in the *New York Times* ran only 2,129 words. In contrast, a single academic journal article on the controversy might run 10,000 words, and this could be just one in a series of articles, commentaries, and rejoinders.

The publication impacts in journalism and academia are also different. A typical news article on the Mead-Freeman controversy in a major metropolitan area could have a hundred thousand readers, perhaps more. A typical article on the controversy in a major anthropological journal might have a few hun-dred actual readers, perhaps fewer, even though the journal has thousands of subscribers. It is not surprising, then, that academics and journalists sometimes have problems communicating with each other. They are writing for different purposes and addressing different audiences.

Reporters and journalists are looking for brief answers, while academics often have difficulty condensing their arguments for public consumption, espe-cially when being interviewed. Reporters cannot use the extended and nu-anced arguments that academics wish to provide. They prefer compelling one-liners and concise statements. For example, prior to an interview that I did for a BBC television documentary on the controversy in 2006, I asked the pro-ducer, who was very well informed, how short my answers should be—thirty seconds, sixty seconds, perhaps two minutes?[5] He asked me to keep my answers to fifteen to twenty seconds per question and to state my opinion clearly and without qualification or nuance. This was a challenge.

Yet the producer faced a more daunting task. He had to edit dozens of hours of interviews with other anthropologists and experts into a one-hour documentary that had to be marketable as well as conforming to the protocol of the series. Which themes would be emphasized? Whose answers would fit into the story line that he and his team were developing for the documentary? Which answers would survive the editing process? Just as in their interactions with print journalists, the scholars on film did not have control of the final product.

For journalists writing about the controversy, the multiple claims by Free-man and the counterclaims by his critics were sometimes confusing and could seem equally valid. One possible conclusion about this chaotic state of affairs was that the controversy told people more about the fractured state of anthro-pology than about Mead or Samoa. As one reporter wrote: "A dispute touched

off by a noted scholar's scathing attack on the late Margaret Mead has provided rare insight into the peculiarities of social science, and may tell more
about anthropology than it does about Samoa."[6] In fact, this kind of argument
encouraged the public to think that there might be something amiss in the
house of anthropology, a point of view that Freeman himself endorsed.

This type of outcome is part of a more general process in which the media
find controversy itself more important than the issues and data. The process
begins with Professor X publishing an idea. The media pick up the story. When
scholars familiar with the evidence question Professor X's work, he denounces
them in the highest moral tones and engages in personal attacks on them. Battle
lines are drawn, and he has now become the "controversial" Professor X. His
ideas are taken seriously by nonspecialists, including journalists. Soon he has
become a familiar figure in the media, while his critics have difficulty finding an
audience to demonstrate the weaknesses in his argument. It was through this
process that Freeman, like Professor X, gained popular attention and that anthropology itself was called into question.[7]

This process repeated itself after the publication of Freeman's second book
on the controversy, *The Fateful Hoaxing of Margaret Mead,* in 1999. Although it did
not receive the attention of his first book, its reception nevertheless reinforced
Freeman's original message about Mead. A review in the *Wall Street Journal*
stated that Freeman's account of Mead's hoaxing was so convincing that the
only logical conclusion should have been that Mead was a charlatan, although
Freeman did not make that claim.[8] Local papers also picked up the mantra.
And when *Time* magazine named Margaret Mead one of the greatest scientists
of the twentieth century and the century's "foremost woman anthropologist,"
this assessment was qualified with the comment: "It seems Mead accepted as
fact tribal gossip embellished by Samoan adolescent girls happy to tell the visiting scientist what she wanted to hear."[9] This, of course, was a version of Freeman's argument, but it had become so commonplace that it was unnecessary to
mention him by name.

The drumbeat of Freeman's message continued. In 2001 the conservative
Institute for Intercollegiate Studies listed *Coming of Age in Samoa* as the *worst* non-
fiction book of the twentieth century, citing Freeman's work as its inspiration.[10]
In 2005 Mead's book received honorable mention on a list of the "Ten Most
Harmful Books of the 19th and 20th Centuries" compiled by the conservative
magazine *Human Events.*[11] In 2008 *Coming of Age* was ranked number nine in
Benjamin Wiker's *Ten Books That Screwed Up the World,* a main selection of the
Conservative Book Club, with Mead now in the company of Hitler, Marx and
Engels, and Lenin.[12] What a change from the 1930s, when *Coming of Age in Samoa*
had been nominated one of the hundred *best* books by women "in this century

of progress."[13] It had been considered a classic. But now things were different. Freeman's message, once controversial, now seemed like common sense.

Coming to Mead's Defense

As a result of the media feeding frenzy surrounding Freeman's initial critique of Mead, there was a professional backlash in anthropology against his work based on the flaws that scholars saw in his refutation of Mead. Whatever valid points Freeman had made were overshadowed by problems so serious that the initial reviews by anthropologists were almost as scathing as Freeman's critique of Mead. Mary Catherine Bateson, dean of the faculty at Amherst College and Mead's daughter, immediately challenged the original *New York Times* story in a letter to the editor.[14] In the first published review by an anthropologist, written for the *New York Times Book Review,* George Marcus called *Margaret Mead and Samoa* a work of "great mischief."[15] Other anthropologists concurred. David Schneider labeled it "a bad book."[16] Annette Weiner found it "deeply destructive."[17] These anthropologists were scholars with high profiles and solid credentials. Even anthropologists who normally disagreed with each other on major theoretical points were virtually unanimous that Freeman had manufactured much of the controversy and that parts of his critique were inflammatory rather than scholarly.[18]

While reviews by people outside of anthropology were often favorable, within anthropology there was increasing criticism of Freeman. In November 1983, a few months after the actual publication of Freeman's book, the controversy came to a head at the annual meeting of the American Anthropological Association (AAA), the largest organization of professional anthropologists in the world, with several thousand members. A special panel of anthropologists was convened to discuss the controversy before an audience of hundreds of professionals.[19] The panelists as a group were almost uniformly critical of Freeman, although their individual critiques differed in focus and content. And while the panel was about Freeman, Mead, and Samoa, Freeman himself had not been invited to respond.

Then, in its business meeting, the association passed a motion expressing members' dismay that *Science 83,* a reputable popular magazine, had recommended Freeman's book for holiday gift giving. The motion noted that the book "has been consistently denounced by knowledgeable scholars as being poorly written, unscientific, irresponsible and misleading" and that the magazine's recommendation was a disservice to its readers and social scientists.[20]

When the panelists' papers appeared together in a special section of the association's flagship journal, *American Anthropologist,* Freeman was not invited to respond in the same issue, although he was provided space in a subsequent issue.[21] In all of these actions Freeman had been shut out and condemned by the AAA without, in his view, adequate time or space for a response. Incensed, he wrote a long letter to the AAA that was published in the association's newsletter. Freeman reprimanded the association for treating his work unfairly, believing that there was a rush to judgment about his critique that was decidedly unscientific. He stated: "In both science and scholarship it is a quite fundamental principle that substantive issues must be settled with reference to the relevant empirical evidence, and that this evidence must be objectively considered before any conclusion be reached."[22] Freeman saw the AAA's action not simply as an injustice but as a demonstration of how many cultural anthropologists had come to embrace "a prescientific ideology in which hallowed doctrine lords it over empirical realities." He concluded: "And so, infuriated by what had happened, some American anthropologists turned to rhetorically restoring the mystical aura of their totemic mother [Mead] and the popular repute of her long-acclaimed *magnum opus* while, at the same time, doing everything imaginable to discredit me. This onslaught, which began in February 1983, and was sustained over many months was flagrantly *ad hominem*."[23]

Freeman demanded a retraction of the AAA motion criticizing *Science 83* and his work but did not receive one. He also believed that his critics were an organized cabal, rallying around Mead with one voice. In fact, they were a diverse lot and, for the most part, unorganized. There were dozens of criticisms. Most anthropologists were temperate in their response to Freeman and not critical of Freeman as a person. Some critics accepted parts of Freeman's critique; others rejected it almost entirely. Still others criticized both Mead and Freeman. A few did not take sides but simply tried to provide more context and more data so that there would be greater understanding of the issues. The critics tended to work separately and on different parts of the controversy. Some would stay in for the duration of the controversy, while others moved into or out of the controversy as their interests dictated.

Freeman did not retreat from any of the criticism. He vigorously responded to each of his critics, demanding vindication. He also had his own set of defenders, although fewer in number than Mead's. Anthropologists George Appell and T. N. Madan, Freeman's intellectual biographers, reflected on the controversy, stating:

> Many of us who view anthropology as a scientific and scholarly discipline have been shaken to our foundations by the response Freeman's book has received in American anthropology. The attempts to silence him, to deprive him of the right of adequate reply to published criticism, the failure to weigh the issues critically and put them to Popperian test, the conscious

and unconscious misreading of his argument including denial of the facts on which it is based, and attempts to divert attention from his refutation by *ad hominem* attacks have astonished many of us. We find these reactions counterproductive in a discipline that is supposedly seeking the truth. For all those skilled in social analysis and willing to turn this analysis upon their own social lives, such reactions are the reactions of a belief system that is out of touch with the real world and unresponsive to change.[24]

While deploring the lack of objectivity of his critics and denouncing their willingness to attack him personally, Freeman did not see any evidence that he had manipulated "relevant empirical data," as his critics claimed, or that he had made *ad hominem* attacks on Mead or those who disagreed with him. Instead, Freeman believed that his virtue had been questioned, not just his scholarship, hence the moral indignation in many of his replies. Yet slowly but surely, academic responses to Freeman's critique developed a momentum of their own. Careful scholarship into almost every nook and cranny of the controversy, published in numerous books and far more numerous articles, was overwhelmingly critical. As usual, though, these critiques remained within the halls of academia. The nooks and crannies of the controversy were far too complex for the public to fathom and, in many cases, for anthropologists as well.

\2/

Selling the Controversy

B ECAUSE FREEMAN'S CRITIQUE of mead was so widely reported
and so hotly contested in the media, it is reasonable to assume that his books
were best sellers, or at least that they were widely read. Yet they were not. *Margaret Mead and Samoa* received excellent advance publicity, appeared in headline
stories in most major newspapers and many magazines around the world, received endorsement as a Book of the Month Club alternate, and was excerpted
in *Discover* magazine.[1] Because news coverage was so extensive, Harvard University Press increased the print run from seven thousand to thirty thousand
copies.[2] Nevertheless, for all of the publicity surrounding it, *Margaret Mead and
Samoa* went through only one edition. *The Fateful Hoaxing of Margaret Mead,* released by Westview Press, a small commercial publisher based in Boulder,
Colorado, had more modest sales, with one printing each in the hardback and
paperback editions. It was not the reading of the books themselves that generated so much attention but rather the *publicity* surrounding the books.

In providing Freeman's book to the *New York Times,* Harvard University Press
was doing what publishers normally do. The mainstream media—newspapers,
magazines, and television shows—expect publishers to send galley proofs of
forthcoming books months before actual publication so that reviewers will be
able to review them in time for their arrival in bookstores, that is, when they are
"news." If a publisher waits until a book is available for sale, reviewers may
consider it "old news." When Harvard University Press was criticized for disseminating prepublication copies of the book to the media, the director of public relations at the press responded that buzz sells books: "Academics don't
understand publishing. We have a responsibility to make money and generate
sales for books as well as to publish books with something important to say. . . .
It seemed appropriate to break the story in the news media because we knew
there would be a lot of interest. . . . People say it's been known for years that
Mead made mistakes in interpreting Samoa, but the general public hasn't
known that."[3]

The print media covered the story as a major event, but it was television that provided a broader audience. In fact, Harvard University Press decided to bring Freeman from Australia to the United States for a publicity tour. This was unusual for a university press, but in early 1983 the momentum surrounding the controversy was building, and Freeman was in demand. The controversy was so newsworthy that he was quickly booked on major TV talk shows.

Harvard was taking a risk in asking Freeman to appear on national TV because he was an untested commodity. Would he be media savvy? Or would he be a liability? As it turned out, Freeman was more than up to the task. He appeared on PBS-hosted TV interviews and on ABC's *Good Morning America* with anchor Barbara Walters. Mary Catherine Bateson, a scholar in her own right as well as Mead's daughter, was included on the program for "balance." While these appearances may not have enhanced book sales very much, they did expose Freeman and his message to a wide audience.

In Person:
Freeman's Appearance on the *Donahue* Show

Freeman's most important network television appearance came on March 18, 1983, on NBC's *Donahue* show, which was taped in Chicago. *Donahue* was the top-rated daily TV talk show of its era, with millions of viewers, at least the equivalent of the *Oprah Winfrey Show* today. And Phil Donahue was an intelligent and articulate host, willing to engage his guests, who included not only show business celebrities but also scientists and scholars. During its many years on the air the show earned nineteen Emmy Awards.

Donahue took a keen interest in current events and was no novice when it came to the nature-nurture debate, which became the focus of the show. At the time, Donahue was writing a book on human nature, later published as *The Human Animal,* and so he had a familiarity with this issue. To provide some counterpoint to Freeman, the producers invited Mary Catherine Bateson and Bradd Shore, then an associate professor of anthropology at Emory University in Atlanta. Shore was an excellent scholar who had authored an ethnography on Samoa and had reviewed Freeman's book for a potential publisher prior to its publication.[4] He was therefore one of the very few people truly qualified to appear with Freeman. Bateson, with her deep knowledge of her mother's life and work, was equally appropriate to comment on Freeman's book.

Freeman's appearance gave a broad American audience a look at the person at the center of the controversy. On TV the tone of Freeman's voice and his use of body language, absent in print, were now visible. They provided a dimension to understanding the man that had been missing in the print media.

Donahue was a live, hour-long show, and Phil Donahue did not interrupt the show with constant commercial breaks. He encouraged discussion, give-and-take, and humorous banter, and he was able to draw Freeman out in a way that other appearances and interviews had not.

The first segment of the show lasted for almost twenty uninterrupted minutes, something that could not happen on today's network TV. Yes, the *Donahue* show was commercial television, but Donahue's viewers were being not only entertained but educated. It is worth reviewing this show in some detail because it included not just a disembodied argument by Freeman but the person himself. What follows is an account of the first segment of the show. While the visual dynamic of the show cannot be re-created, this account may provide some understanding of how Freeman communicated his message and how the audience responded to it.[5]

Donahue chose to focus his questions on the nature-nurture debate because he and Freeman shared a common interest in this topic. Although Donahue was sympathetic to Mead (she had been a guest on his show years earlier), she would not be the immediate focus, nor would there be much discussion of Samoa. As Donahue, Freeman, Bateson, and Shore all sat around a small table next to each other in front of the studio audience, Donahue began by joking with Freeman that since the show was now being viewed in Australia, he had "better behave; they're watching you at home."

Donahue then asked Freeman if he was a "nature guy," that is, someone who gave priority to the role of innate biology as opposed to learned culture. Freeman immediately corrected Donahue, stating that he was not a "nature guy." Nor was he in favor of sociobiology, which was a new academic discipline that postulated a biological basis for social behavior. In fact, Freeman declared that he was perhaps anthropology's "most trenchant critic" of sociobiology, forcefully denouncing its formulations as "null, ludicrous, and void" because it did not take into account human choice.[6]

Donahue wondered if this meant that Freeman was discounting the role of biology. After all, Donahue suggested, if humanity is like a pie, then the role of the anthropologist was to determine the size of the piece we call nature and the size of the piece we call culture. Freeman quickly connected this question to Margaret Mead, replying that in Donahue's brief introduction to the show he had stated that Mead believed that nature was part of the pie. However, Freeman argued that in *Coming of Age in Samoa* Mead excluded nature "totally."

Freeman noted that his book was designed to correct Mead's view and that he favored an approach in which both biology and culture were equally important. Quoting a renowned biologist, Freeman stated that it is "silly" to try to determine whether nature or culture is more important. Relishing the moment,

Freeman gestured to the studio audience with outstretched hands and received a round of applause.

Donahue replied that he was not sure that most anthropologists would accept this reasoning and asked Freeman if he was suggesting a simple fifty-fifty split between nature and culture. Freeman responded that he did not know what the exact relationship was and that further research would decide this question. While this exchange had taken only two minutes, it did help clarify Freeman's position and highlight his engaging presence. Freeman clearly enjoyed being on camera and interacting with the audience. He was comfortable, confident, authoritative, and the center of attention.

At this point, Mary Catherine Bateson commented that she did not think that humans were like pies either and that drawing an exact line between culture and nature in that metaphorical pie would be difficult. Nevertheless, she noted that anthropologists were interested in the relationship between culture and biology and that there was never an anthropologist who did not take biology into account. For instance, fieldworkers could hardly ignore activities like eating, sleeping, and giving birth. While Bateson was making this point, the TV camera panned to Freeman, whose head and body were bowed forward with his hands clasped, expressing his silent disagreement with her.

Bateson continued her discussion of the relationship between nature and nurture by noting that every person requires food to survive, but how people satisfy this biological need varies from culture to culture. Biology may help us understand the nutritional components of food consumption, but cultures organize their use of food differently. People share food and have feasts, going well beyond minimal nutritional requirements. Bateson made these points about culture calmly and patiently, ignoring Freeman's negative body language.

Bradd Shore then entered the conversation by noting that Freeman was not entirely wrong to argue that there was a time when anthropologists did not pay much attention to biology as we know it today. They paid attention to "race." In the early twentieth century there was no clear distinction between race and culture, and all too often people thought in terms of racial inferiority and superiority. The concept of culture as separate from race was not firmly established, and Shore noted that Freeman's own book discussed how racist viewpoints, posing as science, led people to believe that biology was destiny. Donahue commented that racist thinking of this kind led to Nazi Germany. He then situated Mead in the 1920s, going to Samoa and discovering that adolescence was not a direct result of biology but a process shaped by culture.

Freeman challenged Donahue once more, instructing the audience that Margaret Mead "quite specifically reached the conclusion, and we can cite the page, that biology could be eliminated *totally* and that behavior could be explained *purely* in cultural terms." Turning to Shore, Freeman stated that Shore's own recent book was in this tradition, entirely excluding biology, and that Shore's work was "cultural determinism to an extreme degree." Turning to Donahue, Freeman explained that "they [Shore and Bateson] like to tell you that they now know about biology," but "they pay no attention to it whatsoever. They couldn't begin to pass an elementary examination in it."

The derogatory intent of these remarks was clear, but Shore and Bateson did not respond directly to this provocation. Instead, Shore took the high ground, noting that science was a cooperative enterprise, not the work of lone individuals. He commented that his job as an anthropologist was to provide the best description of Samoan culture that he could and then let people like Freeman improve on it. Donahue asked Shore what his disagreement with Freeman's book was. Shore said that it was not the book that Freeman should have written. Freeman humorously feigned his dismay, to the delight of the audience.

Shore explained that Freeman had been promising a book about nature and culture in Samoa for the past twenty years. Instead, Freeman's book was a simple refutation of Mead with no other contribution. The logic of Freeman's argument was that Mead said X, but the evidence said Y. Shore deplored the appearance of anthropology as a shooting gallery where someone's work was merely discredited; instead, he felt that scholarly discussion should build on earlier work to produce better scholarship.

"I Am a Scientist"

Freeman was adept in positioning himself in opposition to Shore and Bateson even when they were in apparent agreement. He seemed to understand that the show could be viewed as a sporting event, where opponents could aggressively score points when possible and gently persuade the audience when convenient. His perspective differed from that of Bateson and Shore, who viewed the show as an educational opportunity, offering the public a better sense of anthropology as well as providing a form of damage control to prevent Freeman from further trashing Mead.

Freeman did not feel constrained by the conventional rules of professional etiquette. Responding to Shore's point about logical argument, Freeman lamented: "Dear, dear, dear, Professor Shore, I want to tell you to go away and get educated." He then broke into a short lecture on the philosophy of science, noting that his book was dedicated to the philosopher Sir Karl Popper, who pioneered the idea of falsification. Instead of assembling all the evidence in favor of a particular position, Popper had asked scientists to think about what evidence could count against their position. In this way errors would be corrected, and this is what Freeman said he was doing in his book—eliminating Mead's errors.

Bateson noted that Freeman's logic in refuting Mead was flawed and that while Freeman had done valuable work in Samoa, other anthropologists did not agree with him on many issues. Shore noted that Mead was not absolutely wrong on Samoa but rather was incomplete. He stated that for this reason refutation was insufficient and that what was necessary was to correct, add, and acknowledge what had been learned from earlier work. Shore and Bateson agreed, "That's called science." Speaking to Donahue and ignoring Shore and Bateson, Freeman forcefully interjected that he was "quite sure that these two people had never studied Sir Karl Popper. They don't understand. They don't know what science is about. *I am a scientist!*"

At this point, still prior to the first commercial break in the show, things became more heated, with Freeman passionately enumerating his credentials as an expert on Samoa in an attempt to enhance his standing with the audience. He noted that he

- was fifty years of age when he did his research in Samoa;
- was a professorial fellow at an advanced research institute;
- was asked to write the book by Samoans to correct Mead's "travesty";
- wrote the book for Samoans and gave it to them;
- received support from the Prime Minister of Western Samoa (Shore quietly noted that the Prime Minister had criticized Freeman's book);
- had the book reviewed by Samoan scholars for errors at the National University of Samoa;
- had been appointed as Foundation Professor of Anthropology at the National University of Samoa.

At this point Donahue speculated that this may have been a political appointment. Freeman rejoined: "Now that's not arrogant; that's nasty."

Donahue persisted, raising the issue of Margaret Mead's many accomplishments and commenting that Freeman's book had totally destroyed her reputation. Freeman responded by saying that in his book he did not make a single personal statement about Mead and that he was not interested in her personally. In fact, he said that he admired, indeed deeply admired, many of Mead's achievements. Bateson replied that she was pleased to hear this but that it was not evident in the book and that Freeman's version of Mead was a "caricature" created by quotations taken out of context. Referring to Mead's alleged errors in *Coming of Age,* Freeman stated that when an error is committed in science, it is committed at a particular moment in time. And with a dramatic flourish he exclaimed that it did not matter whether the error was made "a *thousand* years ago!"

Donahue Asks the Difficult Question

Donahue could not resist raising the issue of Freeman's personality, which he had been tiptoeing around during the early minutes of the program. It was the issue that people were most reluctant to discuss because it would seem like a personal attack on Freeman and outside the boundaries of professional etiquette. Yet Donahue raised it directly. "Dr. Freeman, sir. Part of the problem that we have here is your own posture. You do cut a bit of the messianic personality as we speak. Now I'm not here to suggest that you have a personality change in order to be on our show. But it has been called to your attention and some of the reviewers of your book make the point that . . ." Freeman, clearly anticipating this line of questioning, interjected: "I'm a difficult man?" Donahue continued: "You're difficult, somewhat self-indulgent, and appear to be intolerant. Could it be that you erred, this wonderful professor of anthropology from Australia?"

Freeman responded to Donahue with passion and conviction: "*I am a scientist!* Now, a scientist is a difficult man. Do you know what 'difficult' means? It means 'not facile,' and that comes from the Latin [word] *facilis,* which means 'easily done,' and I am not easily done. I am obsessive. Of course, every scientist is obsessive. How do you think they got the DNA molecule? Crick and Watson [the discoverers of DNA] sat there, and that's what 'obsessive' means."

Donahue calmly replied that he knew what Freeman was talking about because, not to brag, James Watson had appeared on Donahue's show. But Donahue felt that if someone attacked Watson he would probably let the argument rise or fall on its own merits. Freeman agreed with Donahue and said that this was exactly what Freeman was doing in his book. Holding up a copy of *Margaret Mead and Samoa,* Freeman slowly placed it in front of the camera and said, "This book may have errors in it. If any of you [in the audience] or any people listening in can find an error, I plead with you to let me know, and I will correct it at once. I might say that there are other books that have never been corrected," a not-so-subtle reference to *Coming of Age in Samoa.*

In the following segments of the show Freeman, Bateson, and Shore took questions from the audience. Freeman continued to cite his own credentials—his love of Samoa, his desire to be buried there, his knowledge of the Samoan language, and his prestigious Samoan princely title. Referring to Shore, he told the audience that "this boy [Shore] is untitled," meaning that Shore did not hold a Samoan chiefly title and was therefore not in the same league as Freeman. Shore wryly replied that he did have a title, a Ph.D. Freeman's body language also conveyed his "alpha male" status as he asserted his own authority and experience while diminishing the authority and experience of others. Unwilling to engage in a dialogue with Bateson and Shore directly, he often referred to them obliquely, even as they sat within an arm's length of each other.

In subsequent question-and-answer segments with the audience, Freeman was more gracious, generous, and far less adversarial. He could be engaging and agreeable and had a sense of humor. Yet Donahue sensed that Freeman believed that right-thinking people should agree with him. If they did not, they deserved his stern judgment. And Freeman's judgment could be severe. During one of the commercial breaks in the show he leaned over and quietly informed Shore that he would ruin his career. This was not an idle threat. Freeman contacted the University of Chicago and asked them to rescind Shore's Ph.D. He also requested that Columbia University Press withdraw Shore's ethnography on Samoa from its publications.[7]

While the show did not teach the audience very much about Mead, Samoa, anthropology, or the nature-nurture debate, it did showcase Freeman's personality. By the end of the hour Freeman's self-admitted difficult manner was apparent not only to Donahue but to millions of others who had tuned in, including his sponsors at Harvard University Press. As criticism of Freeman mounted during his tour, he felt that Harvard was not standing up for him and considered the press "rather cowardly."[8] This was especially so after the American Anthropological Association meeting in 1983, where criticism of Freeman's book was quite open. After evaluating the situation, Harvard University Press sold the rights to *Margaret Mead and Samoa* to Penguin, which brought out the paperback edition to a limited readership.

A Documentary Film with "Startling New Evidence"

Although Freeman's 1983 tour of the United States had given him unprecedented exposure, he became disenchanted with media coverage, returned to Australia, and was wary of future appearances. Nevertheless, opportunities arose that offered Freeman new platforms for his views. In the mid-1980s one such opportunity was provided by filmmaker Frank Heimans, who wanted to produce a documentary about the controversy. This effort would involve close cooperation between Heimans and Freeman and yielded a fifty-one-minute documentary entitled *Margaret Mead and Samoa*. Released in 1988, the film won several awards. Not only was it widely available for classroom use, it was also picked up by the Discovery Channel and shown on cable TV. The film was so well made that National Geographic considered purchasing it in 2000 and, with minor changes, reissuing it for TV.[9] The documentary continues to be marketed for teaching purposes and is recommended instructional viewing by the Human Behavior and Evolution Society. It is also the most publicly available form of Freeman's hypothesis about the "hoaxing" of Mead and therefore worth reviewing.

The documentary begins with a narrator introducing the controversy and contrasting the respective positions of Mead and Freeman on Samoa. She then states in dramatic fashion, with Polynesian drums pulsating in the background, that the controversy will "be resolved by startling new evidence presented in this program." About midway through the documentary the "startling new evidence" of Mead's alleged hoaxing is presented by an elderly Samoan woman, Faʻapuaʻa Faʻamū. According to the film, Faʻapuaʻa was "Mead's chief informant" in Samoa during her stay in the islands in the 1920s. Presented as a living witness to Mead's fieldwork, Faʻapuaʻa gives testimony that will decide the controversy once and for all.

In his first book on Mead, Freeman had cautiously *suggested* that Mead *might* have been misled in Samoa by young girls telling her innocent lies about their private lives, but he did not have evidence that this was actually the case. It was not until the making of the documentary in 1987 and the interview with Faʻapuaʻa that the hoaxing argument moved from the realm of speculative possibility to foregone conclusion. In a short interview sequence in the documentary, Faʻapuaʻa remembered with remarkable clarity how, sixty years earlier, she and her friend Fofoa were asked by Mead what girls did at night. These two women, who were slightly older than Mead at the time, jokingly told her that they spent their evenings "out with boys." Faʻapuaʻa swore that she and Fofoa could not believe that Mead would ask them such an inappropriate question and so, in jest, they innocently lied to Mead, never conceiving that she would repeat these innocent lies about their private lives in a book.

As the film continues, other Samoans comment, reinforcing the idea that Mead did not understand their culture. Freeman then appears, declaring his commitment to truth and his love for Samoa. At the conclusion of the documentary he appears once more, this time in outdoor gear driving his modified armored troop carrier through the Australian bush, one of his favorite activities. This final image reinforces the filmmaker's view of Freeman as an intellectual road warrior and iconoclast. With the controversy apparently resolved, Freeman drives off as a heretic in the best sense of the word. To most viewers the film seems objective and definitive in its portrayal of Mead as a naive young woman in contrast to Freeman, the mature and dedicated scholar.

Behind the Scenes

Faʻapuaʻa's testimony took the controversy in a new direction and would become the centerpiece of Freeman's continuing critique of Mead. In his first book Freeman attempted to show that Mead was wrong about Samoa. After Faʻapuaʻa's testimony Freeman focused his attention primarily on *how* Mead got Samoa wrong. He published a crucial portion of the interview in 1989, and it became the basis for his second book in 1999 as well as for several articles on the controversy.[10] Yet there is very little context provided in the documentary about the circumstances surrounding the interview. What seems straightforward to the viewer becomes more problematic when the story behind the filming is presented. Consider the appearance of Faʻapuaʻa. How did she come to be in the film?

Unknown to the viewing audience, Faʻapuaʻa became part of the documentary when the film crew, with Heimans and Freeman, arrived in American Samoa to shoot generic footage of the islands. Before the project began Heimans had requested permission to film from the government of American Samoa, and the official involved happened to be the son of Fofoa, Faʻapuaʻa's friend and accomplice in the alleged hoaxing of Mead. Galeaʻi Poumele, Fofoa's son, was a high-ranking Samoan chief and Secretary for Samoan Affairs in the government in American Samoa. Although Fofoa had died in 1936, Galeaʻi Poumele knew that Faʻapuaʻa was still alive on Taʻū and that she was the only person remaining there who had known Mead in 1925–26. He accompanied Heimans and Freeman to Taʻū and personally introduced them to her. Poumele had read Freeman's book about Mead and was quite critical of her. He filmed the interview with Faʻapuaʻa in Samoan, which was translated with subtitles in the documentary.

Faʻapuaʻa had little prior knowledge of what the interview would entail. As she noted in later interviews, she did not know what had become of Margaret Mead after her visit to Samoa in the 1920s, even though they were so close that she thought of Mead as a sister.[11] Although some Samoans in the islands had been openly critical of Mead for decades, apparently Faʻapuaʻa did not know that Mead was an anthropologist, nor was she aware that Mead was an author. She also did not know that Mead had died over a decade earlier, although this was international news and Faʻapuaʻa was living in Hawaiʻi at the time. Faʻapuaʻa did not know of Freeman's book, of his critique of Mead, nor of the controversy that it had generated. She learned of these things for the first time during Galeaʻi Poumele's visit to Manuʻa with Freeman, Heimans, and the film crew.

Galeaʻi Poumele told Faʻapuaʻa what he believed Mead had written about the private lives of Samoan girls. He thought that Mead had characterized his own mother, Fofoa, as a "slut," and he conveyed this sentiment to Faʻapuaʻa.[12] Under these circumstances and believing that she might be the source of the idea that Samoan girls were sexually active, Faʻapuaʻa responded to Galeaʻi

Poumele by stating that, as a devout Christian, she wished to make a "confession" of her wrongdoing on film.[13]

Freeman recalled: "Fa'apua'a had made this confession, she later explained, because when she had been told by Galea'i Poumele and others about what Mead had written about premarital promiscuity in Samoa, she suddenly realized that Mead's faulty account must have originated in the prank that she and her friend Fofoa had played on her when they were with her on the island of Ofu [part of the Manu'a group] in 1926."[14]

Given the awkward position that Fa'apua'a found herself in, she may have sincerely felt that she was responsible for Mead's views, or at least what had been portrayed to her as Mead's views, and that she should confess. Given the Samoan taboo on women discussing sex with men as well as the etiquette of rank, Fa'apua'a's answers to this high-ranking male chief may have reflected a desire to uphold the virtue of Samoan womanhood as well as the reputations of herself and Fofoa. That is, she may have felt pressure to provide socially acceptable answers to Galea'i Poumele's questions.

The documentary does not mention Galea'i Poumele's relationship to Fa'apua'a or her desire to make a confession, nor does it mention Freeman's relationship to Galea'i Poumele and Heimans. It simply presents Fa'apua'a's testimony as the "smoking gun" that accounted for how Mead got Samoa wrong. And that is how Heimans and Freeman saw it. For Freeman, the interview with Fa'apua'a was beyond anything he had dreamed of in his investigation of Mead's Samoan research. As he listened to Fa'apua'a's confession during the filming of the documentary, he let out a "yelp" of surprise; the sequence had to be reshot.[15] Immediately after filming ended, Freeman privately told Heimans that this interview was the most significant moment of his life.[16]

Margaret Mead and Derek Freeman: The Play

With the release of the documentary in 1988 and the publication of the interview with Fa'apua'a in 1989, the hoaxing hypothesis gave new life to the controversy. This hypothesis was also featured in David Williamson's play *Heretic*, which was performed for audiences in Australia and New Zealand in the late 1990s. It included Mead and Freeman as major characters, imagining them as they might have been and how the controversy might have turned out had Mead lived to debate Freeman.

Freeman met Williamson after the playwright authored a piece in the *Weekend Australian* arguing against a feminist who had stated that there was no human nature. Freeman read Williamson's piece and sent him his own essay on

Mead, "Paradigms in Collision."[17] Williamson faxed him back immediately and asked about the possibility of a play based on Freeman and his critique of Mead. Freeman and Williamson developed a close relationship in the course of writing the play; they also shared a mutual interest in evolution and were members of the Human Behavior and Evolution Society.

Freeman was so taken with the idea of the play that he provided Williamson with very personal information about his life that was little known prior to the play's performance. Freeman informed the playwright about his relationship with his mother, his sexual problems, his mistreatment of his wife, Monica, his obsession with Mead, his delusional episode in Borneo, and his difficulties with his colleagues. Both Derek and Monica Freeman read drafts of the play and provided feedback to Williamson about it. Although quite sensitive about his personal history, Freeman was not angered by Williamson's inclusion of it in the play because he felt Williamson supported his conclusions. At the end of the play the hoaxing hypothesis was presented as evidence that Freeman was ultimately correct and that Mead was wrong. As for the inclusion of his personal flaws, Freeman commented: "Being shown to have foibles is a small price to pay. I also have a defence, which is that this is only David Williamson's version of me. But it is pretty close to the truth."[18]

Williamson did not spare Mead either, basing his portrayal of her mostly on Freeman's characterization. In the text version of the play Mead appeared as a serious but misguided scholar, but in the Sydney Opera House production Williamson set the play in a hallucinogenic dream by Freeman, a setting based on Freeman's negative memories of the turbulent 1960s, which both Freeman and Williamson believed were partly Mead's responsibility. The director of the play suggested an LSD-like theme and dressed the characters in psychedelic costumes, much to Williamson's dismay. In a bizarre twist the Mead character appeared in various celebrity guises as Marilyn Monroe, Jacqueline Kennedy Onassis, and Barbra Streisand.[19]

Freeman loved the play and attended several performances in both Australia and New Zealand, five in Sydney alone. As he proudly announced, "David has bared my soul to the world."[20] Williamson used Freeman's language and arguments throughout the play. He was close enough to Freeman to have written a play not simply about him but for him as well. In the introduction to the play published by Penguin, Williamson candidly stated that he believed that both Mead and Freeman were limited by personal flaws: "Mead's passions for sexual expression and for status and recognition lead her to crucial errors of judgement that result in the generation of one of the century's enduring myths, and perhaps even the social upheaval of the Sixties themselves. Derek's passion to control and dominate, nurtured by his mother's ambitions and his own genetic drive, caused him to mistreat the one person in the world he loves above all others, his wife Monica."[21]

Yet Williamson was convinced that Freeman was a genius and that his achievements went far beyond his critique of Mead. As he said of Freeman: "His intellectual and creative achievements are in fact far more substantial and prescient than this. It is my belief that he stands among a handful of thinkers in this century who have brought us close to answering David Hume's question about our ultimate nature."[22] This view was shared by Freeman, who explained: "The world is such a complicated place and so complex that understanding it is something that must be reserved for just a few people. I think I'm one of them."[23]

From Heretic to Hero

In 1996, the year that the play was first staged, Freeman's updated version of *Margaret Mead and Samoa* was republished in Australia as *Margaret Mead and the Heretic* and became the number one best seller in the sciences in Australia. A feature story about him appeared in Sydney's major newspaper.[24] And a small society, the Australian Skeptics, named Freeman their Skeptic of the Year. In Australia in the late 1990s Freeman had become a celebrity once more. And in 1999, when his second book on Mead was published, favorable media coverage continued.

The endorsements on the dust jackets of Freeman's two books demonstrated that support for Freeman's critique of Mead came from some very well-known, intelligent people, including distinguished scientists like Ernst Mayr, Niko Tinbergen, and Richard Dawkins; prominent science writers like Martin Gardner and John Pfeiffer; and academics in the humanities like Bruce Mazlish and Mary Lefkowitz.[25] Only one of the endorsements came from an anthropologist, Ashley Montagu. None of these endorsers was familiar with the breadth of research on Samoa, and only Gardner had written anything more substantial than a dust jacket comment or review or provided more than passing reference in support of Freeman's critique. Nevertheless, this list of individuals was impressive, and their praise was often lavish.

Mary Lefkowitz, a professor of classics at Wesleyan University, stated on the dust jacket of Freeman's second book on Mead her belief that "in *Margaret Mead and Samoa*, Derek Freeman showed conclusively that Margaret Mead was wrong; in *The Fateful Hoaxing of Margaret Mead* he shows how she managed to misunderstand Samoan customs so completely. Both anthropologists and everyone who cares about the truth should regard Freeman (rather than Mead) as a 'culture hero' for our times and society."

On the same dust jacket Martin Gardner, a science writer and former mathematics columnist for *Scientific American,* observed: "Margaret Mead's admirers will continue to raise howls of protest, but Derek Freeman's conclusions are unshakable. Mead's reputation will continue to go downhill, and her most famous book has become worthless. The sad facts are all detailed in Freeman's account of Margaret's gullibility." Gardner's endorsement was especially significant because he had made a career of exposing scientific frauds and hoaxes, and he had followed the controversy over the years. Gardner's conviction that Freeman's exposé was "irrefutable" was a tribute to Freeman's skills of argumentation.[26]

So it was that the controversy sprawled across the public landscape during its first two decades, with Freeman receiving substantial support and recognition from publishers, writers, scientists, columnists, reviewers, filmmakers, playwrights, and intellectuals. Despite his notoriety within anthropology, many people outside the discipline found Freeman's critique persuasive and worthy of praise. Indeed, they provided him with a measure of fame.

PART 2

Derek Freeman

\3/

Derek Freeman, the Critic

FAME CAME LATE IN LIFE for Freeman, and it was almost entirely based on his role as Mead's critic, a term that often accompanied his obituaries.[1] His name would be forever linked to hers. For most of his career, though, Freeman was not famous or even well known. Rather, he was an academic recognized for his solid scholarship on the Iban, a tribal culture in Sarawak on the island of Borneo. Freeman studied the Iban for thirty months between 1949 and 1951, writing his Ph.D. dissertation on them. Trained in the tradition of British social anthropology, Freeman was also known for his more general work on social organization.[2] Although not considered a great theorist, he was considered to be a very good ethnographer, one of the highest compliments that a cultural anthropologist can receive.

It was only after Margaret Mead and Samoa was published, more than a year into his retirement, that Freeman gained international visibility. Freeman's extensive research in Samoa had taken a back seat for most of his professional career. He had gone to Samoa as a schoolteacher in the early 1940s, spending three years there and becoming a very good amateur anthropologist in the process. In the mid-1960s he spent two more years conducting research in the islands. Yet he published relatively little on Samoa and almost nothing on Mead for most of his professional career. In the 1940s he authored some short archaeological reports on the islands, in 1959 and 1978 he wrote two historical essays on Samoa, and in 1964 he published a critique of other anthropologists' work on Samoan social organization.[3]

So when and how did Mead's Coming of Age in Samoa and Mead herself come to occupy a place in Freeman's work, indeed becoming the project of a lifetime? Fortunately, we have learned a good deal about Freeman from his career history, brief biographies, his personal and professional correspondence, interviews, and anecdotes told by friends and colleagues.[4]

The Early Years

Freeman was born in New Zealand in 1916 and grew up into a very tall, imposing young man. His father owned a fashionable men's barbershop in Wellington, and his mother was a member of a prominent local family. Although neither of his parents had attended university, his mother was nevertheless dedicated to her son receiving a good education. Young Freeman was very bright and independent. At sixteen he renounced his Presbyterian upbringing and avidly read Darwin and Huxley as well as the rationalist philosophers.

Freeman attended Victoria University College in Wellington, where he studied psychology and philosophy. As a college student, Freeman was outspoken on political issues. In his own words, he was very much a radical and a "firebrand."[5] Freeman was secretary for a campus group opposing the fascists in the Spanish Civil War, and in 1937 he publicly challenged the German consul in New Zealand over Germany's treatment of Jews. Freeman was also a member of a successful debating team, was prominent in drama, won poetry prizes, and was literary editor of the student newspaper. He was a fine track athlete and an accomplished mountaineer.

Anticipating that he would have to support himself, Freeman enrolled in a teachers' training college program and taught young schoolchildren for two years before going to Samoa. In 1938, while still an undergraduate, he took a graduate seminar from Earnest Beaglehole, a psychologist who had done ethnographic work in Polynesia and who knew Margaret Mead. Beaglehole became his mentor, and Freeman accepted from him the view that culture shaped behavior from birth through childhood and into adulthood. Although he did not formally study anthropology during his university education, Freeman nevertheless became an ardent believer in the importance of culture as the key determinant of human behavior.

But this was not the only intellectual influence on Freeman. As literary editor of the student newspaper, Freeman reported on various speakers who came to Wellington, often debunking them. In 1939 he attended a talk by Jiddu Krishnamurti, the prominent Telugu mystic, expecting to be disappointed. Yet Freeman was impressed as Krishnamurti lectured the audience on how to reach enlightenment through critical inquiry. He took two weeks off from teaching in order to have private meetings with Krishnamurti. The philosopher would have a powerful influence on Freeman. Later in life and after more fully studying Asian religions, Freeman became, in his own words, "an evolutionary Buddhist."[6]

By the late 1930s Freeman was becoming increasingly disenchanted with his home country and a world that was on the brink of war. As he stated, "I wanted to escape from New Zealand society and the whole suffocating atmosphere there."[7] After seeing an ad for schoolteachers in Western Samoa, then a New Zealand colony, Freeman signed up. Although he knew very little about the islands, Freeman did have a strong interest in other cultures.

Samoa and World War II

Freeman arrived in Western Samoa in April 1940, shortly after World War II began in Europe but before the Japanese attack on Pearl Harbor. He was twenty-three years old, almost the same age as Mead when she arrived in American Samoa fifteen years earlier. As a schoolteacher, he instructed European and part-Samoan children in the port town of Apia, where the New Zealand colonial government was headquartered. During his free time he became interested in archaeological research. Freeman also struck out on his own, meeting Samoans and learning the Samoan language, in which he became quite proficient. He was also sympathetic to the organized Samoan resistance movement against colonial rule known as the Mau.

By 1942 Freeman was spending much of his time in the village of Sa'anapu on the south coast of the island of Upolu, a few hours by horse from Apia. At that time there was no road to the village, so it remained quite traditional. In Sa'anapu he was adopted by a Samoan family and given a princely title in the Samoan system of rank. He thus became a true participant-observer in Samoan village life. The emotional bond that Freeman forged with his Samoan family and the villagers of Sa'anapu led him to further identify with Samoans and especially Samoan chiefs.

Freeman was fascinated with Samoan culture and learned a good deal about it. The islands became one of the great interests in his life. Nevertheless, Freeman did not "go native." He associated with Europeans as well. Part of the time he lived with a European physician in a large European house across from the hospital in the port town. Freeman loved sailing and became secretary of the Apia Yacht Club. He also had a personal relationship with a Samoan nurse.[8] However, World War II would soon take priority over these interests.

Freeman had been a pacifist prior to the Japanese bombing of Pearl Harbor on December 7, 1941. As the war overwhelmed the Pacific, he became a member of the New Zealand Defense Force in Western Samoa. Although this set of islands was never attacked, it did serve as a staging base for tens of thousands of American troops headed to the western Pacific front. After three and a half years in Western Samoa, Freeman left in November 1943, returning to New Zealand, where he joined the navy. Viewed as officer material, Freeman was sent to the United Kingdom for further training. He would serve in the Far East for the remainder of World War II and was in Borneo when the war ended.

Freeman's sometimes eccentric and contentious personality made him a memorable figure even then. During his naval service in World War II he worked with Keith Sinclair, another seaman who would become one of New Zealand's best-known historians. In his autobiography Sinclair recalled:

> Freeman was an extraordinary person, a big man with a big voice. He was an intellectual extremist or fanatic. At one time he had been a Marxist and had helped start Wellington's left[-wing] bookshop. Later he was converted to the doctrines of Krishnamurti. After we reached England he broadcast to the Pacific in Samoan for the BBC, greatly impressing our officers. Near the war's end, and after we were commissioned, he went to the Admiralty and convinced someone he was a linguist. He was sent to a course in Japanese. He had gone over the heads of our own officers and displeased them. Whether for that reason I do not know, but he was taken off the course and sent out East in a landing-ship tank, a hazardous assignment. However, he was in Borneo when the Japanese surrendered, and some officers surrendered to him. He acquired an impressive collection of their swords.[9]

Sinclair also remembered their drinking and carousing. Well before his academic career formally began, Freeman was already a larger-than-life personality.

Although Freeman did not see actual combat during his tour of duty, he ended up convalescing in an Australian hospital.[10] While there he was able to spend two months at the Mitchell Library in Sydney poring over records of missionary work in colonial Samoa. Freeman was serious about learning as much as he could about the islands. In 1946, after the war, Freeman applied for and received support for further education. He became a student in anthropology at the London School of Economics and Political Science (LSE), where he wrote an academic postgraduate diploma thesis titled "The Social Structure of a Samoan Village Community" in 1948. The thesis was long and detailed and remains his most important ethnographic contribution on Samoa.[11]

While at LSE Freeman continued to make an impression. His friend and colleague Robin Fox recalled that Freeman was a "living legend" in the department. Once, while doing research, Freeman went missing for days, and "people got worried. They searched through a warren of dusty rooms that was the library then, and finally found him way back in some recess, unshaven and glassy eyed, poring over early volumes of a professional journal. 'I've been reading backwards through the Journal of the Royal Anthropological Institute,' he explained. 'I'm at 1907.'"[12]

Freeman's knowledge of Samoa was very helpful to him in seminars, where he was surrounded by more advanced students. In 1947 Freeman was invited to lecture on Samoan social structure at the University of Oxford and LSE. These presentations, vital to his professional development, drew uneven evaluations. As Freeman remembered, one of the great British social anthropologists in attendance, Meyer Fortes, found his ideas about social structure to be "exceedingly brilliant," but his own advisor, Professor Raymond Firth, who had done fieldwork in Polynesia, described the analysis as "pretentious" and "nonsense." Maurice Freedman, a fellow graduate student, called it "mere phantasy."[13]

Although Samoa was the subject of his postgraduate diploma thesis and of continuing interest to him, Freeman took advantage of an opportunity to return to Borneo, where he had been stationed when the war ended. He began his doctoral research in 1949, studying the Iban, a truly exotic tribal culture most noted for their practice of head-hunting. As Freeman stated, they were "the first really wild people I'd seen."[14] Yet Freeman was not interested in sensationalizing the Iban and instead gathered data on social organization and agriculture. He received his Ph.D. from the University of Cambridge in 1953 and, after a year of teaching in New Zealand, took an academic position at the Australian National University (ANU) the following year.

Freeman's works on the Iban became standard references and secured his reputation as a careful fieldworker, astute observer, and sophisticated analyst. He became known as a Southeast Asian specialist at the Research School of Pacific Studies at ANU, one of Australia's most prestigious universities. But a series of events was about to change Freeman's life and his intellectual direction and ultimately lead him back to Samoa and Margaret Mead.

A Series of Events in Sarawak, 1961

Freeman's position at ANU was unusual by academic standards. The Research School of Pacific Studies was exactly that, a research school within a major university. Faculty members were researchers first, with ample leave time and excellent support. Faculty taught only graduate students, not undergraduates. This was a position of great privilege that allowed faculty members to focus on research in ways that most faculty rarely, if ever, experience. Freeman had the time and resources to read widely and to continue his work among the Iban.

By now Freeman was a well-established academic. Yet as the 1950s ended he had become dissatisfied with the intellectual frameworks that he had embraced earlier in his career. In the late 1930s and early 1940s he had been a cultural determinist, believing that behavior was determined by culture. In the late 1940s and 1950s he believed that social structure determined behavior. But these perspectives were of little help to Freeman as he attempted to fathom the meaning of certain Iban head-hunting rituals. In 1960 he decided to alter his theoretical perspective. He also considered returning to Samoa.

Shortly thereafter, while on a study leave, Freeman was asked by a vice-chancellor at ANU to go to Sarawak to investigate a serious problem that had arisen between one of Freeman's graduate students and the curator of the Sarawak Museum. It would become one of the most profound experiences of Freeman's life. Freeman's intellectual biographers recount what happened, based on Freeman's own description:

> Freeman found himself in the center of a complicated social situation in which he was able to study firsthand a whole series of deep psychological processes. He writes that for one who had reached this state of mind about the significance of psychological and behavioral variables for anthropological enquiry, this was an educational experience of a most fundamental kind, and led to what he has described as a "cognitive abreaction." He suddenly saw human behavior in a new light.
>
> So momentous was this experience, Freeman writes, that he returned to Canberra rather than continue on his study leave and in March 1961 began systematic reading in ethology, evolutionary biology, primatology, the neurosciences, psychology and genetics, all of which from his changed perspective he judged to be relevant to the development of a unified science of anthropology.[15]

What happened in Sarawak influenced the intellectual direction of Freeman's career. He began to incorporate biology and psychoanalysis into his work in ways that were very different from standard British social anthropology. And this experience would later contribute to his critique of Margaret Mead. But this account seems incomplete in terms of detail.

What exactly happened to Freeman in Sarawak? What do the terms "cognitive abreaction" and "educational experience" mean? In addition to their more literal meanings, they seem to be euphemisms that Freeman used to refer to a delusional episode—what some have referred to as a mental breakdown—that he experienced in 1961. Although Freeman would deny having a breakdown throughout his life, there is little doubt about what took place. Author Judith Heimann painstakingly reconstructed these events after communicating with several individuals who were there, including Freeman himself. Hiram Caton, an emeritus professor of politics and history at Griffith University in Australia and a colleague of Freeman, also carefully reviewed correspondence and other primary documents at ANU relating to this delusional episode.[16] Together Heimann and Caton have provided a detailed picture of what happened. Caton's account is more comprehensive and his reconstruction is used here.

Freeman had gone to Sarawak to help resolve a conflict between Tom Harrisson, the curator of the Sarawak Museum in Kuching, and one of Freeman's own students, whose work in the field was interrupted by Harrisson. Freeman's official duties on behalf of ANU were to return his student to his research site in good standing and to revise ANU's commitment to collaborate with Harrisson. Harrisson was a very gifted but notoriously unstable individual. He had done fieldwork before World War II and led an indigenous counterinsurgency in Borneo against the Japanese during the war. By all accounts he was a difficult person and had been labeled a "madman" by many. Among other things, he harassed anthropologists and denigrated their work.

Nevertheless, Harrisson considered himself a competent ethnographer and had become close enough to Freeman on an earlier trip to bestow on him a gift of tribal carvings. At this time, in 1957, Freeman was having marital problems, and the carvings, with their supposed hidden power, were given to help improve his relationship with his wife. Freeman took them home to Australia and hung them in their bedroom. At the end of that same trip, though, there was an incident in which Harrisson verbally abused Freeman with a violent tirade that left Freeman silent and trembling for hours afterward. The Freeman-Harrisson relationship was thus already fraught with conflict.

Dangerous Statues and a Communist Plot

When Freeman returned to Sarawak in 1961, there was the potential for additional conflict between the two men over Harrisson's treatment of Freeman's student. But Freeman resolved his official duties on this issue promptly and without incident. He could have returned to his study leave but instead chose to remain in Kuching on a personal matter that was at odds with his official role. Freeman had decided to use his broad network of government contacts to build a case against Harrisson that would demonstrate to the government that Harrisson was a dangerous psychopath suffering from extreme paranoia who should immediately be relieved of his administrative duties and expelled from the country.

Over the course of the next few days in Kuching, where the Sarawak Museum was located, Freeman became further convinced that Harrisson was quite mad and that his evil nature had to be reported to the proper authorities. He questioned those that he knew about Harrisson and believed that he had made an important discovery at the museum that Harrisson curated. Freeman alleged that Harrisson was desecrating Iban culture by producing counterfeit pornographic tribal carvings with large phalluses and then displaying them in the museum. This insight had come to Freeman in a matter of seconds in the middle of the night, and it made his new mission all the more urgent.[17] Freeman was convinced that the erotic statues not only were a perversion of authentic tribal culture but were also exerting a form of mind control over him through their hypnotic power, a power that Freeman was determined to break.

Freeman also believed that the statues were being used by Harrisson and the Soviet Union to subvert the local government itself. Indeed, Freeman thought Harrisson's wife was a Soviet agent. In Freeman's eyes the statues in the museum were a front for a local cult; as a member of the cult, Harrisson was thought to be in league with the Soviets in trying to undermine the colonial government. Given these beliefs, Freeman felt that he had to do something to get the attention of local authorities. His plan was to stage a symbolic protest, be arrested, and then be taken before a magistrate, where he could reveal Harrisson's diabolical plot.

So Freeman entered the museum and destroyed one of the statues. He then informed the local authorities of what he had done. By this time the chief secretary of the colonial government had become concerned about Freeman and aware of his attempts to undermine Harrisson. In fact, he supported Harrisson against Freeman. The authorities therefore did not arrest Freeman, and he had no forum to present his accusations. For Freeman, this turn of events simply demonstrated the degree of mind control Harrisson exerted over the government.

Freeman believed that only a psychiatrist would give his story credence, and he attempted to fly to London to see his psychiatrist friend Morris Carstairs, who could properly appreciate Harrisson's alleged plot. His journey to London began in Kuching with a flight to Bangkok. But as he boarded the plane, Freeman became alarmed, believing that he was being pursued by police officers; in fact, the officers on the plane were going to a conference in Kuala Lumpur and were not interested in Freeman at all. When the flight reached Bangkok, Freeman phoned the Australian ambassador to ask for an urgent meeting during which he could discuss Harrisson's alleged plot; the ambassador declined. The same thing happened on the next leg of the trip, in Calcutta. By then news of Freeman's erratic behavior, including his request for a gun from an airline captain to protect himself, was spreading like wildfire. The entire Australian Southeast Asia diplomatic corps was on alert. Finally, at the end of the next leg of his flight, in Karachi, Pakistan, Freeman found someone to listen to him, a high-ranking diplomat with close connections to ANU. The diplomat listened patiently and promptly notified ANU.

The head of Freeman's department at ANU was dispatched to Karachi to accompany him back to Australia; a psychiatrist in Karachi had met with Freeman and determined that he should not be allowed to fly unescorted. There would be no trip to London. Back in Australia, Freeman received another psychiatric evaluation—his fourth—and diagnosis of a breakdown.[18] Administrators at ANU wanted to give Freeman medical leave, but he rejected it, saying that he had never been more physically or mentally fit. Indeed, Freeman did not seem to experience any long-term disability as a result of this episode. He also saw these events as enabling him to view the world in a new and different way, almost as if it was a conversion experience in the religious sense. In fact, "conversion" was the word that Freeman sometimes used to describe what happened in Sarawak.

Point of No Return

Freeman immediately returned to his university duties convinced of the new direction in his intellectual life and concerned about the continuing existence of Harrisson's alleged plot. Although he rejected psychiatric help for himself, he was willing to meet with a psychiatrist to discuss his own important discoveries about Harrisson's alleged paranoia. Freeman then wrote a report on Harrisson and the colonial government, but ANU considered it an embarrassment and kept it under wraps. Harrisson himself was untouched by Freeman's attack, which was largely pointless because Harrisson, like all expatriate civil servants in Sarawak, was about to be replaced by a local counterpart as Sarawak came under Malaysian control. Freeman then turned his attention to the diplomat with whom he had met in Karachi, the psychiatrist whom he had seen at ANU, and the head of his own academic department, all of whom he targeted with correspondence.

Although Freeman viewed what happened in Sarawak as a psychological and theoretical breakthrough, the institutional fallout from his high-profile delusional episode would alter the course of Freeman's professional career. His research activities in Sarawak had been underwritten by an institutional agreement between ANU and the governing body of the area. After the episode Freeman was viewed as a problem by the government of Sarawak, and a new research agreement prohibited him from returning to the site of his most important work and the area that had made his professional reputation. This would have been a severe setback for any anthropologist, but because Freeman was at a premier research institution, it was an even greater problem. He would now have to find another research site. If he began research in a culture other than the Iban, he would have to learn a new language, master a new literature, and slowly immerse himself in a new field situation. If Freeman could not immediately return to the Iban, a return to Samoa was a possibility, and the islands were already on his research agenda before his delusional episode.

Among some of his colleagues, knowledge of the events in Sarawak confirmed that Freeman was more than just an eccentric scholar. Yet he retained his position, denied that he had any psychological difficulties, and scoffed at those who believed he was mentally ill. Although many people had private knowledge of Freeman's history of psychological difficulties and although his colleagues at ANU often discussed Freeman's most recent problems among themselves, it was taboo to discuss them publicly during the first two decades of the Mead-Freeman controversy. With few exceptions, such as Williamson's play about Freeman and Judith Heimann's account, Freeman's mental state was off-limits for friends and critics alike during his lifetime.

Most of those close to Freeman and to the controversy felt that Freeman's problems were irrelevant to evaluating his critique of Mead, since arguments should be evaluated on their academic merits alone. The source of the critique and the critique itself were regarded as separate. To mention Freeman's mental state was viewed as a desperate measure by those who, unable to pierce Freeman's intellectual armor, were trying to discredit him as an unbalanced individual. So critics of Freeman's work did not discuss his psychological problems in public, a courtesy that worked to his advantage. As one exasperated professor stated during the question-and-answer period after a talk that I gave on the controversy, "We all know he's crazy, but we can't say it!" Freeman was not reluctant to discuss the details of Mead's personal life as he saw them, but his own life was, for the most part, not discussed. Yet Freeman's autobiography highlighted the events in Sarawak as a major turning point in his career. His "cognitive abreaction" there would lead him toward psychoanalysis, back to Samoa, and into a personal confrontation with Margaret Mead.

\4/

Psychoanalysis, Freeman, and Mead

IN THE EARLY 1960S, following the events in sarawak, Freeman's growing interest in psychoanalysis had both personal and professional dimensions. Psychoanalysis might help Freeman the scholar unlock the mysteries of Iban ritual symbolism that neither British social anthropologists nor the Iban themselves could fully explain. It might also help Freeman the person understand some of his own unresolved conflicts, although he publicly denied their existence.

One of the people to whom Freeman turned for assistance in psychoanalytic training was Margaret Mead.[1] Although Freeman and Mead had not yet met and although he privately disparaged her work, he knew that Mead was well connected to the American psychoanalytic community and could provide contacts to scholars and therapists with whom Freeman wished to study. So Freeman sent Mead a series of long letters in 1961, including one that asked her directly for sponsorship in the American psychoanalytic community. Mead had heard of Freeman's reputation as an unstable individual, and she knew of his private criticism of her work. She therefore avoided assisting Freeman directly.

In 1962 Freeman wrote his British psychiatrist friend Morris Carstairs soliciting his assistance with a bold ten-year project that he believed would result in a new, "unified view of man and so point the way to a genuine anthropology." Carstairs, who had done anthropological fieldwork, had known Freeman years earlier at the University of Cambridge and liked him. Carstairs wrote Mead about Freeman's project, trying to enlist her cooperation, but Mead responded to Carstairs with a three-page, single-spaced letter, noting that, while Freeman was a "brilliant" man, he had not recognized that a good deal of work on the significance of psychological forces in human life had already been done by American anthropologists.[2]

Mead also noted that Freeman had a messianic streak and was a difficult individual. She remarked, "The experience of everyone I have talked to, unfortunately without exception, in the last five years has been very negative." Mead worried that Freeman might not fit well in the small, closely knit American psychoanalytic community. Yet she did not want to exclude Freeman, so she provided Carstairs with some alternative possibilities that he could present to Freeman. Carstairs replied to Mead that he was surprised that Freeman had become difficult to get along with but agreed with Mead that the "grandiosity of his intentions . . . makes one fear that he may be passing through a period of emotional instability."[3]

Freeman turned to England for psychoanalytic training and was able to take a study leave for a year at the Institute for Psychoanalysis in London, where he attended lectures and seminars in 1963–64 as well as undergoing 154 sessions of personal analysis.[4] Several of Freeman's articles from the late 1960s and early 1970s were published in psychoanalytic journals and reflect this new influence. Freeman also learned more about ethology and primatology, visiting ethologist Konrad Lorenz at the Max Planck Institute for Behavioral Physiology in Germany and observing monkeys and apes at the London Zoo; he would later author articles on aggression and human nature.

As his work was taking him in new directions, Freeman anticipated going back to Samoa, having been away for almost two decades. After completing his psychoanalytic training in England, Freeman traveled to Australia by sea in July 1964; on this voyage he reread *Coming of Age in Samoa,* more than twenty years after initially reading it. But now he saw it in a somewhat different light. Freeman's biographers comment that as he anticipated returning to the islands, "Freeman realized that . . . it would be incumbent upon him, in the course of his other researches, to reexamine and test the evidence on which Dr. Mead in 1928 based her conclusion that biological variables are of no significance in the etiology of adolescent behavior, evidence of which he was decidedly skeptical as a result of his own Samoan researches."[5]

Freeman himself stated it somewhat differently. His responsibility was definitively to *refute* Mead, not simply to "reexamine and test" her ideas. Freeman noted that this had become evident to him in the early 1940s while he was still in Samoa during the war. As he recalled in the preface to *Margaret Mead and Samoa,* by the time he left the islands in 1943 he knew that he would "one day have to face the responsibility of writing a refutation of Mead's Samoan findings."[6] Yet there is little in Freeman's professional scholarship on Samoa to lend credibility to this claim. Until the 1960s Freeman's professional writings do not discuss Mead; it was almost as if he was publicly avoiding her.[7] Of course, Freeman had been focused on the Iban, but as he was planning a return to Samoa in the 1960s, after Sarawak and his psychoanalysis and after his correspondence with Mead on psychoanalytic matters, Mead became the object of Freeman's attention, indeed his obsession.

What was it about Mead and her work that was so important to Freeman? Again, the answer is not immediately obvious. At the time Freeman returned to Samoa in the mid-1960s, *Coming of Age* was almost forty years old and showing its age. Mead did not think it was her most important work. The book was not used in graduate seminars as a model for research, and it was not considered much more than a popular best seller by most anthropologists. In fact, a number of her colleagues thought of Mead as a popularizer rather than a serious scholar. And this had been the case from the beginning of her career. In 1931 A. L. Kroeber, one of the great anthropologists of that period, labeled Mead "an artist" rather than an ethnographer after reviewing her popular works on Samoa and New Guinea.[8] In much of British social anthropology, according to Robin Fox, Mead was viewed as "whoring after cheap fame instead of doing a professional job of fieldwork."[9]

In the early 1960s *Coming of Age* was still an interesting read for undergraduates and the public at large, but academic research on the islands rarely discussed the book. Mead's professional monograph on Samoa, *Social Organization of Manu'a*, was more durable. Yet anthropologists working in American Samoa and Western Samoa had new interests, better methods, and different theories. Mead's stature in the public eye was at its apex, yet within anthropology she had become a historical figure, a pioneer and professional resource person but not a cutting-edge thinker. As for the nature-nurture debate, new research was changing the terms at issue. So why, at this time in the early to mid-1960s, did Freeman think that *Coming of Age* was of such momentous significance?

A Meeting in Canberra

In November 1964, only a few months after rereading *Coming of Age in Samoa* and prior to returning to the islands, Freeman received Mead as a visitor at the Australian National University. She had notified him that she would be visiting ANU, and she asked to meet with him; he agreed. Mead had known for years that Freeman was critical of her work on Samoa, yet the two had never met. The meeting in Canberra would be their first and last.[10] Given their interests, they might have been expected to discuss psychoanalysis, ethology, Freeman's planned fieldwork on cultural change in Samoa, or other topics in which they shared a mutual interest. But this did not happen.

According to Freeman, Mead visited his office and initiated the conversation by bluntly asking what he really knew about Samoa. Over the course of the next two hours and forty minutes Freeman laid out in detail the data he had assembled, allegedly demonstrating that Mead's account of Samoan adolescence was wrong. He also told her that he intended to do further fieldwork in

Samoa and write up the results in a published critique. According to Freeman, Mead was "very agitated" and "shaken."[11]

During their meeting Mead asked to see Freeman's postgraduate diploma thesis on Samoan social structure, since she had published a professional monograph on the same subject in 1930. Freeman stuttered as he said he would find it for her. He recalled, "I had never stuttered in my life. And she said, 'You're trembling like a jelly.' I was a bit scared of her." Freeman gave her the thesis for overnight use, but she forgot to take it with her. The following day, in her seminar with faculty and graduate students, according to Freeman, they were arguing about Samoa when Mead asked Freeman why he had not brought the thesis to her university residence. In an unguarded moment Freeman responded: "Because I was afraid that you might ask me to stay the night." Freeman did not mean to utter these words; it was a Freudian slip: "I don't know why I said that. I was mortified after I said it."[12] Yet these words spoke volumes about Freeman's symbolic relationship with Mead.[13]

Of course, Freeman did not literally imagine Mead as a seductress. At the time of their meeting she was sixty-two and grandmotherly and had a physical disability that required her to use a staff for walking. As Freeman observed, "She dressed frumpishly. She had no allure about her."[14] Freeman himself was fourteen years her junior, well over a foot taller than Mead, and in good physical condition, having followed a health and fitness regimen. But on another level Freeman viewed Mead as having a powerful presence. As he remembered, "She could cast a spell. . . . [S]he certainly mesmerized me."[15]

Freeman's imagery of Mead involved her power over men. He stated, "Mead was known as a castrator; she went for men and put them down. She also had this [sexual] reputation [and] I was not going to be bullied by her."[16] He repeated this charge elsewhere, stating, "She was a great castrator of men. She had huge power. She did this kind of schoolmarm thing. I mean, there were lots of cases where she would intervene in an appointment and speak against you and you wouldn't get promoted or you'd lose your job, and the people were really scared of her. I fortunately was outside that system, so I could stand up to her completely."[17]

Freeman's perception of Mead is somewhat puzzling. In their private meeting it was Freeman who had forcefully critiqued her work and told her there was more to come. He was in the driver's seat and had posed a challenge if not a direct threat to her; yet he imagined himself as a potential victim of Mead, a powerful and bullying woman who caused him to stutter and whose spell he had to resist. Mead's request for his unpublished thesis had become a test of his manhood. Although Freeman had made his points with Mead in their private meeting, he seemed to believe that she had victimized him there and in her public seminar.

In one of Freeman's accounts of the seminar he noted that everyone had laughed at his remark about Mead spending the night with him, and that was the end of it. He would write an apology, stating, "I would very much hope that, however we disagree, there should be no bad feeling between us. You have my assurance that I shall strive towards this end." Freeman quoted Mead as responding, "What is important is the work."[18] Their relationship was thus professional if not amicable.

But in a second account of the seminar Freeman acknowledged that he and Mead became involved in a very heated public exchange. As he remembered, "There was a great deal of tension."[19] The argument was about the value of virginity in Samoa, with Freeman forcefully contending that the "sacrosanct" defloration of ceremonial virgins was a central element in Samoan culture during his fieldwork in the 1940s. Mead replied that during her work in the 1920s this was not the case, partly because ceremonial deflorations had ceased to exist. Mead did not yield to Freeman's sharp criticisms.

In this version Freeman also wrote Mead a letter of apology to which she responded about two and a half weeks after their meeting in Canberra. In her letter from New York she reviewed their differences on the issue of the value of virginity in Samoa and then pointedly noted: "As a matter of fact I rather enjoyed the seminar, although I think it is unfair to expose students who have not been analyzed to that kind of exchange. However, you asked for it, and you got it. It didn't offend my personal susceptibilities [sensibilities?] except on the grounds of taste and estimates of what other people can stand."[20] In this version of what happened in the seminar, Mead and Freeman openly fought about the importance of ceremonial defloration. Mead responded, "You asked for it, and you got it." She accepted Freeman's apology while giving no quarter.

During their encounters in the private meeting and the seminar, it seems that Freeman may not have been in full control, that he had embarrassed himself first by stuttering in their private meeting and then by a Freudian slip in the seminar. All of this involved Margaret Mead, a woman whom Freeman personally disliked and professionally disdained. Moreover, Freeman would have interpreted this exchange with Mead through the lens of his own recent psychoanalysis, which presumably dealt with issues like sex, dominance, and aggression that were of personal significance to him.[21] While it is possible to understand this incident in different ways, the meeting between Freeman and Mead may shed some light on how she had come to occupy a central place in Freeman's psychological universe, representing not only an intellectual challenge but a

personal threat to him, to men in general, and to the integrity of Samoan custom. This meeting may have been a significant catalyst in further motivating
Freeman to critique Mead.

The aftermath of the meeting was less clear. According to Mead's colleague
Lola Romanucci-Ross, Mead left Canberra upset over Freeman's critique of
her Samoan work, stating to Romanucci-Ross that Freeman had proven Mead
wrong and that she did not know what to do.[22] Romanucci-Ross reassured
Mead that her reputation did not rest on her Samoan work alone, and there
was no further discussion of the meeting with Freeman. But if Mead thought
that she was wrong about Samoa immediately after meeting with Freeman, she
did not believe so for very long. In fact, her letter responding to Freeman indicates that she strongly defended herself both during the seminar and afterward.

Mead also mounted a published defense of *Coming of Age*. She had responded to other, earlier criticisms of *Coming of Age in Samoa* with new prefaces
to her book. Anticipating Freeman's published critique of *Coming of Age,* she
chose to comment on it in the second edition of *Social Organization of Manu'a,*
which was published in 1969. Although Mead did not know exactly what Freeman would say about *Coming of Age* in print, she concluded her monograph
with a section on how different anthropologists (men and women, for example)
might produce different accounts of the same culture. Mead noted that she had
studied Samoan culture from the point of view of the adolescent girl, a point of
view very different from that of the older male chiefs and removed from their
concerns over rank and status. Adult Samoan chiefs embraced and promoted a
public morality in ways that adolescent girls might not. A second line of defense Mead offered was that there might have been a "felicitous relaxation" of
Samoan public morality at the time she was there, hence the difference between Freeman's account and Mead's. Her defense against Freeman was brief
and generic. Because Mead did not know what Freeman would ultimately publish, her preemptive remarks would hardly scratch the surface of his critique.
Mead diplomatically stated that she looked forward to reading Freeman's findings from his fieldwork in the mid-1960s.[23]

Freeman, however, saw this olive branch and Mead's continuing defense of
her Samoan research as a weak excuse for shoddy scholarship. According to
Freeman, she was unrepentant about her views on Samoan sexual conduct and
the relationship of culture to biology. This is what he says spurred him to advance his critique and to believe that Mead should suffer for her views.[24] Privately, Mead was now even more cautious about her correspondence with Freeman, who was sending her letters requesting the actual names of her Samoan
informants, whose identities she wished to keep confidential. Mead politely
parried these requests.

Return to the Islands

Freeman had planned a brief return to Samoa in 1961 in order to set up more extensive fieldwork for the mid-1960s. Due to the events in Sarawak in 1961, he was not able to return to Samoa as soon as anticipated. Nevertheless, after his psychoanalytic training in London, Freeman did spend two years in Samoa, from late December 1965 to early January 1968, his first lengthy stay in the islands since the early 1940s.

Originally, this new research in Samoa was to be on change, especially population growth and environmental change, as well as on ethological and psychoanalytic approaches to Samoan culture. There was no direct mention of revisiting Mead's work as part of the research plan. Yet by the time Freeman, with his wife and two daughters, arrived in Samoa, he was privately committed to refuting Mead. After spending most of his time in Western Samoa, Freeman made a special trip to Taʻū in American Samoa, the island where Mead had done most of her research over forty years earlier.

Freeman hoped to find some of Mead's original informants, and he had connections to Taʻū through the village of Saʻanapu, where he had resided in the early 1940s. Although he did not find any of Mead's original informants at that time, Freeman did ask chiefs and others about Mead's claims concerning sexual conduct, among other topics. They told him that her writings, and especially *Coming of Age in Samoa*, were defamatory to Samoans and that "if she ever dared to return they would tie her up and feed her to the sharks."[25]

Freeman also gathered sworn testimony from two older Samoan males that Mead had an affair with a Samoan man whose pseudonym was Aviata and that she danced bare-breasted with him. These Samoans were shocked by her behavior and said that she behaved "like a vagrant, like an animal." For Freeman, this testimony provided him "with an explanation of Mead's fantastically erroneous account of Samoan sexual behavior—and especially that of young women."[26] He thought:

> In reality, her account (as I had long half-suspected) is a *projection* on to Samoan females of her *own* sexual experiences as a young woman, in the faraway, romantic South Seas.
>
> I have, indeed, been long interested in the way in which anthropological fieldwork presents immature personalities with massive opportunities for what might be called cultural regression. And of which not a few anthropologists avail themselves. . . .
>
> These discoveries came as a shock too, and I found that my feelings were deeply stirred—both for the sake of Samoa and the science of anthropology, both of which mean much to me.[27]

Indeed, these discoveries, real or imagined, were truly upsetting to Freeman in a way that he could only partially express, and they may have precipitated another event somewhat similar to the delusional episode in Sarawak when he discovered Harrisson's allegedly diabolical plot.

Shortly after Freeman learned of these allegations about Mead's conduct, his Samoan hosts found him on the beach in an agitated and possibly disoriented state. A local news bulletin reported that Freeman was "verbally violent" to such an extent that the government on the main island of Tutuila was contacted. A Coast Guard cutter was dispatched to Taʻū in order to bring Freeman back to Tutuila for observation at the islands' hospital.[28] There are different versions of the seriousness of this incident. Some Samoans who witnessed Freeman's behavior believed that he may have been possessed by spirits, or *aitu*, possibly related to his research on Mead. Spirit possession was not unusual in the islands, but the possession of a European would have been alarming to Samoans. Some Americans in the islands thought that Freeman might be experiencing severe psychological problems. Freeman himself would claim that the incident was the result of exhaustion from fieldwork and possibly dengue fever. Whatever the case, he recovered quickly.

Freeman did not view this episode as a symptom of an underlying problem, nor did he mention it in his intellectual autobiography, in contrast to the episode in Sarawak, to which he gave great significance. In retrospect, though, this episode may have been part of a pattern in which he saw himself acting on behalf of the Iban and the Samoans against allegedly decadent and deviant Europeans whom he believed threatened the integrity of these indigenous cultures.

Reality Check

To verify the Samoan testimony that he solicited about Mead's personal conduct on Taʻū, Freeman wrote to Lowell Holmes, an anthropologist who in the 1950s had done a restudy of Mead's Samoan work and found it to be generally reliable.[29] Freeman informed Holmes of Mead's alleged affair with Aviata and asked him if he had heard about it. Holmes replied that he had not. Freeman also informed Holmes of his desire to make the affair public knowledge. Roughly a month and a half later Freeman again wrote to Holmes, this time stating that he had decided not to write about Mead's personal life in Samoa and vowing: "Inasmuch as the motivations of an investigator must be kept entirely distinct from the evidential value of any report that he might make, I have now decided to vigorously *exclude* from any reappraisal of Mead's publications on Samoa that I might write any mention of her personal behavior as reported to me by witnesses in Manuʻa."[30]

Yet Freeman did not keep this solemn pledge. Although there was no mention of the affair with Aviata in his two books on Mead, Freeman did publish an academic article in 1991 in which he discussed this alleged affair.[31] He stated that he did so only after his private letter to Holmes was published in 1990, and so, he reasoned, the affair had become public knowledge.[32] However, Freeman seemed to have forgotten that he had already published information in 1983 on another alleged affair by Mead with a Samoan named Andrew Napoleon.[33] He repeated this allegation in a letter to the *Royal Anthropological Institute Newsletter*.[34] He also used this allegation in private conversations to deprecate her.

The allegations about Mead's personal life on Ta'ū may have been unwarranted. As we shall see in chapter 13, it is questionable whether affairs with Aviata and Napoleon ever occurred. And the sworn testimony that Mead had danced bare-breasted was clarified in an unpublished interview with Fa'apua'a in 1993 that was in Freeman's possession but not discussed by him. In the interview Fa'apua'a affirmed that Mead had danced bare-breasted but did so only in her role as a ceremonial virgin, or *taupou,* having been appointed by a high chief and with the possible encouragement of Fa'apua'a herself.[35] Fa'apua'a also volunteered, without prompting, that as a *taupou* she too had performed the same ceremonial dance bare-breasted, as was the cultural norm, on the same island at about the same time. Since *taupou* were representatives of the dignity of Samoan women and the pride of the village, for Fa'apua'a there was nothing scandalous or immoral about the dance.

Nevertheless, disturbed by what he thought he had learned about Mead on Ta'ū, Freeman returned to Australia with a renewed sense of purpose in writing about Mead and Samoa. In early 1968 he gave a paper to the Australian Association for Social Anthropology titled "On Believing as Many as Six Impossible Things before Breakfast."[36] It was his first written critique of *Coming of Age in Samoa* and took its title from *Alice in Wonderland,* implying that Mead, like Alice, was unable to distinguish fantasy from reality. The critical arguments that Freeman presented linked Mead as a person to her allegedly unreliable professional findings. According to Freeman, Mead had gone to Samoa with preexisting beliefs about the power of culture. She had an emotional attachment to these beliefs and blindly clung to them. Freeman also included his argument that Samoa was a sexually repressive society, marked by rape, conflict, and adolescent delinquency. This unpublished paper, privately circulated to colleagues, contained much of the argument that would appear in *Margaret Mead and Samoa* fifteen years later. Freeman did not send a copy to Mead.[37]

In 1972 Freeman authored his first published critique of Mead in a professional journal. It was a note, not an article, in the *Journal of the Polynesian Society* about Mead's alleged misspelling of Samoan words in her professional monograph on Samoa, *Social Organization of Manu'a.*[38] The implication of this note was that if Mead could not properly spell Samoan words, she could not speak the language, and therefore the actual substance of her book must be unreliable. Yet Freeman did not say this in print and did not take the opportunity at that time or later to review and critique this monograph, which was Mead's major academic contribution on Samoa.

Instead Freeman concentrated on *Coming of Age,* and by 1977 he had completed most of *Margaret Mead and Samoa.* In a letter to her he offered to send Mead a copy of an "acutely critical" chapter on sexual behavior, but Mead's assistant wrote back that she was very ill.[39] Mead would die of cancer in 1978. After her death Freeman submitted his manuscript to several distinguished academic presses. Oxford University Press asked for revisions that Freeman did not wish to make. Then, in 1982, Harvard University Press accepted it for publication. So did Princeton University Press and Yale University Press. Freeman chose Harvard. In early 1983, five years after Mead's death, *Margaret Mead and Samoa: The Making and Unmaking of an Anthropological Myth* was published.[40] It had been a long journey, and the route was circuitous, but the moment had finally arrived. And once the controversy began, Freeman continued to pursue Mead and her work with a determination and focus rarely encountered in academia.

A History of Controversy

The dogged and highly personal approach that Freeman embraced attracted attention but also alienated a number of colleagues and readers. Some of his own friends and relatives privately asked him to leave well enough alone. One colleague and friend regretted that Freeman's unabashedly adversarial style made him "his own worst enemy." Why did Freeman not heed their advice? His critique was scathing and replete with rhetorical absolutes. Mead was judged to be "fundamentally in error" and "grossly hoaxed" and her conclusion "preposterous." His critique could have taken a less confrontational form and more measured tone. As a senior scholar, Freeman did not have to press his case to gain attention. Was it necessary to use an intellectual sledgehammer on someone he considered an academic butterfly and on a book that in an unpublished interview he considered "frivolous and romantic"?[41] Freeman might have used gentle persuasion rather than polemical refutation. So why did he choose this style and tone?

Certainly, Freeman's perception of Mead, whom he imagined to be a scholarly pretender and a castrating feminist, was part of it. His belief that she was immoral and a disgrace to anthropology were also factors. And there was Freeman's deep identification with Samoans and his belief that Mead's portrayal of them was an intellectual "travesty." Yet this was not his first controversy, and Freeman insisted on winning controversies, not simply engaging in debate. Controversy and confrontation were part of his professional career and personal style; they were fundamental to how Freeman saw himself.

This style was also part of his relationship with his colleagues. Long before the Mead-Freeman controversy, a number of colleagues at ANU kept a careful distance from him. Some, particularly women, described Freeman as "paranoid" and a "bully." Others privately complained about Freeman's confrontational style but remained silent in public. Some pretended to be cordial to Freeman in order to avoid conflict, while others gave his work favorable reviews in order not to become potential targets of his uneven temperament. They worried about his personal history. When discussing their encounters with Freeman, several of his colleagues specifically asked me not to disclose their identities, fearing retaliation if word got back to Freeman.

At the same time there were also colleagues and former graduate students who respected and admired Freeman. Speaking on their behalf, his intellectual biographers stated:

> To many of us the most salient trait of Professor Freeman's character is his absolute insistence on intellectual integrity. Not only does he demand that we endeavor to make ethnography as accurate and comprehensive as possible, he also insists on unswerving dedication to the scientific truth in the analysis and presentation of data. His moral outrage at shoddy or self-serving scientific work is well known, and he has told innumerable scholars about to set out on ethnographic fieldwork to make sure to "get it right."[42]

Anthropologist Michael Jackson also spoke of Freeman's passionate pursuit of the truth, commenting: "What many find dogmatic and self-assertive in his manner, I have construed as dedication, enthusiasm, and an unrelenting pursuit of the truth that underlies the conventional defenses that we construct against it."[43] Supporters also describe Freeman as having "a deep sense of moral responsibility": "Though Freeman presents a stern exterior, at heart he is a person of broad sympathy and gentle disposition."[44] Indeed, Freeman could be generous, thoughtful, and caring. He could also be threatening and hostile.

Whatever their opinion of him, Freeman's colleagues knew of his penchant for controversy long before the Mead-Freeman controversy developed. As Freeman himself admitted, they looked on him "as a bit of a wild card, you see. I was liable to go off the deep end, which I am [*sic*]."[45] At faculty colloquia he was known for interrupting speakers. And his confrontations with colleagues sometimes bordered on physical contact. In fact, many faculty and students at ANU as well as the residents of Canberra knew of Freeman and his argumentative persona.

In 1979, well before his critique of Mead was published, Freeman initiated another controversy when he publicly protested the donation of an Aztec calendar stone (a replica, not the original) to ANU by the Mexican government. This stone was to be displayed in a prehistory exhibit. The donors believed that the purpose of the original stone was to provide the Aztecs with accurate calendrical readings. Freeman, however, believed that the donation was a replica of an Aztec sacrificial altar upon which thousands of humans had been ritually murdered.

In a private letter to the vice chancellor of ANU and then in a public letter to the *Canberra Times,* Freeman stated that Aztec culture was the most barbaric and deluded in history. He declared that there were no objects "on this green and pleasant earth more deserving of the repugnance of civilized men and women than the sacrificial stones of the demented and blood-thirsty Aztecs of ancient Mexico." Freeman concluded that "to have a massive and malignant sacrificial stone from the most barbaric culture in all human history, an object that out-Molochs Moloch, towering over authentic pieces from ancient Greece, is an abomination of a kind that I have never before witnessed."[46] He demanded the stone be immediately removed from the campus. Despite his protest, the scheduled dedication ceremony was held, and Mexican delegates presented the replica to the ANU Department of Prehistory and Anthropology. By now the controversy had attracted so much public attention that one reporter noted, "Little wonder then that a goodly portion of the crowd was there to see whether the Professor of Anthropology himself would attend and, if he did, what he would do."[47]

Freeman did attend, with his dog, but he remained in the background. During his presentation at the ceremony the vice chancellor pointedly noted that sacrificial altars did exist among the Aztecs but that the donated replica was not one of them. At the conclusion of the ceremony Freeman approached the vice chancellor and privately exchanged words with him. The event ended without incident.

In the retelling of this story over the years it has become an urban legend. In one version Freeman allegedly poured blood on the calendar stone to symbolize the Aztecs' bloody sacrifice. In another he merely stalked the ceremony with a cup of blood. Neither of these versions is true. What is true is that in a series of articles and letters in the *Canberra Times* readers learned of Freeman's strong opinions. Australian columnists and readers noted that Freeman seemed to have a double standard of morality. For example, one writer commented that there was a model of the Roman Coliseum at ANU, but Freeman did not deplore it, although innocent Christians and others were sacrificed in the original. Furthermore, the ancient Greeks and Romans, to whom Freeman traced the roots of Western culture, had built their civilizations on slavery, yet Freeman did not criticize them.

In addition, the two cultures that Freeman had studied practiced head-hunting in the Iban case and the public defloration of ceremonial virgins, with death as a possible consequence for failure, in the Samoan case. Yet for Freeman, the Iban and the Samoans, as well as the Greeks and the Romans, were cultures worthy of study and of great value to humanity as a whole, while the Aztecs were "blood-thirsty" and "demented."[48] In this local but well-publicized controversy the residents of Canberra became familiar with Freeman's outspoken views years before the American public would learn of them.

When the controversy over Mead and Samoa was in full swing and the play *Heretic* was about to open in Australia in the mid-1990s, Freeman was asked how he felt about being at the center of controversy. He replied: "I'm a hardened campaigner. And I enjoy it. I'm rather looking forward to it! There's nothing more invigorating."[49]

Thus Freeman's involvement with Mead and Samoa was partially academic, but it also included a complex intersection of his personal history, intellectual development, and proclivity for controversy. While the substance of his two books on Mead appeared to be academic, the background that contributed to their writing, exposition, and style was personal.

PART 3

Margaret Mead and
Coming of Age in Samoa

\5/

Young Margaret Mead

Having discussed freeman's life and his connections to
Samoa and Mead, we now turn to Mead's life and her connections to Samoa.
How did her career begin? What led her to study adolescence in Samoa and to
write the book that made her famous?[1]

Mead was born in Pennsylvania in 1901, the eldest of four surviving children. Her mother was a highly educated sociologist and feminist. Her father
taught at the Wharton School of Finance and Commerce at the University of
Pennsylvania. Mead's family was unusual in its commitment to education, especially for women. Both her mother and grandmother were professionals.
Mead loved the world of books, poetry, and ideas. While in high school she met
Luther Cressman, who was four years older and would soon study to become a
minister. They became engaged when Mead was sixteen and a senior. She did
not tell her parents about the engagement until some time later. At this point
in her life young Margaret Mead believed that she could live happily as a minister's wife and be the mother of several children. Their engagement would
last nearly six years, though, and during this period both Mead and Cressman
would undergo major changes in their life goals.

Mead spent her first year of college at DePauw University in Indiana, a
school that her father had attended. DePauw was a small liberal arts school,
and Mead's experience there was mostly painful. She did not fit into the sorority system that dominated the lives of most young women, and although she attended sorority rush parties, she did not receive a bid to pledge.[2] Her engagement to Cressman lessened the sting, but she nonetheless felt like an outsider,
an outcast. Her taste in clothes was different from most of the other young
women that she knew. Her intelligence, so highly valued by her family, was now
a liability; the young men in her classes resented her for it. After class Mead
would read avidly about the literary and artistic scene in New York City, where
Cressman was now living and studying. She became acutely aware of the constraints of small-town life. At DePauw she said she felt like "an exile."[3]

Margaret Mead's graduation portrait in the 1923 Barnard yearbook, *The Mortarboard*. Courtesy of the Barnard College Archives.

For her sophomore year Mead transferred to Barnard, a women's college in New York City where sororities had been abolished in 1913. Here she flourished, becoming involved with a new group of friends and a new set of experiences. If post–World War I America had one city that exemplified the Roaring Twenties, New York was it. Art, poetry, literature, music, and alcohol (even though it was Prohibition) were everywhere, and there was great interest in politics and psychoanalysis. Bohemian and avant-garde, New York was the cultural epicenter of cosmopolitan America. The city seemed made for Mead.

In some ways Mead's experience at Barnard in the early 1920s was similar to Freeman's college experience in the 1930s in New Zealand. College was a liberating experience for each of them. Mead and Freeman considered themselves radicals, although Freeman was more politically active than Mead. Both were interested in writing; both had considered careers in writing, and both worked on school publications. Both wrote poetry and were interested in debate. Both took psychology courses and were strongly influenced by them. Mead and Freeman were very much engaged with the wider world of great ideas. They were both assertive and had a flare for the dramatic. But while Mead's memoirs of college discuss her personal relationships and her views on sex, these subjects are absent from Freeman's. He married at thirty-two, and was committed to monogamy.

Sex and the City

Mead was also committed to monogamy, as her long and chaste engagement to Luther Cressman attested. But in New York and other major metropolitan areas a "singles culture" was emerging in which young women, working or getting an education, lived apart from their parents. These independent living arrangements provided opportunities for relationships with men that were frowned on in many other parts of the country. In the 1920s most single women still lived at home until marriage and were chaperoned as men came courting.[4] Until the early twentieth century, courtship often took place at the young woman's home and was under the control and auspices of the young woman's family. If a couple went out, they continued to be chaperoned. Making a good impression on the young woman's parents was part of courtship, which ideally led to marriage. In contrast, "dating" did not and therefore was discouraged by girls' families. Sex outside of engagement and marriage was not only forbidden but risky. Contraceptives were unreliable by today's standards, and pregnancy outside of marriage was deeply shameful. There were limited opportunities for relationships to be consummated, and when young women first left home at marriage, the overwhelming majority of them were virgins.[5]

In New York City, though, sexual norms were changing. The city had been at the center of early-twentieth-century movements for women's suffrage, access to birth control, sexual freedom, and equal pay for equal work. Prior to World War I a budding feminist movement flourished, especially in Greenwich Village.[6] Authors promoted free love; there were gay men and women. During World War I "charity girls" became part of the urban scene.[7] These young women were willing partners who often saw soldiers outside the narrow parameters of engagement and marriage. They followed their desires instead of social convention and were often arrested and imprisoned by local vice squads because they were suspected of spreading sexually transmitted diseases.

Since the late nineteenth century sex had become a central fact of life in the city.[8] There was a gradual separation of sex from the rhetoric of sin. Although there was still a great deal of sexual repression by today's standards, sex was now being studied and thought about as a social good.[9] It was something that people wanted to know more about. After World War I the sexual ambience of the city continued to evolve. With a number of young single women living independently, there were more opportunities for young men and women to meet. And private women's colleges like Barnard provided opportunities for lesbian relationships, which were very much forbidden at the time. In fact, many mothers of this period worried that their daughters might enter homosexual relationships if they attended these schools.

Coming of Age in New York

Among Mead's close-knit group of friends at Barnard, known to each other as the Ash Can Cats, there were many lengthy discussions about sex, pregnancy, sexual repression, marriage, and homosexuality. Mead wrote about this brave new world of problems and possibilities in her autobiography, *Blackberry Winter:*

> Sophisticated as we were, we were still remarkably innocent about practical matters relating to sex. During that first year, the sixteen-year-old daughter of a friend of my mother's was found in bed with a boarder and was forced by her mother to get married. We knew that she ought not to have a baby yet, and I compiled a five-page typed list of home remedies that could be used for a douche. However, our young friend in due course had a baby. . . .
>
> We knew that repression was a bad thing, and one of our friends—not a member of the inner circle—described how she and her fiancé had made up a set of topics to talk about on dates so that they would not be [sexually] frustrated. When she heard that I had been engaged for two years and did not intend to get married for three years more, she exclaimed, "No wonder your arm hurts." [At the end of her first year at Barnard Mead began to have chronic pain in her right arm that would continue intermittently for the rest of her life.]
>
> We learned about the existence of homosexuality, too, mainly from the occasional covert stories that drifted down to us through our more sophisticated alumnae friends and through upperclassmen who were close to some members of the faculty. Allegations were made against faculty members, and we worried and thought over affectionate episodes in our

past relationships with girls and wondered whether they had been incipient examples.[10]

For these young women, sex was on the table, not in the closet. It was not secret or considered unseemly. Mead felt at home with this group of young women. She also felt that she was part of something larger and more significant, the next wave of feminism, the new woman of the 1920s. As Mead commented:

> We belonged to a generation of young women who felt extraordinarily free—free from the demand to marry unless we chose to do so, free to postpone marriage while we did other things, free from the need to bargain and hedge that had burdened and restricted women of earlier generations. We laughed at the idea that a woman would be an old maid at the age of twenty-five, and we rejoiced at the new medical care that made it possible for a woman to have a child at forty.
>
> We did not bargain with men. After college many of us fell in love with an older man, someone who was an outstanding figure in one of the fields in which we were working, but none of these love affairs led to marriage. Schooled in an older ethic, the men were perplexed by us and vacillated between a willingness to take the love that was offered so generously and uncalculatingly and feeling that to do so was to play the part of a wicked seducer. Later most of us married men who were closer to our age and style of living, but it was a curious period in which girls who were too proud to ask for any hostage to fate confused the men they chose to love.
>
> At the same time we firmly established a style of relationships to other women. "Never break a date with a girl for a man" was one of our mottoes in a period when women's loyalty to women was—as it usually still is—subordinate to their possible relationships to men. We learned loyalty to women, pleasure in conversation with women, and enjoyment of the way in which we complemented one another in terms of our differences in temperament, which we found as interesting as the complementarity that is produced by the difference in sex.[11]

For Mead and her cohort, sexual politics were a matter of serious ethical concern. They read the new literature on the philosophy of free love and learned about sexual technique in manuals by influential authors such as Havelock Ellis. Mead, as a modern young woman, embraced the idea of free love and promoted it in conversations with her fiancé and her friends. On a philosophical level Mead believed that free love meant following one's heart rather than conventional norms about commitment to one partner, marriage, and heterosexuality.[12] If marriage and passion coincided, so much the better, but love itself was paramount. Free love also meant that multiple relationships were possible, as were bisexual relationships. Jealousy was considered a negative

Margaret Mead and her social circle at Barnard, the "Ash Can Cats." *Left to right*: Mead, Léonie Adams, Deborah Kaplan, Pelham Kortheuer, and Viola Corrigan. Library of Congress, Margaret Mead Papers, Box Q44, folder 8. Courtesy of the Institute for Intercultural Studies, Inc., New York.

emotion because it implied possessiveness and prevented free love. As an idea, free love appealed to Mead. It also became a matter of practical concern, for she was becoming involved with a number of young women.

Brilliant and charismatic, Mead attracted women to her. She loved conversation. Historian Lois Banner found that Mead appealed to young women on many levels: "She could be childlike and maternal, playful and mature, sweet

and dependent, needing mothering and able to give it. More than that, her body matched the 1920s ideal of beauty. Take a look at [actresses] Mary Pickford and Clara Bow. Both are slim and tiny; the ideal woman of the 1920s was around five feet tall."[13]

Mead's marginal status at DePauw was transformed at Barnard. She was now intellectually exciting and attractive. She was also daring. For these reasons, young women loved her.[14] Banner's detailed reconstruction of Mead's college years indicates that, while she was chaste in her relationship with her fiancé, she had a number of lesbian relationships inside and outside her social circle. Although Mead enjoyed these relationships, she kept them secret. They were passionate and complicated, and they left Mead feeling torn as she tried to manage them simultaneously. Despite her belief in the ideal of free love, Mead was uncertain of her sexual orientation and troubled by it. Homosexuality was generally taboo, and bisexuality was even less well understood, although in the early twenties both were considered fashionable in some New York social circles.

Apart from the personal issues that were so important in her development, Mead's academic direction changed. She had wanted to be a writer, journalist, or poet, and she continued to major in English, which she had chosen at DePauw. However, she became interested in psychology and added it as a second major at Barnard. Mead was a quick study and an excellent student whose ability to process information was remarkable. Yet at this time a very painful bout of neuritis in her right arm rendered her unable to write with that hand. So Mead learned to write with her left hand. When the neuritis subsided, she was able to write with both hands simultaneously. As Patricia Francis learned from examining Mead's notes, she could now take down class lectures with one hand and, if bored, write letters with the other. Later, during her fieldwork, Mead could type her field notes with one hand and take written notes with the other on what was going on around her.[15]

Mead's interest in anthropology came late in her undergraduate career. In her senior year at Barnard, after committing to psychology, she took a course from Franz Boas, the German-born founder of American anthropology. It was a life-altering experience. As a result of her upbringing Mead already believed in the equality of "races" and that cultures were neither inherently superior nor inferior to each other.[16] But Boas introduced her to the idea of human evolution, which strongly influenced her. She also met Boas's teaching assistant, Ruth Benedict, who would become her close friend and colleague.

After taking one course from Boas, Mead attended all the others that he taught and got to know Benedict better. Nevertheless, Mead entered the graduate program in psychology at Columbia and earned an M.A. in that discipline

Franz Boas, Mead's advisor at Columbia University and the founder of American anthropology. Library of Congress, Margaret Mead Papers, Box P2, folder 3. Courtesy of the Institute for Intercultural Studies, Inc., New York.

while preparing for a Ph.D. in anthropology. Her background in psychology, her mentors in that discipline, and the psychology courses that she took would provide her with valuable assistance in her future work in Samoa, but she did not know that then.[17] At one of their lunches Benedict told Mead that she and Boas hoped that Mead would pursue anthropology, but they had nothing to offer her except "the work itself," which could not wait because cultures around the world were rapidly disappearing.[18] Mead had already made up her mind. Anthropology would become her career.

From Cape Cod to American Samoa

In New York City, Mead and Cressman saw each other once or twice a week. He was now in training to be an Episcopal priest and was a graduate student in sociology at Columbia. They married in September 1923 and spent their honeymoon on Cape Cod. However, despite all their discussions and reading about sex, and despite the liberal environment that their friends provided, they were still novices, and their wedding night was not quite what they had hoped for. Mead wrote that, after more than five years of engagement, there were "moments of strangeness and disappointment to overcome": "We had read so many books written by sex specialists of the 1920s who believed that sex was a matter of proper technique—that men should learn to play on women's bodies as if they were musical instruments, but without including in the calculations that women must be very good musical instruments in order to please the men who played on them."[19] Cressman was more candid: "We came to each other at marriage as virgins. Although quite sophisticated intellectually and verbally, we were both physically and emotionally immature. I, four years Margaret's senior and with much wider experience, was the more mature. During these early days of our honeymoon we both, I think, had a sense, an awareness we could not quite conceal that something expected, hoped for, was lacking." During their honeymoon the couple used separate bedrooms because Mead insisted that she had to prepare for a seminar. Cressman did not quite believe her, recalling, "Margaret, as she so often did, was dramatizing a situation and, I think, seeking to avoid an experience and a possible emotional commitment she preferred not to have. . . . I am afraid we were both rather relieved when our days on the cape came to an end."[20]

While their honeymoon was not ideal, the newlyweds settled in and lived together comfortably for two years in a small apartment in the city. They each had their own work, although neither had much money. Mead's father had cut off her school funding after she refused his offer of an enormous sum of money to travel around the world and forsake marriage to Cressman.[21] Instead, she

worked as an assistant for one of her professors and received a generous three-hundred-dollar gift from Ruth Benedict.

Mead prided herself on her independence, even within the bonds of marriage. She kept her own name, shocking her relatives, and was pleased that her marriage, unlike her mother's, allowed her to be herself. In retrospect she saw it as "the ideal student marriage," unclouded by the fear of pregnancy. Cressman did household chores, and they shared expenses. She would write, "We never quarreled and never had a misunderstanding even of the kind roommates often have over leaving the light on or keeping the bathroom tidy."[22] Cressman agreed that their marriage was virtually conflict-free.[23] Mead thought that she had what she wanted—a thoroughly modern marriage.

Mead and Benedict became closer when one of Mead's friends, Marie Bloomfield, committed suicide. Mead wondered if she could have done more to save her friend. Mead had spent the weekend with another close friend whom she was helping with a health problem.[24] When college administrators tried to convince Mead that Bloomfield was mentally ill and that the college was not responsible for her suicide, Mead felt alone and tormented; Benedict offered her sympathy. Mead and Benedict had been friends, and later, after Mead chose anthropology, they became intimate.

As Mead recalled in her autobiography:

> By electing anthropology as a career, I was also electing a closer relationship with Ruth, a friendship that lasted until her death in 1948. When I was away, she took my varied responsibilities for other people; when she was away I took hers. We read and reread each other's work, wrote poems in answer to poems, shared our hopes and worries about Boas, about [Edward] Sapir, about anthropology, and in later years about the world. When she died I had read everything she had ever written and she had read everything I had ever written.[25]

Both Mead and Benedict knew that if their relationship became public, it would cost them their careers and reputations. Benedict was a married woman at this time, and so was Mead. There was not only a sexual dimension to their relationship but a teacher-student dimension as well. Although the sexual aspect of their relationship ended in the early 1930s, they remained close friends

Facing page top: Margaret Mead with Luther Cressman, her first husband. Library of Congress, Margaret Mead Papers, Box Q44, folder 7. Courtesy of the Institute for Intercultural Studies, Inc., New York.

Facing page bottom: Ruth Benedict in 1931. Photo by Arthur Muray. Courtesy of Special Collections, Vassar College Libraries.

and intellectual companions until Benedict's death in 1948. The intimate nature of their relationship did not become public knowledge until 1984, sixty years after it began and several years after Mead's death.[26]

Meanwhile, Mead's marriage was showing signs of stress. She thought of her marriage to Cressman as a student marriage, one that allowed each of them time to study without the distraction of looking for permanent companionship. But Mead had a good deal of additional companionship from Benedict and her other female friends. As she juggled these relationships, she thought of them in terms of a poem by Amy Lowell in which significant others were like sparkling wine or daily bread. Mead told Cressman that he could never be like wine to her, and he accepted her interest in an open marriage with the understanding that other relationships were temporary, while their marriage was permanent.[27]

Although Cressman was very committed to the marriage and its future, he sensed Mead's ambition and realized that her career might supersede it. In his autobiography, Cressman commented:

> Margaret and I, young, idealistic, naïve, and avant garde, entered marriage in 1923 under conditions that would make heavy demands upon us. Full-time academic schedules and extracurricular duties left little time and energy to devote to our new, extremely important process: learning to live together in marriage. Too often it was probably taken for granted that the very inner dynamic of marriage itself would insure success, and I say this without animus: by Margaret more than by me. When we returned from our honeymoon on Cape Cod we were, even at that very special time, aware of tensions arising from the competing demands for time and attention made by the desire for high academic performance and the winning of love. That Margaret had chosen academic performance was a storm flag of warning we both recognized for the voyage ahead.[28]

There were other storm flags that Cressman recognized but did not fully appreciate. Mead's relationship with Benedict, as well as her other female partners, was one. Another was Mead's relationship with Edward Sapir, a Boas protégé and brilliant linguist who had been recently widowed. Mead and Sapir met at a professional meeting in Toronto and were immediately attracted to each other. Benedict was also close to Sapir and attracted to him, but Mead and Benedict ultimately put their love for each other ahead of their interest in Sapir. Cressman knew of Sapir's interest in Mead, but he did not realize until years later that the relationship was so close that Sapir had tried to persuade Mead to divorce Cressman and marry him. Ruth Benedict was the person who told him.[29]

Margaret Mead was now twenty-three years old. She had read about human sexuality and had many conversations about it with her group of close friends. She believed in free love and had encouraged both her husband and Ruth Benedict to agree to it in principle. In a relatively short period of time she had sexual experiences with both men and women; she was bisexual. She had married and made pivotal choices about her personal and professional life. Mead and Cressman had come a great distance from dreams they had shared when they became engaged. She was now fully immersed in an academic career and no longer thought of herself as being a priest's wife with the ambition of having several children. Cressman himself was questioning his dedication to the priesthood and would soon abandon that career altogether.

Thinking about Samoa

Mead entered the Ph.D. program in anthropology at Columbia in 1923 as one of only four graduate students in the department. In the United States at that time there were only two major departments of anthropology—at Columbia and Harvard. There were very few anthropologists, even fewer female anthropologists, very few positions in academia, little financial support, and a minimum of professional training by today's standards. It took Mead only two years after graduating from Barnard to receive her M.A. in psychology and then to complete her Ph.D. dissertation in anthropology. Today it takes an average of over eight years to complete a Ph.D. in anthropology, partly due to the time-consuming nature of fieldwork in another culture.

Mead had not done fieldwork for her dissertation. She had written a library-based study of the distribution and stability of certain Polynesian cultural traits, including tattooing, canoe building, and house building.[30] This kind of dissertation was not unusual at the time, but it was a liability in a discipline where fieldwork was already a measure of professional credibility. Time spent in another culture doing ethnographic fieldwork was, and continues to be, considered the best way to learn about another culture. It was also a professional rite of passage. While receiving her graduate education, Mead attended professional meetings and listened to anthropologists talking about their fieldwork and "their people." Mead wanted a "people" of her own. She knew that as soon as she finished her dissertation she would go to the field. Cressman already had a scholarship to study in Europe for 1925–26, and the couple agreed that each of them needed a period of further professional training.

After completing her Ph.D. dissertation, Mead was still under the professional guidance of her mentor, Franz Boas. He would continue to be an important resource for future academic positions and research opportunities in the small but growing profession of anthropology. Mead wanted to engage in fieldwork that examined how cultures changed, but Boas had his own agenda. As the founder of a field that was still in its infancy, he chose his students' projects very carefully, based on his vision of research that he thought necessary.

Many of Boas's early students had done "salvage ethnography," reconstructing vanishing cultures, particularly those of Native Americans. They looked for connections between cultures as a way of determining past cultural history. But Boas's research agenda was not static. He became interested in learning more about how cultures shaped the individuals growing up in them. As Mead remembered: "Now he wanted me to work on adolescence, on the adolescent girl, to test out, on the one hand, the extent to which the troubles of adolescence, called in German *Sturm und Drang* and *Weltschmerz,* depended on the attitudes of a particular culture and, on the other hand, the extent to which they were inherent in the adolescent stage of psychobiological growth with all of its discrepancies, uneven growth, and new impulses."[31]

Since Mead had written her Ph.D. dissertation using Polynesian material, she wanted to do fieldwork in that region of the world. She hoped to travel to the remote Tuamotu Islands in French Polynesia, but Boas, concerned with her safety, told her that she would have to choose an island where a ship came at least once every three weeks. Mead agreed and chose American Samoa, which was administered by the U.S. Navy. By chance, Cressman's father knew the surgeon general of the navy, who agreed to have his staff in American Samoa keep an eye on Mead and assist her with contacts in the islands.[32] While Boas, Sapir, and other colleagues of Mead worried about her ability to survive in the field, she nevertheless applied for a National Research Council fellowship to study adolescence in American Samoa and received it.

In the summer of 1925 Mead prepared herself for the long journey to the islands and fieldwork. Then she and Cressman took a last vacation together and said good-bye. They planned to meet again in France the following year. Mead made her way west, visiting Benedict in New Mexico. On the train she wrote to Cressman about her relationship with Sapir in order to share with him what she had not been able to tell him in person.[33] Then, just before departing to Hawai'i from San Francisco, Mead wrote Cressman another letter with a sentence stating: "I'll not leave you unless I find someone I love more."[34]

\6/

First Fieldwork in Samoa

M EAD'S PROFESSIONAL GOAL of fieldwork abroad took precedence over her personal life. And fieldwork for a young woman traveling abroad and working alone was not easy in the 1920s. Mead had never visited another culture prior to Samoa. She had never been west of the Mississippi. She had not spent a day alone before her fieldwork began, and, according to her autobiography, she had not even spent a night in a hotel by herself.[1] Her mentors worried that Mead might be setting herself up for failure.

Traveling by ship from San Francisco to Hawai'i, Mead stopped to meet with colleagues at the renowned Bishop Museum in Honolulu.[2] There she agreed to conduct a general study of Samoan ethnology for the museum while also studying Samoan adolescence funded by her fellowship from the National Research Council. In return, Mead received the title of associate in ethnology at the Bishop Museum and entered into an agreement to have her findings published in the museum's monograph series. These were good career moves. After Honolulu, Mead continued her voyage to American Samoa, about 2,300 miles to the southwest, arriving in the port of Pago Pago in late August 1925. Cressman's father's naval connections were available to help her.

Apart from official recognition, Mead's presence in Pago Pago drew the attention of the local expatriate community. Her unconventional marriage, which allowed her to be away from Cressman for long periods of time, did not go unnoticed. As she wrote to Ruth Benedict: "And this sweet little group of gossips are just seething with speculation about why 'I left my husband.' Of course, they are sure I have. And I know I oughtn't to mind but it's so depressing to be greeted with suspicious unfriendly glances."[3] Nevertheless, Mead focused on her project. Naval personnel provided her with a Samoan nurse to help her learn the language, which she began to study almost immediately.

Mead was interested in Samoan culture, but American Samoa was not a pristine, untouched culture and had not been for some time. Samoans had become devout Christians many decades earlier; they were part of a cash

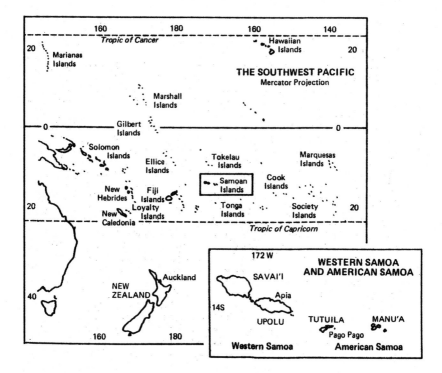

Map of the Southwest Pacific with Western Samoa and American Samoa. In 1997 Western Samoa was renamed Samoa. Mead did her fieldwork in American Samoa. Freeman did most of his fieldwork in Western Samoa.

economy, selling copra on the world market; and this group of islands was an American territory under the jurisdiction of the U.S. Navy. Pago Pago, the port town, had one of the best harbors in the South Pacific and was an important coaling station for naval ships. So American Samoa, with a population of about twenty thousand Samoans, was not paradise awaiting discovery. It was a small colonial outpost. In this setting relations between Samoans and the naval administration were strained. American Samoan resistance to naval policies coalesced into an organized opposition, just as Western Samoan opposition to New Zealand colonial policies was occurring.[4]

Finding a Field Site

Mead was aware of these administrative problems, but she was more concerned with finding a village where she could begin her study of adolescents. The island of Tutuila, where she was learning Samoan, was a logical place to look for a field site, but, after touring the island's numerous villages, Mead wondered if she would find a suitable site there. In a letter to Boas she wrote that villages were either Westernized because they were on the bus line or small and isolated. The Westernized villages were not of interest to Mead, while the small villages presented two disadvantages. According to Mead, "They are very difficult to reach and very small. No one of them boasts more than four or five adolescents, and so the difficulty of getting from one to the other makes them impossible places to work. To find enough adolescents I would have to spend my time climbing mountains or tossing about in the surf in an open boat, both extremely arduous and time-consuming activities."[5]

On the other hand, Ta'ū Island in the Manu'a group seemed ideal. This group of islands was about seventy miles by boat to the east of Tutuila, less Westernized, and more culturally conservative. However, the high chief, Tufele, had been educated in Hawai'i and was not part of the anticolonial opposition to the American naval government. The only Americans on Ta'ū were the Holt family, who ran the naval medical dispensary, and two navy corpsmen. Mead wrote to Boas:

> Tau is the only island with villages where there are enough adolescents, which are at the same time primitive enough and where I can live with Americans. . . . In Tau I will be living at the dispensary with the only white people on the island and right in the midst of the village. I can be in and out of the native homes from early in the morning until late at night and still have a bed to sleep on and wholesome food. The food will be much better than the hotel food [on Tutuila] because Navy people have canteen privileges. Mrs. Holt is a sweet woman, was a school teacher, and I think I shall enjoy living with them. . . . It is really optimum in every way because I will have infinitely better care than I could possibly have in one of the remote villages on Tutuila.[6]

Mead's rationale for doing fieldwork on Ta'ū had to do largely with the sheer numbers of adolescents readily available, the lesser effects of Westernization on the villages of this island, and the comforts of living with the Holts. Ta'ū provided a unique setting in which several hundred Samoans lived in close proximity to each other in three different villages.[7] While still on Tutuila Mead realized that Ta'ū could yield a sample of dozens of adolescent girls.

Mead thought about living with a Samoan family but weighed the costs and benefits in another letter to Boas:

> This is the only place where I can live in a white household and still be in the midst of these villages all the time. This is the point about which I am particularly anxious to have your advice. If I lived in a Samoan house with a Samoan family, I might conceivably get into a little more intimate touch

with that particular family. But I feel that such advantage as might be reaped would be more than offset by the loss of efficiency due to the food and the nervewracking conditions of living with half a dozen people in the same room, in a house without walls, always sitting on the floor and sleeping in constant expectation of having a pig or a chicken thrust itself upon one's notice. This is not an easy climate to work in; I find my efficiency diminished about one-half as it is, and I believe it would be cut in two again if I had to live for weeks on end in a Samoan house. It is not possible to get a house of my own, which would of course be optimum.[8]

Becoming a Participant-Observer

Should Mead have been concerned with such "nervewracking conditions"? Aren't anthropologists supposed to be "dirt fieldworkers," living with indigenous families, eating their food, speaking their language, and enduring whatever inconveniences and hardships that may occur? Ideally, this is the way in which cultural anthropologists become true participant-observers, people who not only know about the culture but become part of it. Extended immersion in the field as a lone ethnographer is what Freeman eventually experienced in Samoa. For this reason Freeman faulted Mead for her cautious approach to fieldwork, stating that because she did not want to live as a Samoan with a Samoan family she was allegedly unable to obtain detailed, firsthand accounts of how Samoans really lived. She therefore had to rely on hearsay in her study of adolescents.[9]

Becoming a participant-observer is not easy. Read any anthropologist's field diary or letters from the field, and one quickly learns that fieldwork requires an enormous amount of time, energy, and patience.[10] Although it remains the best way to learn about another culture, it is notoriously inefficient. It is a lengthy process, not a single event. There is culture shock, misunderstanding, frustration, embarrassment, and possible illness. The ethnographer's path is filled with potholes. Today ethnographers readily admit what they have long known privately: they are not always perfectly attuned to their surroundings. Even under the best of circumstances ethnographers cannot always shed their biases and attitudes. Nor do they always cope well under difficult circumstances.

Mead was no exception. Her private letters reveal that during her fieldwork she was lonely, homesick, self-critical, frustrated, and sometimes worried that she was not learning enough or acquiring enough good data to please Boas. The physical challenges of the islands were trying. On Tutuila the painful neuritis in her arm flared up, the mosquitoes were ravenous, and the heat and humidity were exhausting. Mead sometimes felt that she was going to fail. In a letter to

Ruth Benedict she declared, "I'm just going to give up and get a job taking change in a subway."[11]

Mead did try to anticipate her own limitations, for example, her concern about Samoan food. She candidly admitted, "I can eat native food, but I can't live on it for six months."[12] In fact, it was not easy for Americans to adjust to the high-carbohydrate Samoan diet, consisting at that time mainly of taro, bananas, and breadfruit. This was not just a matter of taste; one young fieldworker was hospitalized for malnutrition after living with a Samoan family for several months.[13]

There were social challenges in living with Samoans as well as physical ones. Samoan families could be extremely hospitable, generous, and helpful. Mead's letters to Boas and her friends show her appreciation of the privileges of rank that she was given when she was appointed a ceremonial virgin, or *taupou*, in the chiefly family that she stayed with. Yet rank also had its drawbacks, restricting her contact with other girls and preventing her from studying the general population of adolescent girls. She wrote to Boas in October 1925: "Comfortable and happy as I was [on Tutuila], I could not live like that and do my problem, because I was too sheltered. As a taupo [ceremonial virgin] I could go nowhere alone nor could I enter the houses of common people."[14] This was another reason that Mead wanted to live with the Holts. For her study of adolescents she needed to have a residence that did not identify her too closely with the rank of a particular Samoan family.

Privacy was also a consideration. Even the most rudimentary Western conventions of privacy could not be taken for granted. Samoan families lived together in open-sided houses known as *fale*. There were no walls and hence no doors or windows. As a result, social life was very public, and Samoans viewed privacy as dangerous because they felt that people only sought it when they wished to do "bad things." When anthropologist Tim O'Meara asked a Samoan work group to build him a *fale* with low walls for minimal privacy, they resisted, saying that it was against Samoan custom. O'Meara asked one of the men why. "When people see that your house has walls," Selesele said, "they will think that you are doing something bad that you must hide."[15] O'Meara was able to persuade his hosts that the walls would protect him from the curiosity of village children, and his *fale* was built as he requested. Mead also became the object of such curiosity, but as a single American woman she could not live alone in her own *fale*.

Mead became familiar with these problems—food, comfort, rank, and privacy—after spending ten days living in a chiefly household in the village of Vaitogi on Tutuila. This firsthand experience was largely pleasant, but it had an impact on her selection of a field site. She wrote:

It was there [in Vaitogi] I had all my essential training in how to manage Samoan etiquette. His daughter Faʻamotu was my constant compan-
ion. We slept together on a pile of mats at the end of the sleeping house.
We were given privacy from the rest of the family by a tapa curtain, but of
course the house was open to the eyes of the whole village. . . . I learned to
eat and enjoy Samoan food and to feel unabashed when, as a guest, I was
served first and the whole family sat about sedately waiting for me to finish
so that they, in turn, could eat. . . . Day by day I grew easier in the language, sat more correctly, and suffered less pain in my legs. In the evenings
there was dancing and I had my first dancing lessons. . . . I learned how to
relate to other people in terms of their rank and how to reply in terms of
the rank they accorded me.[16]

An additional problem in Vaitogi and elsewhere on Tutuila was that Mead
was not only an honorary ceremonial virgin in the Samoan system of rank but
also associated with the U.S. naval administration and therefore considered by
Samoans to be a very important person. Her status in the colonial order made
fieldwork with children and adolescents difficult; from a Samoan perspective
she was too important for that.[17]

Mead tried to negotiate where and how to do her research given these
constraints and her own preferences. She did not want to avoid Samoans; she
wanted to maximize her research time with them, and she thought that the Holt
household would provide the best base of operations. Mead's concerns about
comfort and company were not unrealistic, and they were secondary to her
research goals. She did not choose Taʻū for comfort's sake alone. Had Mead
sought more familiar surroundings, she could have remained in Pago Pago, residing at the hotel where the British writer Somerset Maugham had penned his
famous short story "Rain." Yet Mead was eager to go to the remote Manuʻa
group and, while there, travel without naval escort. So, after two months of language training and exploration on the main island of Tutuila, she set off for
Taʻū and settled in with the Holts.

Mead used her room at the back of the Holt house to meet with Samoan
girls individually and in small groups, as it was a very convenient place for visiting. The room opened onto a village, and the girls enjoyed Mead's company
and attention. At 5 feet 2 ½ inches and 98 pounds, Mead was often smaller than
they were. Samoan parents allowed their daughters to visit her because Mead
was associated with education, something they greatly valued. Mead also "borrowed" a schoolhouse and gave the girls psychological tests that she called "ex-
aminations" as well as talking with them alone.[18] By getting to know the girls
one-on-one, away from their homes and peer groups, she was able to obtain information that would not have been available in more public settings. Mead

Margaret Mead standing between two Samoan girls, ca. 1926. Library of Congress, Margaret Mead Papers, Box P25, folder 7. Courtesy of the Institute for Intercultural Studies, Inc., New York.

also preferred the casual give-and-take of unstructured conversations to more formal interviews.

Most of the girls of Ta'ū assumed that Mead was like them, young and single. She did not tell them that she was married, although some certainly knew.[19] Over a period of five months Mead became part of their lives just as they became part of hers. They addressed her informally as Makelita (Margaret in Samoan). Her perceived status as an unmarried young woman led to her courtship by at least one young man. On another occasion Mead received a marriage proposal from a high chief, which she politely declined. Mead fit well into the role of a young, single woman and was appointed as an honorary *taupou* on three different occasions.[20] This was quite unusual. As she became a participant-observer she felt that she was beginning to understand Samoan culture from the perspective of adolescent girls.

Although Mead spent much of her time with adolescents and women, she also spent time with men, including chiefs, because of her interest in social organization and her appointment as a *taupou*. While she could not attend some chiefly occasions because she was a woman and did not participate in village political life, she nevertheless conversed with chiefs and untitled men.[21] And Mead combined her interests in adolescence and social organization, working on both topics at once when possible. As she explained:

> In connection with my psychological research I became acquainted with every household group in these three villages [on Ta'ū]. My material comes not from half a dozen informants but from scores of individuals. With the exception of two informants, all work was done in the native language. I found it particularly useful to utilize the Samoan love of pedantic controversy and to propound a question to the group and listen to the ensuing argument. As my fellowship did not provide field funds I had to rely upon the friendliness and the good will of Samoans for my material. Very little of it was gathered in formal interviews but was rather deviously extracted from the directed conversations of social groups, or at the formal receptions which the chiefs of a village accorded me on account of my rank in the native social organization.[22]

Ethnographic Standards in the 1920s

Based on the letters and bulletins that she sent home, Mead's fieldwork seems to have gone well despite a number of difficulties. Yet Freeman found her fieldwork inadequate and believed that this inadequacy explained her alleged misunderstanding of Samoan culture. Freeman's role model for proper fieldwork was the great ethnographer Bronisław Malinowski. In the 1920s and for decades thereafter Malinowski was regarded as the godfather of modern field-work. In his classic account of the Trobriand Islands, *Argonauts of the Western Pacific,* published in 1922, he discussed his lengthy immersion in Trobriand culture and the advantages of in-depth fieldwork. He also insisted that ethnographers should indicate clearly and concisely which data came from direct observation and which came from indirect knowledge.[23] Malinowski, a British-trained anthropologist of Polish nationality, spent almost two years in the Trobriands. He learned the language and studied an indigenous culture more deeply than most previous ethnographers, and he wrote a series of detailed monographs on the Trobriands that were considered models for presenting ethnographic data.

In the 1920s, though, Malinowski's work was just being introduced in the United States. Being in the field for a lengthy period was not yet part of the training for most young American ethnographers. At that time fieldwork for American anthropologists often consisted of a summer—sometimes only a few days—on a Native American reservation. Many of Mead's peers visited reservations with short vocabulary lists to be used for the purpose of reconstructing vanishing cultures. They did not have the time or resources to learn a field language. American ethnographers had little training in fieldwork, and this was true of Mead as well, although her training in psychology and her work as an editorial assistant on a professional journal may have given her a methodological edge over some of her peers.

In contrast, today's ethnographers often have prior language training and have visited their field sites before settling in for actual research; ideally, they are able to spend at least a year or more in the field. Mead did not initially have the funding for research or transportation that would have made this possible. In fact, her father, rather than the organizations that sponsored her research, paid for her travel expenses. Mead spent a little over eight months in American Samoa. By American ethnographic standards at that time this was an extended period of fieldwork.

Malinowski's work on the Trobriands was exemplary, but these islands were his second field site, not his first. And while Malinowski's ethnographic goals were noble, his actual fieldwork, even in the Trobriands, did not involve living as a "native." At age thirty Malinowski began his ethnographic career in the South Pacific by conducting preliminary fieldwork on Mailu, an island off the New Guinea coast near the Trobriands. But he did not live among the people for a lengthy period of time, nor did he speak the language well at first. On Mailu he often lived with expatriates, used interpreters, relied on the local European missionary as well as an indigenous police constable for help with his ethnography, had a "cook boy," and retreated into reading novels and old newspapers when he became bored with fieldwork.[24]

In fact, Malinowski's experience in Mailu was filled with sickness, loneliness, and sometimes a raging dislike of the people he was studying. After one encounter in which the natives walked away from a photographic session with him, Malinowski expressed his displeasure by quoting the character Kurtz from Joseph Conrad's *Heart of Darkness;* in his personal diary Malinowski wrote: "On the whole my feelings toward the natives are decidedly tending to 'Exterminate the brutes.'"[25] Moreover, for Mailu Malinowski did not write the compelling ethnographies for which he would later become famous as a result of his Trobriands research. Even in the Trobriands Malinowski lived in a tent in the village, using indigenous people to assist him with his daily tasks. At best, Malinowski lived among the people but not as one of them. This was true of Mead as well. They did not "go native," although both became participant-observers.

Samoa was Mead's maiden voyage. She was considerably younger than Malinowski when he began his first fieldwork, and she did not have the prior training that Malinowski had. Although Mead had read some of Malinowski's findings on the Trobriands before her own fieldwork, she did not read *Argonauts of the Western Pacific* until her return from Samoa and therefore may not have fully appreciated his emphasis on long-term, British-style fieldwork at the time. Nevertheless, Mead knew the value of learning Samoan and of interacting with Samoans over a period of several months. In fact, her field experience in Samoa seems to have been more positive than Malinowski's in Mailu. But if Mead did not meet Freeman's standard of ethnographic experience set by Malinowski in the Trobriands, how good an ethnographer could she have been?

Malinowski himself provided an answer to this question. After reading *Coming of Age in Samoa* he lavishly praised Mead's work in comments that appeared on the book's cover, endorsing it as an "absolutely first-rate piece of descriptive anthropology and an excellent sociological comparison of primitive and modern conditions in some of the most problematic phases of human culture. . . . Miss Mead's field work seems beyond cavil or criticism. Her style is fascinating as well as exact and the book provides excellent reading; convincing to the specialist, attractive to the layman . . . an outstanding achievement." Malinowski also wrote Mead personally to express his admiration for *Coming of Age.*[26]

Could Mead Speak Samoan?

What of Mead's language competency, that essential prerequisite for understanding another culture? Could she, in the relatively short period of time that she spent in the islands, have learned Samoan? According to Mead, she not only spoke with a wide variety of Samoans, she spoke with them in their own language. Yet Freeman questioned this claim in *Margaret Mead and Samoa*, stating that Mead had a "far from perfect command" of Samoan.[27] Initially, he criticized her language competency as a way of explaining how she was allegedly hoaxed by Samoans.

Freeman was also implicitly comparing his own proficiency in Samoan to Mead's. He was justifiably proud of his ability to speak the language, which he learned after arriving in Western Samoa in 1940. Freeman spent over two years learning Samoan, passing an examination that certified his proficiency in 1943. Yet Freeman was a schoolteacher at this time, not an anthropologist. He resided primarily in the port town of Apia, and his fieldwork in the village of Sa'anapu was intermittent, totaling fifteen months over a more extended period of time. Most anthropologists, even today, do not have this kind of time to learn a field language.

With limited funding for her fieldwork, Mead had a relatively brief period of time in which to do her research. So she pressed ahead, learning the language as quickly as possible. Although she could have applied for an additional year of research funding from the National Research Council and stayed longer, providing her more time to learn the language and the culture, she did not because, while in Samoa, she received a cable offering her the position of assistant curator at the American Museum of Natural History beginning in the fall of 1926. It was an offer that was too good to refuse.

Mead had not studied Samoan in detail before she began her research. She did spend a week studying Samoan as well as two related Polynesian languages, Marquesan and Tahitian, while at the Bishop Museum in Honolulu in transit to American Samoa. But she believed that it would take at least a year or more to learn Samoan well. Furthermore, she spent only eight weeks on Tutuila learning the language before traveling to the Manu'a group for roughly five more months of fieldwork there. Under these circumstances, how well could she have learned the language?

Samoans themselves raised questions about Mead's fluency in their language. In 1967 Samoans on Ta'ū told Freeman that Mead required an interpreter, and in 1978 Samoans on Ta'ū told ethnobotanist Paul Cox that, contrary to her claim, Mead did not speak Samoan with them in the 1920s.[28] In 1990 photojournalist Larry Gartenstein visited Ta'ū on assignment for *Geo* magazine and asked Fa'apua'a directly if Mead spoke Samoan. "Very little," she replied. "We always had someone to translate for us."[29] Thus, according to many Samoans, Mead hardly spoke their language. Could they have been mistaken?

A more complete picture of Mead's language competency comes from Freeman himself. Although he originally questioned Mead's language ability in his first book on Mead, to his credit Freeman continued his research on her fieldwork in the Mead archive at the Library of Congress after *Margaret Mead and Samoa* was published. In *The Fateful Hoaxing of Margaret Mead,* his second book on Mead, he gave her solid marks for her language competency and provided a detailed record of how she learned Samoan.

Freeman elaborated on Mead's language training in Hawai'i. While briefly visiting the Bishop Museum, she spent several hours a day studying Polynesian languages and their structure, and she was given Pratt's *Grammar and Dictionary of the Samoan Language,* the standard guide to Samoan at the time. As a result, Freeman found that she was off to a "flying start" in her language studies. In addition, "Mead, with the training in linguistics that she had had from Boas, was well equipped to achieve a good working knowledge of the Samoan language."[30]

Within three days of her arrival in American Samoa Mead began learning the language with the aid of the Samoan nurse assigned to her for this purpose. She resolved to do no other work and to study the language eight hours a day. In addition to her study of standard Samoan, one chief took it upon himself to instruct Mead in the more specialized honorific language of chiefs during her ten-day stay in Vaitogi. Mead gradually became more confident in her language ability and after two months on the island of Tutuila was ready to move on to the more remote Manu'a group. As Freeman observed, "Mead, with the knowledge of the Samoan language she had acquired in Tutuila during October and November 1925, was the first female member of the ruling American elite to associate with the young women of Manu'a."[31]

Freeman described how, while on Ta'ū, Mead not only continued to learn Samoan but became an interpreter for the U.S. Navy lieutenant commander. Mead acknowledged that there were three Samoans on Ta'ū who could speak better English than she spoke Samoan. Nonetheless, she translated the chaplain's official letters to high chiefs. Her translations were checked by an official Samoan interpreter who found that they contained very few errors.

Mead was also called on to act as an interpreter in a court case involving a land dispute between chiefs. She was nervous but was able to interpret nonetheless. And she acted as an interpreter in an emergency medical situation when Samoan nurses were not available. Freeman concluded that this is "evidence that by the end of January 1926, she had become reasonably competent in Samoan"; by March 1926 she was "reasonably fluent in Samoan." Thus, within five months of arriving in American Samoa and well before her alleged hoaxing in March 1926, Mead was not only "reasonably competent" in the language but "proficient enough" to act as an interpreter. Whereas Freeman had previously faulted Mead as lacking a "perfect command" of Samoan, he now reported that "with the command of Samoan she had achieved, she was able to work productively on the ethnology of Manu'a."[32]

For Mead, learning Samoan was facilitated by the English-speaking abilities of Samoans, as there was a fair amount of English spoken in the Manu'a group even in the 1920s. Anthropologist Martin Orans suggested that if Samoans had spoken as little English as Mead claimed, she might well have had difficulty understanding the culture.[33] But Orans found Mead's claim that she spoke only Samoan with all but a few informants improbable. Orans's own work in the Mead archive led him to conclude that a number of Samoans on Manu'a, including adolescents, spoke English with varying degrees of proficiency and that Mead spoke English with them, thus mitigating her self-admitted limitations in Samoan during her early months of fieldwork. By February 1926, though, she felt proficient enough to go to the village of Fitiuta, where almost no English was spoken, and work without an interpreter. While Orans is more skeptical of Mead's competence in Samoan than Freeman, there is reason to believe that she developed a degree of fluency in the language.

Mead was also learning more about adolescent girls through informal interactions. Mead worked long days, from dawn until well into the night. She recalled, "The adolescent girls, and later the smaller girls whom I found that I also had to study, came and filled my screen-room day after day and night after night."[34] The girls visited her so often at the Holt residence that Mr. Holt became annoyed at their constant presence. Freeman described how Samoans of all ages and ranks visited Mead on her porch and how "she had to lock the door to keep adolescents out," yawning prodigiously to get rid of them by midnight.[35] And her visitors sometimes discussed sex to such an extent that, in a letter to Benedict, Mead complained that all they wanted to talk about was "sex, sex, sex."[36]

That said, the window for Mead's fieldwork on Ta'ū was narrow. Seven weeks after her arrival there, a major hurricane struck the Manu'a group. Mead and the Holt family sought protection from the storm inside an empty cement water tank.[37] Samoan homes and crops were severely damaged, and in subsequent months all families were engaged in rebuilding efforts. Famine relief was necessary, and most ceremonial activities were suspended. However, the Holt house and medical dispensary were not badly damaged, and their food supply remained intact. Despite the hurricane's devastation Mead continued her fieldwork, forging ahead and completing it in mid-April 1926. She then returned to Tutuila, where she happily revisited Vaitogi, her favorite Samoan village, from which she wrote to a friend, "Here they love me and I love them."[38]

As improbable as it may have seemed at the outset, Mead's fieldwork in Samoa was successful. She not only worked through the challenges of her first fieldwork but also overcame the doubts of her colleagues in anthropology and those of the naval administrators in American Samoa. While Freeman found Mead young, naive, incompetent, and therefore gullible, an alternative view suggests that she was courageous, energetic, resourceful, and a very quick learner. Freeman himself acknowledged Mead's "phenomenal energy" in the field.[39]

7

Writing *Coming of Age in Samoa*

I N E A R L Y M A Y 1 9 2 6 Mead boarded a ship in Pago Pago to begin the long voyage home. During her fieldwork in Samoa she had ended her relationship with Sapir, but her relationships with Cressman, Benedict, and others had largely been placed on hold. With her research completed, the unfinished business of Mead's personal life resurfaced. She had left Cressman uncertain about the future of their marriage. Soon she would reunite with him in Europe. During her shipboard journey, though, Mead fell in love with someone new. Reo Fortune, a young New Zealand–born psychologist, had become the object of her affection, and Mead would now face another personal crossroads.

Although she and Fortune were deeply in love, Mead chose to stay with Cressman because she wanted children and felt that Cressman would be a better father. After returning from Samoa, however, Mead learned that she had a tipped uterus and would probably be unable to carry a child to term. Mead did not tell Cressman, but this was a precipitating event in their divorce. When she found out that she might not be able to have children, Mead chose to pursue more fieldwork, and ultimately marriage, with Fortune.[1] On Mead's advice, Fortune switched from psychology to anthropology at the University of Cambridge in England. He received a grant to work in New Guinea and asked Mead to join him. Cressman accepted the inevitable, and Mead would file for divorce in Mexico. Cressman would not learn of Mead's inability to carry a child to term until years later; once again, the person who told him was Ruth Benedict.[2]

Even as Mead worked through her personal relationships, she began writing up her Samoan field material. One result was *Coming of Age in Samoa*—her first book, her best-known book, and her biggest seller. By the time of her death it had gone through six editions, been translated into sixteen languages, and sold over a million copies. The book is still in print today, eight decades after it was written.

Mead and her publisher wanted the book to be readable by the general public, and it was. Released in 1928, it contained no systematic footnotes or bibliography, as a professional monograph would, although it did have five appendixes. Mead wrote in what she called "literate English," a style later dubbed the "wind rustling in the palm trees" school of ethnographic writing, and for good reason.[3] Passages in *Coming of Age* evoked images of paradise. In her chapter "A Day in Samoa," Mead wrote in a lyrical and idyllic manner, offering sentences like this: "As the dawn begins to fall among the soft brown roofs and the slender palm trees stand out against the colourless, gleaming sea, lovers slip home from trysts beneath the palm trees or in the shadow of beached canoes, that light may find each sleeper in his appointed place."[4] The cover of the first edition of *Coming of Age* repeated this theme, showing a young couple, both bare from the waist up, holding hands and slipping away under the swaying palms.[5]

The structure of the book followed the Samoan life cycle from childhood through adulthood. After the introduction and "A Day in Samoa," Mead described in some detail the many facets of coming of age: child socialization, the Samoan household, the girl in her community, formal sex relations, and the roles of dance, personality, individuality, conflict, maturity, and old age. These chapters were full of interesting anecdotes about the people she knew and studied. Mead incorporated individual stories into her topical coverage in a way that earlier anthropological works had not. What she tried to give readers was a sense of the lives of Samoan adolescents rather than an impersonal narrative about a distant culture. In the last two chapters she drew explicit comparisons between Samoa and America because she wanted her book to be relevant to public concerns. Yet this was not the way the book was originally conceived and written. It began as a professional report.

From Academic Report to Best Seller

One of Mead's first obligations on returning from the islands in 1926 was to write up her data as a scientific report for the National Research Council, one of the two institutions that sponsored her research. So she set about writing an ethnography of Samoan adolescence under the supervision of Boas. At the time there were very few studies of adolescence in other cultures and no models for writing up the results of this kind of field study. Mead pioneered the ethnographic study of adolescence in a report drily titled "The Adolescent Girl in Samoa," which she submitted to the National Research Council in April 1927. This report did not contain most of the social commentary that would eventually appear in *Coming of Age*, including the seductive chapter "A Day in Samoa," nor the two social advocacy chapters that concluded the book. The report was inconsequential and might have remained an obscure and uncontroversial document. However, as it was transformed into a popular work of social criticism

Mead's own views became more explicit. In writing about the contrast between adolescence in Samoa and the United States, Mead became a social critic, not simply an ethnographic reporter.[6]

Even before Mead went to Samoa, Boas and Clark Wissler, a curator at the American Museum of Natural History, saw in her work the potential for something more than professional ethnography.[7] After all, Mead was going to the South Seas, an area that already held a unique place in the American psyche. The Western world had been fascinated with the South Pacific ever since people had read early voyagers' romantic descriptions of Polynesia in the eighteenth century. Additional explorers and authors added to the mystique of the islands. Travelogues, books, short stories, photographs in magazines like the *National Geographic,* and a new medium—silent motion pictures—all contributed to stereotypes of the people Mead would be studying.

While she was in Samoa the *New York Sun Times* ran a story about Mead titled "Scientist Goes on Jungle Flapper Hunt."[8] The mere fact that a young female anthropologist would venture into paradise to study young Samoan women was news. Boas and Wissler sensed that Mead could use this cultural fascination with Polynesia to provide Columbia and the American Museum of Natural History, Mead's new employer, with some public attention. Mead understood this too. She did not need prodding by Boas or Wissler. Hoping to turn her report into a popular book, she asked the National Research Council for permission to do so, and the council approved her request in May 1927. The original report had been written in a straightforward manner, so reworking it for a nonacademic audience was not difficult. And Mead thought she knew how to write for a popular audience.

Mead had conscientiously honed her writing skills as a schoolgirl. From an early age she had wanted to be a writer and a poet; she was aware that good writing was a valuable skill. Mead authored poems, essays, and plays during her school years and continued to do so in college. As a graduate student she worked with the distinguished sociologist William Ogburn as an editorial assistant for a major professional journal. Mead also read books with a critical eye to their writing style and targeted audience. At Columbia she read Boas's popular book *The Mind of Primitive Man* but thought it lacked "the literary persuasiveness which its importance and its subject matter deserved." Mead also knew that within anthropology there were writers like Sir James Frazer in England who did not write in the "heavy German style that had captured the American university dissertation field."[9] So she consciously brought a literary approach to her writing.

Nevertheless, Mead did not have a track record of major publications, popular or academic, before *Coming of Age.* By 1928, the year she received her doctorate, she had published only two articles based on her master's research in psychology, one article on the need for teaching anthropology in teachers' colleges, and two poems.[10] Her Ph.D. dissertation was the longest piece of writing that she had completed prior to her report for the National Research Council. When published by Columbia University Press in 1928, the dissertation was only eighty-nine typeset pages long.[11]

Mead could write very quickly. "The Adolescent Girl in Samoa" took her only ten weeks. The last two chapters of *Coming of Age* were written in two weeks.[12] At this time Mead was engaged in a whirlwind of activities. She was a newly appointed assistant curator who was also trying to complete her writing commitments to the National Research Council and Bishop Museum as well as dealing with her complicated personal life.

To help her revise her professional report for commercial publication Mead sought the advice of George Dorsey, a senior anthropologist who himself had become a popular author. Dorsey advised her to submit the report to Harper and Brothers, but it was rejected. Mead and Dorsey then offered it to William Morrow, a young publisher who saw how it might find a wider audience if Mead added an introduction and concluding chapters to make it more relevant to the general public and if she placed some of the methodological and historical material in appendixes. Mead and Morrow discussed spicing up the manuscript, and she was willing to take his advice.

In the process of writing *Coming of Age*, Mead realized that some of her statements in the book manuscript were frankly speculative. In her correspondence with Morrow she worried that she might be going too far in the text. In one letter to Morrow, Mead noted that the two concluding chapters pushed "the limit of permissibility." Morrow agreed that she might pay a price with her colleagues for popularizing her work, but they were both willing to take that risk.[13] In rewriting her report as a popular book Mead did not see herself as dumbing down her prose to the lowest common denominator. She simply wanted to make anthropology available to a broader audience. At best, her research report might reach a few dozen professionals. A trade book could mean an audience of thousands of interested readers, perhaps more.

In the transformation of her research report into a trade book, Mead inserted her own views in a deliberate manner. Working from her professional report, she rethought the Samoan material through the lens of her experience while anticipating the audience that she hoped to reach. Mead wrote about issues that she knew about from her own life. Her interactions with her DePauw and Barnard classmates as well as Cressman, Benedict, Sapir, and Fortune provided some of the background for the views she expressed in *Coming of Age*. She wrote that adolescence in Samoa was less stressful than in America. Samoan adolescents might have sex with less commitment, with more than one partner, and with partners of more than one gender. Mead knew what this might be like. Her discussions of the absence of romantic love and violent jealousy in Samoa also reflected her own views. Mead noted in a private letter that her Samoan adolescent girls seemed remarkably modern.[14] While Samoa was not her own life writ large, as Freeman believed, the book was a manifesto of Mead's views about America in the 1920s.

Description and Interpretation in *Coming of Age*

Mead offered Samoa as a mirror into which Americans could look for alternatives to their own culture, where adolescence was more difficult. She did not neglect rape, conflict, sexual restrictiveness, and aggression in Samoa, but she did downplay their significance. There are numerous examples of rivalry, competition, jealousy, and conflict in *Coming of Age in Samoa*. Indeed, there is an entire chapter titled "The Girl in Conflict." Yet Mead's *interpretation* of their place in Samoan culture gave them less emphasis and far fewer negative connotations than Freeman did.

For example, Mead noted that children were physically punished with beatings. In a passage on the physical punishment of children by neighbors, Mead wrote:

> Towards a neighbour's children or in a crowd the half-grown girls and boys and even the adults vent their full irritation upon the heads of troublesome children. If a crowd of children are near enough, pressing in curiously to watch some spectacle at which they are not wanted, they are soundly lashed with palm leaves, or dispersed with a shower of small stones, of which the house floor always furnishes a ready supply. This treatment does not seem actually to improve the children's behaviour, but merely to make them cling even closer to their frightened and indulgent little guardians. It may be surmised that stoning of children from next door provides a necessary outlet for those who have spent so many weary hours placating their own young relatives. And even these bursts of anger are nine-tenths gesture. No one who throws the stones actually means to a hit a child, but the children know that if they repeat their intrusions too often, by the laws of chance some of the flying bits of coral will land in their faces.[15]

It was not that Mead ignored or neglected the existence of physical punishment of children, but she did minimize its significance.

The same was true of conflict. In the following passage Mead described a "dramatic" incident involving incest, sexual jealousy, and conflict:

[Moana's] amours had begun at fifteen and by the time a year and a half had passed, her parents, fearing that her conduct was becoming so indiscreet as to seriously mar her chances for marriage, asked her uncle to adopt her and attempt to curb her waywardness. This uncle [Mutu], who was a widower and sophisticated rake, when he realised the extent of his niece's experience, availed himself also of her complacency. This incident, not common in Samoa, because of the lack of privacy and isolation, would have passed undetected in this case, if Moana's older sister, Sila, had not been in love with the uncle also. This was the only example of prolonged and intense passion which I found in the three villages. Samoans rate romantic fidelity in terms of days or weeks at most, and are inclined to scoff at tales of life-long devotion. (They greeted the story of Romeo and Juliet with incredulous contempt.) But Sila was devoted to Mutu, her step-father's younger brother, to the point of frenzy. She had been his mistress and still lived in his household, but his dilettantism had veered away from her indecorous intensity. When she discovered that he had lived with her sister, her fury knew no bounds. Masked with a deep solicitude for the younger girl, whom she claimed was an innocent untouched child, she denounced Mutu the length of three villages. Moana's parents fetched her home again in a great rage and a family feud resulted. Village feeling ran high, but opinion was divided as to whether Mutu was guilty, Moana lying to cover some other peccadillo or Sila gossiping from spite. The incident was a direct violation of the brother and sister taboo for Mutu was young enough for Moana to speak of him as *tuagane* (brother). . . . [Months later, when Mutu] announced his intention of marrying a girl from another island, Sila again displayed the most uncontrolled grief and despair, although she herself was carrying on a love affair at the time.[16]

This single case could probably be the subject of an entire chapter. It demonstrates Mead's ability to present detailed data and analyze them in a Samoan context. But she viewed this dramatic case as an exception, not the rule, concluding a paragraph later:

With the exception of the few cases to be discussed in the next chapter ["The Girl in Conflict"], adolescence represented no period of crisis or stress, but was instead an orderly development of a set of slowly maturing interests and activities. The girls' minds were perplexed by no conflicts, troubled by no philosophical queries, beset by no remote ambitions. To live as a girl with many lovers as long as possible and then marry in one's own village near one's own relatives and to have many children, these were uniform and satisfying ambitions.[17]

One can read example after example in *Coming of Age,* such as those just presented, appreciating the data while wondering to what extent Mead's interpretations, judgments, and conclusions followed from them. Why is this so?

Freeman believed that the problem stemmed in part from Mead's naiveté and inexperience; he claimed that she simply did not know enough about Samoan culture to separate fact from fiction. Yet, as we have seen, Mead was a competent fieldworker who could provide sensitive and accurate descriptions. Freeman added that Mead's slavish devotion to her mentor, Franz Boas, also contributed to the book's skewed interpretation of Samoa. According to Freeman, Mead had internalized Boas's alleged belief in "absolute" cultural determinism, in which culture was everything and biology played no role whatsoever.[18] As Boas's protégée she was simply doing what he wished and writing what she now believed. Yet Freeman read into the relationship more than there was.

True, Boas had been her Ph.D. supervisor and mentor and was Mead's supervisor on her National Research Council fellowship, helping her to formulate her research problem and overseeing her report. Mead wanted to please him, as her letters from Samoa make clear. She even hid her interest in poetry from him, fearing his disapproval. Mead respected Boas and did not wish to "betray" the high standards that he had set for all his students to do more and better fieldwork.[19] But Boas gave his students very little actual direction about the fieldwork process. Before her departure to the islands he met with her only once, for half an hour, and he left her largely on her own during her fieldwork. After her return, when she submitted her report "The Adolescent Girl in Samoa," Boas posed only one question to her: why had she not made clearer the distinction between romantic and passionate love?[20]

In writing *Coming of Age in Samoa,* Mead sought advice from George Dorsey, Ruth Benedict, and others. Boas did not play a major role in this process. While Freeman focused on Mead's relationship with Boas before and during her time in Samoa, *Coming of Age* was largely a product of what happened *after* she returned and especially after she had completed her National Research Council report. It was Mead who wanted to turn her professional report into a more accessible book. Dorsey helped with a new title and advice; Morrow and Mead worked together on the manuscript's transformation. Benedict assisted her in conceptualizing the general argument but did not help her with specific Samoan content. The descriptions and interpretations in *Coming of Age* were Mead's.

Boas saw the book after it was completed, was pleased with the result, and wrote the foreword, giving *Coming of Age* his scholarly support. But the book itself was not a work that he had directed. Similarly, Mead's second book on

Samoa, *Social Organization of Manu'a,* was not a Boasian product. Boas did not demand lockstep conformity from Mead or his other graduate students. And while she was indebted to Boas as her teacher and mentor, Mead was becoming very much her own person. With her appointment at the American Museum of Natural History, her professional career was now fully under way.

Mead's Intent in *Coming of Age in Samoa*

Like Boas, Sapir, and Benedict, Mead saw herself as a citizen-scientist. Not content with being a bookish academic, she wanted to be a public intellectual and activist, using ethnographic data to address important public issues. Although other anthropologists had waded into public debates periodically, Mead's primary goal in *Coming of Age* was to reach a large segment of educated Americans on a subject of concern to them. And she succeeded. Why else would Americans read a book about an unfamiliar culture by a young woman whose profession they did not understand?

Most anthropologists of her era did not write the way Mead did in *Coming of Age.* She was unequivocal and unafraid to offer her own opinions. Mead did not qualify or hesitate; she did not use words like "perhaps" and "probably." Her use of dramatic phrasing suggested just how progressive Samoan adolescent girls were compared to American girls. She stated that they enjoyed "great premarital freedom," could "experiment freely," and had "as many lovers as possible" for as long as possible before marriage. These phrases added a dash of excitement to Mead's staid professional report, but what may have seemed tantalizingly provocative to the American public in the late 1920s seemed truly problematic to a number of academics and popular reviewers at the time she wrote them. Mead herself recognized the discontinuity between her descriptions and what she called the "almost drastic character of the conclusions."[21]

Taken as descriptive statements, the phrases Mead used to evoke casualness and permissiveness often did not follow from her data. Indeed, she herself discussed the *limits* on premarital sex for adolescent girls, *punishments* for premarital sex, and how premarital sex often led to marriage rather than to its avoidance. Thus, the phrasing that Mead chose followed more from the message that she wished to convey and less from the data. Anthropologist Martin Orans substantiated this point in his analysis of Mead's descriptions of Samoans in *Coming of Age.*[22] Orans patiently counted each positive and negative reference to Samoans in the book and added them up. He found that in numerical terms these references were more often negative than positive. Yet overall Mead gave Samoan adolescence a positive spin.

Like Freeman, Orans argued that Mead's conclusions were impressionistic, the result of her beliefs rather than her data.[23] He noted that Mead did not carefully define variables such as adolescent stress, or use representative samples of Samoan and American adolescents, or employ a research design able to adequately test her hypothesis about differences that she perceived between Samoan and American adolescents.

Mead herself understood that she and other young anthropologists of her era were given very little methodological advice on how to approach fieldwork and provided few resources to conduct their research.[24] Nevertheless, as a trained psychologist Mead was aware how her research problem could be studied scientifically in America. In her introduction to *Coming of Age,* she discussed how to set up a controlled experiment on adolescent development in the United States, complete with large samples and multiple variables. Yet as an *anthropologist* Mead chose to use another culture—Samoa—as her control group. In doing so Mead was interested not only in scientifically testing her ideas about adolescence but also in humanistically appreciating cultural differences from, in her words, a more "self-conscious" and "self-critical" perspective.[25]

For Mead, *Coming of Age* was not just another ethnography in the short queue of scholarly monographs on other cultures being produced in the early twentieth century. It was the first book by an American anthropologist to use ethnographic data from another culture as the basis for social criticism of American society. Mead went beyond simply describing and analyzing Samoan adolescence as she would have in a standard ethnography and as she did in her report to the National Research Council. She was no longer a dispassionate ethnographer writing from "the native point of view" or from a purely scientific point of view. Mead was writing from *her* point of view to a nonprofessional audience. And Mead was writing for Americans about America as well as about Samoa. As she noted in the preface to the 1973 edition of *Coming of Age:* "It seemed to me then—and it still does—that if our studies of the way of life of other peoples are to be meaningful to the peoples of the industrialized world, they must be written for them and not wrapped in the technical jargon for specialists."[26]

With this in mind, Mead contrasted a fairly benign period of adolescence in the islands with the more turbulent years of American adolescence, arguing that Americans might learn something from the Samoan experience. The intent of the book was prescriptive, offering lessons for American teachers, educators, and parents. Mead observed: "The strongest light will fall upon the ways in which Samoan education, in its broadest sense, differs from our own. And from this contrast we may be able to turn, made newly and vividly self-conscious and self-critical, to judge anew and perhaps fashion differently the education we give our children."[27] This is why the book was subtitled *A Psychological Study of Primitive Youth for Western Civilization.* The final two chapters of the book, titled "Our Educational Problems in the Light of Samoan Contrasts" and "Education for Choice," were especially important in this regard.

Mead left little doubt about her own views of the personal lives of Samoan and American adolescents:

> From the Samoans' complete knowledge of sex, its possibilities and rewards, they are able to count its true value. . . . The Samoan girl who shrugs her shoulder over the excellent technique of some young Lothario is nearer to the recognition of sex as an impersonal force without any intrinsic value than is the sheltered American girl who falls in love with the first man that kisses her.[28]

> The opportunity to experiment freely, the complete familiarity with sex and the absence of very violent preferences make her experiences less charged with the possibility of conflict than they are in a more rigid and self-conscious civilization.[29]

> The Samoan girl never tastes the rewards of romantic love as we know it, nor does she suffer as an old maid who has appealed to no one or found no lover appealing to her, or as the frustrated housewife in a marriage which has not fulfilled her high demands.[30]

Mead was not writing as a cultural relativist in these passages. Cultural relativism as an ethnographic tool assumes that other cultures are worthy of study and that the ethnographer's own judgment should be temporarily suspended so that cultures can be studied on their own terms. Although cultural relativism requires the *temporary* suspension of judgment and comparison, it does not call for *permanent* suspension. Mead practiced cultural relativism in her fieldwork and professional work on Samoa, but in writing *Coming of Age* she made judgments and comparisons that were very much her own. Writing as a social critic, Mead reiterated that other cultures might teach us something about America: "Realising that our own ways are not humanly inevitable nor God-ordained, but the fruit of a long and turbulent history, we may well examine in turn all of our institutions, thrown into strong relief against the history of all other civilisations, and weighing them in the balance, be not afraid to find them wanting."[31]

Mead's comparisons and personal opinions about Samoan and American adolescence were professionally suspect. As anthropologist Nancy Lutkehaus commented: "The fact that Mead was willing to make such generalizations and to spell out their implications for American society contributed to the denigration of Mead's professional reputation among fellow anthropologists. Paradoxically, it simultaneously endeared her to the general public, for its conclusions presented a utopian vision of a liberal democratic society that generations of Americans read about with enthusiasm."[32]

In fact, *Coming of Age* was utopian in the sense that Mead hoped that American adolescence could become less stressful for adolescents and parents alike. Mead viewed Samoa as a kind of utopia, and in her interpretation she minimized its less pleasant aspects while emphasizing its more positive ones. She was also an early feminist, writing about the lives of young women in a positive manner. There was no hidden agenda in the book, and her direct approach connected with her readers. While her book was utopian, Mead knew that Samoa was not a realistic alternative for Americans. Americans could not become Samoans, but they might learn something about themselves from Samoans nonetheless.

Some scholars have voiced disapproval of Mead's utopian vision. Expressing his concern about Mead's mixing of ethnographic data and personal belief, Martin Orans cautioned: "Anthropologists' voyages to remote parts of the world should be genuine voyages of discovery and not occasions for designing tracts in support of an ideological position. And all of us should be especially on guard when that position is one that has our sympathy!"[33] From a scientific perspective, Orans's concern is well taken. However, for Mead and a number of other anthropologists, the lessons of fieldwork extended beyond ethnography. *Coming of Age* was about framing the choices that Americans might make about adolescence; in this sense it was a work of public advocacy. Mead intended to bridge the gap between the public and the professional, and she did so, going well beyond the information she had gathered in the islands. In the process, questions about her knowledge of Samoa arose.

Mead's Professional Monograph

Had *Coming of Age* been the only book that Mead wrote about the islands, criticism of her knowledge of Samoa might have had some merit. However, in less than two years after returning from the islands, Mead completed not only her professional report for the National Research Council and *Coming of Age in Samoa* but also *Social Organization of Manu'a*, a major ethnographic monograph. For Freeman, *Coming of Age* was Mead's most significant contribution on Samoa, and he believed it to be a disaster of monumental proportions. Yet *Social Organization of Manu'a*, which received very little attention, was her genuine ethnography of the islands. Mead herself regarded it as her most important professional work on Samoa.

This monograph was written for anthropologists, contained almost no social commentary or cultural criticism and no utopian vision, and was published in the obscure Bernice P. Bishop Museum series. It languished in the shadow of its best-selling counterpart to such an extent that Freeman could treat it almost as a footnote to *Coming of Age* instead of acknowledging its importance in understanding Mead's ability as an ethnographer of Samoa.

The two books stood in stark contrast to each other. *Coming of Age* was a popular trade book about adolescence; it bore little resemblance to the ethnographies of that era. *Social Organization of Manu'a,* on the other hand, was a professional monograph on a decidedly unsexy topic. *Coming of Age* was boldly comparative; *Social Organization of Manu'a* was sober and scholarly, building on earlier descriptions of the islands. Had this been the only book that Mead published on Samoa, she would have been remembered as a careful and pioneering ethnographer. And had Mead published it first, *Coming of Age in Samoa* might have had more professional credibility. In fact, a number of Samoan specialists regard it as her best work on the islands. *Social Organization of Manu'a* is not flawless, but it is a very thoughtful study that was ahead of its time in terms of theoretical sophistication.[34]

Yet Freeman and other critics of Mead have neglected it. The third section of Freeman's *Margaret Mead and Samoa* is titled "A Refutation of Mead's Conclusions," covering 11 different topics in the course of 165 pages. However, there is little mention of *Social Organization of Manu'a* and little discussion of social organization. This is all the more interesting because social organization was the topic of Freeman's most substantial ethnographic work on Samoa—his 1948 postgraduate diploma thesis. He and Mead had done research on the same topic less than twenty years apart. Her monograph was a standard reference work on Samoan social organization in English. Freeman's thesis advisor, the great anthropologist Sir Raymond Firth, had read and referred to it in his own ethnography of Tikopia, another Polynesian culture.[35] At over three hundred typewritten pages, Freeman's unpublished thesis would have been an obvious place to recognize Mead's monograph, to note that she had done parallel research on social organization, and to discuss and critique her findings. Yet there is no discussion of any of Mead's published work on the islands in Freeman's thesis.[36]

Social Organization of Manu'a complemented *Coming of Age in Samoa.* They represented the two different projects that Mead had researched. Yet relatively few anthropologists read both of them. One anthropologist who did was Robert Redfield. Reviewing them separately after each was published, Redfield was initially critical of *Coming of Age,* commenting:

For all the intimate association with Samoans the book is somehow disappointing. Why do the Samoans, with whom love is merely one of a hundred unstressed values and who are cynical of fidelity, follow romantic conventions of courtship in speech and song? How is it that in spite of extreme license in word and conduct there nevertheless remains a residue, apparently quite like our own, of what is salacious and obscene? But Miss Mead is interested, one feels, in problems and cases, not in human nature. A little Malinowski, stirred in, would have helped, perhaps.[37]

But after reading *Social Organization of Manu'a* Redfield concluded: "The documentation that was lacking in *Coming of Age in Samoa* is given in this book. It is a monograph of exceptional merit."[38] Anthropologist Ralph Linton, who himself had done fieldwork in Polynesia, concurred, also giving it a very favorable review.

Social Organization of Manu'a provides an effective rebuttal to many of the criticisms of *Coming of Age*. Samoan social organization was an extremely complex subject, requiring subtle ethnographic understanding. Mead tailored this monograph to professional standards, and by these rigorous standards her monograph was an important contribution.

The Reception of *Coming of Age in Samoa*

In *Coming of Age* Mead could have stayed closer to the data, could have been less of a social critic, and could have toned down what Freeman called her "verbal artifice."[39] She could have avoided absolutes in describing Samoans as having "*no* frigidity, *no* impotence," and so on.[40] But *Coming of Age* was a popular book written for the general public. Reviewers understood the book's purpose immediately, and this was a major reason for its enthusiastic reception.

When *Coming of Age* was published in August 1928, it generated exceptional press coverage. Morrow had lined up strong endorsements from Malinowski, Dorsey, Havelock Ellis, and psychologist John W. Watson; their accolades were a major public relations coup and drew attention to the book. Following the book's release, tabloidlike headlines heralded the distant islands, declaring that "Samoa Is the Place for Women" and that Samoa is "Where Neuroses Cease."[41] The praise Mead's book received was often profuse and unqualified. For Freeman, it was the beginning of a "mythic process" that would confer legendary status on Mead and Samoa.[42] Yet a closer reading of these early reviews suggests that while most were quite positive, a number called attention to the inconsistencies between description and interpretation on which later critics would focus.

Some of the early reviews were quite astute in their understanding of the book's strengths and limitations. As Nels Anderson wrote in the *Survey:* "If it is science, the book is somewhat of a disappointment. It lacks a documental base. It is given too much to interpretation instead of description. Dr. Mead forgets too often that she is an anthropologist and gets her own personality involved with her materials."[43] Writing in the *Saturday Review of Literature,* Mary Elizabeth Johnson criticized Mead's generalizations, for example, that there were few neurotic people in Samoa. She wondered how Mead, a person from another culture who had spent relatively little time in the islands, could support this kind of generalization on the basis of the limited data she had gathered. In addition, Johnson found Mead's broad comparisons of Samoa and America questionable, based on "a method extremely precarious in any study of social phenomena." She also was able to accurately discern that the book had been reworked to make it more popular, noting: "The lack of coherence between chapters one, twelve, and thirteen [the chapters Mead added to her report] and the remainder of the volume leads to the inference that they have been added to provide a basis for popular appeal and to give the book its subtitle—'A Psychological Study of Primitive Youth for Western Civilization.'"[44]

The well-known critic H. L. Mencken also thought that Mead's comparison of Samoan and American adolescence was unconvincing, and he remarked, "Miss Mead's book would have been better if she had avoided discussing the woes of American high-school girls and confined herself to an objective account of life in Samoa."[45] These reviewers were not reluctant to express their reservations, but, like most reviewers, they found *Coming of Age* worth reading because the issues Mead addressed were interesting and important.

Early reviews by anthropologists were also favorable, particularly in Great Britain.[46] But there was professional criticism as well, decades before Freeman's books on Mead appeared. One of the first professional reviews, published in *American Anthropologist* in 1929, was by Robert Lowie, a former student of Boas who was also editor of that journal. Lowie began his review by praising Mead, stating, "Miss Mead's graphic picture of Polynesian free love is convincing. It falls into line with the reports of early travelers." However, Lowie immediately followed these words with critical comments, remarking, "Nevertheless, this is not the whole story. The author knows it and even enlarges on it—in an appendix." He then quoted Mead at length on the harsh pre-European Samoan culture and asked how that culture and the seemingly benign post-European culture could be reconciled. Lowie also registered doubt about some of Mead's findings and her overstated conclusions, noting her penchant for "pedagogical sermonizing."[47]

Perhaps the most damning comments came from Edward Sapir, Mead's former lover, who wrote in the *New Republic* in 1929 that *Coming of Age* was "cheap and dull."[48] In addition, he deplored feminists and lesbians, whom he believed were both frigid and ambitious, and accused "emancipated women" of being little better than prostitutes.[49] In private, Sapir berated Mead as a "loathsome bitch" and "pathological liar."[50] Having turned against Mead, Sapir attempted to persuade Malinowski to also do so, and Sapir's influence among some American anthropologists may have influenced their negative views of her work.[51]

Professional criticism of *Coming of Age* would follow Mead for the rest of her career, coming from both those who knew her well and those who did not. In the 1960s anthropologist Marvin Harris took Mead to task in his comprehensive history of the discipline, *The Rise of Anthropological Theory*. Harris, who knew Mead while he was a student at Columbia and later as a faculty member there, agreed that Mead was one of "anthropology's most creative and brilliant personalities." Yet her "sweeping ethnographic generalities . . . leave many of her colleagues in a state of wide-eyed wonder." He cited as an example Mead's statement that "the girls' minds were perplexed by no conflicts, troubled by no philosophical queries, beset by no remote ambitions," commenting, "For a generalization which is at once so sweeping and so thoroughly dependent on 'getting inside of heads,' Mead's style conveys an unnerving degree of conviction." Like many other critics, Harris found that Mead "exaggerated."[52]

Criticism of *Coming of Age* came from many quarters, despite the book's commercial success. Some questioned Mead's data and conclusions, while others questioned her judgment. Anthropologist Maureen Molloy observed in her analysis of Mead's writing: "Her conflation of the modes of science, literature, and journalism was a reason for both her popular success and the ambivalence and hostility with which many of her professional colleagues regarded her work. The quality of her prose aroused suspicion if not wrath in the hearts of her fellow anthropologists."[53]

From the time it was published, *Coming of Age* was the subject of high praise and strong criticism. The book did not receive a free ride from Mead's colleagues or its other reviewers. Moreover, Mead was sensitive to this criticism and defensive about it, especially criticism from Malinowski, who, after initially applauding *Coming of Age,* became quite critical of her work.[54] At the time it was published, though, the book's reception was of limited concern to Mead. She had not anticipated its success; neither had her publisher. Mead was leaving New York when the book was released. Indeed, when the first reviews of *Coming of Age in Samoa* were published, she was not even in the United States. She was on her way to the South Pacific to join Reo Fortune, her soon-to-be second husband, to do more fieldwork.

Mead's American Audience
in the 1920s

As MEAD WAS DEPARTING FOR New Guinea, *Coming of Age in Samoa* reached the shelves of American bookstores. William Morrow had invested $1,500 to advertise and promote the book, a substantial sum for a small publisher. The first edition had the enthusiastic endorsement of Havelock Ellis emblazoned on a red band across the book's cover, a "stunt" that Morrow thought helped sales.[1] And Mead herself had prepared popular articles for magazines like *Natural History* and *Parents' Magazine* to call attention to the book.[2] As a result, *Coming of Age* quickly became a commercial success.

Part of this success had to do with Mead's connection with her readership. Employing an explicitly comparative perspective, her broad argument was that coming of age in Samoa was less difficult than coming of age in America and that the Samoan adolescent experience could help Americans respond more effectively to the problems of adolescence at home. Many Americans were having problems with their adolescents. People were looking for answers, and Mead suggested some. Although she was criticized for not having sufficient data to make her comparisons between Samoa and America, it is worth looking more closely at Mead's American reference point in order to understand the context in which it was received at the time.

Mead assumed that her reading audience shared her basic perception of American youth and so did not specifically document the ways in which American adolescence was more turbulent than Samoan adolescence. Today Mead's references to America at that time seem very general. Yet her reading audience in the late 1920s understood this part of her argument. Why?

On the first page of her introduction to *Coming of Age* Mead observed:

> The spectacle of a younger generation diverging ever more widely from
> the standards and ideals of the past, cut adrift without the anchorage of

respected home standards or group religious values, terrified the cautious reactionary, tempted the radical propagandist to missionary crusades among the defenceless youth, and worried the least thoughtful among us.

In American civilisation, with its many immigrant strains, its dozens of conflicting standards of conduct, its hundreds of religious sects, its shifting economic conditions, this unsettled disturbed status of youth was more apparent than in the older more settled civilisation of Europe.[3]

Mead found a broad consensus among educators, psychologists, and other professionals about the "restlessness of youth" in the 1920s.[4] For her, though, the more interesting question was to what extent this was a uniquely American phenomenon. Was it limited to America, or was it more widespread? Mead noted that the influential psychologist G. Stanley Hall believed that the difficulties and conflicts of adolescence were part of a universal stage in the life cycle found in all cultures. For Hall, idealism and rebellion, parental conflict and peer pressure were typical of adolescence everywhere.[5] For Mead, however, turbulence could not be assumed to be universal without actually investigating adolescence in other cultures. This was, of course, her rationale for going to Samoa.

Young and Restless

To many Americans in the 1920s, adolescents seemed to be going through an especially difficult time. Although adolescents were getting more education, working outside the family, and experiencing a variety of social, religious, and political ideologies, there were costs to all of these new experiences. Mead discussed these costs in *Coming of Age:* "For it must be realized by any student of civilisation that we pay heavily for our rapidly changing, heterogeneous civilisation; we pay in high proportions of crime and delinquency, we pay in the conflicts of youth, we pay in an ever increasing number of neuroses. . . . In such a list of prices, we must count our gains carefully, not to be discouraged."[6] Compared to the problems of contemporary adolescents, the problems of early-twentieth-century adolescents may not seem that serious. But the problems that were encountered, such as crime and delinquency, were real enough for families that were supposed to act as a refuge from the challenges of the city and as a buffer against the unpredictable changes that were occurring.

Mead's view of these problems was confirmed in a number of studies from the 1920s. Willystine Goodsell's book *Problems of the Family* summarized the conventional wisdom of the time:

That the home is not successfully meeting either the demands of society or the deepest needs of its members is evidenced by the prevalence of juvenile delinquency and crime, by outburst of suicidal mania among youth, by the establishment and spread of child guidance clinics, juvenile courts and the probation system. Unsuccessful functioning of the family is further revealed by the alarming growth of mental and nervous diseases, culminating in nervous breakdowns. . . . The conditions of modern life in our huge urban centers are so complex that both the child and his parents find difficulty in adjusting to them.[7]

For American adolescents, and especially girls, there were many choices and no clear roadmap for making the right ones. Among the choices that Mead listed were the number and kind of responsibilities at home, the degree of acceptance of parental authority, the degree of acceptance of religious authority, the amount of schooling a girl would receive, the degree of conformity to her peer group, the amount of knowledge about "sex hygiene" and birth control, the decision about whom and when to marry, and the decision about whether to work and when to stop. Most important, "the basic difficulties of reconciling the teachings of authority with the practices of society and the findings of science, all trouble and perplex children already harassed beyond endurance."[8] For Mead, the answer to the burden of these choices was an enlightened "education for choice" so that young people could make decisions that were right for them, including choices about sex.

The Way We Were

Just as Mead did not document the exact nature of adolescent storm and stress in America in the 1920s, neither did she document changes in sexual conduct of young Americans at that time. Her assumption that America was more restrictive than Samoa was, again, one that she shared with her audience.

As noted earlier, the 1920s were a "period of transition" for young Americans, especially in the realm of sex.[9] During World War I young soldiers sent abroad sometimes became sexually involved with their girlfriends or other young women during their last good-bye. Following the end of the war in 1919, many young soldiers returned from Europe having experienced not only the rigors of combat but also intimate relations with European women. This meant that there was a greater reservoir of sexual experience on which young people could draw.

There were other broad changes taking place in the sexual landscape. As America became more urban and industrial, cars became a common means of transportation and telephones the preferred means of communication. These very basic technological changes shifted control of relationships away from the home and parental supervision and into the hands of young men and women themselves. Relationships were privatized, and chaperones were gradually becoming a thing of the past. In earlier decades courtship leading to marriage had been the norm. This ritualized relationship between proper suitor and chaperoned young lady was now slowly giving way to less formal interaction between boyfriend and girlfriend. Dating was in. Girls expected to be taken out. They met their boyfriends at the door, often arranging a date by telephone and sometimes creating friction with their parents.[10]

There were new places to go. By the 1920s silent movies had become a weekly form of entertainment for millions of young Americans, providing visual models for love and romance. Young couples attended the movies without adult supervision or escort. They could learn manners, fashion, and even how to kiss and flirt at the movies. "Sex adventure films," as they were called, were in vogue, although they were often simple morality tales with lessons about the wages of sin.[11] Some silent movies were more daring. In 1928, the year in which *Coming of Age* was published, Joan Crawford appeared in *Our Dancing Daughters,* one of the most popular films of the era. Audiences watched as Crawford drank, kissed, went on joy rides, and danced the Charleston. This was a daring young woman. F. Scott Fitzgerald, the great writer of the Jazz Age, thought that Crawford was the perfect flapper, the fashionable, pleasure-seeking icon of the 1920s. The following year Crawford starred in a sequel, *Our Modern Maidens,* in which she played a married woman who flirted, got divorced, and—scandalously—lived happily ever after![12]

These trends, already established in the big cities, gradually worked their way into the heartland of the country. Robert Staughton and Helen Merrell Lynd, in their classic sociological study of the period in Muncie, Indiana (known by the pseudonym Middletown), reported that new technologies like cars and movies were changing the way young people interacted:

> The more sophisticated social life of today [1925] has brought with it another "problem" much discussed by Middletown parents, the apparently increasing relaxation of some of the traditional prohibitions upon the approaches of boys and girls to each other's persons. . . . [I]n 1890 a "well-brought-up" boy and girl were commonly forbidden to sit together in the dark; but motion pictures and the automobile have lifted this taboo and, once lifted, it is easy for the practice to become widely extended. Buggy riding in 1890 allowed only a narrow range of mobility; three to eight [p.m.] were generally accepted hours for riding, and being out after eight-thirty without a chaperone was largely forbidden. In an auto, however, a party may go to a city halfway across the state in an afternoon or evening, and unchaperoned automobile parties as late as midnight, while subject to criticism, are not exceptional.[13]

Cars and movies provided new locations for young people to get together. So did public dances and dance halls, no longer sponsored exclusively by religious or civic organizations. Privately owned clubs provided new opportunities for young people of different backgrounds to meet each other. There were "fast" dances, like the Charleston and early swing, which frightened traditionalists. As one female evangelist declared, "Social dancing is the first and easiest step towards hell. The first time a girl allows a man to swing her around the dance floor her instinct tells her she has lost something she should have treasured."[14]

In the traditional American ideal young men were supposed to be gallant gentlemen, protective of a young lady's dignity and virtue; young women were supposed to be modest and chaste. But young people in the 1920s were openly interested in sex. Movies, dances, music, magazines, and literature all used sex as an invitation to imagine new relationships. Popular magazines, such as *Telling Tales,* included stories like "Primitive Love," "Indolent Kisses," and "Innocents Astray." A full-page advertisement for another "sex-adventure" magazine declared: "Until five years ago [1919], there was nowhere men and women, boys and girls could turn to get a knowledge of the rules of life. They were sent out into the world totally unprepared to cope with life. . . . Then came *True Story.*"[15] *True Confessions,* which also began its long publication run in 1919, provided life lessons in stories like "Playing with Fire," with its teaser, "It was only a little indiscretion but it led to another and still another."[16]

By the 1920s a more sexualized culture was developing in the public arena. Smoking and drinking, formerly considered social vices among women, were not only tolerated but accepted in some circles. Women's dress became more revealing as hemlines rose. Silk stockings were all the rage, and advertisements for them were so popular that they were used to sell other products. The use of makeup, formerly associated with prostitutes, was now common, and nail polish was in use among younger girls. Even "permanent" hairstyles, including fashionable "bobbed" hair for married women, were in demand among adolescents. A separate culture for young people was developing, with sex as its central theme; sex marked off youth from age.[17]

More subtle changes were also occurring. Increasing education was deferring the age of marriage for a subset of the population. As more young people completed high school and attended college, some of them postponed engagement and marriage. Dating, in which there was no commitment to engagement or marriage, became more common, creating a sphere where personal expression and the recognition of individual desires took precedence over strict laws and a puritanical public morality.[18]

The new freedoms were accompanied by new problems. Young men going to college now wished to avoid being "trapped" into an early marriage. And young women now became more sexually inviting to attract these educated males while avoiding the appearance of being too "easy" or, far worse, becoming pregnant. A carefully calibrated code of intimate contact developed for different kinds of relationships, from kissing to French kissing to "petting" to "heavy petting" to intercourse, this last supposedly reserved for one's fiancé. "Necking" and "petting" parties, popular with college students, were emulated at high school parties.[19]

People across the country were talking about sex, writing about it, and researching it. In the late nineteenth century in both Europe and America the new science of sex—sexology—emerged to help provide more basic knowledge and often to advocate a more liberal approach to sex. Havelock Ellis, who introduced Sigmund Freud's ideas about sex to Americans, discussed the issue of women's sexual responsiveness. Because elementary knowledge of sex was often lacking, especially knowledge of women's sexuality, there was an almost desperate search for literature on the subject. Sex manuals—formerly written for the medical profession—found their way into the public realm.

Marie Carmichael Stopes was a sexologist whose own life illustrated just how sexually naive people were in the early twentieth century. At the time she was married, Stopes held two advanced degrees, a doctor of science degree and a doctor of philosophy degree, from two major European universities. She was one of the most highly educated women in the world. Yet she remained a virgin for the first six months of her marriage because she did not realize what sexual intercourse involved. Her marriage was not consummated because, as she later discovered, her husband was impotent. Appalled at her own lack of knowledge about sex, in 1918 Stopes wrote a book titled *Married Love: A New Contribution to the Solution of Sex Difficulties* to remedy the situation. By 1924 it was in its sixteenth edition, having global sales of more than a half million copies.[20]

As the recognition of women's sexuality migrated from academic circles into popular consciousness, women began to think of themselves as sexual beings. Women's sexual responsiveness and satisfaction were no longer considered issues to be avoided or to be ashamed of but rather issues to be addressed. Advances in birth control in the form of condoms and diaphragms meant that sex and pregnancy were no longer inextricably linked. It was now possible to imagine sex without children and even outside of marriage. Sex was no longer the ultimate bargaining chip for a marriage contract.

Although none of the available forms of contraception were very effective, they seemed better than withdrawal, the rhythm method, or nothing at all.

Douches had been preferred because women had control over them. Condoms became commonplace among troops during World War I but depended on male initiative. And female-controlled diaphragms were not introduced in New York until the 1920s by sexual crusader Margaret Sanger. Although diaphragms as well as other forms of contraception were at first publicly condemned as a social evil that would inevitably lead to moral decay, they were gradually accepted.[21]

In *Coming of Age* Mead recognized that birth control posed a new set of choices for young people, stating:

> The knowledge of birth control, while greatly dignifying human life by introducing the element of choice at the point where human beings have before been most abjectly subject to nature, introduces further perplexities. It complicates the issue from a straight marriage-home-children plan of life versus independent spinsterhood by permitting marriages without children, earlier marriages, marriages and careers, sex relations without marriage and the responsibility of a home. And because the majority of girls still wish to marry and regard their occupations as stop-gaps, these problems not only influence their attitude towards men, but also their attitude towards their work.[22]

Meanwhile, in Greenwich Village sexual frontiers were being pushed even farther. Cultural radicals of the 1920s embraced a new ethic of self-expression in politics, literature, and sex.[23] Liberty meant the shattering of social convention. Living for the moment and living it intensely were the watchwords of the day. The poet Edna St. Vincent Millay, whose work was widely read, embodied this new ethic. Millay was bisexual and wrote unashamedly about "lust." She expressed her defiance of conventional morality in one of her best-known poems:

> My candle burns at both ends;
> It will not last the night;
> But ah, my foes, and oh, my friends—
> It gives a lovely light![24]

Millay was at the cutting edge of Greenwich Village's sophisticated social scene. Mead and her close friends, the Ash Can Cats, read and admired Millay's poetry. They even went to her home in the Village and visited with her.[25] The Village was also where people read *Lady Chatterley's Lover* and other banned works. Cultural radicals went to Broadway to see actress Mae West in her play *Sex*, which the censors promptly shut down. And they drank alcohol, like so many other Americans, from the ubiquitous hip flasks that were a by-product of Prohibition.

Conventional Morality in the 1920s

If the 1920s were a period in which America was becoming more sexually permissive, the changes were uneven and limited. The dominant morality of the time remained restrictive. In describing Middletown the Lynds wrote: "Sex is one of those things Middletown has long been taught to fear. Its institutions — with the important exceptions of the movies and some of the periodicals it reads, both imported from the outside culture — operate to keep the subject out of sight and out of mind as much as possible."[26]

For all the sexual possibilities of the 1920s, sexual restraint prevailed in actual conduct. Young women were very likely to be virgins when they became engaged. Young men often found their first sexual partners in prostitutes; married men were also frequent clients. As for married women, sexual fulfillment was often unrealized with their husbands, so they purchased a device that was generically advertised by department stores as a useful "household appliance." It had a motor and attachments for kitchen activities like churning, mixing, beating, grinding, buffing, and operating a fan. Advertised in catalogs and in many women's magazines for kitchen tasks, the device was actually employed as a vibrator. Most American husbands did not realize what these appliances were being used for or that their wives were looking for sexual fulfillment until the devices began turning up in underground pornographic films in the 1920s. The catalog ads quickly vanished.[27]

Divorce was also viewed as a threat to conventional sexual morality. As the Lynds observed:

> The truth of the matter appears to be that God-fearing Middletown is afraid of sex as a force in its midst, afraid it might break loose and run wild, and afraid to recognize too openly that those "whom God hath joined together" can be mismatched. In theory, therefore, it averts its eyes and talks about marriage as a "sacred institution," while daily in courtrooms its businessman lawyers work in the matter-of-fact spirit of their world of personal contractual obligations. As one of these lawyers said to a member of the research staff, "I believe that marriage is a contract and that anyone twenty-one years old ought to be able to get out of it just about as easily as he [*sic*] gets into it."[28]

The norms of the time were summarized in Joseph Folsom's book *The Family: Its Sociology and Social Psychiatry*, published in 1934; the following excerpts describe the social environment in which American children were supposed to be raised:

- All sexual behavior on the part of children is prevented by all means at the parents' disposal. . . . For the sake of prevention it has been usual to cultivate in the child, especially the girl, an attitude of horror or disgust toward all aspects of sex. . . .

- Premarital intercourse is immoral though not abhorrent. . . . Violations are supposedly prevented by the supervision of the girl's parents. . . .
- Illegitimate children are socially stigmatized. . . . The chief stigma falls upon the unmarried mother, because she has broken an important sex taboo.[29]

This public morality persisted well into the twentieth century. Author William Manchester recalled that when he grew up in the late 1930s and early 1940s,

marriage was a sacrament. Divorce was disgraceful. Pregnancy meant expulsion from school or dismissal from a job. The boys responsible for the crimes of impregnation had to marry the girls. Couples did not keep house before they were married and there could be no wedding until the girl's father had approved. You assumed that gentlemen always stood and removed their hats when a woman entered the room. . . . You needed a precise relationship between the sexes, so that no one questioned the duty of boys to cross the seas and fight while girls wrote them cheerful letters from home, girls you knew were still pure because they let you touch them here but not there, explaining that they were saving themselves for marriage. . . . Later the rules would change. But we didn't know that then. We didn't *know.*[30]

Thus, in the early twentieth century there was still a socially approved norm in which virginity was highly valued and in which dating or courtship led to marriage, which in turn led to sex and children.

This conservative public morality opposed the individualizing and liberalizing trends of the 1920s favored by Mead and others. The passing of the Eighteenth Amendment to the Constitution in 1917, which banned the "manufacture, sale, and transportation" of alcohol in the United States, was a reminder of just how influential social conservatives were. Religious fundamentalists like Billy Sunday preached hellfire and damnation to those sinners who drank liquor and engaged in sex outside of the institution of holy matrimony. They also deplored thinkers like Freud and Darwin for supposedly reducing sex from a sacred covenant that was part of marriage to an animal instinct that undermined Christian teachings. Through the modern medium of radio these evangelists reached huge audiences sympathetic to their message. Government commissions were created to censor sexual references in literature and the exposure of flesh in movies. Books like *Lady Chatterley's Lover* and James Joyce's *Ulysses* were not only "banned in Boston," but their publication and mailing were prohibited nationwide.

There was also a secular backlash against the liberalization of sex and the sexualization of culture. For a number of public thinkers who were more tolerant than the fundamentalists, the incipient sexual revolution of the 1920s had gone too far. Sex had been so publicized, individualized, studied, and discussed that it had been demystified. Joseph Wood Krutch, writing in 1928, lamented: "Sex, we learned, was not so awesome as once we had thought. God does not care so much about it as we had formerly been led to suppose; but neither, as a result, do we. Love is becoming gradually so accessible, so unmysterious, and so free that its value is trivial."[31] Edward Sapir concurred, commenting: "Sex as self-realization unconsciously destroys its own object by making it no more than a tool to a selfish end."[32]

This was the American context in which Mead wrote *Coming of Age,* a set of cultural understandings that she and her audience shared but that was largely undocumented in her book. An older public sexual morality was in decline but had not been replaced. A new morality seemed to be emerging but had not become widely accepted and would not be for many decades to come. These were the conflicting standards with which maturing adolescents had to cope and were one reason that Mead believed they experienced more turbulence than Samoan adolescents.

When William Morrow suggested that Mead make her report about Samoan adolescence relevant to an American audience, Mead knew what he was talking about. He asked her, "What would you have to say if you wrote some more about what all this means to Americans?" Mead recalled her answer:

> Fortunately, I knew. When I came back from Samoa I was asked to give lectures before an assortment of audiences—in schools, in the Long Island town where a cousin lived, in a new housing project for intellectuals—and, when I was asked about the meaning of what I had found in Samoa, I was compelled to think through the answers. It seemed clear that, to start with, that if girls in Samoa did not have to live through the difficulties that face American girls in adolescence, then the problem is not the inevitable, universal one that it was assumed to be. If one society could bring its children through adolescence painlessly, then there was a chance that other societies could do so also. What then[,] audiences wanted to know, did this mean to us Americans? During the same winter, I was also teaching an evening class of working girls, and their questions, which I had to answer, were very different from those I had thought of.
>
> Fresh from these experiences, I was ready to write the last two chapters—one comparing the lives of Samoan and American girls and one called "Education for Choice." This chapter, written in 1928[,] is still relevant [as of 1965]. The problem of bringing up children who are free to

choose among many new alternatives is one we shall be trying to solve, in new and better ways, as long as we are a democracy. The manuscript was at last complete.[33]

People had questions about adolescent storm and stress. Mead was one of a number of authors who addressed their pressing concerns. This was a major reason so many people read the book. The contrast between Samoa and America had been vivid for Mead as an American of the 1920s and as a novice ethnographer. It also made sense to her American audience.

Fantasy Islands?

If Mead's method of comparing and contrasting American and Samoan adolescence worked well because Americans were interested in the problems of American youth, it was also effective because Samoa conformed to American beliefs about a utopian Polynesia. Mead built on preexisting images of the South Pacific and simplified Samoa for her reading audience. Her basic argument, that Samoan girls experienced fewer choices and therefore less stress and fewer problems growing up, seemed reasonable.

Although Samoan and American girls passed through the same physical stages of puberty, their social experiences as adolescents were very different. American girls in the 1920s were facing choices about education, work, sex, and marriage that most Samoans could not imagine; indeed, most of their own American mothers could not have imagined these choices. American adolescents were part of a rapidly changing society with different classes, religions, educational levels, and political beliefs. In contrast, Mead noted: "We have followed the lives of Samoan girls, watched them change from babies to baby tenders, learn to make the oven and weave fine mats, forsake the life of the gang to become more active members of the household, defer marriage through as many years of casual love-making as possible, finally marry and settle down to rearing children who will repeat the same cycle."[34]

In her idealized summary of the traditional life cycle Mead saw Samoan girls having fewer choices than their American counterparts and making the same choices their mothers had made. When these girls did make choices, Mead found that "in each case she was making concrete choices within one recognized pattern of behavior. She was never called upon to make choices involving an actual rejection of the standards of her social group, such as the daughter of Puritan parents, who permits indiscriminate caresses, must make in our society."[35]

In a general way Mead was undoubtedly correct. Samoan girls had fewer choices, different choices, and choices made within a single cultural standard, differentiated only by rank, age, and gender. But was there really less stress and conflict? Here Mead was emphatic. In her conclusion she found:

> The Samoan background which makes growing up so easy, so simple, is the general casualness of the whole society. For Samoa is a place where no one plays for very high stakes, no one pays very heavy prices, no one suffers for his convictions or fights to the death for special ends. Disagreements between parent and child are settled by the child's moving across the street, between a man and his village by the man's removal to the next village, between a husband and his wife's seducer by a few fine mats. Neither poverty nor great disasters threaten people to make them hold their lives dearly and tremble for continued existence. Wars and cannibalism long since passed away and now the greatest cause for tears, short of death itself, is a journey of a relative to another island. No one is hurried along in life or punished harshly for slowness of development. Instead the gifted, the precocious, are held back, until the slowest among them have caught the pace. Love and hate, jealousy and revenge, sorrow and bereavement, are all matters of weeks. From the first months of its life, when a child is handed carelessly from one woman's hands to another's, the lesson is learned of not caring for one person greatly, not setting high hopes on any one relationship.[36]

Of course, Mead was romanticizing Samoa, for in the very next paragraph, after stating that "no one" plays for very high stakes, "no one" pays a very heavy price, and "no one" suffers for their convictions, she mentions three girls who did and were considered social misfits. These girls and others who did not conform to the benevolent, low-conflict norm inhabit Mead's descriptive chapters in *Coming of Age*. Nor did Mead mention the "great disaster" brought by the 1926 hurricane on Manu'a or the important anticolonial political movements in both American Samoa and Western Samoa that led to exile and even death for some of their leaders. Nevertheless, to her American audience and *in comparison* with urban, middle-class America in the 1920s, Samoan adolescence seemed more orderly and predictable.

The Islands in American Life

Mead's audience shared a common set of images about Polynesia and Samoa that, by evoking an island paradise, made it easier to envision life in the islands as less stressful and more pleasant. These images found their way into American life in books, magazines, and other forms of popular entertainment, including silent films during the early twentieth century. While we take these images for granted today, they had a particular history that contributed to the American understanding of Mead's Samoa in *Coming of Age*.

For Americans living in the late 1800s and early 1900s, Polynesia was not so much a geographic location as a state of mind. Samoa was somewhere out there, but who knew exactly where? Many Americans of that period could not even identify the South Pacific on a map, confusing it with the Caribbean or even Africa. Hawai'i, Samoa, Tahiti—all these islands blurred together.[37] Yet if Americans could not identify individual islands with any certainty, generic images existed nonetheless. People believed that Polynesian life was free and easy and that sexual conduct was permissive.

This image of a South Seas paradise that people found so compelling had its roots centuries earlier in philosophical discussions about "Man" living in a "state of nature" uncorrupted by Western civilization.[38] This idea of "natural man" fed into Rousseau's ideas about the "noble savage." Then came the great voyages of discovery by European explorers that seemed to bear witness to the existence of paradise on earth.

After surviving the perilous passage around the tip of South America, these early explorers often went ashore in Tahiti, where they encountered a bountiful culture with fresh water and abundant food presented to them by dignified and generous chiefs. The weather was tropical and the culture enticing. Most of all, there were beautiful women with flowers in their hair, wearing little or no clothing, and offering their bodies to weary officers and crewmen after their immensely difficult journey. As Capt. William Bligh wrote in the elegant language of the eighteenth century, "The allurements of dissipation are more than equal to anything that can be conceived."[39] Unlike many areas of the world, where women were inaccessible and therefore only a marginal part of travel narratives, Tahitian women were quite accessible. These were fantasy islands, at least in the minds of the Europeans, and the Tahitian experience was generalized to Polynesia as a whole.

As Europeans overwhelmed the islands, native populations were often radically depopulated and their cultures transformed. Epidemics decimated the indigenous populations of Tahiti and Hawai'i to such an extent that by the late nineteenth century there remained only a small percentage of their pre-European numbers. In other island groups like Samoa the effects of disease were initially minimal, and their cultures continued to flourish. At this point in time American and European entrepreneurs realized that there might be a market in "real live" islanders for people in the West who had heard of and perhaps read about these exotic people but who had never seen them in person. If Europeans could not go to Polynesia, Polynesians would come to them.

Samoans on Tour

In the late nineteenth century American showmen began bringing Samoans to the United States, where they performed for audiences as dancers and warriors. In 1889 circus agent Robert Cunningham selected a group of nine Samoan men and women, contracting with them to spend three years on tour in America and Europe.[40] They performed their dances to great acclaim first in San Francisco and then in New York. However, one Samoan woman died early in the tour, and others died as it progressed. The dancers were forced to perform in Samoan costume even in the winter, and this may have contributed to the pulmonary diseases that killed them. Two more Samoans died in Europe just before the remaining dancers were presented to the Berlin Anthropological Society. Another died in Denver, where his body was placed on public display. Of the original nine dancers, only three survived to return to the islands in 1891. Cunningham was clearly more concerned about his finances than the health of his Samoan troupe.

While the Cunningham tour was a disaster for the Samoans involved, more successful tours followed. Perhaps the most important Samoan tours were associated with the great world's fairs of that era. At the Chicago World's Fair in 1893 Harry Moors, a Michigan-born entrepreneur living in Western Samoa, added action and sex to his Samoan dance troupe, which also included a few Fijians and Wallis Islanders. This act featured war dances and sitting sivas, with the dancers in tapa cloth costumes set against a traditional Samoan background.[41]

Although the Samoan women were required to wear tops and the show did not include erotic "night dances," Moors's Samoan dance troupe was a popular success, returning in 1904 for the St. Louis World's Fair. Because traditional Samoan musical accompaniment used only drumming, Moors hired a Mexican orchestra for additional color. No one seemed to mind, as audiences showered the dancers with money. Moors took his troupe on the road for another year and a half, traveling throughout the country and performing two shows a day. Since the Samoan girls were especially popular, Moors had to enforce strict rules against their involvement with members of the audience. These shows helped establish the image of the seductive and sensuous Samoan woman.

The Making of the Polynesian Stereotype

By the early twentieth century, popular images of seductive Polynesian women were already part of an inviting stereotype. In 1912 a play called *The Bird of Paradise* sparked particular interest.[42] Set in Hawai'i, the play opened in New York and would travel the country for two years. It introduced Americans to the hula, the grass skirt, the flower lei, and other stereotypical elements of the islands, including volcanoes, beautiful sunsets, black sand beaches, and pre-European religious idols. The play's featured actress, Laurette Taylor, was Irish, wore brown makeup, and had never been to the islands. She learned the hula in her New York City apartment. Yet her performance embodied the grace and sensual excitement of Polynesian dance for an American audience, and it defined the ideal of the South Seas maiden.

The ukulele was also featured in the play, and songwriters in Tin Pan Alley quickly imitated the music. The ukulele found a home at fraternity parties around the country. Vaudeville, carnivals, and cabarets also embraced musical themes from *The Bird of Paradise* in their own shows. But it was the hula that made the strongest impression. As one young man wrote after seeing the play in Kansas City: "A girl danced. With hands and arms undulant as restless waves, her body supple as a swaying vine, her bare feet moving with caressing lightness, she danced against an exotic background of trailing, tangled lianas and tall, sky-rocketing palm trees."[43] The seductive innocence of *The Bird of Paradise* captivated American audiences.

Pictorial images of Samoan women were also influencing curious Americans. In the late nineteenth century several professional photographers set up shop in the islands, producing glamorous black-and-white and sepia photographs of Samoan women in various stages of costume.[44] Tens of thousands of these photographs flooded the Western market and were shown privately as well as published in magazines.

As these images were slowly absorbed into American culture, motion pictures came of age. By the 1920s, silent films were projecting images of paradise for huge American audiences and contributing to what by now was the nation's love affair with the South Pacific. At the very time that Mead was conducting fieldwork in Samoa, the silent-film documentary *Moana* was being shown on movie screens across the country.[45] *Moana* had been filmed in Samoa over a two-year period by the great filmmaker Robert Flaherty, already known for his earlier documentary *Nanook of the North.*

Moana contained some of the most compelling images of a tranquil Polynesia presented to an American audience in the 1920s, including a sensual dance scene featuring the handsome young Moana and his Samoan girlfriend. Viewers were not aware that Flaherty had spent months in Samoa casting the main characters to conform to preexisting Western notions of Polynesians.[46] Flaherty shot his film on location with foreknowledge of how Americans wanted to see paradise. Mead herself viewed *Moana* after she did her fieldwork, and she would later use it in her exhibit on Samoa at the American Museum of Natural History.

Moana was not the only film on the South Pacific that American audiences saw during this period. In 1928, the year that *Coming of Age* was published, another well-made and popular feature film, *White Shadows in the South Seas*, reinforced the image of graceful Polynesian women. Flaherty's friend Frederick O'Brien had authored the best-selling book of the same title. After reading the book and speaking with O'Brien, Flaherty was so taken with the islands that he went to Samoa to put on film what his friend had captured in prose.[47] After Mead's *Coming of Age* was published, O'Brien's praise for it appeared on the book's cover.

The stereotype of beautiful Samoan women had also been used in the works of gifted writers like Robert Louis Stevenson, who lived the final years of his life in Western Samoa in the 1890s. Somerset Maugham, who spent time in American Samoa before Mead, also drew on ideas about the islands as sites of temptation. Mead stayed at the same small hotel in Pago Pago as Maugham. She had read "Rain," his well-known short story, and had seen the play based on it before going to Samoa. Indeed, two Hollywood versions of the story were released in 1928 and 1932, reinforcing images from other South Pacific–based films. So the general imagery of Samoa actually had a specific lineage, linking O'Brien, Flaherty, Maugham, and Mead, among other purveyors of paradise. Mead used these themes implicitly in *Coming of Age*. She did not cite her predecessors who had constructed the generic South Seas maiden because she did not have to. By the 1920s audiences knew enough about the islands to supply it themselves.

Mead was aware of these stereotypes and their potential uses. She wrote that "in the twenties, there were people who wanted to go to the South Seas as a personal escape from their post-war world, from a dull and empty routine, from the denial of spontaneity, and the trammeling of individual passions."[48] When Mead told people that she was going to Samoa, some gasped with envy, almost as if she were going to heaven. Again, Mead worked with these familiar themes without overtly referring to their presence in the popular culture of the era. Because her audience had already incorporated at least some of these images into their worldview, the tropical setting for *Coming of Age* made the contrast between America and Samoa enticing as well as instructive.

PART 4

Sex, Lies, and Samoans

\9/

What the Controversy Meant
to Samoans

By THE 1920S THE SOUTH SEAS had become part of American consciousness. As Mead wrote *Coming of Age,* she thought about what the islands might mean to her American audience. But she did not anticipate what her book would mean to Samoans. She had written *Coming of Age* for Americans, and although she said that she wrote about Samoans from the perspective of the Samoan girls she had known, she did not write as a Samoan. Mead presented Samoans as potential models for minimizing the problems of American adolescence, shaping them to her message. From her perspective, she had portrayed them in a positive manner. Yet as Samoans heard about her book in subsequent decades or read it in English, many felt that Mead had misrepresented them. Her voice was not their voice. At stake were their identity and the world's perception of them.

When Freeman criticized Mead, he claimed to be speaking on behalf of Samoans and upholding their dignity. To him, Mead's book was a "travesty," not just a potential misunderstanding of another culture. Freeman was particularly adamant about the subject that Samoans themselves found most offensive in Mead's work—her description and interpretation of their private lives. Although most of *Coming of Age* was noncontroversial, with only a single chapter about sex framed within a broader discussion of marriage, this part of the book drew everyone's attention. Freeman believed that he was representing Samoan views in his critique of Mead and providing them with symbolic retribution for Mead's alleged transgression of their culture.

Some Samoans have vigorously objected to *Coming of Age* for decades. Anthropologist Leonard Mason remembered that, while using the book in his course at the University of Hawai'i in the late 1940s, a young Samoan student protested that, contrary to Mead, Samoans greatly valued female virginity.[1] The student, who became a Samoan chief and later governor of American

Samoa, remembered his protest almost four decades later, when he appeared in the documentary film *Margaret Mead and Samoa*.[2] In 1971, when Mead briefly stopped in American Samoa on her first visit there since the 1920s, a young Samoan woman challenged her on this same issue on local television. Many other Samoans, including some Samoan academics, have concurred, believing that Mead disregarded the sanctity of virginity for Samoan women and neglected the institution of the ceremonial virgin, or *taupou*, which was at the center of Samoan public morality. One Samoan academic, Le Tagaloa Fa'anafi, felt that Mead had portrayed Samoans "like animals."[3]

Today, younger Samoans compare themselves to their American contemporaries and view their own sexual conduct as far more restricted. Many have visited America or have relatives there. They note that in America boys can openly ask girls to go out or vice versa; in Samoa relationships are usually secretive due to parental opposition. Younger Samoans view American parents as much easier on their adolescents than Samoan parents. As one young woman informed me, "In America, if you do something wrong, you get a lecture. In Samoa, you get a beating."

There is no doubt that Mead struck a raw nerve among Samoans with her discussion of sex in *Coming of Age*. Mead herself later acknowledged that if she had realized that Samoans would read the book, she would have written it differently. And she recognized that younger Samoans could be embarrassed by its contents.[4] However, she wrote in the 1920s, when Samoans, while literate in their own language, were often not literate in English. And Mead chose not to revise and update the text itself but rather added new prefaces to new editions, explaining that the book should remain faithful to what she observed then.[5] To Freeman, her failure to revise it demonstrated that Mead was unrepentant in her permissive view of Samoan sexual conduct.

For some Samoans, the problem with Mead was not only *what* she wrote about their private lives but *that* she wrote about them without their knowledge or approval. As we have seen, Mead's writing reflected the era in which she did her research and wrote her book. In the 1920s almost no one, including most Americans, knew what anthropology was. Studying other people was the anthropologist's prerogative; indigenous people were ethnographic subjects, not research collaborators. Furthermore, in the 1920s American Samoa was a colony. Samoans were American subjects, not American citizens. Research permissions were not required. There was no concern about informed consent; that is, the idea that the people being studied should know from the outset what the research involves and how it might harm or benefit them. So ethnographers of that era could engage in research without going through extensive Human Research Committee reviews, as they would today, where the appropriateness of the research and the exact wording of each question in the interview protocol would be considered in detail prior to the research itself. They also would not need to obtain prior written consent from those being studied.

Writing too was the anthropologist's prerogative. Mead would write her report for the National Research Council, *Coming of Age* for an American lay audience, and *Social Organization of Manu'a* for a professional audience. Like other anthropologists of her era, Mead did not appreciate for many years that Samoans would have concerns about their image and hence her findings. As Mead looked back on her writing about Samoa, she reminded readers: "Only during World War II did we begin to learn that anyone, anywhere in the world, might be listening. And from that time on the anthropologist had to assume a new responsibility to speak—and of course write—about every people in the world, however remote, in ways that they, their friends and their descendants would find bearable and intelligible."[6]

Can We Talk about It?

Mead was not the only anthropologist whose work has been called into question by the people in their books. Oscar Lewis, author of popular books such as *The Children of Sanchez* and *La Vida,* was among a number of anthropologists who have been criticized by their former subjects and collaborators.[7] This is especially true when the work becomes well known. So who can speak for indigenous people? Can an anthropologist be trusted to do so? And for which groups or individuals can he or she speak? Finally, to what extent can indigenous people express themselves in their own cultures, where some voices are favored while others are suppressed?

This is clearly a challenging set of issues. In the South Pacific today there are Western anthropologists who collaborate with their indigenous counterparts and vice versa. As a matter of practical necessity, both indigenous and Western scholars rely on the work of earlier anthropologists, historians, and other Westerners because there are no other written records. Nevertheless, the authority of Western scholars is no longer unquestioned. As Vilsoni Hereniko, a Polynesian scholar from Rotuma, put it: "Knowledgeable as they are, outsiders can never truly know what it is like to be a Samoan. . . . As [Samoan author Albert] Wendt had written: 'They [outsiders] must not pretend they can write from inside us.' (1987:89) This is good advice, because history has shown that neither Margaret Mead nor Derek Freeman really knew how 'natives' think."[8]

Although Western anthropologists may not be able to become insiders, they nevertheless have tried to represent insiders along a number of dimensions that Samoans themselves consider important, including higher/lower political

rank, male/female, and older/younger. Thus, older, higher-ranking males articulate a public ideology that is often but not always held by others. Younger,
lower-ranking men and women are subject to public ideology but may not fully
share it. Their views may be less public and less well known. The status of the
ethnographer also plays a role. It is not surprising that female ethnographers
like Penelope Schoeffel, Bonnie Nardi, and Sharon Tiffany have been more
interested in Samoan women than male anthropologists and that some of them
have been more sympathetic to Mead than to Freeman, who, as the holder of a
princely title, saw Samoa from a different perspective.[9]

In the 1990s a generation of young Samoan scholars at the University of
Hawai'i and at universities in New Zealand actively initiated research on young
Samoans themselves. Bridging the gap between insiders and outsiders, these
scholars found that in overseas settings, where individuality could be expressed
in a neutral context and in confidence, younger Samoans were more willing to
discuss what has previously been taboo. For young Samoan women, this meant
discussing subjects that had been secret and shameful.

Samoan researcher AnnaMarie Tupuola, who received her Ph.D. in education from Victoria University, found that while initially reluctant, young Samoan women were able to discuss their personal experiences for the first time.
As one participant in her study related:

> This research helped me a lot. It gave me an inspiration of strength and
> inner peace. I felt very safe talking about my sexual experiences . . . even
> though it was hard I felt I could trust the other [Samoan] women and the
> researcher, it made a big difference—we had common ground and that
> helped. I feel this research is so important. It is not very often that young
> Samoan girls get the opportunity to talk about their experiences. In the
> past, this has always been by our Samoan elders, the palagi [European] in-
> tellects or those who are so far removed from our realities.[10]

In Samoa young women's conversations were largely confined to the very
limited sphere of other young women. They could not speak publicly about
their private lives. In fact, as noted earlier, the idea of privacy in traditional Samoan culture has negative associations. Given that Mead was a young American woman talking about Samoan female adolescents and about their private
lives, Samoan disapproval of her work is understandable.

Samoans have expressed their resentment about *Coming of Age* in a variety
of ways. In 1969–70, when I was doing research in the islands on Samoan migration overseas, some Samoans spoke with me about *Coming of Age*, knowing
that I was interested in their culture. Although my research was not about sex,
I was told by one government official to refrain from writing about Samoans as
Mead had. I was also told that if Mead wanted to visit Western Samoa, she

would not be allowed to do so. Moreover, another government employee informed me that because of its objectionable content, *Coming of Age* was not available in the public library in Apia. These Samoans felt strongly about Mead. Yet how did they know about the book if it was not available somewhere in the islands? I visited the library, and the book was there after all.[11]

Although some Samoans had read the book or parts of it in Samoa or abroad, most had not, just as most Americans had not. Samoans nevertheless had heard about it from other islanders or Europeans or from Samoan newspapers after the controversy erupted in 1983. There was a good deal of misinformation. For example, I was told by university-educated Samoans that Mead had done her research in Western Samoa, yet she never visited this part of the Samoan archipelago. I was informed that she did her research in the 1940s and that she only spent a few weeks in the islands, although she actually spent over eight months in American Samoa in 1925–26. And I was told that Mead studied only very young girls, not adolescents, although she had focused on adolescents. The precise details varied, but Samoans' general resentment of Mead was apparent.

Mead was especially disliked because she had openly and publicly discussed sex, representing Samoan women as sexually permissive. Ethnobotanist Paul Cox reported that in the late 1970s, well before Freeman published his critique, Samoans on Manu'a were reluctant to talk about Mead, and among those who would talk she was not held in high regard. Puzzled by Samoans' dislike for Mead, Cox asked a young Samoan with a master's degree in sociology about people's perception of her:

> "So what's the deal with Margaret Mead? . . . None of the chiefs or older women seem willing to say much about her."
>
> "Oh, her," he said. "The old people are really angry at Mead."
>
> "Why? I thought they liked her."
>
> "That was before they knew what she wrote about them," he said.
>
> "Mead argued that Samoans have an easier time passing through adolescence than palagi [American] teenagers do," I offered.
>
> "Maybe they do, maybe they don't," he said. "But it blew the old people's minds when one of the village kids came back from college several years ago and translated a few excerpts from her book for them."
>
> "You mean that for all these years the villagers didn't know what she had written about them?" I asked.
>
> "No. They all assumed it was very complimentary. But when they heard that she claimed that they were having sex with nearly everybody in sight, they burned her book."
>
> "Why do you think Mead wrote those things? You don't think that she just made them up, do you?" I asked.

"Samoans joke about anything, particularly with foreigners. Somebody just fed her a bunch of baloney and she believed it."[12]

Context Matters

Like other visitors to the islands, Cox found that discussing sexual topics and participating in sexual activities were governed by Samoan—rather than American—conceptions of etiquette and sexuality. Privately, Samoans were interested in sex and knowledgeable about it, but public discussion, apart from joking and bantering, was another matter. The same was true for sex education. Although Samoan children grew up learning about their bodies and sometimes secretly witnessing sex, there was no formal sex education by parents. And, of course, Christian churches were quite restrictive.

In the islands sexual conversations that were permissible in some contexts were strictly forbidden in others. Samoans distinguished between public behavior that was culturally appropriate and private behavior that violated cultural ideals; such private behavior could not and should not be discussed publicly.[13] Anthropologist Robert Maxwell discovered this code of etiquette when he attempted to carry out research on Samoan sexual attitudes in the 1960s. As he did his fieldwork, Maxwell realized just how difficult it was to gather accurate accounts of sexual behavior because discussion was so dependent on context:

> First, the range of subjects covered in conversation with a chief is necessarily limited. One does not casually visit a chief in his home and inquire about his attitude toward masturbation, for example. It would be an outrageous breach of etiquette. Second, the untitled men may talk about sex under intimate circumstances, such as all-male parties, but it is difficult to guide this sort of banter into productive channels. Furthermore, the sexual experience disclosed by the speaker has to be carefully edited beforehand, particularly if the girls involved in the story have brothers present at the gathering, for even speaking about flirting with someone's sister can provoke an argument. Finally, it was in conversation about sex that the reciprocal lie [where everyone involved is bending the truth] seemed to acquire epic qualities. The relative utility of entertainment and truth were so disproportionate that it was safest to believe nothing that was said in these contexts. I regularly listened to tales of personal conquests, superhuman masculine endurance, and incredible female responsiveness that were later revealed to be entirely untrue.[14]

Context was also important in cross-sex joking; as writer Joseph Theroux noted:

Sex jokes, for example, wildly obscene, are perfectly acceptable as long as no females present are related to anyone in the group and no female relatives are referred to. The sainted pastor's wife, a pillar of the community, will leer and mutter a *double entendre* with the abandonment of a sailor as long as the audience is appropriate. Makelita's [Margaret Mead's] book, people thought, found a wider, and therefore inappropriate audience.

Walking along the beach at Luma, the village where Makelita stayed, I came across a white-haired old woman, weeding her garden. I asked if she could tell me the site of the first dispensary. She rose and said she would take me there. We chatted as we walked along the beach and came upon another old woman, laying out clothes to dry on rocks. "Where are you taking that young *palagi* [European] man?" she asked.

Without hesitation, my guide replied, "We're going to the plantation to be alone."

"What will you do there?"

"He wants to plant some *ta'amu*" (a large, long root plant, similar to the taro).

"Oh, no, you're too old for the game!"

"And you're so jealous!"

By this time both crones were cackling. It was perfectly acceptable behavior, these two women in their innocent fun. They cackled louder when I put my arm around my guide. But they would be shocked to find that I would publish the story, thereby sharing it with a wider audience, many of whom they would not have joked with.[15]

Anthropologist Tim O'Meara also participated in a sexual joking situation with a group of women as he and a friend from New Zealand were gathering limpets from the shoreline:

As we carefully wrapped our harvest, the women entertained themselves with ribald jokes, using Pascal and me as butts. In the proper company, Samoans find these suggestive comments hysterically funny precisely because they are so outrageous and so improbable. If there was any possibility of following up on the suggestions, they would be highly embarrassing rather than funny. The jokes elicited peals of laughter from the women—the cruder the reference, the wilder the laughter—but only uncomfortable smiles from Pascal and me. We had learned, however, that in this situation the *only* defense is a good offense, and the more offensive the better. Finally giving in to the crudity of the occasion, our own quick and vulgar replies sent the women rolling hysterically on the ground.[16]

Samoans also "see" sex differently than Americans. In the 1980s, when videos and videocassette recorders first arrived in Western Samoa, families would rent R-rated videos with abundant sex and violence. They would watch them with their young children present. When I asked parents whether it was a good idea for children to watch this kind of material, they assured me that it was perfectly acceptable; children could watch sex scenes because they knew that Samoans would never engage in such activities themselves; only Europeans would behave in such a degrading manner.

Samoans have become much more self-conscious about sex as a result of Western contact and missionization over the past 170 years. Samoan cultural traditions involving sex, such as erotic singing and erotic dancing, have diminished. At one time the islands had rich traditions in these activities. However, with the advent of Christian missionaries in the 1830s, they have been gradually suppressed.[17] Samoans now sometimes speak of the premissionary era as a "time of darkness," and they are embarrassed or ashamed about this part of their past, which they now regard as sinful.

Eleanor Gerber, an anthropologist who did fieldwork in American Samoa in the 1970s, also discussed the contemporary reworking of history in her evaluation of Samoan responses to Mead's *Coming of Age:* "So strong is this reconstruction of the past that educated Samoans who have read *Coming of Age* automatically reject what they euphemistically call 'all that sex stuff.' They insist that their parents and grandparents have told them about how 'hard' it was in the old days. They often resolve this discrepancy by claiming that Mead's informants must have been telling lies in order to tease her. That such a re-writing of history should be necessary is an indication of how completely the tone of sexual morality has changed."[18]

Exposure in the media, especially as a result of the Mead-Freeman controversy, has made Samoans acutely aware of the risks of sharing their traditions with outsiders. They are sensitive to outsiders' opinions and may be reluctant to talk about certain aspects of their culture. In writing about this sensitivity, a former Prime Minister of Samoa asked the following question:

> Can or should we tell all we know about Samoan history and culture for general historical examination? The missionaries have imposed a Victorian prudishness on the national psyche to the extent that we have acquired a colossal hangup about ourselves and our culture. We have succumbed to a sanitized version of Samoan history, whether alien or indigenous, authored because it portrays an idealized Samoa. There is a strong sentiment about defending this idealization. There is an awful fear that if all is told the *palagi* [Europeans] will think less of us. Hence the penchant to camouflage, condense and edit.[19]

This dilemma of contemporary self-awareness is also found in other cultures. Anthropologist Annette Weiner, who worked in both the Trobriands and

Samoa, found that "Trobrianders often complained to me about the things that Bronislaw Malinowski had 'got wrong' in his pioneering study in 1915. They rejected his writings that described them as 'savages' and 'primitives' and said that he exaggerated the idea of 'free love.' Today, some Trobrianders, educated and with Western values, are no happier about Malinowski's interpretations than Samoans are about Mead's account, because their perceptions of themselves within their own cultures are integrated with many Western values and ideas."[20]

The Many Layers of Samoan Culture

For the reasons just discussed, it is not easy to study sex in Samoa without understanding how Samoans view it and in what contexts they can or cannot talk about it. If sex in America is difficult to understand as well as to research, even though it is widely and openly discussed, imagine how difficult it is to do research on sexual conduct in a very different culture where conversations about sex are appropriate only in certain limited situations.

How well did Mead comprehend the shifting contexts of Samoan sexual conversations and sexual conduct? This question is part of a more general one that many ethnographers and others have wrestled with: Is it possible to get a single, consistent picture of what is going on? Linguist George Milner, who wrote the *Samoan Dictionary*, has referred to the "dialectical nature" of Samoan culture, in which "it is rare for information to be given, even from a reputedly sound and authentic source, without soon being contradicted from another reputed and equally reliable source."[21] Samoan historian Malama Meleise'a concurred, noting that Samoans operate in a world of multiple truths where "different versions of the truth are told to enhance the dignity of the teller's ancestors, family, or village."[22] A number of anthropologists have also written about how Samoans can behave in seemingly contradictory ways, depending on the situation.[23]

Mead wrote about these problems herself. She spoke of the common Samoan manipulation of social forms, altering things when necessary or convenient, and commented that Samoan "inconsistencies and fabrications were not promoted by any desire for remuneration but by the forces which make for variation in native life: family pride; love for constructing fanciful ceremonial edifices; and a desire to rearrange the social structure for personal preferment."[24]

Freeman argued that Mead did not understand the Samoan tradition of joking, or what O'Meara has called "recreational lying," and that this basic misunderstanding led to Mead's alleged hoaxing.[25] However, Mead herself wrote about how, during her fieldwork, it was necessary for her to "share their jests and above all share their manners."[26] She was certainly aware of Samoan joking. Freeman himself quotes Mead expressing her concern about Samoans being "too ready liars" under certain circumstances.[27] Given Mead's knowledge of the language and her continual interaction with young Samoans, it is difficult to give the hoaxing allegation credence, although Samoans themselves have often believed it. Mead may not have understood everything that she encountered in Samoa, but she did understand a good deal.

Derek Freeman, Local Hero?

If Samoans often resented Mead, how did they feel about Freeman? In the early 1940s he was a well-liked schoolteacher who was adopted into a Samoan family and given a *manaia*, or princely title, and who would come to identify closely with Samoans and their culture. Freeman became a very competent observer of Samoa, with a superior grasp of the language, culture, and history of the islands. He also took the side of Samoans in political matters, sometimes against the policies of the New Zealand colonial government. Given his expertise and his critique of Mead on their behalf, it seems reasonable to believe that Freeman would be viewed as a local hero in the islands. Indeed, this is how he portrayed himself.

Freeman claimed that he was asked to write *Margaret Mead and Samoa* by Samoans, to have written the book for Samoans, to have given it to Samoans for review and criticism, and to have been rewarded by them by being appointed a Foundation Professor of Anthropology at the University of Samoa. Yet, just as with *Coming of Age*, few Samoans read Freeman's first book about Mead and Samoa, and even fewer read his second book. *Margaret Mead and Samoa* was a weighty academic tome and not an easy read, even for educated Americans. Neither of Freeman's books was readily available for most Samoans to read, even if they had wanted to.

Many Samoans nevertheless knew about Freeman's books and about Freeman himself. There were many who liked Freeman, including some Samoan academics who found his work admirable and his "hoaxing hypothesis" convincing.[28] As Martin Orans learned, based on his fieldwork in Western Samoa, most Samoans welcomed Freeman's claim that Mead greatly exaggerated Samoan sexual promiscuity.[29] Yet Freeman's portrayal of Samoan culture, involving high levels of aggression, repression, conflict, delinquency, and rape, has not been viewed as an improvement over their conception of Mead's work. Some Samoans have asked, Are the fear and loathing of Freeman's darker Samoa a suitable replacement for Mead's warm and sunny vision?

Samoan political figures at the highest levels of government immediately weighed in with their opinions after the publication of *Margaret Mead and Samoa*. The Prime Minister of Western Samoa informed the *New York Times* that neither Freeman nor Mead was entirely accurate.[30] In a letter to the editor of *Newsweek* magazine, the wife of a former Samoan Prime Minister complained that "neither Margaret Mead or Derek Freeman represented our ancient land, its customs and its way of life. Both anthropologists missed the subtlety of behavior."[31] In another letter to the editor, the Western Samoan representative to the United Nations, Lelei Lelaulu, asked: "Are we Samoans now to be known as a nation of sex-starved, suicidal rapists? I much prefer my previous reputation as a free-loving orgiast."[32] He then suggested, in jest, that if anthropologists really wanted to study sex and conflict, they should go to another island—Manhattan, where he currently lived. Lelaulu also appeared on an NBC news program delivering the same satirical message.

Freeman cited the accomplished Samoan novelist and poet Albert Wendt as an influential and knowledgeable scholar who endorsed his views. Yet while Wendt was broadly supportive of Freeman's critique of Mead, he was cautious in his evaluation of Freeman's own motives and argument. Writing in the *Pacific Islands Monthly*, Wendt observed:

> He [Freeman] has a deep love and respect for us. This I think helps to explain his almost obsessive quest to correct what he deems the wrong Margaret Mead did to us. Perhaps he has not felt at home in his own society and in understanding us hoped he would find a people to belong to, to champion, to be needed by . . .
>
> The easily discernible flaws in Freeman's book stem mainly from its polemical form. To prove Mead wrong, some of his claims tend toward exaggeration and idealisation. (This idealisation is also perhaps the result of his profound trust in us.)
>
> For instance, he is correct in stating that we place a great priority on female virginity, we institutionalise it in the *taupou*, we forbid premarital and extramarital sex and promiscuity but institutionalise bravado and machismo.
>
> In sexual matters, Mead erred far too much on the side of free love and promiscuity, where Freeman errs on the side of sexual purity, strictness, and abstinence.[33]

Felix Wendt, another knowledgeable Samoan and Albert Wendt's brother, had similar misgivings: "Some people have expressed the view that Freeman has done us (Samoans) a good turn by finally dispelling Mead's illusion of Samoa. Unfortunately, the more I re-read Freeman's book, the more difficulty

I have what constitutes this 'good turn.' Granted he has to a large extent succeeded in refuting Mead. But he has at the same time, contributed significantly
to confirming another stereotype of Samoans—that they are temperamental
and violent."[34] For a number of well-educated Samoans and Samoan scholars,
then, Freeman's critique did not represent them either.[35]

The most outspoken Samoan critic of Mead has been Malopa'upo Isaia, a
young Samoan chief residing in Australia who has written about the controversy. Portraying the controversy as a cultural and political dispute between Samoans and American anthropologists over the intellectual property of Samoans, he believed that *Coming of Age in Samoa* was "professional racism under
the guise of science." Malopa'upo listed thirty points of contention, asserting
that "the truth is, billions of dollars in damages to our tourism industry, was the
direct result of these slanderous 'scientific' claims," and he called for compensation to be paid for "business losses" attributable to Mead as well as other rem-
edies from the American Anthropological Association.[36] This uniquely financial approach to the controversy did not develop a following among Samoans.
In fact, Mead had helped put Samoa on the tourist map. Moreover, the tourism
industry is only one sector of the economies of both American and Western
Samoa, hardly the billion-dollar business that Malopa'upo believed. In light of
these considerations Malopa'upo more recently has tempered his arguments.

Another vocal critic of Mead has been Samoan anthropologist Unasa L. F.
Va'a, who received his Ph.D. from the Australian National University and who
conducted interviews with Fa'apua'a for him. As a result, he has been very
close to the issues in the controversy. Unasa has contended that Mead's "free
love" portrait of Samoa was "full of inconsistencies" and was a "sloppy piece of
work" that "deserves to be ranked as one of the worst books of the 20th century."[37] The remaining question for him has been whether Mead was unwit-
tingly misled by Samoans or whether she was deliberately misleading. Making
many of the same points as Freeman, he has focused on what he believes Mead
missed or misunderstood. Ironically, as a boy, Unasa was featured in the 1953
film *Return to Paradise*, starring Gary Cooper and shot on location in Western
Samoa. The movie draws on some of the stereotypes that Samoans now find
unacceptable.

For most Samoans, though, the controversy has remained something of a
mystery. Samoan author Sia Figiel captured this sense of perplexity in her
novel, *Where We Once Belonged,* in a humorous conversation between two fictional Samoan schoolgirls:

> One day our teacher, Miss Faafouina, showed us an article from *Time*
> magazine, an article which was supposed to be about us . . . one we were
> supposed to be very interested in. The article was written on Samoa and

the "Mead-Freeman Controversy." None of us knew what the controversy was. None of us knew what the word controversy meant.

Because she spoke so quickly, I did not understand anything in the article. Later on I asked a girl from Malifa to explain to me what Miss Faafouina had talked about in class. This is how she explained it.

Mead was a palagi [European] woman who wrote a book on Samoan girls doing "it" a lot . . . and they were loving and loved "it" too. Freeman was a palagi man who said that Mead, the palagi woman, was wrong about Samoan girls doing "it" a lot . . . and the Samoans are jealous, hateful, murderous people who do not know how to do "it."

That evening I told Lili and Moa what the girl from Malifa explained to me. Lili looked at me and laughed.

"How do you think she knew?" she said.

"Who? What?" I asked.

"How did the palagi woman know that we do 'it' a lot?"

"You do 'it' a lot, not *we*," said Moa to Lili.

"Malo [good] Moa!" I laughed.

"And what about the palagi man?" I asked. "What about him? How does he know that we . . . I mean, that people like Lili don't do it a lot?"

"I don't know," said Moa. "Maybe he was talking to someone like Fauakafe, who'll be a spinster for the already rest of her life . . . or to some *matai* [chiefs], like your father, who are too embarrassed to tell palagis where their hundreds of children come from."[38]

The Relevance of the Controversy for Samoans Today

A cartoon in a Samoan newspaper, the *Observer*, in 1983 smartly summarized the contemporary relevance of the controversy for Samoans. A European character asks a Samoan, "Which Samoa is this—Mead's or Freeman's?" The Samoan responds, "Neither—This is the real Samoa!"[39] He is surrounded by graphs showing rising consumer prices, import duties, school fees, and travel charges. For most Samoans, the rapid changes resulting from globalization have transformed the islands in so many ways as to render the controversy academic. In their books on Samoa, Mead and Freeman did not situate their fieldwork in a broader historical context, but this context is important for understanding what the controversy means to Samoans today.

When Mead did her fieldwork in Manu'a in the mid-1920s and when Freeman did his first fieldwork on Upolu in Western Samoa in the early 1940s, most Samoans lived in relatively small villages and supported themselves by growing coconuts, taro, bananas, and breadfruit; by raising pigs and chickens; and by fishing inside and outside the coral reefs that surround the islands. Village life structured adolescent experience. Each village was composed of extended families, and each family selected a chief (*matai*) to lead the family and to represent it in village matters through the village council (*fono*). Chiefs controlled the family labor force and the redistribution of wealth within and between families. Since the village economy was based on agriculture and family membership meant access to agricultural land, young people worked for their families and were expected to serve their chiefs.

The village council controlled the behavior of individual villagers and families through its ability to fine them and to sometimes ostracize a troublemaker. Chiefs were hierarchically ranked and competed with each other for prestige and additional chiefly titles, also requiring family members' labor and support. So there were strong pressures toward conformity within the family and within the village.

For families and villages to run smoothly, individual emotions had to be controlled and mobilized. Boys and girls grew up in the same roles as their mothers and fathers. Christian churches provided a religious justification for the village social order and sanctions of their own. Although it was not a perfectly functioning system, there were fewer roles and fewer choices to be made than in America at that time.

Since Mead's time village life in American Samoa has been greatly eroded by urbanization, a cash economy, migration abroad, and changing traditions. As American Samoa became more urban and more American during the post–World War II era, the traditional system of family and village authority was undermined by the expansion of a nonagricultural cash economy. Young people found wage employment in the islands. The control formerly exercised by the *matai* and the village council decreased. In the urban area surrounding Pago Pago the traditional system of authority has been in decline, and individualism has increased, with predictable consequences.

In 1974 Lowell Holmes reported:

> In the more urban villages of Tutuila, councils do little of a punitive nature. Violations of law tend to become police matters rather than council matters. Pago Pago area households are extremely fluid in composition. People come and go and rarely develop any sense of belonging or loyalty. Delinquency in the form of property destruction, truancy, pilfering, and drunkenness has become a major problem for teenagers. The High Court of American Samoa now employs a juvenile office and special counselors and has inaugurated new procedures to involve the delinquent's *matai*, and thus reinstate something of the *fa'a-Samoa* [Samoan custom] influence in the regulation of behavior among young people.[40]

While young American Samoans are having more problems coming of age in the islands today, the majority of them no longer even live there. Over the past four decades there has been a major exodus from both American Samoa and independent Samoa. American Samoans have migrated to Hawai'i and the West Coast of the mainland United States. People from independent Samoa have migrated to New Zealand, American Samoa, the United States, Australia, and at least three dozen other countries. The majority of Samoans now reside permanently overseas.

This massive emigration has been vital to the economic well-being of relatives remaining in the islands, for relatives abroad send millions of dollars in remittances to the islands each year. In independent Samoa remittances became the single most important source of personal income, providing a much higher standard of living than would have otherwise been possible. Opportunities for employment overseas continue to draw young Samoans abroad, where they often have more individual choice than they had in traditional villages, often marrying non-Samoans.

The two Samoas have had very different economic and political trajectories. American Samoans have been aided by many federally funded programs and by open access to the United States. However, independent Samoa has had to cope with severe economic problems over the last three decades and has had to respond to changing immigration policies in the countries to which its migrants travel. The current economic and political difficulties of Samoa have weighed heavily on the young people remaining behind. They are on the margins of an economy that cannot fulfill their rising expectations. Many are well educated and are not interested in returning to village agriculture, while jobs in the port town are scarce. International migration may be their best option, but permanent visas are sometimes difficult to obtain.

These economic pressures in addition to the obligations to serve one's family have led to an increase in delinquency and alcohol abuse in the Apia urban area in independent Samoa. By the early 1980s the decline of traditional family authority in Samoa had become so pronounced that the Prime Minister wanted to institute military discipline in school with the help of the United States Reserve Officer Training Corps (ROTC). Of course, as a foreign country Samoa was not eligible for ROTC programs, but his concern was nevertheless genuine.[41]

Young Samoans in independent Samoa have often been abroad temporarily and are immersed in American movies, music, and clothes. Pirated CDs of the most recent music and DVDs of the most recent films are readily available; cell phones are becoming ubiquitous, as are iPods. In Apia there is some gang activity based on their overseas experiences. These young Samoans are more aware of overseas lifestyles and opportunities than their parents ever were. They have also been committing suicide at an alarming rate.

Beginning in the 1970s, the suicide rate among young people in independent Samoa increased sharply to one of the highest rates in the world for the age group between fifteen and twenty-four.[42] Although Freeman found that youth suicide in Samoa was already high in the period from 1925 to the 1960s, he did not discuss the sixfold increase in youth suicide between 1970 and 1982. A high rate of suicide has continued into the twenty-first century. Freeman emphasized the persistence of tradition and its interaction with adolescent biology in his explanation of youth suicide, but a more plausible explanation may lie in the different economic and political opportunity structures in the two Samoas, since the suicide rate in American Samoa has been considerably lower than in independent Samoa.[43]

Whatever Samoan adolescence was like during Mead's fieldwork in the mid-1920s or Freeman's fieldwork in the early 1940s, it has become increasingly problematic for young Samoans both in the islands and abroad. In California anthropologist Craig Janes chronicled how high levels of unemployment, poverty, and welfare led to increased stress and diseases like obesity, diabetes, and stroke.[44] On the West Coast and in Salt Lake City gang warfare among Polynesians, including Samoans, has taken a tragic toll.[45] In New Zealand the increasing number of unintended pregnancies among young, unwed Samoan women is viewed by the Samoan community itself as a problem. Between 1990 and 1992 the estimated abortion rate for Pacific Islands women living in New Zealand was almost three times as high as for non–Pacific Islands women.[46] To respond to these and other problems of coming of age abroad Samoans have formed new organizations. In this rapidly changing context the Mead-Freeman controversy, however significant it may have been in terms of Samoan identity, is of only marginal relevance to their lives today.

\10/

Samoan Sexual Conduct

Belief and Behavior

THE CONTROVERSY OVER *Coming of Age* gave Samoans opportunities to respond to the representation of their culture and especially of Samoan sexual conduct. It also provided anthropologists opportunities to discuss what they saw as the issues in the controversy. These issues were often quite different from those that interested Samoans. For anthropologists, many of the issues were not specific to Samoa or sexual conduct but rather involved broader questions about context, rhetoric, ideology, and ethnographic authority. For anthropologists working in other areas of the world, these general issues concerning the politics of representation were as significant as the factual issues concerning Samoa itself. For example:

- Richard Shweder commented that for Mead's audience in the 1920s, it did not matter whether Samoa was in fact a sexually permissive society because somewhere in the world there was undoubtedly a place as permissive as the islands she had described. For Mead's readers, the "mere possibility" of such a place was liberating, even if Samoa was not that place.[1]
- In his careful analysis of the rhetoric in Freeman's first book on Mead, Mac Marshall noted that Freeman's use of language gave authority to his position while undermining Mead's. Yet in reminding readers that there was more to the controversy than the simple reporting of objective facts, Marshall deferred judgment about who was right and who was wrong.[2]
- George Marcus considered Freeman's first book a public nuisance that had an implicit ideological agenda. But while Marcus was uneasy about Freeman's argument, it was not necessarily because his facts were wrong. It was rather that his interpretation was unbalanced and one-sided.[3]
- In a similar vein, Nancy Scheper-Hughes contended that Mead and Freeman each wrote about one dimension of Samoan culture. Each had access to *a* truth about the islanders but not *the* truth. "And this difference

can be explained by the differences between Mead and Freeman and their respective informants."[4]

Although these commentaries raised important issues, the issues were generic and could apply wherever anthropologists work. And this posed a problem. Many anthropologists working in other parts of the world, including other parts of the South Pacific, disagreed with Freeman in terms of these general issues. Yet they often conceded that his factual presentation of Samoan culture and history was meticulous, convincing, and apparently accurate. Relatively few reviewers raised the possibility that substantial portions of his factual portrayal of Samoa, including sexual conduct, might be inaccurate.

After the initial stages of the controversy Freeman could still say with confidence that, to the best of his knowledge, "no significant element of the empirical evidence on which my refutation [of Mead] is based has been shown to be unfactual."[5] Indeed, Freeman's seeming certainty about factual accuracy led critics to focus on other issues. Yet the persuasiveness of Freeman's critique rested on the assumption that his characterization of Samoa was supported by the data that he used and the sources that he cited. For Freeman, the controversy was thus necessarily about the nature of Samoan culture and history, including sexual conduct. This chapter and the next two are about Samoan sexual conduct—what is known and what is not known, what Mead knew and what Freeman knew, and the difference between belief and behavior.

Malinowski on Belief and Behavior

In the 1920s two works had a major impact on how anthropologists thought about sex. The first was Mead's very accessible *Coming of Age in Samoa*. The second was a professional monograph by Malinowski, who not only set the standard for ethnographic fieldwork but also set the standard for studying sexual conduct in non-Western societies. In 1929 Malinowski published *The Sexual Life of Savages in North-Western Melanesia: An Ethnographic Account of Courtship, Marriage and Family Life among the Natives of the Trobriand Islands, British New Guinea*. At just over six hundred pages, this ethnography was very detailed and, in places, sexually explicit, much more so than Mead had been in *Coming of Age*. In fact, it was so explicit for its time that it was banned from some British libraries. It was also so ethnographically rich that it could never become a popular book, even with a preface by Havelock Ellis, the sexologist who had also endorsed Mead's book. Although the monograph itself had limited circulation, Malinowski would write about sex and marriage in the Trobriands for popular periodicals in Great Britain, so people heard about the Trobriands through the intellectual grapevine.

Malinowski was candid about the limitations of *The Sexual Life of Savages*. He acknowledged that some of the documentation was "thin" and that there were topics that he did not cover. He also recognized the difficulties of writing about sex for a European audience, including the danger of moralizing, the problem of appealing to "the seeker after pornography," and the misuse of this material by the very young.[6] Although the Trobriands were a truly permissive culture by Western standards at that time and far more permissive than Samoa, Malinowski emphasized that sex was always constrained by custom. However, these rules were sometimes bent or broken as a result of human interests and passions. For Malinowski, the study of culture was not about how people submitted blindly to custom but about how custom itself was shaped by the interests and passions of individuals. He was therefore interested in the relationship between belief and behavior, between what people said they should do and what they actually did. This distinction had important implications for how data on sexual conduct were gathered and on the results themselves.

In *Coming of Age* Mead was less analytical than Malinowski, focusing more on behavior and less on Samoan belief and public ideology. She wrote about the broad process of coming of age for adolescent girls, of which sex was one component. Mead observed that after puberty girls gradually gained sexual experience. She recognized the existence of a restrictive public morality but found that many maturing girls engaged in sex nonetheless. Mead wrote about punishment for sexual misconduct, the sexual surveillance of adolescent girls, the role of Christianity in altering sexual practices, and the importance of the ceremonial virgin for the village as a whole, but she did not focus on these aspects of Samoan life. She found that a number of the girls in her study were interested in sex and that they had some sexual experience. And this is what she emphasized.

Belief and Behavior in Samoa

Freeman focused on Samoan ideology, arguing that behavior was largely the result of belief. He described Samoans as a deeply religious people who embraced, in his words, "a puritanical Christian sexual morality." As devout Christians, Samoans prayed daily and might attend church twice on Sundays. Citing the guiding principle of Samoa, "Samoa is founded on God," Freeman noted that a Samoan parliamentarian had declared that nowhere else on earth was virginity more highly valued than in their culture.[7] Moreover, for most girls, there was strict supervision of their private lives. Freeman's emphasis on the public ideology of virginity was an important and valuable contribution to the understanding of Samoan sexual conduct.

Yet in Samoa, as in many other cultures, public morality and private behavior could be quite different. What people said they ought to do and what they actually did were often not identical. So cultural beliefs about virginity and proper behavior might not be able to explain actual patterns of sexual conduct.[8] For example, if the dominant public morality was represented by a "cult of virginity," as Freeman believed, why was it that young men deliberately subverted this belief by attempting to engage in intercourse with young women? If virginity was "sacrosanct" for every Samoan, why was it necessary to protect virgins? The answer, paradoxically, was that the same brothers who were supposed to protect the chastity of their sisters were themselves encouraged and expected to seduce someone else's sisters.[9] As a result, according to Freeman, "virgins are both highly valued *and* eagerly sought after."[10] Because there was a double standard of morality for young men and women, public ideology about virginity was not monolithic and did not apply equally to all segments of Samoan society.

Freeman himself demonstrated that young men were permitted and encouraged to engage in premarital sex while at the same time protecting their sisters from potential suitors. He observed that young men were preoccupied with the taking of virginity. Success in deflowering virgins was not only deemed a "personal triumph" but also a "demonstration of masculinity." Young men kept count of their conquests and bragged of them. As Freeman noted, "Young men are greatly given to boasting about having deflowered a virgin," and they felt shame if they were unsuccessful.[11] Furthermore, the high-ranking leader of the unmarried men of a village (*manaia*) was "expected to be something of a Don Juan" and gained great prestige by seducing a succession of ceremonial virgins without marrying them. Freeman knew about this expectation firsthand, since he held a *manaia* title in the village of Sa'anapu in the early 1940s. Even perpetrators of the serious crime of surreptitious rape could, if successful, "gain acclaim" from their peers, according to Freeman.[12]

For young women, however, expectations about virginity were quite different. High-ranking young women were expected to be chaste, and punishments for failure could be severe. If young men were shamed by their peers for failure in seduction, young women could be publicly disgraced if it was discovered that they had sex. Their families would also be shamed, since brothers were supposed to control their sisters' sexual conduct. Yet these expectations were not applied equally to all women. According to Freeman, the ideal of virginity applied "less stringently to women of lower rank."[13] So Freeman himself documented the multiple and conflicting values concerning virginity for both young men and women.

Freeman emphasized the ideology of virginity as opposed to actual behavior. Citing anthropologist Bradd Shore's fieldwork in the 1970s, Freeman stated that chastity was "the ideal for all women before marriage,"[14] and indeed Shore did discuss this ideal, recognizing its symbolic importance for Samoans. But Shore also stated, in passages that Freeman did not cite, that the ideal of virginity was frequently unrealized and that premarital sex, carefully hidden from public view, was "not uncommon."[15] In another publication Shore found that "premarital sex is part of growing up for many Samoan boys and girls. . . . Privately, at least, many Samoan youth see sex as an important part of youthful adventure."[16]

Anthropologist Penelope Schoeffel and her Samoan husband, historian Malama Meleiseʻa, who worked extensively in the islands in the 1970s, also reported the public value on virginity for Samoans while confirming the existence of secret affairs:

> Freeman disputes the testimony of Mead's informants on the grounds that sexual topics are not freely discussed by Samoans and that her informants deliberately duped her with their accounts. Schoeffel's field notes suggest, to the contrary, that clandestine love affairs, not dissimilar to those related by Mead, are not in the least uncommon. But the crucial point is that they are clandestine, and as Freeman points out, severely punished if they became publicly known. The general Samoan attitude is that, without careful surveillance, adolescent girls and boys will engage in illicit sexual relations.[17]

Anthropologist Tim O'Meara provided an example of just how sensitive to clandestine sexual encounters Samoans can be. Like Freeman and Mead, he observed that girls and young women were almost always chaperoned and that opportunities for sex were limited and dangerous. Nevertheless, he described the following scene:

> One day while I was in a village that I visited regularly on the north coast of Savaii, I met a burly young friend named Mona coming down the road from the plantations. He carried no basket of taro, and he was holding his right hand, the knuckles of which were swollen and bleeding. I was not surprised since accidents are frequent in the plantations. In response to my question, however, Mona smiled a vicious smile and told me that he had just broken the jaw of a young fellow he caught sitting under a breadfruit tree with his 20-year-old sister. A bit hasty and overprotective, I thought, to break the poor guy's jaw for sitting and talking with his sister. Mona knew better than I, however, that there was only one reason for a man and a woman to be alone together. And right he was, for nine months later his sister gave birth to twins. The girl's parents tried in vain to force the young man to marry her. He had been visiting from another village, and when he got out of the hospital he returned to his natal village.[18]

So although there were strong cultural prohibitions against premarital sex, and although young women were closely supervised, it occurred nonetheless.

Mead's Quantitative Data on Virginity

What kind of data did Mead use to make her case that Samoan adolescents were more sexually permissive than American adolescents? In the body of *Coming of Age* itself Mead's data on sexual activity were largely anecdotal, which is true of most of the data available on sexual conduct in the islands, including Freeman's. Furthermore, she avoided graphic descriptions of sex or use of explicit language in her book that would cause concern by her publisher and the censors and possibly make her audience uncomfortable. Mead's field notes contained some of the detail that would be expected to appear in a book today but did not appear in her book at that time. Even then, in the late 1920s and 1930s, some American readers considered *Coming of Age* "shocking."[19] Phrases like "the opportunity to experiment freely" and "the lack of frigidity or psychic impotence" were enough to set tongues wagging and cheeks blushing.[20]

Some passages in *Coming of Age* may have given the impression that all Samoan girls behaved in a similar manner, yet Mead collected systematic data on variation in sexual activity, and they appear in an appendix to *Coming of Age*, where she reported on twenty-five unmarried postpubescent girls that she interviewed. In tabular form Mead presented data on time elapsed since puberty, age of first menstruation, periodicity, pain during menstruation, masturbation, heterosexual experience, homosexual experience, and residence in the pastor's household, where some girls were sent by their families for instruction and supervision. Given the era in which Mead did her research, these kinds of quantitative data were unusual, especially on this subject matter. Yet she did not make too much of these findings, noting the small size of her sample.[21] Nevertheless, she believed that the data supported her general observation that sex was common among adolescents.

Mead's published data indicated that slightly fewer than half (44 percent) of her sample of girls were nonvirgins; 56 percent were virgins.[22] A closer look at her data demonstrates that they are internally consistent with respect to age and heterosexual experience; that is, the longer the time since first menstruation, the less likely the girl was to be a virgin. By late adolescence a majority of the girls had heterosexual experience. Freeman disputed the validity of Mead's data. But if Mead's evidence was based on hearsay or if the girls were lying to her, as Freeman believed, why did the data take such a consistent form? And why did her data conform to the pattern found by Freeman?

In *Margaret Mead and Samoa* Freeman presented similar data on forty-one adolescent girls ranging in age from fourteen to nineteen from the village of Sa'anapu.[23] He found that 27 percent were nonvirgins and 73 percent were virgins. The difference between Freeman's 27 percent nonvirgins and Mead's 44 percent nonvirgins may seem large, but the sample sizes were small and not identical in composition. In Freeman's sample, just as in Mead's, girls were more likely to become sexually active as they grew older. Thus, about 20 percent of fifteen year olds, 30 percent of sixteen year olds, and almost 40 percent of seventeen year olds had engaged in premarital intercourse. At age nineteen 60 percent had engaged in premarital sex. For Freeman, these percentages were "far from inconsiderable," but he viewed them as deviations or departures from a strict public morality.[24] These deviations, according to Freeman, were seen by Samoans as illicit and, if discovered, would be subject to social disapproval and punishment. Nevertheless, they were common.

Freeman used Mead's data as well as his own to support his contention that Samoan adolescent girls were overwhelmingly virgins. At first glance, the data seem to support Freeman. The overall percentages of heterosexual activity in both studies seem low, and the majority of adolescent girls in both studies were virgins. Yet sexual activity did not begin with the onset of puberty. As Mead found, after puberty began, "perhaps a year, two or even three would pass before a girl's shyness would relax, or her figure appeal to the roving eye of some older boy."[25] By late adolescence a majority of the Samoan girls in both studies had sexual intercourse. What do these data mean in comparison to adolescent sexual activity in America?

When Mead's and Freeman's data are compared with the limited statistical data on premarital sex among American adolescent girls in the early twentieth century, which was Mead's point of reference, Samoan adolescent girls seem to have been more sexually active than American girls at that time.[26] This was Mead's argument. In addition, using more reliable data on female adolescent virginity in America from the 1930s through the mid-1970s, Freeman's fifteen-, sixteen-, and seventeen-year-old Samoan girls were somewhat more sexually active than their American counterparts from these decades.[27]

In terms of actual behavior, then, the limited comparative data indicate that even at the beginning of the sexual revolution in the 1960s and early 1970s the adolescent Samoan girls studied by Mead and Freeman were somewhat more likely to have been sexually active than their American counterparts. The quantitative data, though, are only part of the story. They do not provide the cultural context or offer the personal experiences of the young women in both Samoa and the United States.

Sexual Belief and Behavior in America

The complex relationship between restrictive beliefs about sexual conduct and more permissive behavior was evident in America as well as Samoa, even in recent decades. A comprehensive Kinsey survey conducted in the late 1980s found that, despite the sexual revolution two decades earlier, most Americans still did not approve of premarital sex.[28] The percentage of the population expressing disapproval hardly changed in the twenty years between 1970 and 1990. Yet during that same period a very real revolution occurred in actual behavior. The percentage of American adolescent girls who remained virgins during adolescence dropped dramatically from about 70 percent in the early 1970s to about 40 percent by the late 1980s.[29] By the late 1970s and especially in the 1980s and 1990s, American adolescents were more likely to be sexually active at younger ages, with more partners, and for a longer period of time before marriage than their Samoan peers of that time period.

A series of public opinion polls further elucidated inconsistencies between sexual belief and behavior in America. One survey of high school students in 2003 demonstrated a strong public commitment to virginity.[30] Of the fifteen to seventeen year olds polled, 92 percent thought that virginity in high school was a good thing. Yet in terms of actual behavior, other surveys found that public morality was a poor predictor of actual behavior. Over 60 percent of high school seniors had sexual intercourse despite their public stance in favor of virginity. On average, boys had somewhat more experience than girls, but a majority of both sexes were active. The percentages of sexual activity among deeply religious Christian adolescents were only slightly lower.

Other polls were also revealing. In the decade between 1993 and 2003, as part of the "abstinence only" movement, millions of teenagers took the "virginity pledge," a vow to remain chaste until marriage that was initiated by the Southern Baptist Convention. Teenagers signed the pledge and committed themselves in public to sexual abstinence before marriage. Of the twelve thousand teens interviewed in a study to determine how well the pledge worked, only 12 percent were able to fulfill their pledge; 88 percent had sex before marriage.[31] On average, male and female pledgers were able to maintain their virginity for eighteen months longer than nonpledgers. However, once they became sexually active, they had roughly as many sexual partners and as many sexually transmitted diseases as nonpledgers. They were also less likely to use condoms and more likely to marry young. A second study of the effectiveness of the government-funded "abstinence only" curriculum found no difference in sexual activity between those who had taken the curriculum and those who had not.[32]

Among married women in America, a study conducted by *Redbook* found that two-thirds wanted to be virgins if they were getting married today.[33] But this survey of five hundred women, published in 1994, also found that 53 percent believed having sex with the person that one *planned* to marry was the same as being a virgin at marriage. That is, slightly over half believed that as long as sex led to marriage, it was permissible and did not compromise a woman's status as a virgin. Such a relationship leading to marriage was not viewed as casual sex but rather as pre*marital* sex. And there was an age consideration as well. Roughly half of the women believed that if a twenty-three-year-old woman was unmarried, she should experience sex; only 27 percent said that a woman of this age should remain a virgin.

Finally, a 1992 *Bride's Magazine* survey found that by the time American women actually married, regardless of their previous commitment to virginity, almost all were sexually experienced.[34] Even if they had been committed to chastity, by marriage virginity was hardly a consideration. This study found the following:

- Brides had an average of six sexual partners before wedlock; grooms had an average of seven.
- 42 percent of the couples surveyed had lived together before marriage.
- Only one in ten said that they wished their partner was a virgin.
- 27 percent of the brides had an abortion before marriage.
- Almost 25 percent of the brides broke off their engagement before the wedding.
- Only 5 percent of the brides were virgins at marriage, as were 3.7 percent of the grooms.

What these statistics demonstrate is that the relationship between belief and behavior is not straightforward. The ideal of virginity may be upheld with sincere conviction at the same time that other beliefs and changing conditions yield very different behavior. In America the declining *rate* of virginity at marriage, as contrasted with the *belief* in virginity prior to marriage, reflected several underlying trends, including the movement of women into the workforce, the increasing importance of higher education for both men and women, increasing age at first marriage (twenty-five for women, twenty-seven for men), the emergence of a singles culture, and the contraceptive revolution. It should not be surprising, then, that the relationship between belief and behavior might be complex in Samoa as well.[35]

\11/

Under the Coconut Palms

GIVEN THE DIFFERENCES BETWEEN belief and behavior, how did young Samoans learn about sex, and to what extent did they engage in sexual relationships? Here Mead's descriptions of child socialization are helpful. In the process of growing up, Samoan children learned informally about sex and about gender roles. Mead described how children were raised within large extended families, where interaction between boys and girls was restricted on the basis of gender and age. She noted:

> Relatives of the opposite sex have a most rigid code of etiquette prescribed for all their contacts with each other. After they have reached the years of discretion, nine or ten years of age in this case, they may not touch each other, sit close to each other, eat together, address each other familiarly, or mention any salacious matter in each other's presence. They may not remain in any house, except their own, together, unless half the village is gathered there. They may not walk together, use each other's possessions, dance on the same floor, or take part in any of the same small group activities. This strict avoidance applies to all individuals of the opposite sex within five years above or below one's own age with whom one was reared and to whom one acknowledges relationship by blood or marriage. The conformance to this brother and sister taboo begins when the younger of the two children feels "ashamed" at the elder's touch and continues until old age when the decrepit, toothless pair of old siblings may again sit on the same mat and not feel ashamed.[1]

Many relationships outside of the extended family were also governed by gender, age, and rank. As children grew up, they became aware of a web of authority, responsibility, and obligation to their families, their broader kin groups, and their villages.

The adult Samoan men and women that Mead studied led largely separate lives. There were no public displays of affection between husbands and wives.

There was no public hand-holding, hugging, or kissing. Girls were usually chaperoned. There was no dating. And brothers were required to protect their sisters from potential seducers. How, then, did young men and women get together, given the restrictive social environment of the rural villages in which Mead and Freeman did their fieldwork?

Opportunities for Relationships

Some girls, mostly from high-ranking families, had almost no opportunity. In addition, some adolescent girls were sent by their parents to live in the Samoan pastor's house; they were less likely to have affairs than girls living with their families. And before the role of ceremonial virgins, or *taupou,* attenuated in the early twentieth century, they were closely guarded by the unmarried women of the village. These high-ranking girls were likely to be formally courted. But other girls and boys of lower rank had more opportunities for heterosexual relationships, as Mead noted, including elopement and clandestine affairs that might not lead to marriage.[2]

Formal courtship was common among families of high-ranking chiefs but much less so among lower-ranking families, who were a substantial part of a village's population. Formal courtship was based on the approval of both families, gift exchange between the families, a public proposal of marriage by the young man and his family representative, and a Christian wedding ceremony in church. Elopement, or *avaga,* on the other hand, was another publicly recognized form of marriage, but it involved the young couple's covertly escaping together, usually to the home of the young man's relatives. It did not involve a church ceremony, nor was it approved by the church. Nevertheless, once a couple lived together, they were recognized as husband and wife. *Avaga* was the most common form of marriage for couples of lesser rank and often occurred after a sexual encounter. Freeman himself noted that girls might use premarital sex to encourage elopement.

Clandestine affairs were the third form of relationship that Mead described, and they were risky. Because privacy was regarded with suspicion, because young men and women were not supposed to be alone together, because girls were closely monitored by their relatives, and because physical punishment could result if a couple was discovered, young men and women had to be very careful. Young men might use intermediaries to approach young women. With the help of these go-betweens, an encounter could be set up in the bush or in the plantations away from the village. Because young men were expected to initiate a relationship, young women did not require intermediaries as often.

The male intermediary, or *soa,* carried messages, arranged meeting places, warned the couple of impending danger, settled lovers' quarrels, and, for serious relationships, might propose marriage.

Visiting Parties

One occasion where clandestine relationships could occur with less scrutiny was the visiting party. For example, a village would send its young men's group to visit another village for work, ceremonials, or entertainment. While there, the young men would be formally entertained by the host village's group of unmarried women. Visiting parties were recognized as potential opportunities for relationships to form, even though they were chaperoned. At visiting parties, young men and women were more likely to be unrelated than within a village and therefore had fewer restrictions on them. They were expected to consider potential partners for marriage and possible affairs, since most marriages occurred between men and women from different villages.[3]

As each group of young men and women performed its dances late into the night, the party could become more raucous and erotic, and couples could slip off into the darkness. A description of one such party comes from Fay Calkins, an American who married a young, highly educated Samoan, Vai Ala'ilima, in the United States in the 1950s. They then returned to Western Samoa, where they lived in a rural village. Calkins recalls a visiting party at which thirty young men from Lefaga and twenty young women from another village danced, sang, and laughed their way through the evening. She and her husband provided adult supervision. Around midnight, each group of men and women produced its comic dancers. "Fat old women jumped and bumped and ground, to everyone's great delight."[4] At about this time, Fay and Vai retired for the evening. The music and laughter continued until dawn. Later that morning, a chief came to the couple and announced with dismay that five women were missing. Everything in the village came to a halt.

The chiefs of Lefaga were immediately called to a meeting at Fay and Vai's home, where they sat cross-legged on the floor and contemplated what to do. The five women had eloped with five Lefaga men. "Four of the elopements caused no concern. The girls were single and would be back in a few days. But the fifth was a poser. The lady was married, and to a high chief at that. Wars have been fought for lesser reasons."[5] The only solution was to arrange a large-scale ceremonial apology to the aggrieved chief during which pigs and fine mats would be presented in a public ritual requesting forgiveness.

Many people from Lefaga, including the young men's group, traveled to the aggrieved chief's village, Sapo'e. They entered in a long procession, carrying mats, pigs, tinned beef, and baskets of taro. The procession then stopped in front of the chief's house; members sat down on the ground under the burning tropical sun and waited silently for him to forgive them. Finally, they were forgiven. With the conflict resolved, the somber mood of the ritual was lifted. Mats were presented, food was consumed, and, later that evening, entertainment commenced. Calkins recalled that "there was much laughter. Rollicking song and dance items passed from side to side and it all seemed vaguely familiar. At midnight Vai and I excused ourselves and drove home to a very quiet plantation. . . . Next morning we were again awakened by pounding on the door. A Sapo'e chief rushed in with indignation written in every crinkle of his brow. Eight Sapo'e girls were missing!"[6]

Sleep Crawling

Apart from plantations and the bush in back of the village, a common location for a clandestine affair was the girl's home. Because girls were so closely watched, this was one of the few places available for a relationship. It was far from ideal. Samoan houses were open, with no formal partitions except mosquito nets. Families of six to a dozen people or more slept near each other on the floor. In these circumstances a young man would attempt to quietly crawl to the girl's mat at night. She was surrounded by relatives determined to protect her from a potential "sleep crawler" (*moetotolo* or *moetolo*). So the young man would wait until everyone in the house seemed to be asleep and then, with great stealth, crawl to the girl's side and quietly awaken her. This encounter might be prearranged or not. If not, the boy hoped that the girl would be flattered by his attention or at least not frightened enough to cry out "Moetotolo!" awakening the household and leading to a chase with possible capture and punishment.

Consummating a relationship under these conditions was difficult, but it occurred nevertheless. The girl had a certain amount of discretion in this situation. She might allow the boy to whisper to her without engaging in sex, or she might simply send him away. She might also allow him to have a sexual relationship with her. It was very important for the girl to have deniability in acquiescing to the encounter. She knew that she would not be held accountable if she screamed "Moetotolo!" If intercourse did occur, she might not acknowledge her willing participation even to her partner. Tim O'Meara reported: "According to both male and female participants, even if a girl does go along, she may feign sleep in order to protect her own sense of modesty and perhaps her reputation should they be discovered. If she is not willing and the young man persists, she has merely to cry out to set the entire household upon the intruder."[7]

For his part, the young man might plan an escape route so that if someone did awaken, he would not be captured. He also might cover his body in coconut oil to make capture difficult. Sometimes, though, the best-laid plans went awry. If caught, the young man would be beaten and ridiculed, and his family fined by the village council.

One contemporary instance of *moetotolo* that I knew of involved a young Peace Corps volunteer who decided to visit his Samoan girlfriend one evening.[8] He had successfully visited her on earlier occasions without being caught. However, that evening he had been drinking "bush brew," a potent alcoholic drink, and as he crawled into the house he passed out against one of the house posts, bumping his head. The noise awakened his girlfriend's sister, who screamed "Moetotolo!" The whole household awoke and gave chase. The young man managed to stagger to the pastor's house, where he stayed under the pastor's protection for the next few days while proper compensation for the offense was worked out. The aggrieved family actually liked the young Peace Corps volunteer, but, under the circumstances, he had breached public morality. He was a *moetotolo* and had to be treated like one. In other cases, a *moetotolo* could be expelled from the village. One *moetotolo* who was a pastor's son was permanently banished from his village.

The danger of being caught in this kind of situation is sometimes difficult for outsiders to appreciate. Anthropologist Robert Maxwell gradually became involved with a young Samoan woman and gained some insight into what might happen if someone awoke. Although his relationship was not strictly analogous to *moetotolo,* he wrote: "In a few months we were pretty close, and I was staying at her hut until quite late, her parents and her half-dozen siblings scattered around us, dozing or asleep. After a while I realized what a dangerous situation this was. An untimely awakening by her father or mother could be catastrophic. It could not go on." Maxwell's visits tapered off, and the young woman found another boyfriend. As Maxwell recounted, "So much for love in the South Seas."[9]

In such situations there may be a variety of motivations for young women and young men. The girl may not want a relationship; she may be genuinely fearful of a *moetotolo.* If she does want a relationship, she may not desire marriage yet. She may want to marry the young man, and premarital sex may assist her in the process. She may even have a sexual relationship in order to hurt her family and possibly shame them.[10]

The girl's parents may or may not approve of the relationship. If they know of and approve of the suitor, they may turn a blind eye. They may even tell their sons not to beat their sister's boyfriend if he is known to them. Fathers and mothers themselves may have participated in such relationships when they were younger, so they are aware how *moetotolo* operate. On the other hand, parents often want to prevent *moetotolo* because they know it may lead to an undesired elopement.

The young men have their own motives. Some may want sex. Others may wish to elope. Still others may be under peer pressure to sleep crawl. Some may wish to be caught in order to hurt their own families or to avenge a perceived wrong by the girl. At the same time, on some level, members of a household may be aware that people living within the confines of the *fale*—parents, young women, and other adult members of the household—engage in sex there. In fact, this is how some children receive an informal sex education. But these private facts of life are not publicly acknowledged.

Consensual versus Coercive Sex

This discussion of clandestine affairs in rural Samoan villages has assumed that when sex did occur it was consensual, and much of it was. Due to constraints imposed by chaperoning and sexual surveillance, young women often actively, if surreptitiously, participated in clandestine relationships. Yet, as O'Meara noted, because "all unchaperoned relationships are clandestine, it is difficult from the public's point of view to distinguish acts of force from those of mutual consent. This causes very serious problems for a girl if she is attacked. People told me a story of a girl who had committed suicide after being attacked, and other stories about girls who, feeling humiliated and defiled, had accepted their attackers as husbands."[11]

While most relationships were consensual, there was rape in Samoa, a point that Freeman has underscored. Mead stated that *moetotolo* was a "curious form of surreptitious rape" in which a young man "stealthily appropriates the favours which are meant for another." She also remarked that "the sleep crawler relies upon the girl's expecting a lover or the chance that she will indiscriminately accept any comer."[12] Yet it is difficult to find an element of coercion in Mead's description of *moetotolo*. And some of Mead's statements about *moetotolo* have not been confirmed by other observers.

Freeman criticized Mead for not recognizing that *manual* rape (or "surreptitious rape") could occur during sleep crawling, and in *Coming of Age* there was no discussion of manual rape, although Mead reported it in her field notes.[13] This act of aggression, which girls greatly fear, may not involve actual intercourse. Freeman described how a young man engaged in this type of sleep crawling would try to manually break the hymen of the girl with his fingers. In doing so he imitated part of the ancient ritual in which a ceremonial virgin was manually deflowered during her marriage ceremony as a test of her virginity.

In depriving a girl of a most important marital asset by force, the act of manual rape left the girl so ashamed that she would not report the assault and might even marry the rapist. According to Freeman, the young man who engaged in this kind of assault was seeking a virgin bride, and the very act of manual defloration could accomplish this end, although in the police cases of *moetotolo* that he examined about half of the victims were not virgins.[14]

Mead briefly discussed *moetotolo* in largely consensual terms rather than as a coercive means to secure a marriage partner. Freeman, on the other hand, approached *moetotolo* in more coercive terms involving manual rape as a means to acquire a virgin bride. However, Freeman recognized that "in many cases the defloration that precedes an avaga is the culmination of a seduction that the girl herself has actively encouraged."[15] And in Freeman's earlier work he also described *moetotolo* as a form of consensual premarital sex and a common precursor to elopement. In his unpublished 1948 postgraduate diploma thesis Freeman stated that most elopements began with sleep crawling, remarking that "in many instances a moetolo is achieved with the conivance [*sic*] of the girl concerned."[16] Here Freeman seems closer to Mead's position on *moetotolo*. On this issue, perhaps what can be said is that sleep-crawling behavior occurs along a continuum, varying from consensual to coercive.[17]

On the issue of forcible rape outside a girl's house—in the bush or on a plantation—Mead and Freeman also differed. Mead wrote, "Ever since the first contact with white civilisation, rape, in the form of violent assault, has occasionally occurred."[18] Freeman believed that rape in the form of violent assault was part of pre-European Samoan culture and that it was very common. This kind of rape might be premeditated or not, just as a meeting in the bush or on a plantation might be prearranged or by chance.

If the meeting was prearranged, the girl had already put herself in a compromising position. According to Freeman, the encounter might begin with the young man attempting consensual sex, knowing that he had the upper hand.[19] He would declare his love for the young woman. She might respond positively. If so, the young man would ask her to "prove her love" to him. If she declined, he would accuse her of loving her brother, an allegation of incestuous desire designed to thoroughly shame her, weaken her defenses, and encourage her to submit without violence.

If the girl rejected the young man or resisted him at any point during the encounter, according to Freeman, he might strike her solar plexus with his fist to knock her out. As Freeman observed, this was a technique that young men taught each other.[20] The blow would render the girl unconscious, at which point he might manually rape her or attempt intercourse. Again, in the aftermath the girl might be so distraught and humiliated that she would not report the rape.

If she did tell her brothers, they would viciously beat the rapist. But girls were reluctant to report rapes precisely because their brothers, after harshly beating the rapist, might, like the rapist, be subject to prison sentences, and rape victims did not wish to "waste" their brothers.[21]

If a rape was made public, it was most often adjudicated within the village rather than involving the police or court system. The village council was the deliberative body that considered the offense and appropriate punishment. Sociologist Cluny Macpherson and his Samoan wife, La'avasa Macpherson, found that reports of rape to authorities beyond the village level were considered unusual by Samoans themselves. Thus, one well-educated young woman who was a victim of rape surprised villagers when she demanded a court trial of her alleged attacker after the village had rendered a judgment in the case.[22]

Freeman examined statistics for thirty-two specific cases of rape and attempted rape in the police files in Western Samoa. He also reported that Samoans have one of the highest rates of rape in the world.[23] Anthropologist Bonnie Nardi and sociologist James Côté have each questioned Freeman's interpretation of these statistics.[24] Nevertheless, Freeman's discussion of rape is an important reminder that sexual coercion existed in Western Samoa. Eleanor Gerber reported that rape was common in American Samoa as well.[25] Why, then, did Mead not report on it more extensively?

Although she did know of two cases of rape, as reported in her field notes, Mead did not view rape as a widespread problem in the Manu'a group in the 1920s.[26] These rapes were apparently not reported to the government. Freeman believed that Mead did not know enough about Samoan sexual conduct to document it properly. After examining police records on rape in Western Samoa, Freeman was allowed access to the historical archives of the High Court in American Samoa for the 1920s. He was able to discover several cases of rape that were reported then.[27] When I asked Freeman in 1984 if any of these cases from the 1920s occurred in the Manu'a group, he replied that all of his cases came from the main island of Tutuila and not Manu'a.[28] Is it possible that there was less rape in Manu'a at that time or that it was under-reported?[29]

The Code of Silence

Complicating the search for accurate data about rape is that, at the time that *Coming of Age* was written, social conventions in both America and Samoa limited discussions of sex, including rape. As noted earlier, explicit descriptions of sex in America were considered immoral and prohibited. Books with excessive sexual content could be banned. Even the tabloids of the 1920s were careful not to cross the line for fear that church organizations or the Society for the

Suppression of Vice might have publishers arrested. This is one reason that *Coming of Age* seems so harmless today; the language of sex is muted.

In America in the 1920s rape was known, feared, and criminalized, but for propriety's sake it was not written about in detail, just as other sexual experiences were not. And it was only hinted at in film for decades to come. Among the first American films to deal directly with rape was *Outrage*, released in 1950. In the early twentieth century rape was not perceived and discussed in the same way that it is today, and many men could not understand how traumatic rape was for women. The perpetrator often saw himself as having done nothing wrong. The standard male explanations for rape were that the girl "wanted it" or "asked for it" by putting herself at risk. In fact, Eleanor Gerber reported that these same rationales were offered by the Samoan males that she interviewed in American Samoa during the 1970s.[30]

In America a code of silence on the subject of rape left victims without a voice and without assistance. As interpreted by police investigators and the court system, these explanations by perpetrators were so plausible that victims thought they were better off remaining silent rather than exposing themselves to questions about their morals, their dress, and their sexual histories. This remains true today, as illustrated by the high-profile sexual assault cases involving Kobe Bryant and William Kennedy Smith. Even with rape shield laws that are supposed to prevent examination of the rape victim's previous sexual history, the first line of defense against the accusation of rape is to question the victim's conduct.

This was true in Samoa as well. A young woman knew of the gossip and public shaming that would result if people knew that she had had sex with a boy, whether consensual or coerced. She could be expelled from school and from her church. Her marriage prospects could be compromised, and her family's reputation tarnished. Moreover, her family might blame her for the rape. This problem has continued as Samoans have migrated overseas, as the following account from a New Zealand–born Samoan woman indicates:

> I am twenty years old and, this is hard. . . . I was raped by a Samoan boy
> when I was sixteen. He was supposed to protect me—huh—he was sup-
> posed to keep me a virgin—huh. I tried to tell my parents the truth but I
> got called the slut, the tart. I was punished and sent away to Samoa for two
> years. I had to be the obedient girl. I had to listen to my aiga [family] and I
> had to earn a good reputation. It was really hard for me. I cried a lot and
> kept thinking back to all the things I did. I was the typical obedient Sa-
> moan girl. I always listened to my parents. . . . I felt betrayed. I felt guilty
> for no reason.

This young woman attempted suicide in Samoa, survived, and was ultimately believed by her parents, but she concluded, "It goes to show what lengths some of us go to just to be listened to."[31]

A code of silence and shame helped keep rape out of the public domain in Samoa. But Samoa was hardly unique. At the U.S. Air Force Academy in 2003 a major scandal erupted involving rape. It emerged that almost one-quarter of the female cadets had been victims of rape or attempted rape by male cadets. The male cadets felt more solidarity with the alleged perpetrators than with the female victims and protected each other.[32] No official at the academy recognized the extent of the problem until there was a congressional investigation, and the alleged perpetrators—who became commissioned officers—were not charged or prosecuted, even after extensive press coverage.

In both Samoa and America victims often expressed shock that they had been raped, since they had done nothing to encourage the rapist, who was often someone they knew, even well. The alleged rapist responded that precisely because they knew each other the relationship was consensual. Young men were emboldened by an asymmetry in power, often wanting to see how far they could go. In America it was not until the early 1980s that "date rape" or "acquaintance rape" was given its own terminology and recognized as a widespread problem that needed to be addressed publicly, especially on college campuses, and prosecuted as a crime. For young women, unwanted sexual advances and even rape itself were often unspoken risks of dating, sometimes referred to as "bad sex" before the term "date rape" was used. It was also at this time that rape within marriage was for the first time defined as a criminal act rather than a husband's prerogative. As for the idea that a rape victim would actually marry her attacker, in 1981 the TV soap opera *General Hospital* depicted a rape after which the victim eventually married the rapist. Their marriage was the most watched soap opera episode of that era. Interestingly, the producers suggested that the rape represented was actually consensual sex, while the viewing audience thought it was coercive sex, siding with the victim.[33]

Pregnancy and Deniability

In Samoa premarital relationships were publicly disapproved of and dangerous for a number of reasons, but they occurred nonetheless, although their actual frequency is unclear. Estimates vary widely. For example, in the 1960s Robert Maxwell asked twelve young American Samoan men whom he knew how often they had intercourse in an average week. All were sexually active, and their estimates ranged from two to ten times a week.[34] Based on her research in Western

Samoa in the 1970s, Bonnie Nardi supported Mead's estimate that roughly half of the adolescent girls were sexually active.[35]

Assuming a certain amount of sexual intercourse prior to marriage, what about pregnancy?[36] This is an important question, for if there were few pregnancies, this would suggest limited sexual activity, while higher rates of pregnancy might suggest greater activity. Mead found that there were pregnancies, with children being born outside of marriage, but in this area her data were not systematic.[37] Lowell and Ellen Holmes, in their restudy of Mead's research, also reported illegitimate children in Manu'a, although they found that the illegitimate birthrate was not high.[38]

If there was an unplanned pregnancy, a couple could elope, although they did not always do so. Either the boy or the girl could refuse this type of marriage; their respective families had an important role in this decision as well. An illegitimate pregnancy was stigmatized and could be the focus of much village gossip. Samoans recognized "good" girls and "bad" girls. The village council could also fine any family in which a member gave birth to a child out of wedlock. Despite these sanctions, though, by the time of their birth illegitimate children were usually adopted into the mother's family without prejudice. Mead found that they were "enthusiastically welcomed."[39]

Mead noted that while pregnant women sometimes practiced abortion, they had little knowledge of effective contraception.[40] Withdrawal was the primary method of birth control. After the contraceptive revolution of the 1960s, though, it became possible for young Samoan women to prevent unplanned pregnancies more effectively. Yet among unmarried women there seemed to be little demand for contraception. Was it because they were not sexually active and therefore did not need it, as Freeman might predict? Or was it because they were sexually active and did not want to use birth control for other reasons?

Viopapa Annandale, a Samoan researcher who studied contraceptive use in the islands in the 1970s, examined the question of why girls were reluctant to use contraception even when they were sexually active:

> The attitude of the Samoans to sex is, like their religious attitudes, rather ambivalent. Strict moral codes are laid down and seemingly enforced. However, for a long time we wondered why it was that so many unmarried girls were getting pregnant in spite of frequent approaches by us [about family planning] until we discovered that these girls were far less ashamed of having an illegitimate child than to be known to be using a contraceptive. Using a contraceptive was an admission of her sexual activities, whereas a pregnancy was said to be caused by a chance encounter.[41]

Annandale had found an important link between maintaining the appearance of supporting a restrictive public morality and participating in premarital sex. For an unmarried woman to use contraception was to acknowledge her sexual desire and her complicity in planned sexual encounters without family knowledge or approval. As long as sex appeared unplanned, it was understandable. Not using contraception reinforced a young woman's ability to deny responsibility for sex even when she was faced with pregnancy.

For Americans who lived through the sexual revolution of the 1960s, this may be difficult to comprehend. Obtaining reliable contraception obviously could prevent unwanted pregnancy. For young American women in the first half of the twentieth century, pregnancy was the greatest fear concerning sex; public shame was a close second. These were reasons not to engage in sex. In the 1960s birth control pills were seen by many young women and men as a godsend. Yet the contraceptive revolution also meant that American girls could no longer say no to their boyfriends based on fear of pregnancy. As Gloria Steinem noted, birth control pills led to the "moral disarmament of Betty Co-ed" and an increase in premarital sex.[42] In contrast, Samoan girls seemed to fear discovery of planned sexual activity as much as pregnancy itself.

Homosexuality

Homosexuality among Samoan adolescents was, like heterosexual sex and rape, another issue on which Mead and Freeman differed. Mead found homosexual practices common among young boys and girls. In her book she reported that a majority of the female adolescents in her sample had homosexual experience. Mead did not define precisely what kind of experience this might have been, but seventeen of the twenty-five girls in her sample had homosexual experience in contrast to less than half having heterosexual experience.[43] For Mead, homosexual experience for both girls and boys was considered "play, neither frowned on or given much consideration." Homosexual activity tapered off as adolescents became involved in heterosexual relationships, culminating in marriage. Because almost everyone married, there were few true homosexuals. According to Mead, among the Samoans that she knew there were no girls who were exclusively homosexual and only one young man who was.[44]

Given Freeman's criticism of Mead on heterosexual sex, *moetotolo*, and rape, some criticism or at least commentary by him on Mead's discussion of homosexuality might be expected. Yet in Freeman's two books there is no mention of homosexuality, either male or female.[45] This lack of discussion raises questions similar to those raised about Mead on the subject of rape. Did Freeman know of adolescent homosexuality and choose not to write about it? Did he not know and therefore was he unable to comment? If Samoans were puritanical Christians, as Freeman believed, why was adolescent homosexuality tolerated? If heterosexual conduct was forbidden and punished, why not homosexual conduct as well?

Freeman's lack of discussion of homosexuality is also puzzling because there is a culturally defined role in Samoa that involves cross-dressing males and what we in America would consider homosexual behavior. This role is especially evident today in the form of the *fa'afafine*. A *fa'afafine* (literally, "according to the way of a woman") is a male who plays the female role and has a feminine identity. In the port towns of Apia and Pago Pago, where many *fa'afafine* reside, they often do women's work as well as men's work. They prefer straight men as sexual partners and play the female role in a sexual relationship, although they do not consider themselves gay, just as their straight male partners do not consider themselves gay.[46] Most *fa'afafine* regard each other as "sisters" and do not have sexual relationships among themselves as gay men might. Moreover, many *fa'afafine* are socially accepted and valued as responsible family members and employees. In some cases families may actually encourage a son to become a *fa'afafine*. There is also a parallel role for women who take on the male role, known as *fa'atama* (the way of a man), although they are far less common than *fa'afafine*.[47]

Fa'afafine and *fa'atama* are important to a discussion of Samoan sexual conduct and to a discussion of gender roles more generally. Because they are social accepted, they pose questions about the rigidity of Samoan sexual conduct and the inflexibility of gender roles in the islands. If it is true that gender roles in Samoa are sharply defined if not mutually exclusive, how do the *fa'afafine* and *fa'atama* fit into this social order? Mead did not provide direct answers to these questions, but she believed that Samoan culture was, at least in some areas, flexible. For Freeman, the existence of adolescent homosexuality, *fa'afafine*, and *fa'atama* is simply not acknowledged, let alone explained.

For Samoans themselves, the subject of *fa'afafine* today is a difficult one, reflecting the public/private dichotomy and their concern about how Samoans are perceived by the outside world. Sociologist Johanna Schmidt found that while Samoans accepted *fa'afafine* within their own culture, they feared that Europeans learning of this role would label Samoa a "gay paradise," even though *fa'afafine* do not consider themselves gay in the contemporary American sense.[48] *Fa'afafine* also worry about their image abroad, having worked together to earn legitimacy within the islands.

Finding a Balance?

This overview of Samoan sexual conduct suggests that it is not easy to classify in a black-and-white fashion. There are things that we do not know and may never know. The data are far from perfect. The statistics on Samoan sexual conduct are open to a number of questions. The interview data are limited. The court materials and the case study materials are suggestive but not necessarily definitive. Should belief be emphasized over behavior, or vice versa? Although we have examined the outlines of Samoan sexual conduct and can compare American data on the same issues, there is a good deal that we do not know.[49] As a result, in looking at the controversy there are two temptations.

The first temptation is to believe that Mead and Freeman saw only what each wanted to see. Metaphorically speaking, Mead, as the Nurturant Mother, allowed Samoan adolescent girls permission to experiment in both heterosexual and homosexual realms, minimized the threat of rape, and did not view the sanctions against sexual encounters and pregnancy as insurmountable obstacles to sex. On the other hand, Freeman, as the Dominating Father, saw adolescent girls as bound by rules forbidding sexual conduct, as being fearful and chaste, while young Samoan men, despite the public value on virginity, were expected and encouraged to aggressively violate young women.[50] He minimized the amount of sexual activity, paid little attention to the interest of Samoan girls in boys, and neglected homosexuality. While it is tempting to view the controversy this way, it is also misleading because it treats Samoans almost entirely as figments of the anthropologist's imagination. It is true that Mead saw pleasure in Samoa while Freeman saw danger, but there is more to Samoa than these two anthropologists' views.[51]

There is also the temptation to synthesize Mead and Freeman on Samoan sexual conduct and call the controversy a draw on this issue. Much of this chapter has synthesized their data and also used the work of other anthropologists and scholars, including Samoan scholars, to increase our understanding as best we can.[52] While such syntheses may help to find commonality in the differing views of Mead, Freeman, and others, they do not always do justice to the complexity of Samoan culture, the views of many researchers and Samoans themselves, and the views of Mead and Freeman that are truly problematic and incompatible. Synthesis is important, as is building on the work of other observers of Samoa. Yet the controversy cannot be resolved simply by reaching an amicable compromise. It is, in part, about the nature of Samoan culture.

There is a real Samoa that exists independently of Mead, Freeman, or any other individual observer. And there are enough good data about Samoan sexual conduct to corroborate or falsify some of the competing claims in the controversy. The synthesis presented in the last two chapters was intended to clarify what we know and don't know about Samoan sexual conduct as much as to keep score of Mead's and Freeman's respective positions on sexual permissiveness and restrictiveness. The next chapter will take a closer look at the institution of

the ceremonial virgin, or *taupou*. This was the very subject that Mead and Freeman publicly fought about in Canberra in 1964. If there was an institution that
could establish to what extent Samoan culture was sexually permissive or sexually restrictive, this would seem to be it.

\12/

Virginity and the History of Sex in Samoa

THE *TAUPOU* SYSTEM OCCUPIES a central place in the Mead-Freeman controversy. Its very existence, according to Freeman and many Samoan critics of Mead, showed that virginity was more than an abstract value; it was part of a *system* of *institutionalized* virginity, where the *taupou* played an important role in Samoan culture and provided a role model for other girls. For Freeman, the *taupou* was one of Samoa's "most sacrosanct traditional institutions." He stated that in pre-European times female virginity was "very much the leitmotif of the pagan Samoans," and even in the late twentieth century, Freeman argued, "the sexual mores of the pagan Samoans are still, in many ways, extant."[1]

In pre-European Samoa a young woman, usually the adolescent daughter of a high-ranking chief, was appointed to the role of *taupou;* she represented the chief's political authority and the prestige of the village as a whole. Her marriage to another high-ranking chief could cement new political alliances. She was therefore an important figure in village political life. Beyond her valuable role in forging alliances, the *taupou* was also leader of the village's association of unmarried women (*aualuma*) that entertained prestigious visitors. The *taupou* made kava for meetings of the village council, was a hostess and dancer, ate special food, wore distinctive dress, and did not engage in the heavy labor of her unmarried female counterparts. She was the pride of her village. At her marriage there were elaborate gift exchanges between the families of the bride and groom. And she was required to demonstrate her chastity in a public defloration ceremony just prior to her formal arranged marriage.[2]

Freeman provided an explicit description of the defloration ceremony:

> The exchange of property having taken place, the bridegroom seated himself on the ceremonial ground of his village. The young woman was

then taken by the hand by her elder brother or some other relative, and led toward her bridegroom, dressed in a fine mat edged with red feathers, her body gleaming with scented oil. On arriving immediately in front of him she threw off this mat and stood naked while he ruptured her hymen with "two fingers of his right hand." If a hemorrhage ensued the bridegroom drew his fingers over the bride's upper lip, before holding his hand for all present to witness the proof of her virginity. At this the female supporters of the bride rushed forward to obtain a portion of the smear upon themselves before dancing naked and hitting their heads with stones until their own blood ran down in streams, in sympathy with, and in honor of, the virgin bride. The husband, meanwhile, wiped his hands on a piece of white barkcloth which he wore around his waist for the rest of the day as a token of respect for his wife. With the bride's ceremonial defloration accomplished, the marriage was usually consummated forthwith, with the utmost decorum, in a screened-off part of a house.[3]

However, if the bride was not a virgin, she was cursed as a prostitute, and the marriage was nullified. Sometimes she was beaten by her relatives, even to death.[4]

Freeman argued that the value of virginity embodied in the *taupou* extended beyond her to all adolescent girls, and this "cult of virginity" continued after European contact. Christianity transformed and reinforced the values of the *taupou* system so that, in Freeman's view, "after the mid 19th century, when a puritanical Christian morality was added to an existing traditional cult of virginity," Samoa was a society in which this religiously and culturally sanctioned ideal strongly influenced the actual behavior of adolescent girls.[5]

Freeman's extensive discussion of the *taupou* system was intended to refute Mead's portrayal of the *taupou* as a girl of high rank whose virginity was closely guarded but who was the exception rather than the rule in terms of virginity. Mead argued that, apart from the *taupou* and other daughters of high-ranking chiefs and despite the ideology of virginity for all girls, adolescent girls from lower-ranking families could and did engage in clandestine premarital sex. Instead of reinforcing a preexisting ideal of virginity, as Freeman would have it, Christianity and colonial government led to a relaxation of the severe traditional standards for the *taupou* in part by completely banning the defloration ceremony. Apart from the virginity of the *taupou,* to which Samoans were committed, Mead believed that they were skeptical of Christianity's message about chastity for all Samoans and that they participated in what, by American standards of the 1920s, were permissive premarital relationships.[6]

Freeman agreed that changes in the *taupou* system had occurred, the banning of the defloration ceremony being the most obvious one, but the value of virginity for all girls remained. Chastity was now upheld by Christian Samoans, and the village pastor now guarded adolescent girls, who often resided in his home under his guidance and protection. The village and the church enforced a system of punishments for those who strayed from the fold, as did individual families. Freeman stated that the values of the *taupou* system began to break down as Samoans started to migrate overseas in the 1950s, but for the previous one hundred years or more the values of the *taupou* system had remained intact and enforced sexual restrictiveness.[7] Thus, according to Freeman, the *taupou* system was in effect before, during, and after Mead's research in the 1920s. So Samoa could not have been sexually permissive, despite Mead's assertions to the contrary.

While Mead and Freeman agreed on the importance of virginity for the *taupou*, they disagreed on virtually everything else—how widely the value on her virginity was held, the role of Christianity, and the actual behavior of adolescent girls. Because Samoa has a reputation for tradition and continuity, Freeman's depiction lent itself to an interpretation involving cultural conservatism and resiliency. Mead's depiction, on the other hand, suggested that as a result of missionization and colonialism, the *taupou* system attenuated and declined. So how persistent was the *taupou* system after European settlement began? What kinds of changes occurred? And how closely was the ideal of chastity observed at different times during the colonial period?

Mead's View of the *Taupou* and Her Use of History

In her 1927 National Research Council report, "The Adolescent Girl in Samoa," Mead discussed the decline of the *taupou* system in a chapter entitled "Samoan Civilisation As It Is To-day." The chapter also dealt with other changes in Samoa that occurred as a result of European contact.[8] But in terms of historical detail the chapter got in the way of what she wanted to convey in *Coming of Age in Samoa*.

Mead wanted to present Samoa in a readable manner, without having to shift awkwardly back and forth between different historical time frames. By excluding history and other external factors, she could achieve a more uniform, if artificial, presentation. This kind of representation, known as "the ethnographic present" among anthropologists, was a commonly used literary tool. It factored out the "contaminating" effects of the past and highlighted what appeared to be a relatively untouched present. Yet the stylistic virtue of using the ethnographic present was also its weakness. It presented a culture in a timeless, enduring manner, as if it were forever traditional and unchanging.

Mead wanted to use the ethnographic present to organize the body of *Coming of Age*. So, in the transformation of her report into a book, she shifted the chapter on historical change to an appendix.[9] Mead knew that it was next to impossible to present a single, coherent picture of the culture without distorting history. Things did change. Thus, she noted that the culture of a Samoan adolescent girl's parents was different from the girl's own culture. But for the sake of the unity of the book, different time frames were lumped together, including "customs which have fallen into partial decay under the impact of western propaganda and foreign example."[10] The *taupou* system was one of those customs.

In the body of *Coming of Age* Mead wrote about how, traditionally, the *taupou* differed from other girls and how she was deflowered in a public ceremony: "From this free and easy experimentation, the *taupo* [*sic*] is excepted. Virginity is a legal requirement for her. At her marriage, in front of all the people, in a house brilliantly lit, the talking chief of the bridegroom will take the tokens of her virginity. In former days, should she not prove to be a virgin, her female relatives fell upon her and beat her with stones, disfiguring and sometimes fatally injuring the girl who had shamed their house." Mead footnoted this discussion by observing, "This custom is forbidden by law, but is only gradually dying out."[11]

She then continued her discussion of the *taupou* and other high-ranking daughters of chiefs:

> These girls of noble birth are carefully guarded; not for them are secret trysts at night or stolen meetings in the daytime. Where parents of lower rank complacently ignore their daughters' experiments, the high chief guards his daughter's virginity as he guards the honour of his name, his precedence in the kava ceremony or any other prerogative of his high degree. Some old woman of the household is told to be the girl's constant companion. The *taupo* may not visit in other houses in the village, or leave the house alone at night. When she sleeps, an older woman sleeps beside her. Never may she go to another village unchaperoned. In her own village, she goes soberly about her tasks, bathing in the sea, working in the plantation, safe under the jealous guardianship of the women of her own village. She runs little risk from the *moetotolo*, for one who outraged the *taupo* of his village would formerly have been beaten to death, and now would have to flee from the village. The prestige of the village is inextricably bound up with the high repute of the *taupo* and few young men in the village would dare to be her lovers. Marriage to them is out of the question. . . . For tradition says that the *taupo* must marry outside her village, marry a high chief or a *manaia* [heir apparent] of another village. Such a marriage is an occasion for great festivities and solemn ceremony. The chief and all of his talking chiefs must come to propose for her hand, come in person bringing gifts for her talking chiefs. If the talking chiefs of the girl are satisfied that

this is a lucrative and desirable match, and the family are satisfied with the rank and appearance of the suitor, the marriage is agreed upon. Little attention is paid to the opinion of the girl.[12]

So Mead had a good understanding of the pre-European *taupou* system and described it in a manner similar to Freeman.

In "Samoan Civilisation As It Is To-day," now an appendix to *Coming of Age*, Mead described the changes that had occurred in the system in the nineteenth century, including less punitive sanctions of the *taupou* for an affair:

Deviations from chastity were formerly punished in the case of girls by a very severe beating and a stigmatising shaving of the head. Missionaries have discouraged the beating and head shaving, but failed to substitute as forceful an inducement to circumspect conduct. The girl whose sex activities are frowned upon by her family is in a far better position than that of her grandmother. The navy has prohibited, the church has interdicted the defloration ceremony, formerly an inseparable part of the marriages of girls of rank; and thus the most potent inducement to virginity has been abolished. If for these cruel and primitive methods of enforcing a stricter regime there had been substituted a religious system which seriously branded the sex offender, or a legal system which prosecuted and punished her, then the new hybrid civilisation might have been as heavily fraught with possibilities of conflict as the old civilisation undoubtedly was.[13]

Mead did not see the church as reinforcing the *taupou* system, as Freeman did. The church was influential in promoting the ideal of virginity, especially for young women who went to live with the pastor, but Mead viewed the *taupou* system as a system of marriage that Christianity sought to replace almost in its entirety. However, neither Mead nor Freeman provided more than a brief review of how the *taupou* system worked or how it changed after the Europeans arrived. A more detailed review of the evidence may help resolve some of these issues in the controversy.

Before the Missionaries Arrived

The *taupou* system was, according to Mead, a system of marriage that governed the relationships of daughters of high-ranking chiefs, idealizing their virginity and protecting them from unwanted seduction. As noted earlier, each village had its own set of chiefs (*matai*), organized as a village council and incorporated into a broader hierarchy of chiefs.[14] In pre-European Samoa chiefly prestige was partly inherited and partly achieved. Chiefs could not simply rest on the status of a title after it was conferred; they had to earn prestige by forging alliances, participating in ceremonial exchanges of wealth, successfully waging war, and gaining new titles through strategic marriages. *Taupou* marriages were vital in all of these political activities. Chiefs used the *taupou* as a social asset to promote political alliances with other chiefly families in a system that allowed high-ranking chiefs to have multiple wives, sometimes a dozen or more. The more important the chiefly title, the more marriages he could contract and the greater his upward mobility and prestige.

Because the Samoan political system was not centralized, consisting instead of shifting, warring alliances, and because chiefly marriages were essential to alliance formation, high-ranking families were especially concerned with controlling their daughters' sexual conduct so that they could be used to cement alliances.[15] If the *taupou* passed the virginity test, the marriage transaction was completed and the alliance solidified. If not, there would be no marriage. After marriage, her role as a *taupou* ended. She was now the wife of a chief, and these marriages were not necessarily permanent. Chiefs taking new wives could discard old ones, and former *taupou* would return to their own villages with their children. They could not marry again without permission of their husbands.

If the *taupou* system was vital for high-ranking chiefs, it was far less relevant for lower-ranking chiefs and for untitled men and women. For them, *avaga* marriages based on elopement and individual choice rather than on prior family arrangement and elaborate gift exchange were the norm. Although virginity was nominally valued for young women of all ranks, in practice the lower the rank, the less the value on virginity.[16] Marriage for lower-ranking families was also typically monogamous. So there were two marriage systems in practice, the *taupou* system for elite chiefly families and *avaga* for almost everyone else.

Most girls were not *taupou* and did not have the opportunity to become *taupou* because of their lower rank. Among them there was enough premarital sex to draw the attention of early missionaries. John Williams, the missionary who brought Christianity to the islands in the 1830s, believed that Samoans were more like the permissive Tahitians he had encountered than the restrictive Tongans in terms of their "lascivious habits."[17] Williams traveled widely in the South Pacific and was a keen observer. He reported that non-*taupou* enjoyed a "roving commission" in sexual matters before marriage.[18] So, important as the *taupou* was, her behavior was not followed by many other girls.

The restrictions on the *taupou* and her proper conduct did not prevent women from the erotic singing and dancing that European observers found obscene. Williams witnessed occasions that included erotic "night" dances, and he provided the following account of them: "The young virgin girls taking the lead they now enter the house entirely naked & commence their dance. The full grown women then follow after. Then come the old women all of whom are entirely naked. During their dancing they throw themselves in all imaginable positions in order to make the most full exposure of their persons to the whole company. . . . During the whole of the time of performing the females are using the most vile, taunting, bantering language to the men."[19] Needless to say, Williams and other missionaries were shocked by this and many other aspects of Samoan culture. There was undoubtedly a great deal about Samoan culture that they did not understand.[20] Nevertheless, from their perspective, they had not encountered a culture committed to chastity for all men and women but rather a culture in which "indecent" sexual activities were common enough to become the missionaries' highest priority for reform.

Missionary Reform

The initial impression of a number of early Christian missionaries was that Samoa was a pagan culture filled with godlessness and immorality. Although they considered Samoans a "race" worthy of Christianity and superior to many other non-Western cultures, "sinful" sexual activities were common enough and public enough to receive the missionaries' fullest attention.

While approving of the ideal of virginity as symbolized by the *taupou,* missionaries did not approve of many aspects of the *taupou* system and other aspects of Samoan sexual conduct. They strongly condemned political marriages, multiple marriages, prostitution, adultery, ease of divorce, erotic dancing and singing, ease of sexual access in living arrangements, sexual activities during intervillage visits, and, of course, public defloration.[21] The missionaries were very interested in assuring that virginity become the ideal for all young women, not just the *taupou,* and that men remain faithful to their wives. Anthropologist Penelope Schoeffel, reviewing the early historical accounts of the *taupou* system, found that "in the past, only high-ranking women had been bound by the rules of chastity; and chiefly polygamy and philandering by men had been encouraged. Under the new Christian order, restrictions were applied to all Samoans, irrespective of rank, who wished for salvation."[22]

Williams and his missionary associates began converting Samoans in the 1830s. He initially thought that, given the low status of women and the chiefly prerogative of polygynous marriages, evangelizing Samoans would be difficult.[23] Yet within three decades they had converted in impressive numbers.[24] The process was so swift and seemingly complete that it was easy to mistake it for wholesale acceptance. Freeman, for example, speaks of the merger between the Samoan "cult of virginity" and a puritanical Christian morality reinforcing the value of chastity for all girls.[25] In reality, though, the two were often at odds, if not open conflict, over a number of matters, especially sexual conduct.

The missionaries moved to abolish public defloration, multiple marriages by chiefs, political marriages of any kind, adultery, fornication, and other acts of "immorality." They also sought to discourage a variety of activities that supported the *taupou* system as an institution. "Night" dances were prohibited and were to be replaced by churchgoing and hymn singing. Even mild forms of dance were forbidden. Although these prohibitions were later relaxed, they undermined the responsibilities of the *taupou* and the role of the unmarried women's association in public entertainment. Kava drinking, thought by missionaries to be a form of intoxication, was also banned for a time, and this too eroded the role of the *taupou*, who was responsible for making it.

Despite missionary teachings, allegedly sinful practices continued among large segments of the population, leading to frustration on the part of the missionaries. George Turner, a Wesleyan missionary who began working in Samoa in 1841, wrote: "Chastity was ostensibly cultivated by both sexes; but it was more a name than a reality. . . . There were exceptions, especially among the daughters of persons of rank, but they were exceptions, not the rule."[26]

There were so few missionaries that they could not realistically attempt far-reaching changes overnight. And there were many other temporary European visitors to Samoa who were more interested in vice than in virtue. The Reverend A. W. Murray recorded that, during the mid-nineteenth century, as many as six whalers with "lawless" crews of thirty men each could anchor at any one time in the port of Apia. The missionaries were almost helpless in the face of these men and their Samoan partners. Murray explained: "There they were— men of our own colour, speaking the same language with ourselves, and some of them our own countrymen, and claiming to be Christians, while giving themselves up to the most shameful immoralities, and telling the natives all manner of lies, so far as they could make themselves understood. . . . [W]e mourned over the moral havoc they wrought, and the influence in drawing the people away from schools and services."[27]

During the late nineteenth century the increasing European population in the port town led to a number of relationships between Samoan women and European men. There were marriages, but many more were short-term unions.[28] Apia was the second busiest port in the South Pacific, and in the latter part of the nineteenth century Europeans and a growing group of poorer, rowdy "part-Europeans" clustered in an area called the Beach, known throughout the region for its grog shops and dance halls. Prostitution, gambling, and drink were all available, much to the missionaries' dismay. Writing in 1892, author Robert Louis Stevenson, who lived in Samoa at the time, bemoaned that until recently "the white people of Apia lay in the worst squalor of degradation."[29] The port town was referred to as a "little Cairo" and a "hell in the Pacific."

Samoans were supplying dancing girls and were rumored to be giving women in exchange for muskets.[30]

Samoans actively sought relationships with Europeans that they hoped would lead to marriage or at least a relationship that could benefit their families. This was simply an extension of pre-European custom.[31] But Europeans took advantage of members of the unmarried women's association who had become available for interethnic unions. This gave Samoan women "a bad reputation in the South Seas regarding their morals," according to Augustin Krämer, a German surgeon and observer of the period.[32] While this reputation was undeserved due to a misunderstanding of Samoan custom, it was nevertheless widespread. And there were increasing numbers of part-European children throughout the islands.

The *Taupou* System in Decline

By the end of the nineteenth century the *taupou* system was in decline. The public defloration of *taupou* was not only forbidden by law but becoming extinct in practice. In the 1890s Krämer found that there were very few public deflorations remaining and that many *taupou* were eloping so that they might have a greater choice in marriage partners. Few true virgins remained, mostly among the very young. Krämer even observed that, in those rare public deflorations that did occur, the hymeneal blood of the *taupou* might be counterfeited in order to preserve the spirit if not the letter of the virginity-testing ceremony.[33]

Krämer did not approve of public defloration, but he found the idea of counterfeiting hymeneal blood to be morally reprehensible. Yet he did not blame Samoans but rather the missionaries for this distortion of Samoan custom. In a comment very similar to Mead's he stated: "Naturally, without wanting to say that the custom of public defloration must be maintained, one must however reproach the missionaries who have not been able to offer an alternative to the people. . . . In any case, also in this respect, the 'old Samoa' is finished."[34]

By the 1890s the *taupou* system of marriage was vanishing. Polygyny was no longer a public practice, while monogamy meant that there was no longer a need for many *taupou*. The abolition of multiple marriages by high chiefs created a surplus of candidates for the position of *taupou* and decreased their political usefulness. Anthropologist Felix Keesing, who visited Samoa shortly after Mead's research in the 1920s but prior to Freeman's in the 1940s, wrote: "In the old days a fresh taupo would be married off probably every two to four years. Since the number of high-born chiefs and chiefs-elect suitable for such matches was limited, the new monogamous marriage system brought what might be called a glut in the taupo marriage mart: many maidens but few available husbands of suitable rank."[35]

Taupou were expensive to appoint, maintain, and marry. Because there were fewer marriages of high-ranking chiefs, fewer *taupou* were appointed. If these young women were unable to marry, what good were they? Keesing asked in 1937:

> What then of the taupo institution in the modern era of mission work, commercial development, schools, and Western political control?
>
> The visitor to present day Samoa passes through village after village without encountering a full-fledged taupo. From the writer's own inquiries and experience of travel, he would judge that the great majority of chiefs entitled to maintain a taupo no longer do so. Even where a taupo is found, as in socially conservative areas like Manu'a [where Mead worked] and in the case of very high chiefs like Malietoa and Mataafa, her activities have become attenuated.[36]

Mead found that, while there were several chiefs who could have appointed *taupou* in Manu'a, only one *taupou* was actually appointed, her friend Fa'apua'a, and she was a woman in her midtwenties, not an adolescent girl. Even where *taupou* were still appointed, their role was limited. Although still a hostess, dancer, and political representative of her village and family, she had fewer responsibilities than in pre-European Samoa. The unmarried women's association had declined in importance as well.

Freeman believed that the *taupou* system and Christianity merged and that this merger reinforced the value placed on virginity. At the level of public ideology, this may have been true, but as a system of marriage, the *taupou* system was attenuating. During his years in Samoa Freeman never witnessed a public defloration ceremony himself because by the 1940s there were none.[37] They had ceased to occur decades earlier, with only an occasional private defloration taking place.

Replacing the *taupou* system was a new and different system of monogamous Christian marriage advocated by missionaries. Virginity as a religious ideal became accepted public belief for all young women, with premarital and extramarital sex strongly condemned. In theory this was true for men as well. In practice, though, Christian weddings were rare and mostly for higher-ranking families, while *avaga* marriages continued for the majority of families. In the village of Sa'anapu, for example, Freeman reported that of sixty-four marriages he recorded, only four began with a church ceremony. The other sixty were *avaga* marriages, although a number of couples had a Christian ceremony at a later date.[38]

World War II and Sexual Permissiveness

By the 1940s the role of the *taupou* had been transformed from an essential part of the traditional Samoan political and economic system to a far less significant part of a changing culture. Freeman argued that there was "general stability of Samoan culture" in the first half of the twentieth century, including sexual conduct.[39] Yet he neglected the most important event of the period—World War II.

The war years were a period of major change in the islands, including a dramatic increase in unions between outsiders and Samoans. Tens of thousands of American military personnel occupied both Western Samoa and American Samoa from 1942 through 1945, overwhelming the Samoans themselves. Although the islands were not the site of military action, with the exception of one relatively harmless Japanese submarine attack, both sets of islands had major military bases.

W. E. H. Stanner, an anthropologist and postwar observer, described the situation in wartime Western Samoa as follows:

> Before the main body of troops moved to forward areas in 1943–44 there may have been as many as 25,000 or 30,000 troops in Western Samoa at any one time. The turnover, of course, was much higher because of transfer of units and movement of reinforcements. The troops were dispersed throughout the islands, many defended zones were constructed, and there was an enormous temporary building programme. The troops concentrated in camps or bivouacs along the coastline, in the main areas of native settlement, so that segregation was impracticable. . . . The Samoan islands experienced immensely heightened activity, intimate contact with Europeans *en masse*, and economic "prosperity," all in a degree greater than in any previous period in their history.[40]

The military needed Samoan labor and Samoan products; 2,600 Samoans were initially employed by the Americans. Samoans also quickly became effective small traders, restaurant and café owners, and brewers of crude but potent spirits, leading to increases in Samoan income. Historian Mary Boyd commented: "Wine, beer and spirits were manufactured from cocoa washings and sold at great profit. Gambling, drinking, promiscuity, and prostitution flourished. Samoan relations with the Americans were notably more friendly, hospitable and generous than with New Zealanders."[41]

In terms of Samoan culture, "some native ceremonies were cheapened, and in cases debauched, to attract gift-bearing Americans. A few *matai* [chiefs] appointed new *taupo* virgins, as often as not girls lacking the technical attributes, to assist hospitalities." More generally, "during the military occupation men fraternized very freely with native people, approaching them, accosting them, using their houses as sprawling huts, doing violence to one cherished courtesy after another with complete indifference. The barriers were down, and easy association became epidemic."[42]

Wartime interethnic unions were common. Stanner found:

> A great deal of sexual promiscuity occurred between Samoan or part-Samoan women and American troops. Responsible Samoans said that actual prostitution was restricted to a very small group of women. Romantic, at least friendly, relationships are very common. One mission society reported that in Upolu alone there were 1,200 known instances of illegitimate children by American soldiers from Samoan girls. The official statistics were not revealed, but put the number of known illegitimate children much lower. Only a few incidents were caused by the jealousy of Samoan men, and not much was made of them by either side. Some villages were said to have set up a special curfew for their girls, and at Falefa (near Apia) no troops except officers on business were allowed to enter *fale* [houses]. With troops so widely dispersed in an area so densely settled it is impossible to prevent familiar association. Many soldiers regularly visited girlfriends within the villages, by no means only with single intention, but the entrance-gates to the airport, it was said, became known among Samoans as "the gates of sin." At least one *matai* [chief] was summarily expelled from his church congregation and from the society of the village on suspicion of procuring girls for prostitution.[43]

The well-known author James Michener reported in a discreet but detailed manner his own participation in one such relationship. As a lieutenant Michener was responsible for base security. Early in his Western Samoan tour of duty he found a base where, during the day, sixty to seventy-two American men were on duty, yet at night there were only six. Concerned about security, Michener learned that military vehicles took the men to villages at dusk, where they were dropped off to meet their Samoan girlfriends for the evening. Michener saw firsthand that these evening arrangements were openly welcomed by Samoans. In the morning servicemen were picked up and returned to their base. Michener himself was invited by a high-ranking Samoan chief to enter into such a relationship with his daughter and to father her child. As a result of his involvement Michener felt so compromised that he never reported these relationships to his superior officers.[44]

These accounts of wartime Samoa suggest that relationships between American servicemen and Samoan women developed quickly and often, although many villages away from bases and roads had little contact with

American troops. Where relationships took place, young women were allowed and even encouraged by their families to enter into them, with contact to a large degree under the control of parents and the village. There were relatively few overt conflicts between families and American troops. Although Samoans were perfectly capable of secluding their daughters and punishing them for affairs with Americans and for having children with them, they did not do so for the most part. This pattern of permissive sexual conduct during World War II is very difficult to reconcile with Freeman's portrait of a "severe Christian morality" and a culture in which "female virginity was probably carried to a greater extreme than in any other culture known to anthropology."[45] It is also at odds with Freeman's assertion that major changes in Samoan sexual conduct did not begin to occur until the 1950s.

Because the wartime occupation of Western Samoa began in 1942, perhaps the best opportunity to view these changes would have occurred shortly before and immediately after that date. Freeman arrived in Western Samoa in April 1940 as a schoolteacher and departed in November 1943. He was therefore in a position to have observed or at least known of these relationships. As a New Zealander whose country was the governing power in Western Samoa at that time Freeman served in the Local Defense Force and would go on to serve in the Royal New Zealand Volunteer Naval Reserve. Yet the war and its effects on Samoa, including the relationships between American military personnel and Samoan women, were not discussed in Freeman's work. At that moment, when the world's political future was in great peril and when premarital sexual activity in Samoa was perhaps most apparent, Freeman's focus was elsewhere. He maintained that it was then he realized that he would "one day have to face the responsibility of writing a refutation of Mead's Samoan findings."[46]

Does History Matter?

Because Freeman's critique of Mead was primarily a historical critique based on what Samoan sexual conduct was like before, during, and after the time that Mead did her research, an extended look at the history of Samoan sexual conduct is important in evaluating Freeman's argument. The historical data just reviewed indicate major problems with Freeman's reconstruction of the history of the *taupou* system. Historically, Samoa was less restrictive than Freeman allowed, and there were more variability and permissiveness in some areas of Samoan sexual conduct than he discerned. Especially puzzling is the absence of any discussion of interethnic relationships during World War II in the islands.

Could there be a problem with the sources Freeman used? Most of the sources used here were known to and employed by Freeman in *support* of his argument about the maintenance of the *taupou* system. Yet he neglected passages in source after source that did not conform to his argument. These problems were noted in an article I published in 1996 that included much of the material reviewed in this chapter.[47] Freeman was outraged by the article and sent me a five-page handwritten letter in which he threatened to ruin my career. He also recommended that I immediately come to the islands to offer a ceremonial apology to Samoans for having misrepresented their history.[48] Freeman later published a reply to my article titled "All Made of Fantasy: A Rejoinder to Paul Shankman," declaring that I did not know what I was talking about. Yet Freeman did not refute any of the article's major arguments about the decline of the *taupou* system. Why not?

After Freeman's death in 2001 I had the opportunity to read his postgraduate diploma thesis, "The Social Structure of a Samoan Village Community," which was based on his Samoan fieldwork in the early 1940s, a source that had been previously unavailable to interested scholars. As noted earlier, this was Freeman's most important ethnographic work on the islands, and I was surprised by the data in it. Although Freeman had scoffed at my argument about the decline of the *taupou* system, in his thesis he stated that by the 1940s "the *taupou* system has now become *virtually defunct* in Western Samoa."[49]

To illustrate this point he noted that in the village of Saʻanapu there were five high-ranking families that possessed *taupou* titles. Yet "in 1943 none of these five *taupou* titles was occupied." When necessary, a girl from one of the extended families would be temporarily appointed *taupou* but not maintained on a full-time basis. Freeman then listed the reasons for the decline of the *taupou* system in Saʻanapu:

> Principal among the reasons for this change has been the rigorous suppression of customs associated with it by the Christian missions. Economic factors have also operated. Like a *matai* [chief], a *taupou* is obliged to have her title ratified by the other lineages of her village community. This is established at a feast (*saofaʻiga*) provided by the *taupou*'s lineage. Such a feast is a serious drain on a lineage's resources. Again, following the introduction of money into the Samoan economy, marked discrepancies have developed in the value of the property (*oloa* and *toga*) exchanged at marriage ceremonies. This has resulted in a situation in which a *taupou*'s lineage and village gain nothing from her marriage or formal election.

As for *taupou* marriages, they had become so infrequent that Freeman commented: "This type of marriage, now relatively rare, does not here concern us."[50]

So Freeman knew about the decline of the *taupou* system from his own fieldwork. His unpublished thesis had provided an important ethnographic account of this decline, yet his unpublished account differed from his published statements about the importance of the *taupou* system before, during, and after Mead's fieldwork in Samoa in the 1920s. And Freeman continued to insist on the viability of the taupou system in the 1920s even after my article appeared. In 1998 he wrote: "In fact, in Samoa in those days there was a virginity cult with ritual defloration at marriage."[51]

Freeman certainly knew the history of Samoa, and he gave great weight to his expertise in that area, stating that his work "would involve much research into the history of early Samoa."[52] Furthermore, he believed that "if I had not systematically completed my researches in the way that I have described, my refutation [of Mead] would certainly not have the cogency that it does."[53] He commented that his refutation of her work was "based on most carefully researched evidence, meticulously checked by native scholars, of a kind that could be submitted to a congressional or royal commission." Furthermore, he said that he used so many different sources that they could not "possibly have been affected by any projection of my personality."[54] The issue, though, is not the number of sources or their overall reliability; rather, it is *how* the sources were used.

Freeman not only misrepresented the historical work of others but neglected his own personal experiences in the islands during World War II and his unpublished work on the *taupou* system. To what extent these omissions were conscious and deliberate or unconscious and inadvertent is unclear. What is clear is that Freeman himself, not his sources, misrepresented and distorted the historical record so as to favor his interpretation of the *taupou* system and his critique of Mead. Mead's interpretation of the decline of the *taupou* system, however brief, is more in accord with the historical record presented here.

PART 5

The Broader Issues

\13/

The Many Versions
of the Hoaxing Hypothesis

WITH A BETTER UNDERSTANDING of the complexity of Samoan
sexual conduct and the decline of the *taupou* system, we can now return to
Freeman's hoaxing hypothesis, the most damning part of the controversy for
Mead's reputation as an ethnographer. After all, what could be worse for an
anthropologist than to be fooled by one's informants and collaborators? Some
of the issues in the hoaxing argument have already been addressed in chapter
2, but Freeman advanced different versions of how Mead was "hoaxed" into
believing that Samoan girls were sexually permissive. These versions ranged
from his general observation in 1983 that Mead *may* have been misled by Samoans to his unequivocal assertion in 1997 that Mead was "grossly hoaxed" by
two very specific women on the night of March 13, 1926, and that she "completely misinformed and misled virtually the entire anthropological establishment."[1] As noted earlier, these allegations have been repeated so often that they
have become conventional wisdom. In fact, they are easily challenged. Freeman
provided an exact chronology of the hoaxing, used the testimony of Fa'apua'a
to establish its occurrence, and relied on written documents by Mead to support both the chronology and Fa'apua'a's testimony. How well does this evidence stand up?

Panic in the Field?

In his reconstruction of Mead's fieldwork for his second book on Mead, Freeman determined that she had set herself a difficult research agenda. In attempting to study both Samoan adolescence *and* ethnology, Mead did not allow
herself adequate time to do systematic research on adolescence. Freeman further reasoned that she had spent so much time studying ethnology that by
March 1926 she had reached a point where she realized that she had not carried

out a "systematic study of the sexual lives of her sample of adolescent girls."
With time in the field running out, according to Freeman, Mead panicked. She
wrote to Boas of this crisis in her research and was ultimately forced to rely on
a single evening's conversations with two Samoan women for information
about adolescent sexuality.[2] In answering Mead's questions about what they
did at night, the two women joked with her; it never occurred to them that she
would believe their innocent lies as the truth and publish them in a best-selling
book. As Freeman saw it, this was "a scandal, of [a] kind unique in the history
of twentieth century anthropology."[3]

Yet Freeman's chronology of Mead's alleged hoaxing is based more on con-
jecture than evidence. While Mead was supposedly running out of research
time in March 1926, a letter that she sent a month earlier reported her satisfaction with her research progress to that point. Mead wrote on February 9:

> Yesterday it poured and I had a couple of hours when no children
> came. I spent it taking stock. And that resulted in a feeling of intense relief,
> for if anything should happen to my work now I'd still have a sizable
> amount of material to show for these months. Which relieves my mind im-
> mensely. For it seemed such a gamble to put a long trip and all the time it
> took to learn the language into a doubtful venture which might have been
> hopelessly cut short by illness or hurricane or what not. And when I add to
> this the assurance which everyone gives me that the last few weeks are al-
> ways the most fruitful, then truly I have cause for rejoicing.[4]

Furthermore, on March 7, roughly a week before her alleged hoaxing, Mead
wrote:

> I've been very lucky. In this village [Ta'ū], living with white people and
> because of the very *papalagi* [European] character of the chiefs at this end
> of the island, I've escaped high rank entirely. The children call me Make-
> lita and treat me as one of themselves, which is just what I needed for my
> problem. . . . But school has begun and it's practically impossible to get
> hold of the children any more. Anyway my problem is practically com-
> pleted. So I'll spend the rest of the time filling in gaps in the problem and
> getting ethnology.[5]

Do these passages sound like someone in a state of distress? Mead was certainly concerned about making the most of her time in Manu'a, and she had
written Boas in December 1925 and January 1926, worrying about the ade-
quacy of her statistical data on adolescents, but by mid-February Boas had reassured her that this was not a major concern. The idea that she panicked at
the last minute and therefore had to rely on two Samoan women for data on
adolescent girls is implausible based on Mead's own assessment of her work.
What, then, of the alleged hoaxing itself?

An Evening with Fa'apua'a and Fofoa

In an early version of the hoaxing hypothesis published in 1989, Freeman identified the two Samoan women whom he believed had told Mead innocent lies.[6] In March 1926, six months into her fieldwork, Mead was a member of a visiting party that included Fa'apua'a Fa'amū and Fofoa. Fa'apua'a, who was still alive in 1987, was interviewed by Freeman's Samoan associate, Galea'i Poumele, for the documentary film *Margaret Mead and Samoa*.

As noted in chapter 2, there was an interesting backstory to Fa'apua'a's participation in the film. Galea'i Poumele was the son of Fofoa and a high-ranking chief, and it was he who had suggested to Fa'apua'a that she may have been the source of Mead's notion that Samoans were sexually permissive.[7] Fa'apua'a then asked for an opportunity to literally "confess" on film to what she thought she had done. To Freeman this testimony was conclusive evidence that Mead had been "hoaxed," and the videotaped interview of Fa'apua'a became the centerpiece of the film and Freeman's second book, *The Fateful Hoaxing of Margaret Mead*.

The relevant section of the interview, with Galea'i Poumele's questions and Fa'apua'a's answers in translation, is as follows:

> *Galea'i Poumele:* Fa'amu, was there a day, a night, or an evening when the woman [Margaret Mead] questioned you about what you did at night, and did you ever joke about this?
>
> *Fa'apua'a Fa'amū:* Yes, we did; we said that we were out at nights with boys; she failed to realize we were just joking and must have been taken in by our pretences. Yes, she asked: "Where do you go?" And we replied, "We go out at nights!" "With whom?" she asked. Then your mother, Fofoa, and I would pinch each other and say: "We spend the nights with boys, yes, with boys!" She must have taken it seriously but I was only joking. As you know, Samoan girls are terrific liars when it comes to joking. But Margaret Mead accepted our trumped up stories as though they were true.
>
> *Galea'i Poumele:* And the numerous times that she questioned you, were those the times the two of you continued to tell these untruths to Margaret Mead?
>
> *Fa'apua'a Fa'amū:* Yes, we just fibbed and fibbed to her.[8]

If the interview seemed conclusive to Freeman and to filmmaker Frank Heimans, sociologist James Côté, after reading the interview and relevant materials in the Mead archive in the Library of Congress as well Martin Orans's book on the controversy, found Freeman's interpretation questionable.[9] There were obvious problems, including Galea'i Poumele's personal stake in Fa'apua'a's testimony and the leading questions that he asked her. Côté also took a closer look at *Coming of Age* itself. He noted that Mead had collected and presented a good deal of information on individual adolescent girls in the text of *Coming of Age* as well as systematic data on a sample of twenty-five Samoan girls summarized in an appendix. Côté found it difficult to believe that Mead would ignore all of this information that she had gathered on adolescents and believe only Fa'apua'a and Fofoa, two unmarried women already in their midtwenties.

Côté also asked why, if Fa'apua'a and Fofoa were such important sources of information on adolescent sex, they received so little attention in *Coming of Age*? According to Freeman, Fa'apua'a believed that she was Mead's "very closest Samoan friend."[10] And Freeman reiterated that Fa'apua'a was Mead's main informant. Yet in *Coming of Age* Fa'apua'a is only one of many Samoans described, and she received no special attention or recognition in the book. The pseudonym that Mead used to protect Fa'apua'a's true identity was Pana. In her book Mead described Pana in just four sentences; she was presented as a ceremonial virgin, with no reference to adolescent sex. Aware of her identity and her portrayal in Mead's book, Freeman nevertheless continued to refer to Fa'apua'a as Mead's chief informant.[11]

Martin Orans drew a conclusion similar to Côté's, commenting that "when one compares the data on sexuality that Mead had collected from sources other than Fa'apua'a and Fofoa with the paltry data to which Fa'apua'a testifies, it is evident that such humorous fibbing could not be the basis of Mead's understanding. Freeman asks us to imagine that the joking of two women, pinching each other as they put Mead on about their sexuality and that of adolescents, was of more significance than the detailed information she had collected throughout her fieldwork."[12] Orans further questioned Freeman's argument by noting that Fa'apua'a herself was a *taupou*, the only one in all of the villages in the Manu'a group at the time of Mead's research. As Mead wrote, these ceremonial virgins were carefully guarded, and their chastity was highly valued by the village as a whole. If Fa'apua'a had told Mead that she and other girls "spent nights with boys," and if Mead had believed her, then Mead should have written in *Coming of Age* that ceremonial virgins engaged in premarital sex. Instead, Mead wrote that the entire village protected the virginity of the *taupou*, a statement with which Freeman agreed. Furthermore, Orans found no change in Mead's description of the chastity of the *taupou* in Mead's field notes before and after the alleged hoaxing took place. Nor was Orans able to find a single statement attributable to Fa'apua'a in *Coming of Age*. Even more interesting, he did not find a single piece of information attributable to Fa'apua'a in Mead's field materials.[13] Where, then, is the evidence of Fa'apua'a's influence on Mead?

While it is possible that the two young women may have told Mead innocent lies, Orans observed that there is no evidence that she *believed* them. For hoaxing to have taken place, it is not sufficient for the two women to have told

Mead innocent lies; it is also necessary for her to have found them credible, and there is no evidence of this.[14] While Fa'apua'a may have sincerely believed that what she was telling Galea'i Poumele was true, swearing on a Bible that her testimony was accurate, there is no evidence in Mead's work or field notes that she believed Fa'apua'a and Fofoa.

As noted in chapter 10, Mead was well aware of the possibility that Samoans could present alternative versions of the truth. This became a working assumption of her fieldwork. And, as her field notes make clear, she knew about Samoan joking, including sexual jokes and recreational lying, as does anyone who has spent time in the islands.[15] Mead had also reached a point in her research where she spoke Samoan proficiently enough to work without an interpreter. So it is unlikely that she consistently misinterpreted Fa'apua'a's and Fofoa's jokes. Finally, given that these women were traveling companions who spent their days and nights together, it is difficult to believe that Mead asked only very general questions (What do you do at night? Where do you go? With whom?) and accepted their very general answers as convincing testimony about their private lives. Were these answers ("We spend the nights with boys") the best innocent lies that these women could provide?

No Joking Matter:
Unpublished Interviews with Fa'apua'a

To his credit, Freeman recognized that the 1987 interview with Fa'apua'a could benefit from additional corroboration and that she might be able to provide more detailed information about Mead's fieldwork in Samoa. So in 1988 and again in 1993 he commissioned lengthy interviews with her, conducted by Samoan anthropologist Unasa L. F. Va'a.[16] Although Freeman himself was not present during these interviews, each lasting several hours and conducted in Samoan, he composed the dozens of very detailed questions and provided them to Unasa, who had been a graduate student at the Australian National University before becoming a faculty member at the National University of Samoa. Following the interviews, Unasa immediately sent the questions and answers to Freeman in Canberra.

In his second book on Mead, Freeman cited these two additional interviews as support for the hoaxing hypothesis, stating that Fa'apua'a's "sworn testimony is of the sort that could be presented in a court of law." Since Fa'apua'a was eighty-seven in the 1988 interview and ninety-two in the 1993 interview, Freeman posed questions that checked the accuracy of her memory, and he determined that there was "quite definite evidence that Fa'apua'a, in 1993, as in 1988, had substantially accurate memories of Manu'a in 1926, including the time that she and Fofoa had spent with Mead on the islands of Ofu and Olosega in that year."[17] However, these interviews with Faʻapuaʻa were not published and did not become available until after Freeman's death in 2001. What they demonstrate is that her testimony was sometimes contradictory or unclear and that it is inconsistent with Freeman's argument on key issues.

Faʻapuaʻa's memory may not have been as reliable as Freeman believed. For example, in 1988, when asked if elopement (*avaga*) occurred on Taʻū in 1926, Faʻapuaʻa replied that she had not heard of any cases, although it was the most common form of marriage. Nor could she remember any cases of sleep crawling (*moetotolo*), illegitimate children, adultery, or rape. In notes to himself on the interview transcripts, Freeman placed question marks next to Faʻapuaʻa's answers concerning elopement, sleep crawling, and illegitimate children.[18] Her answers were not in accord with what Freeman knew about Samoa and Manuʻa in the 1920s. Nevertheless, Freeman vouched for the "historical reliability" of Faʻapuaʻa's testimony.[19]

When George Stocking, the eminent historian of anthropology, expressed skepticism about Faʻapuaʻa's testimony, Freeman arranged another interview with her in 1993. After researching the chronology of Mead's fieldwork through her papers in the Library of Congress, Freeman constructed a detailed set of questions for Unasa to pose to Faʻapuaʻa that would yield more systematic answers. After reviewing her answers, Freeman felt that Stocking's concerns about Faʻapuaʻa's memory had been laid to rest. He wrote that in 1993 Unasa had found Faʻapuaʻa still "lucid" and "still able to remember well."[20] On a number of matters this was certainly true, but on other matters Faʻapuaʻa seemed to be losing her memory. So, according to Unasa, in 1993 Faʻapuaʻa had forgotten that Mead had died (an event she learned of in 1987 and remembered in the 1988 interview), expressing her sorrow when Unasa reminded her of it.[21]

In the two unpublished interviews Faʻapuaʻa reaffirmed her belief that she and Fofoa had innocently joked with Mead in response to her inappropriate questions about their private lives and that Mead believed them. In framing the interviews Freeman reinforced this narrative by reminding Faʻapuaʻa of her previous testimony to Galeaʻi Poumele in 1987 and of the stakes involved in the hoaxing argument. Thus, in his instructions to Faʻapuaʻa at the beginning of the 1993 interview, Freeman asked Unasa to "please impress on her how important a figure she has become, being known to thousands of anthropologists and others, throughout the world. The information that she can still provide is thus of the greatest importance. As a Christian she has certainly made full amends for the hoaxing of Mead in March, 1926. Please convey to her my *alofa*, my appreciation of her action in telling the truth about the hoaxing of Mead, and as well my very best wishes for her future."[22] Unasa did as Freeman requested. After each of the interviews Faʻapuaʻa received payment of $100.

At times during the interviews Faʻapuaʻa offered differing answers to key questions. Although identified as Mead's main informant, Faʻapuaʻa herself was unclear about this role. In the 1988 interview she was asked if she was Mead's "*closest* Samoan friend and informant," to which she replied, "Yes." But later in the same interview she was asked if she actually worked with Mead as an informant at the medical dispensary on Taʻū where Mead resided, to which she replied, "Only once." When asked what kinds of questions Mead posed at that time, Faʻapuaʻa said that she did not remember. Unasa commented parenthetically, "Faʻamu gives the impression that she was not a good informant for Mead. If she did not know anything, she told Makerita [Mead] so, and encouraged her to ask others."[23]

Faʻapuaʻa also offered differing accounts of Mead's language proficiency in Samoan. In one published interview she stated that Mead spoke "very little" Samoan and that a translator was "always" used in their conversations.[24] But in the unpublished interviews Faʻapuaʻa stated that Mead understood Samoan well, that no one else was present at the time of the alleged hoaxing, that Mead asked Faʻapuaʻa and Fofoa questions in Samoan, and that Faʻapuaʻa "always" spoke to Mead in Samoan since she did not speak English well.[25]

In another instance of differing answers Faʻapuaʻa was asked to recall the chronological sequence of the hoaxing in more detail. Freeman stated that it occurred on the night of March 13, 1926, and that he used Faʻapuaʻa's testimony to corroborate it. But in the unpublished 1993 interview Faʻapuaʻa actually stated that she and Fofoa had joked about sex with Mead over an "extended period" of time. Unasa commented parenthetically: "What Faʻapuaʻa is saying is that there was no one specific time when she and Fofoa misled Mead about Samoan sexual mores."[26] Moreover, the geographic location of the hoaxing is unclear. In the 1988 interview Faʻapuaʻa was asked when and where she was questioned by Mead about what girls of Taʻū did at night. Faʻapuaʻa replied that she was questioned during an ordinary conversation in the village of Fitiuta on the island of Taʻū. But later in the same interview she stated that it was during a trip to the island of Ofu.[27] In the 1993 interview, after being prompted by Freeman's questions about the chronology and location of the hoaxing, she stated that it had occurred in the evening on Ofu or during walks between the closely linked islands of Olesega and Ofu.[28]

There were clearly problems with Faʻapuaʻa's testimony in the unpublished interviews. Faʻapuaʻa was probably not an important informant for Mead; neither was Fofoa. And without agreement on when and where the hoaxing took place and in what language it took place, the most basic facts about it were ambiguous. In this context Freeman's continuing reliance on Faʻapuaʻa's testimony and the hoaxing hypothesis is puzzling. There were other informants who were far more influential, especially on sexual conduct. One of the most important was a young Samoan, Andrew Napoleon, whom Freeman, Mead, and Napoleon himself all recognized as a key source in providing Mead with extensive information in English on sexual conduct from a male perspective.[29] Napoleon was cited in Mead's field notes. In fact, he was corresponding with Freeman before his first book was published and was available for interviews like those conducted with Fa'apua'a. Nonetheless, it was Fa'apua'a's testimony that Freeman sought and upon which he relied.

The unpublished interviews with Fa'apua'a, including Unasa's comments on them, and Freeman's annotations to them, suggest that Freeman knew that key elements of Fa'apua'a's testimony were questionable six years before the publication of *The Fateful Hoaxing of Margaret Mead*. In that book, though, Freeman reiterated that her testimony would stand up in a court of law and that, in conjunction with Mead's field materials, the interviews with Fa'apua'a "effectively resolved" the question of how Mead got Samoa wrong.[30] Freeman did not mention the obvious problems with her testimony in the book or related articles. Instead, he continued to promote the hoaxing hypothesis as if there were no inconsistencies, no ambiguities, no contradictions, and no lapses in Fa'apua'a's memory. And he encouraged others to do so as well. When Côté and Orans published criticism of the hoaxing hypothesis in the mid-1990s, Freeman responded swiftly and sharply but kept the problems in the 1988 and 1993 interviews to himself.[31] As a person who prided himself on attention to detail, Freeman could have addressed them or at least acknowledged them. Instead, the interviews were filed away, and, employing the hoaxing hypothesis as the most damaging part of his critique, Freeman escalated his attack on Mead.

An Affair to Remember?

In 1991 Freeman offered another version of the hoaxing hypothesis.[32] To explain Fa'apua'a's and Fofoa's motivation for lying to Mead, he argued that, because Mead had taken a particular honorary *taupou* title, she was viewed by Fa'apua'a as a potential rival. That is, Fa'apua'a was jealous of Mead. However, Freeman did not indicate why Mead's *honorary* title would lead to such a rivalry when Fa'apua'a held a *real* title. Nor did he suggest what that rivalry might involve. When asked in one of the unpublished interviews if Fa'apua'a or Fofoa were in any way angry with or disapproving of Mead, Fa'apua'a's reply was "No."[33]

Still another possible motivation cited by Freeman for Mead's hoaxing was the women's knowledge of an affair that Mead allegedly had with a young Samoan whose pseudonym was Aviata. He was the son of a high chief who lived near Mead while she resided at the naval dispensary. As noted earlier, Freeman learned of this affair in 1967 from Samoans on Manu'a. Whether or not the affair actually occurred, according to Freeman, Fa'apua'a and Fofoa were *"fully convinced* that Mead, early in 1926, had an affair" with Aviata.[34] If so, the couple would have violated Samoan public morality, and Mead would have violated the sacred requirement of virginity necessary to hold a *taupou* title. In this version Freeman hypothesized that Fa'apua'a and Fofoa felt that Mead's allegedly immoral behavior justified their joking with her when she began asking about their own sexual behavior.

There are a number of problems with this explanation of the women's motivation. One problem is that while Fa'apua'a had stated in 1988 that Mead and Aviata were undoubtedly lovers, when asked in 1993 if she actually saw Aviata with Mead or just heard about the relationship, Fa'apua'a was more circumspect. Unasa commented, "I prefer her 1988 statement. It is clear that she [Fa'apua'a] did not want to delve too deeply into Makelita's relationship with Aviata. Or perhaps she forgot the details."[35]

Had Fa'apua'a and Fofoa known and disapproved of the alleged affair with Aviata, the telling of jokes would hardly be adequate retribution for this serious offense. Samoan villages are hives of gossip, and this affair probably would have been widely known. Fa'apua'a and Fofoa would have told others, who would have been very upset. As a very visible American woman holding a *taupou* title, even an honorary one, Mead could have faced serious consequences from her Samoan hosts. In 1967 Samoans told Freeman that if Mead returned to Manu'a, they would tie her up and feed her to the sharks for her alleged transgressions of their strict morality. Yet, according to Freeman, in 1926 the best Fa'apua'a and Fofoa could do was joke with Mead in response to her unwanted questions.

Freeman also alleged that Mead had another affair, stating that she became "intimately friendly" with Andrew Napoleon.[36] Freeman told me that he and Napoleon loudly joked about this affair in a bar in Pago Pago, although, when asked by a reporter from *Life* magazine in 1983 if it was true, Napoleon stated that his evenings with Mead were "always innocent."[37] Since Napoleon was married in 1926, if he and Mead had an affair and it became public knowledge, she could have been in physical danger from Napoleon's wife. Even Fa'apua'a had beaten one of her rivals in a similar situation.

What did Mead herself say about her relationships with Samoan men? Had Mead been intimate with Samoans, she probably would have written about it in her letters to close friends. In her correspondence from Samoa she was extremely candid about her personal relationships with everyone from Sapir, her lover; to Cressman, her husband; to the Holts at the medical dispensary on Ta'ū. Historian Margaret Caffrey examined all of Mead's correspondence in the Library of Congress about her relationships with Samoan men and found that Mead did not write about affairs with any of them, including Aviata and Napoleon. Furthermore, near the end of her stay in Samoa she wrote to Ruth Benedict and Eleanor Steele that she had been without adult affection for nine months, a sentiment that she repeated in her autobiography.[38]

Mead did consider the possibility of an affair. Indeed, in late March 1926 she wrote her friend Eda Lou Walton about one such prospect:

> I have met one Samoan, too, who I think would make a perfect lover, for a bit—However I remembered the white population [of American Samoa] and that I represented the Bishop Museum, the Research [C]ouncil and Columbia University and refrained. But he does have a very accurate notion of the place of casual amours. One could be quite sure that ten years later he would tell the story, as he told me a dozen like these—"And so we loved each other very much. But three weeks later I eloped with another girl and she wrote me and told me she was thru with me—and I say, I am sorry, but what could I do."[39]

So Mead had thought about the possibility of an affair; understood the consequences for herself, her lover, and her institutional sponsors; and decided against it.

The "Smoking Gun" Letter to Boas

Faced with problems in each of the versions of his hoaxing hypothesis, Freeman nevertheless continued to pursue his argument in *The Fateful Hoaxing of Margaret Mead*. After reviewing Mead's correspondence with Boas from Samoa, he claimed that he had discovered a letter from Mead to Boas dated March 14, 1926, that provided new "smoking gun" evidence of hoaxing. In the letter Mead supposedly stated that there was "no curb" on adolescent sex.[40] Given the date and content of the letter, Freeman believed this information could only have come from Fa'apua'a and Fofoa, who were alone with Mead on the previous night, when the hoaxing allegedly took place.

Having reviewed this same letter, Martin Orans demonstrated that Freeman selectively quoted from it and omitted a crucial portion of it, thus misrepresenting Mead.[41] The passage from Mead's letter that Freeman quoted is as follows:

> So, the sum total of it all is adolescence is a period of sudden development, of stress, only in relation to sex, and where the community recognizes this and does not attempt to curb it, there is no conflict at all between the adolescent and the community, except such as arises from the conflict of personalities within the household (and this is immediately remedied, as

I have shown by the change to another relationship group); and the occasional delinquent—of any age from 8 to 50, who arouses the ire of the
community.[42]

Freeman *interpreted* this wordy passage as meaning that the community placed
"no curb" on adolescent sex, as if it were the only relevant passage in this fairly
long letter. He repeated the phrase "no curb" in quotation marks a number of
times to underscore its importance in providing "hard evidence" of hoaxing
and to imply that Mead had used these precise words, which she did not.[43]

Freeman did not cite or quote other parts of the same letter, including the
paragraph immediately preceding it. In that paragraph Mead stated that it was
the *family* that attempted to preserve a daughter's virginity, *except* in the case of
the *taupou,* where the community was responsible for preserving her virginity.
Mead wrote: "It is the family and not the community (except in the case of the
taupou) which attempts to preserve the girl's virginity—and this attempt is usually secretly frustrated rather than openly combatted by the adolescent."[44]
Mead never said that there was "no curb" whatsoever on adolescent sex. Freeman misrepresented her letter and chose to focus on the passage that seemed to
support his position. The letter provides no evidence of hoaxing, and Mead's
understanding of the responsibility for protecting girls and the *taupou* is factually correct.

In Freeman's view Mead's encounter with Fa'apua'a and Fofoa on the night
of March 13 was the research breakthrough that she had been waiting for, and
this is what led her to write the so-called smoking gun letter of March 14 to
Boas. However, if this was a research breakthrough, Mead probably would
have shared it with Ruth Benedict and the other close friends with whom she
corresponded about her fieldwork experiences. And Mead did send a letter to
Benedict on March 14, the same day as her letter to Boas, but it contained no
references to Samoa. Rather, it was about a dream she had about Boas and religion and about her relationships with Sapir and Cressman.[45]

The Final Version of the Hoaxing Hypothesis

In his last attempt to establish the "hoaxing" argument Freeman called attention to his "discovery" of an autobiographical chapter by Mead that allegedly
provided "direct evidence" from Mead herself of the purported hoax in her
own words.[46] The source was a popular adventure book from 1931 entitled *All
True! The Record of Actual Adventures That Have Happened to Ten Women of Today.*
Mead's chapter was titled "Life as a Samoan Girl" and was written primarily
for a reading audience of adolescent girls. Since her work in Samoa was not a

typical "adventure," as the title of the book suggests, Mead began by stating: "It was not to climb mountains nor beat trails into an unknown wilderness that I went to Samoa. Instead I had been sent to the South Seas to study not the sea corals nor the bird life, but simply the life of the Samoan girls."[47]

What evidence of hoaxing is there in this chapter? Freeman quoted a single potentially relevant sentence in which Mead stated that she became acquainted with "the Samoan girls" and received "their whispered confidences and learned at the same time the answer to the scientists' questions."[48] Freeman interpreted this sentence as "definitive historical evidence" of hoaxing by taking these very general phrases and assigning them very particular meanings.[49] He assumed that the phrase "their whispered confidences" referred to innocent lies about sex allegedly told to Mead by Fa'apua'a and Fofoa. However, in Mead's chapter there was no discussion of sex; "their whispered confidences" referred to the general subject of Samoan etiquette and how Samoan girls helped her learn proper social behavior, especially in situations involving chiefs.[50] Freeman also assumed that the phrase "the Samoan girls" referred to Fa'apua'a and Fofoa. While they were described in part of Mead's chapter, this phrase was used elsewhere in the chapter without reference to these two women.

Freeman also suggested that the phrase "the scientists' questions" referred to specific questions about sexual conduct. But the first paragraph of Mead's chapter states that the scientists' questions were "about what sort of life girls lived in Samoa, whether they, like American girls, had years of tears and troubles before they were quite grown up." To do this, Mead was "merely to go to Samoa and get to know as many Samoan girls as possible."[51] Again, there is no direct reference to sexual conduct. And it would have been inappropriate for Mead to write about sex in a chapter for adolescent American girls in 1931. So there is no "direct historical evidence" of hoaxing in the chapter.

Who Hoaxed Whom?

The "hoaxing" argument is implausible because the evidence that Freeman used did not support his hypothesis. It is also unnecessary, for Mead's portrayal of Samoa as a sexually permissive society was not based on her conversations with Fa'apua'a and Fofoa but rather on the data that she collected from Samoan adolescent girls and from Samoan men and women, her comparison of Samoa and America in the mid-1920s, and the social agenda that she advocated given her own personal background and interests.

The hoaxing hypothesis was constructed retrospectively by Freeman to answer the question of how he believed Mead got Samoa wrong. Assuming this was the case, Freeman called Mead's ethnographic competence into question.

In doing so he believed he was *absolving* Mead from engaging in the deliberate misrepresentation of Samoan culture, finding instead that she was fatefully "misled" by Fa'apua'a and Fofoa.[52] That is, she was the unwitting victim of her own inexperience rather than the conscious perpetrator of ethnographic fraud. In Freeman's words, Mead was in "a chronic state of cognitive delusion."[53] In this way he believed that he salvaged Mead's reputation and brought the controversy to an end. It was an ingenious argument. It was also an intellectual house of cards.

Given the weaknesses of the hoaxing hypothesis and given his misrepresentation of Mead, it is worth remembering Freeman's claims for his argument:

> We are here dealing with one of the most spectacular events of the intellectual history of the twentieth century. Margaret Mead, as we know, was grossly hoaxed by her Samoan informants, and Mead in her turn, by convincing others of the "genuineness" of her account of Samoa, completely misinformed and misled virtually the entire anthropological establishment, as well as the intelligentsia at large. . . . That a Polynesian prank should have produced such a result in centers of higher learning throughout the Western world is deeply comic. But behind the comedy there is a chastening reality. It is now apparent that for decade after decade in countless textbooks, and in university and college lecture rooms throughout the Western world, students were misinformed about an issue of fundamental human importance, by professors who by placing credence in Mead's conclusion of 1928 had themselves become cognitively deluded. Never can giggly fibs have had such far-reaching consequences in the groves of Academe.[54]

This was a good story—a story that sounded plausible and that people wanted to believe. It was also a story too good to be true.

\14/

The Nature-Nurture Debate
and the Appeal of
Freeman's Argument

Had the controversy been confined to the details of Samoan culture, it would have had little importance beyond the narrow playing field of academia. For Freeman, however, *Coming of Age in Samoa* mattered a great deal because of its relevance to the nature-nurture debate. Mead allegedly had tried to demonstrate that nature was unimportant and even irrelevant, a message that Freeman saw as having disastrous consequences for anthropology and the world at large. Attributing this antibiological perspective to Mead was the final component in his assault on her reputation; it was the penultimate point of his critique. Freeman believed that the controversy his work generated was, "at heart," about evolution.[1] The antievolutionary "Mead paradigm" was, for Freeman, the most significant and far-reaching consequence of what he called "Mead's mistake" in Samoa.

The nature-nurture dimension of the controversy was also the issue that attracted many nonanthropologists to Freeman's cause. Since 1983 Mead and Samoa have become pawns in the intellectual war between those who favored a more biologically oriented approach to human behavior and those who favored a more culturally oriented approach. Intelligent people with an interest in biology, genetics, sociobiology, and evolutionary psychology often assumed Freeman's critique of Mead was correct and used it to condemn her with the same certainty and zeal that Freeman brought to his argument. Mead was demonized as a representative of the *tabula rasa* school of human nature, in which individuals were regarded as blank slates on which anything could be written. She was excoriated as hopelessly lost to the archaic and misguided cause of cultural determinism. Of course, there was nothing inherently wrong in criticizing Mead and *Coming of Age,* but on the nature-nurture debate her critics had accepted Freeman's allegations to such an extent that they often missed what Mead had actually written on this subject.

According to Reliable Sources . . .

Reading the chorus of criticism against Mead provides some insight into the widespread influence of Freeman's argument. Many very bright individuals took Freeman's message at face value. In his 1997 book, *How the Mind Works,* the distinguished Harvard psychologist Steven Pinker criticized Mead for conclusions "based on perfunctory fieldwork" that turned out to be "perversely wrong."[2] In his 2002 work, *The Blank Slate: The Modern Denial of Human Nature,* Pinker proclaimed that Freeman had demonstrated that Mead got her facts "spectacularly wrong."[3]

David Buss, a prominent evolutionary psychologist, contended that Mead believed in both the "Blank Slate" and the "Noble Savage" ideologies that were also the basis for the romantic political ideologies of the 1960s. For Buss, Freeman's critique of *Coming of Age in Samoa* therefore provided some "unpleasant surprises" for those who shared her beliefs. Citing Freeman, Buss noted: "Mead turned out to have lived in a comfortable hotel nearby, not actually among Samoans, so the depth and accuracy of her ethnography became suspect. She apparently relied on two female informants rather than on direct observation or systematic behavioral scans. But these two women later confessed to others that what they had told Mead was factually false."[4]

Like many others who employed Freeman's critique of Mead, Buss did not represent Mead's fieldwork accurately. She lived in the back of a small medical dispensary, not in a comfortable hotel on Taʻū; she relied on a number of Samoans, including twenty-five adolescent girls, for her data, not simply two women; and only one woman, Faʻapuaʻa, confessed to hoaxing—the other had died decades earlier. These problems aside, Buss was just one of a number of evolutionary psychologists who have deplored Mead's work.

Matt Ridley, an influential science writer and author of *Genome* and *The Red Queen,* also criticized Mead's fieldwork based on the hoaxing hypothesis: "In fact, it is now known that she had been duped by a handful of prank-pulling young women during her all-too-brief visit to the island, and that Samoa in the 1920s was if anything slightly more censorious about sex than America."[5]

In *The Origins of Virtue* Ridley provided a broader critique of Mead's work, noting that "for fifty years Mead's Samoans stood as definitive proof of the perfectibility of man." He also found Mead guilty of the "naturalistic fallacy," arguing that because something ought to be, it must be: "This logic is known today as political correctness, but it was shown in the drive launched by Boas, Benedict, and Mead to argue that human nature must be infinitely malleable by culture because (they thought, wrongly) the alternative is fatalism, which is unacceptable." For Ridley, the belief in human perfectibility and the absence of a fixed human nature was a misguided ideology that ultimately led to the crimes committed under Soviet and Chinese communism.[6] By implication, Mead's idealistic hopes for a better world led to a political nightmare.

Ridley was particularly harsh toward Mead's supporters: "The reaction of anthropologists to Freeman's revelation was itself the perfect refutation of Mead's creed. They reacted like a tribe whose cult had been attacked and shrine desecrated, vilifying Freeman in every conceivable way except by refuting him. If even cultural anthropologists, supposedly devoted to empirical truth and cultural relativism, act like a typical tribe, then there must be a universal human nature after all."[7] This sweeping indictment by Ridley is incorrect on several counts, including the implication that Mead's belief in the possibility of social change somehow was associated with communism. The Russian Revolution took place in 1917, when Mead was still an adolescent, and the Chinese Revolution took place after Mead had worked tirelessly on behalf of Western democracy during World War II.[8] Mead was never a Marxist.[9] She did not endorse totalitarian ideologies because she believed in the freedom of the individual and education for choice. Ridley's resort to this kind of argument is reminiscent of Freeman's belief that Mead somehow caused the cultural upheaval of the 1960s in the West. But Ridley and Freeman are far from alone in attributing social ills to Mead.

Primatologist Michael P. Ghiglieri also faulted Mead based on his reading of Freeman. In his 1999 book, *The Dark Side of Man: Tracing the Origins of Male Violence,* he commented on the widespread use of *Coming of Age* in anthropology courses: "Why? Because in it, free love flourished in a guiltless, pacifist society, where violence existed only in occasional stylized war, almost as an afterthought. Samoans, Mead told us, lived in a societal paradise. Mead's message? We could, too. The 'right' cultural upbringing could free us from the evils of violence, sexism, sexual guilt, dysfunction, and jealousy engendered by Western civilization. Inadvertently perhaps, Mead kicked off America's era of social junk food."[10]

On an empirical level, Ghiglieri asserted:

> Samoans in 1925–1926 commonly raped girls. Brothers assiduously guarded the highly prized virginity of their sisters. Sexual jealousy led to mutilation and murder. Samoan men killed in warfare, often in staggering numbers. By contrast, New York City was more idyllic.

In short, because Mead ignored biology in favor of her own wishful thinking—and made things worse by spending only twelve weeks on the job, by neither living with nor interviewing Samoan adults, and by not even learning to speak Samoan very well—many of her major conclusions on human behavior were on a par with the flat-earth hypothesis.[11]

As was the case with Ridley and Buss, there are a number of errors in Ghiglieri's characterization of Mead and Samoa, ranging from the frequency of rape (debatable) and the deadliness of war (which ceased long before Mead arrived) to the duration of her fieldwork (at least thirty-two weeks, not twelve), not speaking Samoan well (she spoke it with some proficiency), and her neglect of Samoan adults (with whom she interacted throughout her fieldwork). But his overall point was that those who favor a biological approach are up against an enduring myth about Samoans created by Margaret Mead. She was not merely an intellectual speed bump along the great highway to knowledge but a genuine road hazard.

Was *Coming of Age* really that mistaken? According to sociobiologists Martin Daly and Margo Wilson, the authors of *Homicide*, "Mead's ideological and popularizing goals seriously compromised her ethnographic research, as has been made painfully clear by Derek Freeman's (1983) surgical exposé of the fantastic misrepresentation of Samoan culture that constituted her doctoral thesis [*sic*] and made her famous."[12] Historian of science Frank Sulloway, in his book on birth order, *Born to Rebel: Birth Order, Family Dynamics, and Creative Lives*, took issue with Mead, using Freeman for support, as did science writer Robert Wright in *The Moral Animal: The New Science of Evolutionary Psychology*.[13] Christina Hoff Sommers, author of *The War against Boys: How Misguided Feminism Is Harming Our Young Men*, also cited Freeman as demonstrating that Mead had been misled by Samoan girls and her own prior beliefs.[14] And in *The New Age: Notes of a Fringe Watcher*, noted science writer Martin Gardner referred to Mead's book as "the great Samoan hoax."[15] Mead was lumped with those who hopelessly embraced cultural determinism.

The Appeal of Freeman's Argument

While some of these criticisms of Mead were carefully considered, such as those by anthropologist Don Brown in *Human Universals*, many were made without looking further into what Mead actually wrote or into the academic critique of Freeman's work. His work was often used because Mead *symbolized* a position that people disagreed with, and Freeman's critique of her work made their own position easier to argue. A number of sociobiologists and evolutionary psychologists saw Freeman's critique of Mead as supportive of their views about the relationship of biology and culture, although, as noted earlier, Freeman had been a forceful critic of sociobiology in the early 1980s.

Freeman was able to reach a wider audience because he presented his arguments about Samoa and Mead's fieldwork as arguments about much larger issues, such as the use of scientific method, the nature-nurture debate, evolution, the intellectual direction of anthropology, and, of course, Mead's place in social and intellectual history. Identifying himself as a proponent of science, reason, truth, evolution, and the future, Freeman linked Mead with prescientific reasoning, "absolute" cultural determinism, antievolutionary thought, and cultural relativism.[16] Although readers may not have comprehended the narrower issues in the controversy, these broader surrogate issues were easy to identify with. They gave the controversy seemingly greater significance.

Other issues drew people to the controversy as well. In 1983 Freeman's critique of Mead struck a chord with an audience of conservatives interested in pushing back the sexual revolution. Mead was peripherally associated with this revolution and became a target of the conservative counterrevolution. The early 1980s were the first years of the Reagan presidency. Divorce rates were rising. The family was seen as under siege. Sexually transmitted diseases such as herpes and HIV seemed to demonstrate the unforeseen consequences of nonmonogamous sex. The women's movement and the gay liberation movement frightened many people. Pornography, denounced by conservatives as well as some feminists on the left, was being investigated by the U.S. attorney general's office. And there was a backlash against *Roe v. Wade,* the 1973 Supreme Court ruling that had made abortion legal.

Conservatives felt that things had gone too far. A cover story for *Time* magazine by John Leo announced: "The Revolution Is Over." The Moral Majority was ascendant, and Mead became vulnerable as a public intellectual and a feminist, embodying the alleged evils of liberalism and permissiveness for this audience. In these ways conservatives and evolutionary psychologists found common cause against Mead. Although these groups disliked and disparaged Mead for different reasons, they were able to use Freeman's critique to advance their own agendas. Their strong reservations about the 1960s also made them unlikely allies.

It was the nature-nurture debate, though, that was most interesting to the scientific community because it spoke to Mead's reputation as a scientist. Could she really be so doctrinaire as to believe that biology played no role in human behavior, that human beings were simply blank slates, that there was no human nature, and that evolution was irrelevant to the study of human beings? Or was this a caricature of Mead that Freeman and others nourished? As we shall see,

Mead discussed the complex relationship between culture and human nature throughout her long career, developing an evolutionary position that was very similar to the one Freeman would later embrace as his own.

Interactionism and Cultural Determinism: What Is the Difference?

Freeman advocated an approach that he called *interactionism*. For him, interactionism sensibly addressed the interplay of nature *and* nurture rather than the separation of nurture from nature. Using almost identical wording to end both of his books on the controversy, he stated: "The time is thus conspicuously at hand for an anthropological paradigm that gives full recognition to the radical importance of both cultural and biological factors, and of their past and ongoing interaction." In *The Fateful Hoaxing of Margaret Mead,* Freeman added one final thought: to enact this is the principal task of the anthropology of the twenty-first century.[17]

Interactionism was a necessary corrective because, in Freeman's view of the history of American anthropology, the discipline had taken an unfortunate direction, preventing any consideration of the role of biology. During the nature-nurture debate of the early twentieth century Freeman believed that there was a crucial intellectual turning point in the 1920s during which Mead's *Coming of Age* led anthropologists to subscribe to cultural determinism completely and reject biology altogether.[18] In this process Mead was strongly influenced by Boas and Benedict, who Freeman believed were the original "absolute" cultural determinists.[19]

Mead became, according to Freeman, a "Boasian ideologue" committed to "absolute" cultural determinism.[20] This prior belief led her to submit findings about Samoa that were "profoundly wrong"; nevertheless, this belief endured over the course of Mead's life and became the cornerstone of what Freeman called the "Mead paradigm," which, he argued, was the reigning paradigm in anthropology that effectively deterred theoretical progress in the discipline for roughly half a century. This was, like Freeman's hoaxing hypothesis, an attractive theory for those unfamiliar with the history of American anthropology. And like the hoaxing hypothesis, it led people to believe that there was something to the controversy.

Taken at face value, interactionism seems so reasonable that it is hard to imagine why anthropologists did not think of it before Freeman. In fact, they did; it had been one of the cornerstones of American anthropology from its inception. Since the early twentieth century American anthropologists had accepted and studied the interaction of biology and culture, initially stimulated by the thinking of Boas. Nevertheless, in reconstructing the background that led to *Coming of Age,* Freeman suggested that Boas, Benedict, and Mead were of one mind as "absolute" cultural determinists.[21] What does this term really mean in historical context?

Boas, Benedict, and Mead agreed that culture mattered, as do most anthropologists today. In this sense they *were* cultural determinists. The very notion of culture was an almost revolutionary idea at the time. In the early twentieth century *race* was the common explanation of cultural difference. Racial superiority and inferiority were assumed to explain differences in technology, social organization, and religion. If these differences were fixed and unchangeable because they were allegedly rooted in race and biology, then theories about "the master race" and other totalitarian ideologies were more acceptable. Indeed, eugenics and ideas about sterilization of the "unfit" were popular throughout Europe and America at this time. Totalitarian solutions based on racial classifications of "inferior" and "superior" populations were just around the corner. Discussions of culture, then, were more than a scientific matter concerning the misuse of the concept of race; they were a political matter of looming importance as fascism spread across Europe.[22]

In his excellent book *In Search of Human Nature: The Decline and Revival of Darwinism in American Social Thought,* historian Carl Degler described how Boas, Benedict, and Mead played a major role in moving America away from thinking about human differences in terms of race and toward thinking about them in terms of culture. This great intellectual and social shift, which we take largely for granted today, was perhaps anthropology's most important contribution to the world in the first half of the twentieth century. But this hardly made Boas, Benedict, and Mead "absolute" cultural determinists.

Boas wrote about and taught human evolution. He was strongly influenced by Darwinian thinking.[23] Freeman's belief that Boas was interested only in culture is refuted by Boas himself in *Science,* the leading scientific journal of the period. Writing in 1931, Boas stated: "There is no doubt in my mind that there is a very definite association between the biological make-up of an individual and the physiological and psychological functioning of his body. The claim that only social and other environmental conditions determine the reactions of the individual disregards the most elementary observations."[24] In this and many other similar statements Boas could not have been clearer about his interest in the interaction between biology and culture. Much of his own research throughout his long career was devoted to the study of human growth and development, with his first paper on the subject appearing in 1892 and his last in 1941.

Even before Mead switched to anthropology, she considered the interaction of culture and biology, specifically using the word "interaction" in relation to adolescence. In 1922, in her notes from a course in developmental psychology, she wrote: "In the same way, adolescence is not a phenomenon which comes bursting from some mysterious source and [it is] a phenomenon determined by the interaction of indiv's at a special stage of development & his environment."[25]

In the classes that she took from Boas, Mead was moved by his interest in human evolution.[26] She also took a course from a renowned zoologist, learning more about the process of biological evolution.[27] From its beginnings in the early twentieth century, American anthropology included biological anthropology (or physical anthropology) as one of its four subfields. Biological anthropology was part of undergraduate and graduate curricula in North America for most of the twentieth century. Even today, general anthropology textbooks begin with chapters on human biology and human evolution. Some use the familiar example of sickle-cell anemia to illustrate the interaction of biology and culture and the contribution of the theory of evolution to understanding this disease.

For Boas, Benedict, and Mead, as for most anthropologists, cultural determinism meant that cultural differences could not be explained by biology alone. Although human beings shared a common biology and evolutionary heritage, the human ability to learn and symbolize allowed for cultural differences, and these differences could not be explained exclusively by a common evolutionary past. So, for example, some cultures practiced infanticide, while others did not; some worshiped gods that were world redeemers, while others worshiped gods that were world destroyers; some cultures were egalitarian, while others were highly stratified; and in some cultures adolescence was more stressful than in others. How could a common human nature explain this variability? Cultural determinists did not deny that biology was important; rather, they argued that biology was not destiny.

Culture and Biology in *Coming of Age in Samoa*

Freeman nevertheless stated that Mead thought that culture "wholly" determined human behavior and that biological factors played no role whatsoever. He also argued that this belief endured throughout Mead's life. Moreover, he asserted that *Coming of Age in Samoa* became a sacred text in anthropology and that the antievolutionary "Mead paradigm" became "the hallowed dogma" of American cultural anthropology.[28]

Freeman believed that the absolute cultural determinism of the "Mead paradigm" was self-evident in *Coming of Age*, quoting her as unequivocally stating: "We cannot make any explanations of adolescence in terms of the biological process itself."[29] Yet as anthropologist Roy Rappaport reported in *Scientific*

American in 1987, this was a partial quotation.[30] The full passage from Mead reads as follows:

> A further question presents itself. If it is proved that adolescence is not nec-
> essarily a specially difficult period in a girl's life—and proved it is if we can
> find any society in which that is so—then what accounts for the presence
> of storm and stress in American adolescents? First, we may say quite sim-
> ply, that there must be something in the two civilisations to account for the
> difference. If the same process takes a different form in two different envi-
> ronments, we cannot make any explanations in terms of the process, for
> that is the same in both cases. But the social environment is very different
> and it is to that we must look for an explanation. What is there in Samoa
> which is absent in America, what is there in America which is absent in
> Samoa, which will account for the difference?[31]

Rappaport noted:

> The "same process" that takes a "different form" in "different environ-
> ments" is identified [by Mead] on page 196 as "the process of growth by
> which the girl baby becomes a grown woman." Mead assumes the "devel-
> oping girl is a constant factor in America and in Samoa" and asks if "the
> sudden and conspicuous body changes which take place at puberty [every-
> where]" are necessarily accompanied by the kinds of emotional and cog-
> nitive upheavals common in American girls. Are conflict and stress inevi-
> table concomitants of "change in the girl's body"?[32]

Mead, it seems clear, recognized the biological character of puberty, never claimed that biological factors had nothing to do with behavior, and simply stated that differences in the emotional and cognitive correlates of "the same [biological] process" in "different environments" were to be accounted for by differences in environment.

This was the crux of *Coming of Age in Samoa*. Mead viewed puberty as a universal biological process but with differences in the way this process was shaped by different cultures. These differences suggested to Mead that there was no unitary social outcome of adolescence. Americans could therefore make choices about shaping this stage in the human life cycle.

Questions about how adolescents experienced this process and how cultures interpreted and shaped it were interesting for Mead and others in the first half of the twentieth century because they were concerned with the description of cultural variability.[33] At that time, priority was given to the documentation of cultural differences rather than cultural regularities and similarities because relatively few good descriptive ethnographies existed on non-Western cultures. This did not mean that regularities were nonexistent or that there was no human nature. As Boas stated in his foreword to *Coming of Age in Samoa*: "Courtesy, modesty, good manners, conformity to definite ethical standards are universal, but what constitutes courtesy, modesty, good manners, and ethical standards is not universal. It is instructive to know that standards differ in unexpected ways."[34]

Biology and Evolution in Mead's Later Work

In reexamining Mead's work for his second book on the controversy, Freeman found that, in fact, she did incorporate biological factors, but he contended that it was only much later in her career that she mentioned them and then only in a peripheral manner. He summarized his reading of her work as follows:

> In her introduction of April 15, 1961, to the Pelican edition of *Male and Female,* she noted that if she had been writing this book in the early 1960s rather than in the late 1940s, she would have laid "more emphasis on Man's specific biological inheritance from earlier human forms." This was largely due to the friendship she had formed in 1954 with the eminent ethologist Konrad Lorenz, whose photograph she had on the wall of her office in the American Museum of Natural History. However, this recognition by Mead in 1961 of "man's specific biological inheritance" did not lead to any reconsideration of her conclusion of 1928 that "we cannot make any explanations" of adolescent behavior in terms of the process of adolescence itself, this being the doctrine on which her anthropological reputation is based.[35]

Here Freeman compounded his initial error in *Margaret Mead and Samoa* by further misreading Mead's intellectual biography. Why would Mead need to reconsider a conclusion that she never reached in the first place?

Freeman's interpretation of Mead's allegedly belated and limited interest in biological factors was effectively countered by Mead's own discussion of her early interest in evolution as a graduate student in the early 1920s and her interest in biology and evolution in the 1930s and 1940s, which she discussed in her autobiography, *Blackberry Winter,* and in *Continuities in Cultural Evolution.*

After Samoa and during her research in New Guinea in the 1930s Mead continued to explore the relationship between biology and culture with her husband at the time, Reo Fortune, and her future husband, Gregory Bateson. In a small tent that they shared in the Sepik, Mead, Fortune, and Bateson had long and deep discussions about these issues. Mead thought that these discussions would be of great theoretical significance, but she realized that the international political environment was changing and that this would affect the study of the roles of biology and culture: "We knew how politically loaded discussions of inborn differences could become; we knew that the Russians had

Margaret Mead with Gregory Bateson (*left*) and Reo Fortune (*right*), July 1933. Fortune was Mead's second husband; Bateson was her third husband. Library of Congress, Margaret Mead Papers, Box P23, folder 3. Courtesy of the Institute for Intercultural Studies, Inc., New York.

abandoned their experiment in the rearing of identical twins when it was found that, even reared under different circumstances, they displayed astonishing likenesses. As yet, however, we were not aware of the full terror of Nazism, with its emphasis on 'blood' and 'race.' The very limited news that reached us gave us no real sense of Hitler's political potential." By 1935, though, after their return to the United States, it became clear to Mead and Bateson that "further study of inborn differences would have to wait upon less troubled times."[36]

In 1949, in the post–World War II era, Mead clarified her position on the roles of biology and culture in a chapter in *Male and Female* titled "Basic Regularities in Human Sexual Development," in which she noted: "Different as are the ways in which different cultures pattern the development of human beings, there are basic regularities that no known culture has yet been able to evade. After excursions into contrasting educational methods of seven different societies, we can sum up the regularities that must be reckoned with by every society. Every attempt to understand what is happening in our own society, or in other societies, every attempt to understand ourselves, or to build a different life for our children, must take these into account."[37]

She restated her position again in the preface to the 1950 edition of *Sex and Temperament in Three Primitive Societies,* this time commenting that biology not only limited human development but also provided potentialities: "The biological bases of development as human beings, although providing limitations that must be honestly reckoned with, can be seen as potentialities by no means fully tapped by our human imagination."[38]

Mead's views on the interaction of biology and culture were carefully thought out and developed over her long career. In her early work Mead did argue that human nature was extremely malleable, but she did not call for the elimination of biological variables in understanding human behavior. Her views on human nature developed over four decades, during which the political and intellectual climate changed dramatically. Thus, when arguing against racial and exclusively "biological" explanations that were common in the early twentieth century and that were at the core of Nazi ideology, Mead emphasized culture; when discussing sex roles near the middle of the twentieth century, she gave more attention to biology, explaining:

> These two approaches to man—one of which sees man as a creature with species-characteristic instinctual patterns that play a continuing part in the forms that civilizations take, and the other which views man as lacking species-characteristic behavior patterns and as capable of being conditioned to almost any kind of system that takes into account survival needs—cross and recross each other. The optimism of the Watsonian position has been tempered by the experience of the following three decades,

during which "techniques" of conditioning were used in the service of absolute or irresponsible power.[39]

Although Freeman believed that Mead's interest in biology and evolution came after 1954, Mead described her renewed interest in biology and evolution as developing much earlier:

> My interest in evolution was reawakened in 1948, when I was asked to review *Touchstone for Ethics* and, while I was doing so, also took time to reread *The Origin of Species*. This reading in turn reawakened memories of discussions, in the mid-1930s, with C. H. Waddington and Gregory Bateson. Renewed interest in the study of animal behavior, an interest which I owe originally to Kingsley Noble and Ray Carpenter, was stimulated by contacts with Konrad Lorenz in the World Health Organization Study Group on the Psychobiological Development of the Child, and later by work with both American and European students of comparative animal behavior in the Macy Conferences on Group Processes.
>
> Two pieces of writing—*Male and Female,* written in 1948, and "Cultural Determinants of Sexual Behavior," first written in 1950 for the compendium, *Sex and Internal Secretions*—which I was able to discuss extensively with Evelyn Hutchinson, focused my attention on the need to integrate more specifically our knowledge of man's species-characteristic behavior, the peculiarities introduced by domestication, and our knowledge of cultural evolution. An invitation to participate in the second of two Symposia on Behavior and Evolution, organized by Ann Roe and George Simpson in 1955, created the necessary focus.[40]

Mead also referred to additional colleagues and conferences that stimulated her thinking about evolution as well as the changing perspectives on biology and culture that occurred from the 1930s through the 1950s.[41] Her writing on basic biological differences between men and women in *Male and Female* was, in fact, the subject of criticism from feminist Betty Friedan, who in her 1963 best seller, *The Feminine Mystique,* sharply reprimanded Mead for stereotyping women's roles and preventing them from realizing the career possibilities that Mead herself had enjoyed. For Friedan, Mead was too biological.

One of Mead's clearest statements on the significance of biological factors and evolution can be found in her presidential address to the 1960 annual meeting of the American Anthropological Association, later published in the discipline's premier journal at that time, *American Anthropologist.* Here Mead had an opportunity to talk about the future of anthropology to one of the world's largest gatherings of anthropologists. She used this opportunity to state that genetics was "enormously relevant to problems absolutely central to our discipline" and was concerned that research on genetics had been largely confined to physical anthropology. Mead also urged her colleagues to take advantage of "the opportunity provided by the new upsurge of interest in the whole field of evolution, in which human evolution is one part and cultural evolution a smaller one."[42] And she reminded anthropologists that distinguished biologists such as Theodosius Dobzhansky and George Gaylord Simpson, as well as other natural scientists, were interested in communicating with them about evolution.[43] In her presidential address to the American Association for the Advancement of Science in 1976, titled "Towards a Human Science" and subsequently published in *Science,* Mead again referred to the importance of evolution.

Given Mead's public statements about evolution to major scientific organizations over which she presided as well as her autobiographical accounts and academic publications, it is not possible to take seriously Freeman's assertions that Mead believed that all human behavior is the result of social conditioning to "the complete exclusion of biological variables."[44] Freeman simply neglected those sections of Mead's work and autobiography that did not support his views while misrepresenting her published record.

Apart from the many professional statements that she made about biology and culture, Mead could hardly have avoided issues concerning biology and culture in her personal life. Her third husband, Gregory Bateson, whom she married in 1935, was trained as a natural historian, and she admired his ability to see life through the lens of biology.[45] Another reason that Mead was interested in both nature and nurture involved watching their daughter grow up. Mary Catherine Bateson was born in 1939 and was a welcome surprise to her parents. After being diagnosed with a tipped uterus in 1926, Mead had a number of miscarriages before carrying Mary Catherine to term.[46] Prior to 1939 Mead had been deeply immersed in academic debates over child rearing. Yet after her daughter's birth and after personally observing her own child grow up, Mead asked: "How much was temperament? How much was felicitous accident? How much could be attributed to upbringing? We may never know."[47]

Finally, had Mead really been the "absolute" cultural determinist that Freeman contended, she would have opposed the inclusion of sociobiology symposia at the 1976 meeting of the American Anthropological Association. Sociobiology had emerged in the 1970s as one way of reintegrating culture and biology. This new discipline was roundly criticized by most anthropologists, including Freeman, for its linkage of genes to social behavior.[48] However, E. O. Wilson, the founder of sociobiology, recalled that Mead publicly defended the open discussion of sociobiology among anthropologists. In his autobiography Wilson remembered: "At the 1976 American Anthropological Association meeting, a motion was made to formally censure sociobiology and to cancel two symposia on the subject that had previously been scheduled. During the debate on the matter Margaret Mead rose indignantly, great walking stick in hand, to challenge the very idea of adjudicating a theory. She condemned the motion as a 'book-burning proposal.' Soon afterward the motion was defeated—but not by an impressive margin."[49]

The following year, at a conference on human behavior, Mead invited Wilson to dinner to discuss sociobiology. He recalled: "I was nervous then, expecting America's mother figure to scold me about the nature of genetic determination. I had nothing to fear. She wanted to stress that she, too, had published ideas on the biological basis of social behavior."[50] So Mead was a cultural determinist, although not an "absolute" one, who encouraged thinking about biology and evolution in her scholarly work and in her leadership roles in major scientific organizations. She was also very much part of anthropology's dialogue with academics in the biological sciences on the nature-nurture debate.

Freeman and Mead on Biology and Culture

What of Freeman's views on biology, culture, and evolution? They were very similar to Mead's. Freeman often emphasized the importance of culture. Like Mead, he believed that since humans could learn nongenetically and transmit information symbolically, culture often gave meaning to behavior. He noted that people could attribute very different cultural meanings to the same genetically prescribed behaviors. As an example, he cited the eyebrow flash, which means "yes" in Samoa while meaning "no" in Greece. According to Freeman, "It is the existence of such conventional behaviors, in great profusion, in all human populations, that establishes, indubitably, *the autonomy of culture*." Moreover, he found that human history reveals "boundless diversity and often extreme variableness of action" that "cannot possibly be explained by changes in gene frequencies."[51]

On the issue of choice Freeman was as much a cultural determinist as Mead: "Because cultural phenomena are particular alternatives, created by human agency in the course of history, it is always possible for these alternatives to be rapidly, and even radically changed. . . . [T]he choice of new alternatives is, in many instances, not connected in any significant way with the process of genetic evolution, or, for that matter, with human physiology."[52] He concluded that humans, "with their biologically given and culturally nurtured capacity for alternative action, cannot be said to have any kind of 'ultimate' nature."[53]

Freeman stressed the primate heritage of humans, our evolutionary history, and the emergence of culture as a biologically based means for allowing choices to be made and transmitted through nongenetic mechanisms.[54] This view of culture, based on a common biological heritage, was one he shared with Mead. She stated that "cultural systems will be treated as extensions of the power to learn, store, and transmit information, and the evolution of culture as dependent upon biological developments of these abilities and the cultural developments to actualize them."[55]

Both Mead and Freeman emphasized cultural variables at one point in time and biological variables at another, giving the appearance of the existence of two very different paradigms in their thinking. However, for Mead, the focus on culture or biology was a matter of emphasis, not one of irreconcilable differences. She recognized that "at some points in the history of anthropology it has been important to stress the discontinuity between man as a culture-building animal and all other living creatures. It has also been important to stress that man is a mammal with certain types of behavior appropriate to mammals and to identify these behaviors which can be recognized as related between monkeys, apes, and man."[56]

Mead, along with most anthropologists, would have agreed with Freeman when he noted that "humans, like our chimpanzee cousins, far from being empty tablets at birth, are born with phylogenetically given primate nature, components of which remain with us throughout our lives beneath all of the conventional behaviors that we acquire by learning from other members of the society to which we belong."[57]

Freeman advocated an interactionist paradigm in which the genetic and exogenetic (i.e., cultural) were distinct but interacting parts of a single system and in which genetic factors combined with environmental factors to influence behavioral differences among individuals. Mead had also thought about this perspective when discussing the role of innate temperament and its interaction with culture in her 1935 book, *Sex and Temperament in Three Primitive Societies*. In *Behavior and Evolution*, published in 1958 and edited by biologists Anne Roe and George Gaylord Simpson, she briefly noted, "We can get some picture of how change occurs only when each individual is fully specified in his genetic and experiential peculiarity."[58]

From the Very General to the Very Specific

At the most general level Mead's cultural determinist position and Freeman's interactionist position were very similar; both acknowledged a relationship between culture and biology. Of course there was a relationship, but what *exactly* was the nature of the relationship? Did these broad statements really help explain particular phenomena in Samoa and elsewhere?

Mead asked, Why was adolescence in Samoa less stressful than in America in the 1920s? For her, the answer was cultural and could be tested using an elementary compare-and-contrast approach. Samoa was a simpler culture with fewer choices than America. The implication was that all such "simpler" societies could have a relatively easy adolescence. Yet current cross-cultural studies suggest that this is not necessarily so.

In the 1920s cross-cultural studies were in their infancy, so Mead lacked comparative data on which to base her explanation. In recent decades, though, there has been more systematic research on adolescence. Alice Schlegel and Herbert Barry III's 1991 work, *Adolescence: An Anthropological Inquiry,* employed data from over 170 societies to answer some of the questions that Mead had posed. They found that Mead's argument about the relative ease of adolescence applied to only a small minority of societies. In most cases adolescence was a period of increased responsibility, problematic choices, and, for boys, a period of training for war.[59] Mead was correct that adolescence was culturally variable, but her explanation of why that variability occurred was limited by the comparisons she was able to make in the late 1920s.

On the question of the value placed on virginity there was also wide cultural variation. In another study Schlegel found that in societies where there were payments or property exchanges at marriage virginity was more likely to be valued. In societies lacking such payments virginity was less valued. For Samoans, because there were two different marriage systems—one with gift exchange for elite chiefly unions and one without exchange for those of lesser rank—Schlegel found that the islanders fell somewhere in between the most restrictive and most permissive cultures.[60] Comparatively speaking, there were societies that were more permissive and more restrictive than Samoa in the 1920s.[61]

What about the incidence of rape? Although studies indicate that no culture is rape-free, cross-cultural research has demonstrated that some cultures have a higher incidence of rape, while others have a lower incidence.[62] Freeman believed that Samoa had one of the highest rape rates in the world, but he offered no general explanation as to why Samoa should have this very high rate or why other cultures had lower rates.

Freeman's explanation of rape and the "cult of virginity" *within* Samoa associated rape with dominance hierarchies among Samoan men. These dominance orders had cultural aspects, according to Freeman, but they could not be understood unless the relevant biological variables were also taken into account. The biological variables that Freeman noted were the age of the rapists and the hormonal states of the relatively few individuals involved, especially their testosterone levels.[63] This was an interesting hypothesis, but Freeman offered no Samoan data on hormonal states or testosterone levels to support it. Moreover, he had already proposed a cultural determinist hypothesis to explain rape in Samoa.

As noted in chapter 11, Freeman found that "many Samoans aver that the principal aim of a male who engages in either surreptitious or forcible rape is to obtain for himself a virgin wife." But where does the idea that the rape of a virgin will yield to marriage originate? According to Freeman, it derives from *fa'a-Samoa*, or Samoan tradition, which has carried the "cult of female virginity" to perhaps "a greater extreme than in any other culture known to anthropology." The Samoan incidence of rape, "certainly one of the highest to be found anywhere in the world," was linked to Samoan culture and its values. As Freeman described in some detail, young men learned how to rape from their peers. "Both surreptitious and forcible rape, it is important to emphasize, involve *culturally transmitted* male practices."[64]

These practices included manual rape and "the *culturally* standardized stratagem of knocking her unconscious with a heavy punch to her solar plexus" should she resist. "Both of these practices are part of Samoan *culture,* and I have witnessed them being communicated by one individual to another within groups of Samoan males." Thus, "both surreptitious and forcible rape have long been intrinsic to the sexual mores of Samoan men and are major elements in their sexual behavior."[65] So while Freeman believed in principle that biological variables were quite relevant to the explanation of rape, his own explanation of rape in Samoa was cultural. Interestingly, in comparative perspective rape for the culturally approved purpose of obtaining a virgin bride is statistically unusual. So it seems unlikely that biological variables could provide an explanation of this relatively rare cultural practice.

From these examples we can see that while both Mead and Freeman made broad statements about the relationship of biology and culture, neither adequately explained cultural variability.[66] Additional cross-cultural and intracultural research has provided more comprehensive tests of each scholar's ideas.

What the Controversy Was Not About

Because Freeman's interactionism and Mead's cultural determinism were so similar, the Mead-Freeman controversy was not about the nature-nurture debate in a scientific sense. Freeman employed this issue to give his critique of Mead a higher profile, enlisting the legitimacy of evolution and interactionism to cast doubt on her work. Yet Mead's views on the relationship of biology and culture and her advocacy of evolution in the study of humanity were articulated long before Freeman developed his views on these subjects in the 1960s and thereafter.

By misrepresenting Mead's views and by presenting himself as the guardian of evolution and interactionism, Freeman asked his readers to dismiss Mead's work as mistaken, misguided, anachronistic, and unscientific and accept his position as accurate, responsible, thoroughly scientific, and a harbinger of the future. A number of intelligent people found this seemingly clear-cut choice attractive. After all, who could oppose evolution, science, and responsible scholarship? The real choice, however, was not between Mead, on the one hand, and Freeman, on the other. It was between wondering whether Freeman read what Mead had written about culture, biology, and evolution and, for whatever reason, omitted entire passages and works that did not support his argument, *or* whether he did not carefully read Mead and therefore was not fully aware of what she wrote.

Conclusion

OVER THE COURSE OF THE CONTROVERSY Derek Freeman became increasingly frustrated with his colleagues in American anthropology: Why were they unable to see that Mead had been misled by Samoans? He thought that his refutation had made this obvious. And why were they unable to appreciate the magnitude and consequences of her error? As he declared in 1983, "There isn't another example of such wholesale self-deception in the history of behavioral sciences."[1] Although his colleagues seemed reluctant to acknowledge the "fateful hoaxing" of Margaret Mead, Freeman would nevertheless pronounce the controversy over in 1989, claiming closure as the result of Fa'apua'a's testimony. With this supposedly decisive evidence in hand, Freeman stated: "All that now remains to be sought is a full and accurate explanation of the passionate and irrational reaction to my refutation of 1983, and an understanding of how it happened that a demonstrably false doctrine was given credence for so many decades within American cultural anthropology."[2]

Of course, this was not the end of the controversy. After Freeman's second book was published in 1999 there was additional criticism, along with his responses and a river of letters and faxes to his critics. Although the many versions of his hoaxing hypothesis had been effectively questioned, Freeman remained unbowed, demanding vindication.

Oceans of Assertions

Why were many anthropologists reluctant to accept Freeman's verdict on the controversy? Some of it had to do with his assertions about the history of anthropology and Mead's place in it. Freeman argued that the publication of *Coming of Age in Samoa* constituted a decisive moment for the entire discipline, leading scholars to accept and perpetuate the false doctrine of "absolute" cultural determinism.[3] According to Freeman: "All in all, it is one of the most momentous stories in the history of anthropology."[4] These assertions, stated with

225

great authority, were a problem for his colleagues. Freeman probably did not strengthen his argument by referring to them as a "cult" that worshiped a "mother-goddess."[5]

In attempting to rewrite the history of anthropology and Mead's place in it, Freeman shaped the discipline to his argument in the same way that he accused Mead of shaping Samoans to her argument. Yet his assertions were misleading and inaccurate. Neither Boas nor Mead believed in "absolute cultural determinism," nor did most anthropologists of that era. They argued that cultural variability could not be explained by biology alone, hardly a controversial position today. Freeman's assertion that the publication of *Coming of Age in Samoa* was a seminal event in twentieth-century anthropology mistook the popularity of *Coming of Age in Samoa* among the public for its professional influence inside the discipline. He did not understand that Mead's fame outside anthropology did not translate into acceptance within it. Rather than being a central figure within anthropology, Mead herself felt somewhat marginalized.[6]

Many anthropologists were uneasy about Mead's role as a popularizer. In fact, her best-selling books on Samoa and New Guinea were the subject of stinging criticism by some of the major figures in the field. While appreciated by her colleagues for making anthropology available to the public, Mead was not considered a significant theoretical figure. In their review of Mead's place in the discipline at midcentury, Stephen O. Murray and Regna Darnell candidly observed: "Rather than being admired as single-handedly vanquishing biology and establishing cultural anthropology, Mead was widely regarded with contempt as an overheated romancier and popularizer by American anthropologists during the 1950s. . . . Although she was embraced by some as a female role model in her last few years, she was not taken seriously as a theorist, even by those who admired her pioneering accumulation of diverse kinds of data."[7]

Freeman's assertions about Mead's fieldwork and Samoan sexuality are similarly misleading and inaccurate. Although he portrayed Mead as an unwitting victim of her own personal and professional shortcomings, she was an energetic and resourceful fieldworker. In Samoa, Mead became a capable ethnographer who spoke the language with some proficiency. Her professional monograph, *Social Organization of Manuʻa*, demonstrated her ethnographic competence. Mead was not a naive and gullible fieldworker, and there is no compelling evidence that she was "hoaxed."

In claiming that Samoans valued virginity to an exceptional degree, Freeman neglected evidence to the contrary, including the many unions that took place between American servicemen and Samoan women while he was in the islands during World War II. He also maintained that the system of institutionalized virginity was central to Samoan culture during the first half of the twentieth century, an assertion contradicted by his own unpublished description of the *taupou* system as "virtually defunct" by the time of his fieldwork in the 1940s.

What is interesting about Freeman's assertions is not just that they were misleading and inaccurate but that they were unnecessary for his refutation of Mead. He did not need them to critique her work. *Coming of Age in Samoa* did include errors of fact and questionable interpretations as well as overstatements. In retrospect, Mead could have been a more scientific ethnographer of Samoan adolescence. These were not difficult points to make. However, Freeman used his knowledge not merely to reinterpret the ethnographic record but to damage Mead's reputation in a deliberate and personal manner. Freeman could have criticized Mead's work, revised it, and improved our knowledge of Samoa without diminishing her record as an ethnographer, without resorting to the accusation of hoaxing, without portraying her as antievolutionary, and without trashing her reputation.

Freeman's critique of *Coming of Age in Samoa* also contained errors of fact and interpretation as well as overstatements. This would not be news either except that he was a senior scholar. Given his vast knowledge of Samoa, he could have authored a substantial ethnography or a problem-oriented study of the islands, but he did not do so. These were opportunities missed, a sense of perspective lost.

Freeman's continuing research during the controversy did provide new information on Mead's linguistic competence in Samoan, additional interviews with Fa'apua'a, and more detailed study of Mead's letters and other correspondence from Samoa. But this information was often misused in the service of his conclusions. For reasons that are still not fully understood, Freeman became obsessed with Mead and compromised his own scholarship as he damaged hers. Perhaps it was the intellectual shadow Mead cast over him as he worked in Samoa. Perhaps it was his close identification with Samoan custom and the culture of Samoan chiefs. Perhaps it was his personal issues with women, dominance, and sex. Perhaps it was his psychological difficulties, which became apparent during Freeman's delusional episode in Borneo. Perhaps it was the heated encounter with Mead in Canberra in 1964 or his experience on Ta'ū in 1967. It may have been some combination of these and other factors as well.

Whatever the reasons, Freeman systematically used sources out of context or omitted them altogether. He failed to disclose crucial parts of Fa'apua'a's testimony that cast doubt on his hoaxing hypothesis. He even neglected parts of his own scholarship that did not support his arguments against Mead. Freeman carefully cloaked his critique of Mead in what appeared to be exhaustive scholarly detail and reference to great issues of the day. Yet the controversy was not primarily about Samoa or the nature-nurture debate or new scientific paradigms as Freeman conceived them. It was, in large measure, about Mead's reputation and, by implication, Freeman's as well.

In 2001 Derek Freeman died in Australia at age eighty-four. His passing was duly noted in newspaper obituaries, as was his irrevocable connection to Mead. But what would be his legacy? As a visionary, Freeman had thought about and planned for the future. In the mid-1980s, when the controversy was in full swing, Freeman developed the idea of a "new anthropological ark" populated by a small group of knowledgeable scholars interested in a genuine science of anthropology and in furthering his interactionist paradigm.[8] Presumably, the ark would survive the troubled waters of anthropology and establish a discipline more congenial to Freeman.

He hoped to bring together perhaps a dozen scholars—half men, half women—at a conference in La Jolla, California, to consider his ideas. This group would issue a white paper outlining where interactionism might lead, drawing attention to it, and providing a platform for future work. The ark was to be funded by corporations and would provide five-year fellowships to develop the project. Freeman suggested potential participants, including two anthropologists from the University of California at San Diego as well as a well-known biologist.

This new anthropological ark would be oriented toward the future, including interactionist approaches at the molecular level. Yet this ambitious project never got off the ground. One reason was that primatologists and ethologically oriented anthropologists, who would have been an important constituency for interactionism, provided little support for Freeman during the controversy. In fact, some were critical of his work.[9] Without their assistance it would be difficult for Freeman to realize his particular vision of anthropology. At this same time a good deal of research using interactionist approaches was already under way in the sciences and continues to flourish today; it simply was not done under Freeman's auspices. So his ark failed to launch. Paradoxically, Freeman's stance as a "heretic" going against the conventional wisdom of his own discipline may have made it difficult for him to enlist participants and lead such an intellectual movement.

Nevertheless, Freeman took a longer view. In an interview near the end of his life he discussed how the new discipline of evolutionary psychology would eventually revolutionize the behavioral sciences and how his work would ultimately come to be appreciated: "But those books of mine if you read them, they are not the books of a madman. They are extremely closely argued and they will come into their own in about 50 years from now, I reckon." In the same interview he commented that he was "centuries ahead of my time."[10]

Requiem for a Controversy?

Now in its third decade, the controversy that Freeman initiated has become part of intellectual history. Quite apart from Freeman's own pronouncements about the controversy's importance, it has been elevated to the status of one of the most significant controversies in the history of science. In Hal Hellman's *Great Feuds in Science* the Mead-Freeman controversy was listed as one of the ten "liveliest" scientific controversies of all time, on a par with the controversy over evolution set off by the discoveries of Charles Darwin. In Ron Robin's *Scandals and Scoundrels* the Mead-Freeman controversy was selected as one of "seven cases that shook the academy." And in terms of the number of books, articles, and chapters generated, it has certainly been the "greatest" controversy in cultural anthropology. But was it really that important?

When the controversy began in 1983, Freeman's refutation called into question Mead's reputation. Sparks flew and tempers flared. Commentaries were vigorously exchanged. The manner in which the controversy initially appeared in the media governed its course. The more dramatic Freeman's claims ("the establishment was fooled," "Mead was hoaxed"), the more media attention they drew. Relatively few people actually read Freeman's books or the responses that they generated, but his message found an audience nevertheless.

In the public mind Margaret Mead was a popular icon, and the controversy was more easily understood by the public as being about specific individuals and their reputations rather than about abstract academic issues and complex substantive data on Samoa. Freeman's message—that Mead was wrong and that she was a naive young woman—was and still is widely believed. The counterarguments that anthropologists and others tried to provide were often too academic for the public and the media as well as too late to matter.

Freeman seems to have understood the public's interest in winners and losers, heroes and villains. And the media felt a responsibility to broadcast his claims as part of "the controversy." Their role was not to choose sides or referee the controversy; it was to cover the controversy in a "balanced" manner. Very few people, journalists and academics alike, realized how personal and all-consuming Mead and the controversy had become for Freeman. Events in his life seemingly unrelated to the controversy became relevant to it. For example, in 1998 he gave a public lecture on the controversy that ended with a remembrance of the tragic death of one of his mountaineering companions sixty years earlier. Freeman, then twenty-one, and two other young men had been climbing Mount Evans in New Zealand when one of them slipped and fell to his death, dragging his companions with him. They survived. For Freeman, this event had special significance. He concluded, "If I had been killed, it is unlikely in the extreme that the Mead myth about Samoa would have ever been exposed. Such are the vicissitudes of human history."[11]

In some academic controversies there are clear-cut outcomes. Yet in this controversy there have been few winners, and there has been considerable damage: to Mead, to Samoans, to anthropology, and to Freeman. So what did the controversy accomplish? It has encouraged anthropologists and other scholars to look more closely at the history of anthropology, the lives of Mead and Freeman, the times in which they wrote, the nature of Samoan culture, and a number of related issues. But it has been of little value in situating Mead's very real accomplishments in historical perspective and minimal value as an important scientific controversy.

Although general questions about human nature and the roles of biology and culture are of great significance and deserve the best research and scholarship, this controversy did not move that research forward. And while there are anthropologists, sociologists, and scholars in the humanities who view the role of biology as insignificant or as entirely "historically situated and culturally constituted," Mead was not one of them. If she were alive today, Mead would be as deeply involved in exploring these issues as she was during her lifetime. So, as important as such issues may be in other contexts and to other controversies and as divisive as they have been within anthropology in recent decades, in the Mead-Freeman controversy there were no "paradigms in collision," no earth-shaking insights into the nature-nurture debate, and no new interactionist paradigm for the twenty-first century led by Freeman himself.[12]

With his passing the controversy has lost much of the immediacy that Freeman brought to it. Since 2001 there have been no further claims of "startling new evidence," new "smoking guns," or "final" verdicts of the kind that he regularly announced. What, then, will be the future of the controversy? On the academic front it will no doubt continue, although perhaps in a less contentious and more muted form. Despite all that has been written and despite attempts to resolve the issues or at least clarify them, the controversy is not over. It has many layers. More commentary will appear. Samoans may have a greater voice. More research may be done on Mead's field sites. And, at some time in the future, Freeman's personal diaries may become available to researchers. There is still more to be learned.

The Legacy of Margaret Mead

The year of Freeman's death was also the one hundredth anniversary of Margaret Mead's birth. To commemorate her centennial a number of public events were held around the country, including four panels organized for the 2001 American Anthropological Association annual meeting in Washington, D.C. Over a two-day period experts on these panels sought to rethink and re-evaluate Mead's contributions.[13] Dozens of scholars examined her work as a whole—more than fifty years of it and in its many different facets. This was no small task because her work was so broad and so voluminous. Mead's bibliography alone ran to an astonishing 110 printed pages—a small book in itself.[14] During her life she had produced almost 1,400 publications, including almost forty books (many coauthored or coedited), as well as films, tapes, and videocassettes. And there were people's memories of Mead as a person; almost everyone who met her or heard her speak remembered the occasion.

At the AAA meeting there was some discussion of Mead's Samoan work, but not very much.[15] And there was little mention of Derek Freeman. Mead was not entirely free of Freeman's ghost, but there was a sense that her work could now be considered without constant reference to him. Scholars at the meeting critically reviewed Mead's wide-ranging ethnographic career. Samoa was Mead's first field site and *Coming of Age in Samoa* her first best seller, but there was much more to come. For anthropologists, it was Mead's entire body of professional work, not one particular study, that was impressive. After Samoa, within a period of fourteen years, Mead went on to do research among the Manus off the coast of New Guinea; the Tchambuli, Arapesh, Mundugumor, and Iatmul in New Guinea; the Balinese; and the Omaha of North America. Because Mead's professional monographs on these cultures are far less well known than her popular works on these same cultures, including *Growing Up in New Guinea, Sex and Temperament in Three South Pacific Cultures,* and, later, *New Lives for Old,* her ethnographic work may not have been fully appreciated.[16]

Panelists also discussed Mead's contributions to applied anthropology and museum work, her place in anthropology and in the wider world. One evening event was held at the Library of Congress, where thousands of Mead's letters and other documents are housed. In conjunction with these events National Public Radio produced a program about Mead.[17] In addition, a number of Mead's books were republished in light of their relevance to the twenty-first century.

As a professional, Mead used her anthropological expertise in public policy forums. In this capacity she made many appearances before U.S. congressional committees, testifying on a variety of subjects, including nuclear reactors, the use of the behavioral sciences in foreign policy, the role of science in long-term problem solving, renewal of funding for the National Science Foundation, the establishment of a National Anthropological Film Center at the Smithsonian, American participation in the United Nations, and the implications of recombinant DNA, to list just a few.[18] In other government forums she testified on behalf of Samoan cultural rights and in defense of bowhead whales.

Some of her critics felt that Mead spoke on subjects about which she knew very little and that she was spreading herself too thin. But Mead had enormous energy and a desire to make a difference. She was very interested in government and actively networked with politicians. She often wrote President Carter, whose presidency she supported and whom she addressed as "Jimmy." She offered him unsolicited advice about marketing his policies, and sometimes he listened. Just before her death in 1978 Mead sent Carter an urgent message from her hospital bed asking him not to veto the Child Nutrition Act, which he was about to do. Instead, he approved the act and sent her a personal thank-you note.[19]

Margaret Mead as a Public Figure

If anthropologists were beginning to rethink Mead's professional legacy, for the public and much of the media, rehabilitating Mead's reputation would take longer.[20] Mead had been a familiar figure during her lifetime and a great public presence, still significant for an older generation of Americans. Yet the controversy had taken a toll on her image. Would the public now be able to remember Mead as something more than the object of Freeman's critique? Could she even be remembered in a culture where celebrities have only a fleeting moment of fame?

During her lifetime Mead's widely read columns for *Redbook* attempted to arbitrate significant public issues over a sixteen-year period between 1962 and 1978. But popular as they were, her columns sometimes reinforced the fault lines of American culture and drew criticism as a result. Hailed as a moving force behind the sexual revolution of the 1960s, Mead was demonized for the same reason. She could be praised for her recognition of sex as an important topic of discussion yet vilified for promoting sexual permissiveness. While a critic of Alfred Kinsey's studies of human sexuality, Mead was often regarded as being in the same camp with him. On the Internet it is easy to find cultural conservatives deploring Mead as an intellectual huckster who not only was wrong about Samoa but who also had led Americans down the garden path to moral degeneracy.

This kind of criticism followed Mead throughout her career. After the publication of *Coming of Age in Samoa* in 1928 the American Legion condemned it as a "sex book." Decades later, after Mead advocated the decriminalization of marijuana, the governor of Florida denounced her as a "dirty old lady."[21] She was a lightning rod on public issues. Mead could be brilliant and outrageous, difficult and contentious, as well as wrong and misinformed, faults to which she occasionally admitted.

Mead recognized that she could be criticized for almost any position that she took. In remembering the responses to two of her popular books—*Sex and Temperament* and *Male and Female*—she found herself accused of being both overly feminist and not feminist enough. As Mead mused:

> How very difficult it was for Americans to sort out ideas of innate pre-dispositions and culturally acquired behavior was evident in the contradictory responses to the book [*Sex and Temperament*]. Feminists hailed it as a demonstration that women did not "naturally" like children, and recommended that little girls not be given dolls to play with. Reviewers accused me of not recognizing the existence of any sex differences. Fourteen years later, when I wrote *Male and Female*, a book in which I dealt carefully with cultural and temperamental differences as these were related in the lives of men and women and then discussed characteristics that seemed to be related to primary sex differences between men and women, I was accused of anti-feminism by women, of rampant feminism by men, and of denying the full beauty of the experience of being a woman by individuals of both sexes.[22]

Much of the general public thought of Mead as a crusader whose work was relevant in their lives. Among those who loved her Mead's positive contributions were easy to recognize, as her editor at *Redbook*, Sey Chassler, recalled in his tribute shortly after her death:

> New York cab drivers knew her and admired her. Octogenarians and teenagers in the South Pacific honored and loved her and looked forward to her comings and goings. Scientific societies sought her leadership. Children visited with her in the American Museum of Natural History, where she made her office for more than fifty years. Scores of organizations at home and abroad asked her to speak to them every year. In an average year, she spoke to more than one hundred groups, roughly two a week, many of them for no fee. She went everywhere. She was tireless and disregarded time. . . .
>
> In behalf of all of us, she worried constantly about the dangers of nuclear radiation, the piling up of nuclear weapons, the distribution of nuclear wastes, the pollution of our air, our earth, our water, and our general disregard for the safety of humanity. She sought ways for women and men to learn to live together rationally and in comfort. She worried that our communities did not care well enough for homeless children, and the handicapped and the aged. . . .
>
> She tried to help us all to see that we share the world and must live in it and work in it together.[23]

Even her critics acknowledged Mead's influence. Betty Friedan was emphatic about Mead's importance to women, stating in 1963:

> The most powerful influence on modern women, in terms of both functionalism and the feminist protest was Margaret Mead. Her work on culture and personality—book after book, study after study—has had a profound effect on the women of my generation, the one before it, and the generation now growing up. She was, and still is, the symbol of the woman thinker in America. She has written millions of words in the thirty-odd years between *Coming of Age in Samoa* and her latest article on American women in the *New York Times Magazine* or *Redbook*. She is studied in college classrooms by girls taking courses in anthropology, sociology, psychology, education, and marriage and family life; in graduate schools by those who will one day teach girls and counsel women; in medical schools by future pediatricians and psychiatrists; even in theological schools by progressive young ministers. And she is read in the women's magazines and the Sunday supplements, where she publishes as regularly as in the learned journals, by girls and women of all ages—and her influence has been felt in almost every layer of American thought.[24]

Although her readers did not know Mead personally, they nevertheless felt that she was speaking to them and perhaps for them. She was not just another anthropologist speaking on important issues, she was *their* anthropologist. It is this quality that made her unique. There was no one quite like her then, and there has been no one in anthropology like her since.

In the early decades of her career anthropology was almost unknown, and Mead herself spent a good deal of her time making the public aware of the discipline. As a museum curator rather than a university-based academic she had more freedom to do so than a regular tenure-line faculty member. Yet within anthropology her efforts in the public realm were regarded as a mixed blessing, as anthropologist John W. Bennett reflected:

> No anthropologist could equal her for sheer chutzpa and nerve; she was a shameless self-promoter; self-appointed national sales agent for the discipline of anthropology; scourge of various Classic-era anthropologists and their picayune quarrels and preoccupations; a friend and tireless mentor of bright young anthropologists. . . . So what precisely was her role and influence? Her public role is easy to describe: First and foremost was her advocacy of the discipline and her conviction that anthropology had something that the world needed and could use. This certainly instilled confidence in young anthropologists. I recall going to social events and when questioned, admitting that I was an anthropologist, to be met with eager questions about Margaret Mead. She *was* professional identity: and

while it was embarrassing to have to say that one had doubts about her probity with respect to research, her name and persona always opened a line of conversation. And of course her example was especially important for young women anthropologists.[25]

If Mead helped garner attention for anthropology, in recent years concern has shifted away from creating an awareness of anthropology to concern about the *image* of anthropology in the public mind. Because of the dedication of earlier generations of anthropologists like Mead, the subject is no longer the mystery that it was in the early twentieth century.[26] Anthropology is now popular; the number of undergraduate majors and concentrations in North America has more than doubled in just the last two decades. Anthropology is even "sexy," as reflected in the constant stream of articles and documentaries about early humans, primates, great archaeological sites, and remote tribes. Television shows and movies feature fictional anthropologists as major characters, such as Indiana Jones and Lara Croft. *Digging for the Past* was one of the History Channel's most popular shows, and the television series *Bones* has attracted a number of undergraduates to forensic anthropology. This is what the anthropology franchise looks like today.

Despite this apparent success, anthropologists have been concerned about respect from the public in light of their sometimes unflattering appearance in the media, including the Mead-Freeman controversy. In her presidential message to the American Anthropological Association in 1990 Jane Buikstra stated that in the future "the central issue for anthropology will be respect from the public."[27] She urged her colleagues to become more involved in the effort to communicate with the broader public and the media, but this has been more difficult than expected and anticipated.

Recently, anthropology has often been represented in the media by journalists and nonanthropologists rather than by scholars in the field. Very few of the news stories, reports, or opinion columns surrounding the Mead-Freeman controversy or the more recent controversy over Napoleon Chagnon's research among the Yanomami of Amazonia were actually written by anthropologists, although anthropologists were often quoted as experts.[28] In the media's coverage of these controversies most anthropologists have watched from the sidelines and this is a major reason why anthropologists have conflicting feelings about the media. They need the media but do not usually control the message.

A related problem is that most anthropologists do not write for the public but write instead for their peers, who comprise small, highly specialized audiences. The norm of "publish or perish" is widespread, filtering down even to junior colleges. As higher education has expanded in recent decades there have been more scholars and more professional journals, and there has been greater pressure to publish in them. While professional publications are vital for the accumulation of knowledge of the world's peoples and cultures, past and present, they do not often reach the general public. The current academic environment is not conducive to popular writing because it is not recognized as important for academic promotion and tenure.

Just as Mead was dismissed for being a popularizer, so too are other anthropologists who speak to the public. As two younger anthropologists candidly commented, "We face censure from our colleagues when we try to break out of the confines of scholarly publication and move into the arena of accessible writing."[29] In an era when anthropologists have important work to share with the public the relevance of that work may be restricted by the structure of professional rewards as well as by the nature of media coverage. As a result, the people most responsible for the public dissemination of anthropology are often generalists outside the discipline such as Jared Diamond, the Pulitzer Prize–winning author of *Guns, Germs, and Steel: The Fates of Human Societies* and *Collapse: How Societies Choose to Fail or Succeed.*

Missing Margaret Mead

Anthropologists concerned about the diminishing influence of their professional scholarship in the public sphere have been revisiting the legacy of Mead and other intellectual ancestors who did so much to bridge that chasm. Earlier doubts about Mead and her ethnographic work are now tempered by recognition of what she accomplished in the public arena.[30] In this context anthropologist Richard Handler noticed a sense of despair among contemporary scholars who found that their insights have had almost no impact on public policy: "This lament is heard from scholars in many fields—it is sometimes discussed as the demise of the public intellectual. Among North American anthropologists, that lament may be particularly heartfelt, as we have great interdisciplinary ancestors (whose work we continue to study), who even long after their deaths seem to cast a longer shadow than we current practitioners are able to do."[31]

The desire for a greater presence by anthropologists in the public arena is understandable, and this is why Mead's presence is missed. From the beginning of her career she was unique among American anthropologists in giving priority to studies that could inform our everyday lives.[32] In writing about Samoa she was also writing about America, recognizing the cultural and political crosscurrents of the post–World War I era. Mead was aware that the late 1920s were a time of youth and hope but also a time of self-criticism and despair. Mead knew of the simmering issues at home and the dangers of rising totalitarianism abroad.[33] For her, anthropology was ideally suited to the understanding of these contemporary issues. As she stated just prior to the publication of *Coming of Age in Samoa:* "By the study and analysis of the diverse solutions to the problems that confront us today, it is possible to make a more reasoned judgment of the needs of our own society."[34] Mead set her agenda accordingly and lived by it for the rest of her life.

Appendix

True Confessions

READERS MAY WONDER ABOUT my personal relationships with Freeman and Mead. Did I know them well? Did my relationship with them influence my scholarship about them? These questions are especially relevant in the case of Freeman because, as he did with many of his critics, he raised the issue of intellectual bias in his correspondence with me. I was in his view an adversary, not a colleague. And worse, I was a defender of Mead. So how did I become his adversary? And what was my relationship with Mead?

Coincidence or Conspiracy?

Freeman did not believe that his critics were capable of questioning his arguments on purely academic grounds. He suspected that we might have ulterior motives or perhaps a hidden connection to Margaret Mead herself. In his correspondence with colleagues who were his friends he would sometimes ask for personal information that would help him understand those he considered his adversaries. In 1999 Freeman wrote to me to report that he had discovered a connection to Mead in my academic background that allowed him to finally understand why I had been a critic of his work.

After speaking to an unnamed mutual acquaintance, Freeman learned that my academic advisor at Harvard, where I attended graduate school in the late 1960s, was John Whiting, the noted psychological anthropologist. As Freeman breathlessly wrote me: "I have just been told, by someone who was there at that same time as yourself, that while at Harvard you were a devoted student of John Whiting."[1]

According to Freeman, Whiting had been strongly influenced by Mead in the 1930s, and he concluded that I was therefore a direct intellectual descendant of Mead through Whiting. As Freeman stated:

> You have been acting throughout [the controversy] as a faithful student of John W. M. Whiting, and in defense of what you were taught at Harvard long, long years ago. And this being the case, the revelations about young Margaret Mead's actions in my recently published book (all of them based on the relevant primary sources) are going to be deeply disturbing to you. . . . May I wish you well then (even though I consider your actions to be quite pathetic) as you doggedly persist in your patriotic campaign to have Margaret Mead's conclusions of 1928 reinstated in the esteem of the anthropologists of Bill Clinton's America. . . . May your nights be wholesome, then, and no planets strike, as you persist in your Whiting-esque endeavors![2]

So there we were all together—Mead, Whiting, Shankman, and Bill Clinton. Was this a coincidence or a conspiracy? As was often the case with Freeman's observations, appearance and reality could be quite different. Mead had far less influence on Whiting than Freeman imagined. Although Whiting was my advisor at Harvard and was very interested in child rearing and adolescence, just as Mead had been, he was not intellectually or personally close to her. His courses on psychological anthropology included Mead as a historical figure but not as a model for contemporary research. Furthermore, when I was a graduate student in the mid-1960s, Whiting taught a graduate seminar with Harvard primatologist Irven DeVore, exploring some of the very biocultural issues that Freeman himself would later pursue using his interactionist approach.

In his own research Whiting had gone well beyond Mead, and his theoretical orientation was different from hers. Mead had also not endeared herself to Whiting, giving his work less than stellar reviews. For example, in a 1943 review of Whiting's first book, *Becoming a Kwoma*, Mead faulted Whiting for not asking the right questions and for not enriching cross-cultural understanding.[3] Later, during the 1950s, Whiting and his wife, anthropologist Beatrice Blythe Whiting, conceived and supervised the most ambitious cross-cultural study of childhood, fatherhood, and motherhood conducted to that point in time.[4] In Mead's review of the first volume of their study, prominently published in *American Anthropologist*, she criticized the project's hypothesis-testing research design as "quite insufficient" and their use of comparative method as "uncritical."[5] Whiting, I'm sure, did not appreciate these professional slights.

As a graduate student, my own research interest was in economic anthropology rather than psychological anthropology. In the late 1960s Whiting generously invited me to become part of his project in Kenya for my doctoral dissertation research. I declined because I wanted to focus on economic development in Samoa, which I had first visited in 1966. Whiting nevertheless continued to be my graduate advisor and graciously encouraged my work. He did not, however, recommend that I read Mead's work or contact her before conducting my dissertation research.

Freeman could have learned more about the relationship between Mead and Whiting by simply asking Whiting, who was alive and well during much of the Mead-Freeman controversy. In fact, had Whiting been as positive about Mead as Freeman suggested, he would have entered the controversy himself. But he did not. Freeman also could have asked me about my relationship to Whiting and Mead. We had spent many hours together in Canberra discussing the controversy in 1984. As an avid correspondent, he could have written me about Whiting. Yet Freeman seemed to believe that the intellectual connections were so obvious that no further information was necessary.

Margaret Mead

I had learned about Mead's work in courses at both the undergraduate and graduate levels, but none of my professors was a great admirer of Mead, and some were quite critical of her and her work. At the time I did not have a strong opinion in either direction.

In the early 1960s, when I was in college, Mead was at the height of her powers. She was so well known that a fictional character based on an anthropologist studying sex in Polynesia was featured in Irving Wallace's 1963 best seller, *The Three Sirens*. In this trashy novel, which I read as a junior, the thinly disguised Mead-like character finds her world turned upside down by the discovery of an untouched island. The dust jacket of the novel managed to capture every undergraduate's fantasies about anthropology, asking:

> What happens when a varied group of men and women, married and unmarried, from our own complex culture is thrown together for six dramatic weeks with people from a simpler, happier society, free from the inhibitions and tensions of the 20th century? Irving Wallace's provocative new novel is the story of this confrontation, as an American team of anthropologists descends upon a remote Polynesian island to study a unique and hitherto undiscovered way of life. The visiting Americans are supposed to be dispassionate observers. Yet each brings to the island his own problems, attitudes, and prejudices. The team consists of nine oddly assorted Americans, led by Dr. Maud Hayden, the world famous woman who is America's leading anthropologist. . . . On The Three Sirens [the

islands], these visitors are brought face to face with uninhibited behavior and customs that seem to be a shocking assault, a challenge, to their most cherished beliefs about love, sex, marriage, child rearing, and justice.

In this Polynesian village they find a society where the monotony of marriage is relieved by the freedom to enjoy other mates for one week of the year; where the dissatisfactions and repressions of men and women, both married and unmarried, are relieved by a mysterious Social Aid Hut; where women over forty can enjoy life without the destructive feeling that youth is the only happiness; where unattractive girls are desired for those attributes that are ignored in our own cult of beauty; where confused teen-agers are given the security of learning firsthand the facts of life; and where grown men do not have to prove their virility by means of their careers. . . .

Irving Wallace's powerful novel tells the story of the shattering impact of this seemingly Utopian way of life on the Americans who have come to study the people of The Three Sirens and who suddenly find themselves instead studying their own desires, fears, and passions.[6]

As I read *The Three Sirens*, which had no redeeming social value whatsoever, I thought to myself, If this is anthropology, I'm glad I majored in it. For this was how many people of that era thought about anthropology and about Mead. She was not a geeky academic but an adventurous individual who studied something that we were all interested in. And the real Margaret Mead was a celebrity, just like the fictional Maud Hayden.

Shortly after reading *The Three Sirens* a small group of anthropology majors from the University of California at Santa Barbara (UCSB) drove up to San Francisco to see what the meeting of the American Anthropological Association was like. Quite by accident, there in the hall of the hotel where the meeting was held, was Mead herself! Even at a distance she was immediately recognizable with her walking stick, cape, and retinue of followers. Although small in stature, she seemed to fill the area.

I did not meet Mead personally then; it was enough to have caught a glimpse of her. I did meet her a little later when she came to UCSB as a guest of the university and the Department of Anthropology. Mead needed transportation, and I volunteered. Since I was the proud owner of a 1953 Studebaker Champion V8 with white sidewall tires and a new metallic paint job, I became Mead's chauffeur, and this vehicle was her chariot. During her captivity in my Studebaker I was able to ask Mead all the ridiculous questions a typical undergraduate of that era might ask a world-famous anthropologist. Yet she took no offense and answered them directly. After her public lecture to an audience of hundreds the department hosted a private party for her. On our way there we stopped at a liquor store, and Mead bought two bottles of Black & White scotch whisky. She told me that one bottle was for the party. The other was for her. The party was a memorable event.

That same year I read *Coming of Age* in a course on cultures of the South Pacific. The book did not make a major impression on me. It was an assignment and not a part of real life. The sexual revolution of the 1960s was already under way, and *Coming of Age* seemed a little dated. Furthermore, the stereotypes of the South Pacific that we held did not come from Mead or the excellent courses that we took but rather from the culture of that period. The closest we had come to the real Polynesia was a visit to the Enchanted Tiki Room at Disneyland as kids. We had never been to Hawai'i; the actual islands were worlds away. Nevertheless, we imagined them through movies (*South Pacific, Hawaii, Endless Summer*), TV (*Gilligan's Island*), travelogues, magazines, novels, our interest in surfing and bodysurfing, and Polynesian-themed bars, like Don the Beachcomber (named after the owner, Donn Beach) and Trader Vic's, where we enjoyed parts of our misspent youth in Southern California.[7]

In 1965 I headed east for graduate work at Harvard without a clue as to what area of the world I would study and without my Studebaker. By pure serendipity, in the summer of 1966 I spent a month in American Samoa and Western Samoa with anthropologist Judd Epling of the UCLA School of Public Health. Judd had been my supervisor on an unrelated summer research project in Los Angeles, and he asked me if I wanted to go with him to the islands. I leapt at the opportunity, although I had virtually no preparation and no prior research interest in the islands. It was an experience that would lead me to spend much of my professional life researching and thinking about Samoa. Judd was also married to a Samoan woman, and I became part of their family, as they became part of mine.

We arrived in American Samoa on a cool early morning in 1966. At that time American Samoa was becoming even more American, complete with a U.S. naval base, tuna canneries, and a brand new hotel getting ready to host a Ford Motor Company convention. We spent two weeks based in Pago Pago doing medical research and then flew to Western Samoa. This second Samoa was an independent country, part of the global economy, and had been Christian for 130 years. Although not traditional in the pre-European sense, it was more traditional than American Samoa. The young Samoans I met there were part of a social hierarchy where proper conduct was required and expected. At the same time, beneath the formal structure and proper etiquette of Samoan culture younger Samoans seemed adept at working around the rules as well as within them.

In 1969 I prepared to do my dissertation fieldwork on the developing economy of Western Samoa. I now knew a little more about the islands and had an opportunity to have lunch with Margaret Mead in New York City at a greasy spoon across from the American Museum of Natural History, where she was a curator of anthropology. We talked about Samoa, but Mead had not been there for over forty years, so much of our discussion was historical rather than contemporary, and it was about American Samoa rather than Western Samoa, where I would be working. There was no discussion of Derek Freeman, although Freeman had been critiquing Mead for some time. I appreciated Mead's taking time to have lunch with yet another aspiring graduate student. But because she was not closely connected to contemporary Western Samoa, our conversation was of limited value in terms of assisting my research. This was our only extended professional encounter.

Since my research was on economic development and, more specifically, on current Samoan migration to New Zealand, Australia, and the United States, Mead's work on adolescence and social organization was of marginal relevance. I completed my dissertation on Samoan migration and remittances in 1973 and continued to do research on this set of problems as well as deforestation and local politics, with short visits to the islands in 1973, 1977, 1984, 1986, and 2001. I also worked with Samoans in the United States.

Derek Freeman

When I taught my first undergraduate course on the South Pacific at the University of Colorado, Boulder, in 1975, I included a section on sex in Samoa; it seemed to be more interesting to students than migration, although I had done no systematic research on the subject. For readings, apart from *Coming of Age*, I used Freeman's unpublished manuscript titled "On Believing as Many as Six Impossible Things before Breakfast," which was an early version of his critique of Mead. The manuscript had been given to me by Richard Goodman, an independent scholar who spent a good deal of time in Western Samoa and who wrote his own critique of Mead well before Freeman's book was published.[8] My students read Mead, Freeman's manuscript, and other sources as well. They then wrote papers wrestling with the issues and the very different perspectives of Mead and Freeman on the private lives of Samoans. This was a good assignment for undergraduates. By the time Freeman published his book in 1983 I had unintentionally been teaching a version of the controversy for several years.

When the controversy broke in late January 1983, I learned about it the same way everyone else did—through the newspapers and television. One morning in the winter of 1983 I received a call from a representative of the *Donahue* show in Chicago. He asked me if I would like to appear on the show with Freeman. I was stunned by the offer and quickly replied that I had not seen or read the book. He told me not to worry, that a prepublication copy would immediately be shipped to me by express mail and that I would have the weekend to read it before appearing with Freeman in Chicago the next week in front of an audience of millions of people. I thought to myself, This could be a disaster, and made one of the few wise decisions of my life: I thanked the *Donahue* representative for the opportunity and said no. As it turned out, a number of other anthropologists had made the same decision before me. To their credit, Mary Catherine Bateson and Bradd Shore said yes and appeared on the show.

Although I had read Freeman's limited published work on Samoa and his 1968 unpublished manuscript on Mead as well as becoming acquainted with him through the media, my personal introduction to him occurred after the Mead-Freeman controversy began in 1983. That is when Freeman and I began to correspond. We had both worked as cultural anthropologists in Western Samoa, but we had never met or written each other. After the controversy started I was invited to write an article for a special issue on the controversy in *Canberra Anthropology*, a journal that was published at the Australian National University (ANU), Freeman's academic home. Freeman responded negatively to all the articles in the issue, quickly dismissing my critique of his work as a feeble attempt to make excuses for Mead and calling my thinking "a disgrace to the profession of anthropology."[9]

In the fall of 1983 I convened a small conference at the University of Colorado to review the controversy with three other scholars—Bradd Shore, Mary Catherine Bateson, and Lowell Holmes; Loia Fiaui, then a Samoan graduate student at UCLA, also participated.[10] We could not afford to bring Freeman from Australia, and he was not pleased. He was also unhappy with criticism of his work by conference participants. Later I applied for funding for a much larger, international conference on the controversy; this time Freeman was on the list of participants, but the conference was not funded. Freeman again informed me of his displeasure.

Freeman and I eventually met in 1984, when my family and I were visiting friends at ANU. I was a visiting fellow in ANU's Research School of Pacific Studies for five weeks. I wrote to Freeman in advance and looked forward to meeting him. During my stay we had several long conversations, lasting up to two hours each, about the controversy and more generally about anthropology. I was grateful for Freeman's willingness to share his time and his arguments. In reality, though, the conversations were more like extended lectures by Freeman because he clearly believed that I was misguided, having already written pieces that questioned his work and defended Mead.[11] At that time Freeman believed that I could be persuaded by and perhaps converted to his position. His first words to me when we met were "We'll set ya right."

Freeman wasn't unpleasant; he was, however, authoritative and interested primarily in what he could tell me. Of course, his knowledge of Samoan culture, history, and language was far superior to mine. So I would ask him questions about his work in Samoa, Mead, and anthropology, and he would provide very thorough, articulate, almost rehearsed replies, sometimes quoting verbatim from his own publications. During my stay at ANU he was so focused on the controversy and his own work that we almost never discussed the islands in general, nor was he curious about my work on migration.

While I was visiting ANU a number of faculty members and graduate students shared their "horror" stories about Freeman's personality, his biases, his formidable presence, his conflicts with them, and his rudeness to visitors during department talks. I had already heard some of these stories in the United States but not in Freeman's own backyard. Almost everyone seemed to have one, and soon I would have my own.

During the last part of my visit I was to give a talk on the work of Clifford Geertz, the well-known American anthropologist with an international following. Having listened to stories about Freeman's conduct during such talks, including interruptions and hostile comments, I asked the moderator beforehand to insure that Freeman did not interrupt the talk prior to the question-and-answer period. Acknowledging that this was almost expected behavior from Freeman, the moderator agreed.

The room for the talk was relatively small and filled to capacity. Freeman sat immediately to my right in his usual seat. Knowing that the moderator would keep the situation in hand reassured me. I also thought that because I was speaking about Geertz, not Mead or the controversy, things would go smoothly. I was kindly introduced and began my presentation. Almost immediately I heard a loud ripping sound. Freeman was noisily opening his mail and conspicuously attracting attention. I glanced at the moderator, who at this point seemed to have melted into the far wall of the room. I continued to speak, and Freeman continued to open his mail. I stopped speaking and looked at Freeman. The room was completely silent, perhaps anticipating this awkward moment. I said politely but firmly, "Derek, I want you to stop opening your mail and pay attention." This was sufficient, and Freeman did not disturb the talk further, even to ask a question afterward.

It was a very minor incident, but I was puzzled about why Freeman had interrupted the talk. Our relationship had been courteous. The talk had hardly begun, so the content could not have offended him. Moreover, he had invited my wife and me to dinner at his home, which we later attended. Whatever the reason, Freeman seemed to enjoy the minidrama that the situation provided.

Over the years, according to Freeman's colleagues, he had more or less successfully interrupted, harassed, and intimidated a number of speakers. This pattern had become normal and even predictable. While some people who attended the talk commended me for daring to ask Freeman to be courteous, I was chastened that this group of very intelligent people had come to view Freeman's conduct as an expected part of department functions and could not prevent it, apart from sharing stories about him. A number of them did not respect Freeman as a person, and they acknowledged that his behavior was corrosive. Of course, they knew far more about him than I did; they also knew that, as problematic as Freeman was, the university administration had not taken disciplinary measures against him.

Another incident at ANU gave me additional insight into Freeman. There was a symposium on campus, and one of the participants presented a paper on the Mead-Freeman controversy. Freeman was in the audience near the front of the auditorium. After listening to the paper he rose and stated that the speaker had "really meant" something different from the wording in the talk; he then proceeded to provide the "correct" wording. The speaker replied that he had employed that very wording in an *earlier* draft of his presentation, but he had used Liquid Paper to erase the original wording and revise it for the talk. Did Freeman know of the original wording? Freeman declared that he had a copy of the paper and that when he held it up to the light, he could see through the Liquid Paper *and* discern for himself the speaker's intent. Furthermore, Freeman would hold him to the earlier wording. The speaker was dumbfounded. Freeman was holding him responsible for wording that he had already changed! It was another moment of high drama for Freeman. The audience expressed some dismay at Freeman's behavior, for the speaker had no hidden agenda; he had simply revised his paper. Members of the audience shook their heads, wondering what Freeman was trying to accomplish.

I was sitting in the back of the lecture hall, and after seeing how Freeman used the speaker's words I realized that any correspondence with Freeman had the potential to be quoted out of context. This is why I rarely corresponded with him and why I had almost nothing to do with the controversy for the next eight years. I was not alone in my reluctance to write to Freeman. A number of other scholars also discontinued correspondence with him for similar reasons. He nevertheless wrote regularly, accusing me of a litany of sins, from being incompetent to being unprofessional and unscholarly, all in my allegedly vain attempt to defend Mead. These letters were often generic correspondence that he sent to others and did not require a response. Even knowing this, I experienced a strange feeling whenever I received an envelope from Australia in the mail. Sometimes I received two a week. Fortunately, Freeman did not use e-mail.

In his letters Freeman would sometimes ask a very specific question, such as "Do you believe that Margaret Mead was correct in her 1928 conclusion that only cultural variables can explain human behavior?" His goal was to get respondents to take sides and go on record as being for or against Mead and, by implication, for or against Freeman. He explained this calculated strategy in an interview with Hiram Caton: "And then I asked them if they agree with me to the conclusion in *Coming of Age*, and quoting her exact words, and that they seem to find [it] most difficult to answer, because if they say, No they don't agree with those words, they must side with me. If they say Yes, they're demonstratively wrong in the light of modern knowledge." This was Freeman's version of the classic question: "Have you stopped beating your wife recently?" Either a yes or a no answer would get you in trouble. Freeman would batch-mail these letters and send them again if there was no reply: "I'm still sending them greeting cards, and saying to them 'When are you going to reply to my letter and so and so . . . ?' and I also point out to them that this whole process is a part of history, and that their failure to reply is an historical artefact now."[12]

In fact, Freeman's ability to lift words out of context and use them for his own purposes became a central issue in the Mead-Freeman controversy. It was the issue that eventually drew me back into the controversy in the early 1990s. At that time Mel and Carol Ember asked me to write a chapter introducing the controversy to a college audience.[13] As I was writing I returned to the original sources that Freeman was quoting. To my surprise I found that Freeman took a number of quotations out of context, misrepresented authors, or neglected them altogether in advancing his critique of Mead. So I reentered the controversy in the mid-1990s by documenting just how often and how seriously Freeman misrepresented original sources.[14] Indeed, I continue to do so in this book, quoting those sources at some length so that readers can understand how Freeman used them. Even now, when I reread Freeman on Mead, he is so convincing that I find myself revisiting original sources once again to appreciate how cleverly he assembled his argument.[15]

In summary, I hardly knew Margaret Mead, and I knew Derek Freeman only slightly better. They were major figures. Their work was different from mine, and our intellectual paths rarely crossed. It was only after the controversy became a significant event for anthropologists, the media, and the public at large that they became an important part of my own work. As a result, even though I did not know them well on a personal basis, I came to learn a good deal about them. Because of who they were many people who did know them went out of their way to help me understand both Mead and Freeman. In this book I have tried to share some of what they conveyed to me as a means of furthering our knowledge about the controversy.

NOTES

Foreword

1. See, for example, Brown, *Charles Beard and the Constitution*; McDonald, *We the People*.
2. See Lefkowitz, *History Lesson*; for a thoughtful review of *History Lesson* and the larger controversy it describes, see McCabe, "Grey Matter."

Introduction

1. These statistics are from the introduction to the documentary film *Margaret Mead and Samoa*, directed by Frank Heimans. For the definitive work on Mead as an American icon, see Lutkehaus, "Margaret Mead."
2. "Margaret Mead Today."
3. Courtesy of the Institute for Intercultural Studies, Inc., New York. No one seems to know when or where these words were actually spoken.
4. See "I Let These Words Guide Me."
5. Mead's testimony appears in the documentary film *Margaret Mead: Taking Note* by Ann Peck.
6. Mead can be seen discussing these themes in Jean Rouch's documentary *Margaret Mead: A Portrait by a Friend*.
7. Kristof, "The Texas Governor."
8. Mead was awarded the medal in 1979.
9. McDowell, "New Samoa Book"; also in Caton, *Samoa Reader*, 211–16.
10. Caton, "What the Fighting Was About," 208.
11. See Mead's introduction to the 1928 edition of *Coming of Age in Samoa*.
12. Freeman, *Mead and Samoa*, 295.
13. Heimans, "Recorded Interview," 74.
14. Caton, "The Mead/Freeman Controversy Is Over," 587.
15. For bibliographies on the controversy see Caton, *Samoa Reader*; Côté, *Adolescent Storm and Stress*; Côté, "Implausibility."
16. Howard, "Angry Storm," 67.
17. Freeman, "Paradigms in Collision: Margaret Mead's Mistake," 68.
18. Freeman, "Paradigms in Collision: Margaret Mead's Mistake," 68.
19. Freeman, "Paradigms in Collision: Margaret Mead's Mistake," 68.

20. Freeman, "Paradigms in Collision: Margaret Mead's Mistake," 68.
21. Freeman, *Mead and Samoa*, 302; see also Freeman, *Fateful Hoaxing*, 217.
22. Freeman, "Paradigms in Collision: The Far-Reaching Controversy," and "Paradigms in Collision: Margaret Mead's Mistake."
23. Freeman, "Margaret Mead's *Coming of Age*," 110.
24. Côté, "Much Ado."
25. Heimans, "Recorded Interview," 95.
26. Freeman to Shankman, May 12, 1997.
27. Freeman to Shankman, May 12, 1997.
28. Heimans, "Recorded Interview," 97.
29. Freeman to James Côté, September 10, 1994, with a copy to Shankman.
30. Heimans, "Recorded Interview," 96.
31. Freeman, "Controversy," 64–66.
32. Michael Shermer, personal communication, 2000.
33. Frazier to Freeman, December 22, 1998.
34. Frazier to Freeman, July 23, 2000.
35. Freeman, *Mead and Samoa*, xiii.
36. Freeman, *Fateful Hoaxing*, 205–6.
37. For Freeman's assessment of Mead's achievements see Freeman, *Mead and Samoa*, xiii.
38. Freeman, *Mead and Samoa*, 295.
39. Freeman on the *Donahue* show, March 18, 1983.
40. Mac Marshall noted this in "Wizard of Oz," his article on the style of Freeman's argument.
41. Freeman, *Mead and Samoa*, 301.
42. Freeman, personal communication, April 1984.
43. Freeman, *Fateful Hoaxing*, 160.
44. Freeman, "There's Tricks," 116.
45. Fox, *Participant Observer*, 339.
46. Howard, "Angry Storm," 67.
47. Dembart, "Attack."
48. See Freeman, "All Made," "Controversy," and "Inductivism"; and Shankman, "All Things Considered," "History of Samoan Sexual," "Samoan Conundrum," and "Sex, Lies."
49. Fox, "A Life," 7.
50. Orans, *Not Even Wrong*, 14.
51. Mead, *Blackberry*, 315.

Chapter 1. The Controversy in the Media

1. McDowell, "New Samoa Book."
2. Rusher, "Margaret Mead: Her Facts are Suspect."
3. Goodman, "Muckraking."
4. Dembart, "Attack."
5. *Tales from the Jungle: Margaret Mead*, directed by Peter Oxley.
6. Dembart, "Attack."
7. This general scenario was envisioned by Sahlins in "Cannibalism."

8. Price, "Coming a Cropper."
9. Jaroff, "Margaret Mead," 183.
10. Henrie, Myers, and Nelson, "The Fifty Worst."
11. Human Events.com, "Ten Most Harmful."
12. Wiker, *10 Books*.
13. Molloy, "Margaret Mead," 40.
14. Bateson, letter to *New York Times*.
15. Marcus, "One Man's Mead."
16. Schneider, "The Coming," 4.
17. Weiner, "Ethnographic Determinism," 918.
18. For example, Schneider, Weiner, Marcus, and Marvin Harris ("The Sleep-Crawling Question") come from very diverse theoretical positions, yet each strongly criticized Freeman's book.
19. The chair of the panel was Ivan Brady, and members included Bradd Shore, Lowell Holmes, and Annette Weiner. Their papers were published in a special issue of *American Anthropologist* 85, no. 4 (1983).
20. Quote from Caton, editor's note, *Samoa Reader*, 229.
21. Freeman, "O Rose Thou Art Sick."
22. Freeman, "Open Letter," 7.
23. Freeman, "Paradigms in Collision: Margaret Mead's Mistake," 70.
24. Appell and Madan, "Derek Freeman," 23.

Chapter 2. Selling the Controversy

1. Angier, "Coming of Age"; Freeman, "The Case."
2. Howard, "Angry Storm," 66.
3. Fields, "Controversial Book," 27.
4. Shore, *Sala'ilua*; Shore, "Evaluations."
5. I transcribed the show from a videotape. I am grateful to Lowell Holmes for lending me his copy of the tape.
6. Freeman had written one chapter criticizing sociobiology in an edited volume on sociobiology (Freeman, "Sociobiology"). However, after the controversy began Freeman found that sociobiologists and evolutionary psychologists were among his supporters, and he would later recommend their works in his correspondence.
7. Bradd Shore, personal communication, July 8, 2008.
8. Heimans, "Recorded Interview," 73. Freeman was unsuccessful in these attempts.
9. Christine Ullrich, personal communication, April 10, 2000.
10. The interview portion appeared as Freeman, "Fa'apua'a Fa'amū."
11. Unasa, "Research Materials" (1993), 39.
12. Galea'i Poumele, interviewed by Frank Heimans, in Unasa, "Research Materials" (1993), 4.
13. Freeman, "There's Tricks," 116; Freeman, *Fateful Hoaxing*, 3.
14. Freeman, "There's Tricks," 116.
15. Heimans, "Recorded Interview," 85.
16. Heimans recalled Freeman's reaction in the 2006 BBC documentary on the controversy, *Tales from the Jungle: Margaret Mead*.
17. Freeman, "Paradigms in Collision: The Far-Reaching Controversy."

18. Insert in the program for the Sydney Theatre Company's World Premiere Production of *Heretic*, which opened at the Sydney Opera House on March 28, 1996.

19. Monaghan, "Fantasy," 8.

20. Dust jacket cover from the 1996 paperback edition of Williamson, *Heretic*.

21. Williamson, *Heretic*, 10.

22. Williamson, *Heretic*, 7.

23. Heimans, "Recorded Interview," 91.

24. Barrowclough, "Sex, Lies."

25. See the dust jacket cover endorsements on the cloth editions of both of Freeman's books (*Mead and Samoa* and *Fateful Hoaxing*).

26. Gardner, "Margaret Mead's Great Samoan Hoax," 38.

Chapter 3. Derek Freeman, the Critic

1. See Freeman's obituaries in the *Los Angeles Times* (Staff and Wire Reports, "Derek Freeman; Professor, Mead Critic," August 6, 2001, B9) and the *New York Times* (John Shaw, "Derek Freeman, Who Challenged Margaret Mead on Samoa, Dies at 84," August 5, 2001, 24).

2. Freeman received the Curl Bequest Prize for his essay "On the Concept of the Kindred."

3. See Appell and Madan, "Derek Freeman," 27–30, for these references and Freeman's complete bibliography to 1988.

4. This chapter is based on several sources, including Freeman's unpublished intellectual autobiography ("Culture and Human Nature"), Appell and Madan's intellectual biography of Freeman ("Derek Freeman"), Hempenstall's introduction to Freeman's study of a Samoan village community (Freeman, *Social Structure*), and, on the events in Borneo, the work of Judith Heimann (*The Most Offending*) and Hiram Caton ("Conversion"). Caton's work has been especially valuable, and I have benefited from his extensive knowledge of Freeman. Caton's anthology, *The Samoa Reader*, is an important resource on the controversy. On an informal level I spoke with dozens of Freeman's colleagues long before I thought about writing this book as well as during its writing. These conversations have informed this chapter and the book as a whole.

5. Heimans, "Recorded Interview," 8.

6. Freeman, "The Question of Questions." This unpublished manuscript was provided to me by Ray Scupin. It is now available in a collection of Freeman's essays (Freeman, *Dilthey's Dream*).

7. Heimans, "Recorded Interview," 12.

8. Hempenstall, introduction to Freeman, *Social Structure*, xiv.

9. Sinclair, *Halfway Round*, 85–86.

10. Hempenstall, introduction to Freeman, *Social Structure*, xiv.

11. Now published as Freeman, *Social Structure*.

12. Fox, *Participant Observer*, 338.

13. Appell and Madan, "Derek Freeman," 6.

14. Heimans, "Recorded Interview," 24.

15. Appell and Madan, "Derek Freeman," 12.

16. For this section I have drawn more heavily on the work of Caton ("Conversion" and "The Exalted Self") and Heimann (*The Most Offending*). In "The Exalted

Self," Caton provides a diagnosis of Freeman's condition. See Monaghan, "Archival Analysis."

17. Caton, "Conversion," 5.

18. Caton, "Conversion," 10.

Chapter 4. Psychoanalysis, Freeman, and Mead

1. Mead, Benedict, and Sapir were all deeply interested in psychoanalysis during the 1920s. Mead's interest in and involvement with psychoanalysis continued throughout her life (see Silverstein, "Boasian Cosmographic Anthropology").

2. Côté, "The Correspondence," 66. Côté examined Mead's correspondence from this period.

3. Côté, "The Correspondence," 66.

4. Heimans, "Recorded Interview," 49.

5. Appell and Madan, "Derek Freeman," 15.

6. Freeman, *Mead and Samoa,* xiv.

7. Shankman, "Margaret Mead's Other Samoa."

8. Kroeber, review of *Growing Up in New Guinea,* 248.

9. Fox, *Participant Observer,* 339.

10. In 1974 Richard Goodman received a letter from Mead mentioning that she had talked with Freeman again in the fall of 1973. To my knowledge neither Mead nor Freeman has discussed this exchange. Mead, "*Coming of Age* Defended," 115.

11. Heimans, "Recorded Interview," 52, 55.

12. Barrowclough, "Sex, Lies," 37.

13. This relationship is explored in Williamson's play *Heretic* and in a popular article about Freeman published in the *Sydney Morning Herald Magazine* (see Barrowclough, "Sex, Lies").

14. Heimans, "Recorded Interview," 55.

15. Caton, "Talking to a Heretic," 78.

16. Barrowclough, "Sex, Lies," 37.

17. Heimans, "Recorded Interview," 56.

18. Freeman, *Fateful Hoaxing,* 205, 206.

19. Barrowclough, "Sex, Lies," 37.

20. Caffrey and Francis, *To Cherish,* 316.

21. In his interview with Barrowclough, Freeman mentions that he took psychoanalytic notes on Mead during their private meeting (Barrowclough, "Sex, Lies," 37).

22. Romanucci-Ross, "Mead Recognizes," 323.

23. Mead, "Social Organization," 228.

24. Freeman, personal communication, February 20, 1999.

25. Holmes and Freeman, "From the Holmes-Freeman," 319.

26. Holmes and Freeman, "From the Holmes-Freeman," 318.

27. Holmes and Freeman, "From the Holmes-Freeman," 318.

28. A letter from J. G. Crawford to Dr. and Mrs. Freeman, October 27, 1967, quotes from an American Samoan news bulletin dated September 20, 1967. Crawford himself discounted the bulletin as irresponsible. The letter was provided to me by Hiram Caton. Far less is known about this incident than the episode in Borneo. Williamson refers to it briefly in his play (*Heretic,* 69–70), but no one else has written about it to my knowledge.

The different versions of what happened were related to me by people who were there, by others who heard the story from Freeman, and by third parties.

29. Holmes, "The Restudy."

30. Holmes and Freeman, "From the Holmes-Freeman," 316–20, emphasis in original.

31. Freeman, "There's Tricks," 116.

32. Freeman, "There's Tricks," 115–16.

33. Freeman, "Inductivism," 179.

34. Freeman, "Samoa and Mead," 7.

35. Unasa, "Research Materials" (1988), 58–59. There is no independent confirmation of Fa'apua'a's account.

36. I am grateful to Richard Goodman for providing me with a copy of this paper.

37. I first noted this in print in 1983 (Shankman, "Samoan Conundrum"). Freeman responded that it was simply a work in progress and that he had already communicated his findings to her at their meeting in 1964 (Freeman, "Inductivism," 172).

38. Freeman, "*Social Organization of Manu'a* by Mead."

39. Heimans, "Recorded Interview," 71–72. In his book Freeman states: "I offered to send her an early draft of my refutation of the conclusions she had reached in *Coming of Age in Samoa.* I received no reply to this offer before Dr. Mead's death in November of that year" (*Mead and Samoa*, xvi). There are other differences between Freeman's published and unpublished accounts of this period. In an interview he stated that but for Mead's death the book would have been published in 1979 (Heimans, "Recorded Interview," 72). In *Mead and Samoa* Freeman provides a somewhat different chronology. See also Appell and Madan's chronology ("Derek Freeman," 21–22).

40. Freeman states that although he could have published his book earlier, he wanted to give Mead a "decent period" after her death (Heimans, "Recorded Interview," 73).

41. Freeman, *Mead and Samoa*, xii; Freeman, "Paradigms in Collision: Mead's Mistake," 68; Freeman, "Controversy," 64.

42. Appell and Madan, "Derek Freeman," viii.

43. Appell and Madan, "Derek Freeman," viii.

44. Appell and Madan, "Derek Freeman," ix.

45. Heimans, "Recorded Interview," 45.

46. Freeman, "Aztec Abomination," 2.

47. Goldie, "Presentation," 2.

48. Freeman, "Aztec Abomination."

49. Interview with Derek Freeman by Joan Fitzgerald for promotion of *Heretic.* Provided by Derek Freeman.

Chapter 5. Young Margaret Mead

1. This chapter draws heavily on Mead's autobiography, *Blackberry Winter*; Jane Howard's biography, *Margaret Mead: A Life*; Luther Sheeleigh Cressman's *A Golden Journey: Memoirs of an Archaeologist*; Lois W. Banner's *Intertwined Lives: Margaret Mead, Ruth Benedict, and Their Circle*; and Hilary Lapsley's *Margaret Mead and Ruth Benedict: The Kinship of Women*. See also Phyllis Grosskurth's *Margaret Mead: A Life of Controversy*.

2. Banner, *Intertwined Lives*, 156.

3. Mead, *Blackberry*, 107.
4. Bailey, *From Front Porch.*
5. Modell, *Into One's Own*, 39–44.
6. Wetzsteon, *Republic*, 162–292.
7. Peiss, "Charity Girls."
8. Adickes, *To Be Young.*
9. Petersen, *Century of Sex.*
10. Mead, *Blackberry*, 110–11.
11. Mead, *Blackberry*, 116–17.
12. Banner, *Intertwined Lives*, 215–19.
13. Banner, *Intertwined Lives*, 160.
14. Banner, *Intertwined Lives*, 176.
15. Francis, "Something to Think With," 5.
16. Mead, *Blackberry*, 122.
17. See Francis, "Margaret Mead and Psychology," for information on Mead's background in psychology.
18. Mead, *Blackberry*, 123.
19. Mead, *Blackberry*, 126.
20. Cressman, *Golden Journey*, 92–93.
21. Mead, *Blackberry*, 129.
22. Mead, *Blackberry*, 132, 134.
23. Cressman, *Golden Journey*, 129.
24. Banner, *Intertwined Lives*, 176–77; Lapsley, *Margaret Mead*, 67–68.
25. Mead, *Blackberry*, 125.
26. Mead's relationship with Benedict was made public in her daughter's sensitive memoir (Bateson, *With a Daughter's Eye*).
27. Caffrey and Francis, *To Cherish*, 55.
28. Cressman, *Golden Journey*, 126.
29. Lapsley, *Margaret Mead*, 124.
30. Mead, *Coming of Age.*
31. Mead, *Blackberry*, 137.
32. Cressman, *Golden Journey*, 114.
33. Caffrey and Francis, *To Cherish*, 54.
34. Banner, *Intertwined Lives*, 268.

Chapter 6. First Fieldwork in Samoa

1. Mead, *Letters*, 19.
2. This chapter, like the previous one, relies heavily on Mead's autobiography (*Blackberry Winter*) and the work of her biographers Howard (*Margaret Mead*), Banner (*Intertwined Lives*), and Lapsley (*Margaret Mead*).
3. Caffrey and Francis, *To Cherish*, 54.
4. Chappell, "Forgotten *Mau*"; Field, *Mau.*
5. Mead, *Letters*, 29.
6. Mead, *Letters*, 28.
7. See Orans, *Not Even Wrong*, 24, on the number of Samoans Mead studied.
8. Mead, *Letters*, 29.

9. Freeman, *Fateful Hoaxing*, 161.
10. See, for example, Barley, *Adventures*; Raybeck, *Mad Dogs*.
11. Banner, *Intertwined Lives*, 240.
12. Mead, *Letters*, 28.
13. This was the experience of Richard Goodman, an independent scholar.
14. Mead, *Letters*, 35.
15. O'Meara, *Samoan Planters*, 41.
16. Mead, *Blackberry*, 161.
17. Mead, *Blackberry*, 162.
18. Mead, *Blackberry*, 163.
19. Freeman, *Fateful Hoaxing*, 228.
20. Orans, *Not Even Wrong*, 19–20.
21. Mead, *Blackberry*, 163.
22. Mead, *Social Organization*, 5.
23. Malinowski, *Argonauts*, 15. See Stocking, "Ethnographer's Magic," on the origins of British field method.
24. Young, *Malinowski*, 331–52.
25. Young, *Malinowski*, 351.
26. Malinowski, letter of September 22, 1928, cited in Tiffany, "Narrative, Voice," 30.
27. Freeman, *Mead and Samoa*, 286.
28. Cox, *Nafanua*, 65.
29. Gartenstein, "Sex, Lies," 23.
30. Freeman, *Fateful Hoaxing*, 72.
31. Freeman, *Fateful Hoaxing*, 83, 97, 98, 6.
32. Freeman, *Fateful Hoaxing*, 139, 116, 123.
33. Orans, *Not Even Wrong*, 20–23.
34. Mead, *Blackberry*, 162.
35. Freeman, *Fateful Hoaxing*, 102.
36. Banner, *Intertwined Lives*, 239.
37. Mead, *Blackberry*, 43–44.
38. Caffrey and Francis, *To Cherish*, 204.
39. Freeman, *Fateful Hoaxing*, 157.

Chapter 7. Writing *Coming of Age in Samoa*

1. Mead, *Blackberry*, 177, 178.
2. Mead, *Blackberry*, 177–78; Lapsley, *Margaret Mead*, 167. For another version of how Cressman learned of Mead's condition, see Howard, *Margaret Mead*, 48.
3. Mead in Gordan, *Margaret Mead*, 3; Lutkehaus, "Margaret Mead."
4. Mead, *Coming of Age*, 14.
5. Tiffany, "Imagining," 25.
6. Tiffany, "Imagining," 24.
7. Banner, *Intertwined Lives*, 231.
8. Molloy, "Margaret Mead," 33.
9. Mead in Gordan, *Margaret Mead*, 2–3.
10. Molloy, *On Creating*.
11. Mead, *An Inquiry*.

12. Gordan, *Margaret Mead*, 67.

13. Côté, "The Correspondence," 64.

14. Banner, *Intertwined Lives*, 243.

15. Mead, *Coming of Age*, 25.

16. Mead, *Coming of Age*, 155–56. Although Mead completed her dissertation in 1925, she did not receive her Ph.D. degree until 1928, when the dissertation was actually published, as required by Columbia at that time (Cressman, *Golden Journey*, 113).

17. Mead, *Coming of Age*, 157; Mead, "Apprenticeship," 30.

18. Freeman, *Mead and Samoa*, 295.

19. Mead, "Apprenticeship," 30.

20. Mead, *Blackberry*, 147–49, 139, 131.

21. Mead, *Coming of Age*, 195, 261.

22. Orans, *Not Even Wrong*.

23. Orans, *Not Even Wrong*, 153.

24. Mead, preface to *Coming of Age*, n.p.

25. Mead, *Coming of Age*, 3–13.

26. Mead, *Coming of Age*, ii.

27. Mead, *Coming of Age*, 13.

28. Mead, *Coming of Age*, 222.

29. Mead, *Coming of Age*, 222.

30. Mead, *Coming of Age*, 211.

31. Mead, *Coming of Age*, 253.

32. Lutkehaus, "Margaret Mead," 191.

33. Orans, *Not Even Wrong*, 157.

34. Shankman, "Margaret Mead's Other Samoa."

35. Firth, *We the Tikopia*.

36. Shankman, "Margaret Mead's Other Samoa," 55. Anthropologists George Marcus and Michael Fischer provided a perceptive analysis of *Coming of Age in Samoa* as cultural criticism decades ago in their important book *Anthropology as Cultural Critique*. See also Clifford, "On Ethnographic Allegory," 102–3.

37. Redfield, review of *Coming of Age*, 729–30.

38. Redfield, review of *Social Organization of Manu'a*, 512.

39. Freeman, "There's Tricks," 118.

40. Mead made very brief mention of these problems in her field notes but provided no data.

41. Molloy, *On Creating*, 51.

42. Freeman, *Fateful Hoaxing*, 191.

43. Anderson, "In the Light," 514.

44. Johnson, "Polynesian Culture," 778.

45. Molloy, *On Creating*, 52.

46. Murray, "On Boasians."

47. Lowie, review of *Coming of Age*, 532.

48. Sapir, "Franz Boas," 279.

49. Molloy, "Margaret Mead," 39.

50. Banner, "The Bo-Cu Plant," 24; Caton, "Talking to a Heretic," 32n12.

51. Banner, *Intertwined Lives*, 281.

52. Harris, *The Rise*, 411, 410.

53. Molloy, *On Creating*, 6.

54. Mead, *Blackberry*, 172–73.

Chapter 8. Mead's American Audience in the 1920s

1. Tiffany, "Imagining," 24, 23.

2. Molloy, "Margaret Mead," 38.

3. Mead, *Coming of Age*, 1.

4. Mead, *Coming of Age*, 244.

5. Mead, *Coming of Age*, 2.

6. Mead, *Coming of Age*, 247.

7. Goodsell, *Problems of the Family*, 420, quoted in Holmes and Holmes, *Samoan Village*, 141–42.

8. Mead, *Coming of Age*, 244.

9. Petersen, *Century of Sex*, chap. 3.

10. Bailey, *From Front Porch*.

11. Lynd and Lynd, *Middletown*, 242.

12. Editors of Time-Life Books, *This Fabulous Century*, 45.

13. Lynd and Lynd, *Middletown*, 137–38.

14. Editors of Time-Life Books, *This Fabulous Century*, 41.

15. Lynd and Lynd, *Middletown*, 241–42.

16. Moriarty, *True Confessions*, 48.

17. Modell, *Into One's Own*, 67–120.

18. Modell, *Into One's Own*, 85.

19. Modell, *Into One's Own*, 97.

20. Petersen, *Century of Sex*, 83.

21. Petersen, *Century of Sex*, 92–95.

22. Mead, *Coming of Age*, 243–44.

23. Wetzsteon, *Republic*, 162–289.

24. Millay, *A Few Figs*, 9.

25. Mead, *Blackberry*, 144.

26. Lynd and Lynd, *Middletown in Transition*, 169.

27. Maines, *The Technology of Orgasm*, 20, 108–9.

28. Lynd and Lynd, *Middletown in Transition*, 162.

29. Folsom, *The Family*, 10–25, quoted in Holmes and Holmes, *Samoan Village*, 141, my formatting.

30. Manchester, *Goodbye, Darkness*, 542–43.

31. Modell, *Into One's Own*, 98.

32. Sapir, "Discipline of Sex," 417.

33. Mead, *Anthropologists and What They Do*, quoted in Holmes, *Quest*, 10.

34. Mead, *Coming of Age*, 197.

35. Mead, *Coming of Age*, 204.

36. Mead, *Coming of Age*, 198–99.

37. Even today, nearly 30 percent of Americans cannot identify the South Pacific on a map of the world, although it constitutes one-third of the planet's surface area (*Rocky Mountain News*, January 16, 2006, 1D).

38. Sturma, *South Sea Maidens*; O'Brien, *The Pacific Muse*.

39. Horwitz, *Blue Latitudes,* 42.
40. Poignant, *Professional Savages,* 198–200.
41. Furnas, *Anatomy,* 419–21.
42. Furnas, *Anatomy,* 412–14.
43. Furnas, *Anatomy,* 414.
44. Nordström, "Early Photography" and "Paradise Recycled"; see also Blanton, *Picturing Paradise.*
45. Flaherty, "Setting Up House."
46. Flaherty, "Behind the Scenes."
47. O'Brien, *White Shadows.*
48. Mead, "Arts in Bali," 336.

Chapter 9. What the Controversy Meant to Samoans

1. Freeman, "There's Tricks," 103.
2. Mason's former student was Chief Albert Lutali, shown in *Margaret Mead and Samoa,* directed by Heimans.
3. *Margaret Mead and Samoa,* directed by Heimans.
4. Mead, preface to *Coming of Age,* n.p.
5. Mead, preface to *Coming of Age,* n.p.
6. Mead, *Blackberry,* 13.
7. See Critchfield, *Villages,* 189–208, for his interview with Jesús Sanchez, the head of the Sanchez family.
8. Hereniko, "Indigenous Knowledge," 89.
9. Nardi, "Height"; Tiffany, "Imagining" and "Narrative, Voice."
10. Tupuola, "Learning Sexuality," 66.
11. Orans had a similar experience (*Not Even Wrong,* 13–14).
12. Cox, *Nafanua,* 67.
13. See Shore, *Sala'ilua,* on this distinction.
14. Maxwell, "Comparison," 469–70.
15. Theroux, "Coming of Age."
16. O'Meara, *Samoan Planters,* 94–95.
17. Moyle, "Sexuality."
18. Gerber, "Cultural Patterning."
19. Tuiatua, "Riddle," 76.
20. Weiner, "Ethnographic Determinism," 914.
21. Milner, *Samoan Dictionary,* xii–xiii.
22. Meleise'a, *Making of Modern Samoa,* vii–viii; see also Meleise'a, "Postmodern Legacy."
23. Shore's early critique of Freeman, "Paradox Regained," makes this point especially well.
24. Mead, *Social Organization,* 5.
25. Freeman, "There's Tricks," 113; Freeman, *Fateful Hoaxing,* 161.
26. Mead, "Life," 15.
27. Freeman, *Fateful Hoaxing,* 125.
28. Unasa, "The Mead-Freeman Debate."
29. Orans, *Not Even Wrong,* 14.

30. Trumbull, "Samoan Leader Declares."

31. Mataʻafa, letter to the editor, 7–8.

32. Lelaulu, letter to the editor, 8.

33. Wendt, "Three Faces," 12, 14.

34. Wendt et al., Untitled, 98–99.

35. Stover, "Samoan Responses," reviews the variety of Samoan positions on the controversy.

36. Malopaʻupo, *Coming of Age*, 2, 11, 12.

37. Unasa, "The Mead-Freeman Debate," 4–5.

38. Figiel, *Where We Once*, 204–5.

39. *Observer,* April 6, 1983, 2.

40. Holmes, *Samoan Village,* 102.

41. Shankman, "Samoan Conundrum," 52.

42. Shankman, "Samoan Conundrum"; O'Meara, *Samoan Planters,* 109–12; Macpherson and Macpherson, "Towards an Explanation."

43. Shankman, "Samoan Conundrum," 52.

44. Janes, *Migration.*

45. Sullivan, "Gangs of Zion."

46. Tupuola, "Learning Sexuality," 61.

Chapter 10. Samoan Sexual Conduct

1. Shweder, "Storytelling."

2. Marshall, "Wizard of Oz," 605; see also Feinberg, "Margaret Mead and Samoa," 662.

3. Marcus, "One Man's Mead."

4. Scheper-Hughes, "The Margaret Mead Controversy," 90.

5. Freeman, "Reply to Ember's Reflections," 911–12.

6. Malinowski, *Sexual Life,* xxvi, xxiii.

7. Freeman, *Mead and Samoa,* 239, xx.

8. Tuzin, "Discourse," 259.

9. Richard Goodman, in *Margaret Mead and Samoa,* directed by Heimans.

10. Freeman, *Mead and Samoa,* 236.

11. Freeman, *Mead and Samoa,* 245, 234, 236.

12. Freeman, "Inductivism," 161, 125.

13. Freeman, *Mead and Samoa,* 23, 236.

14. Shore, *Salaʻilua,* 229.

15. Shore, *Salaʻilua,* 229–30.

16. Shore, "Sexuality and Gender," 197. Bonnie Nardi, who worked on reproductive decision-making in Western Samoa, reached similar conclusions in "The Height of Her Powers," 329.

17. Schoeffel and Meleiseʻa, "Margaret Mead," 59.

18. O'Meara, *Samoan Planters,* 105.

19. This comment came from a senior auditor in my course on the South Pacific. She had read *Coming of Age in Samoa* in the 1930s.

20. Mead, *Coming of Age,* 160, 215.

21. Mead, *Coming of Age,* 282–95, 285.

22. Mead, *Coming of Age*, 285. Orans uses the figure 44 percent rather than Mead's 47 percent because one of the adolescents was raped as a young girl (*Not Even Wrong*, 44). I follow his calculations. Orans provides a thorough reanalysis of Mead's quantitative data, finding a number of simple numerical errors in her work.

23. Freeman, *Mead and Samoa*, 239.

24. Freeman, "Inductivism," 124.

25. Mead, *Coming of Age*, 146.

26. Seidman, *Romantic Longings*, 22.

27. Hofferth, Kahn, and Baldwin, "Premarital Sexual Activity," 48.

28. Klassen, Williams, and Levitt, *Sex and Morality*.

29. Rubin, *Erotic Wars*, 61.

30. Kaiser Family Foundation and *Seventeen*, "*SexSmarts* Survey."

31. Altman, "Study."

32. Freking, "2003 Study"; see also Herzog, *Sex in Crisis*, 93–125.

33. EDK Associates, Telephone Survey.

34. *Rocky Mountain News*, February 25, 1992.

35. On the complex relationship between belief and behavior in Brazil see Goldstein, *Laughter*, 310.

Chapter 11. Under the Coconut Palms

1. Mead, *Coming of Age*, 44.

2. Mead, *Coming of Age*, 86–96.

3. Meleiseʻa, *Lagaga*, 157.

4. Calkins, *My Samoan Chief*, 121.

5. Calkins, *My Samoan Chief*, 121.

6. Calkins, *My Samoan Chief*, 122.

7. O'Meara, *Samoan Planters*, 108, 105.

8. This story was told to me by a Peace Corps volunteer in 1970.

9. Maxwell, "Comparison," 476.

10. O'Meara, *Samoan Planters*, 108.

11. O'Meara, *Samoan Planters*, 107.

12. Mead, *Coming of Age*, 93.

13. Orans, *Not Even Wrong*, 52.

14. Freeman, *Mead and Samoa*, 245–48.

15. Freeman, *Mead and Samoa*, 240.

16. Freeman, "Social Structure of a Samoan Village," 208.

17. Freeman, *Mead and Samoa*, 240.

18. Mead, *Coming of Age*, 93.

19. O'Meara, *Samoan Planters*, 107.

20. Freeman, *Mead and Samoa*, 248–49.

21. O'Meara, *Samoan Planters*, 107.

22. Macpherson and Macpherson, "The Ifoga."

23. Freeman, *Mead and Samoa*, 248, 249.

24. Côté, *Adolescent Storm*, 43–46; Nardi, "Height," 331.

25. Gerber, "Cultural Patterning," 136.

26. Freeman, *Fateful Hoaxing*, 154.

27. Freeman, *Mead and Samoa*, xvi.

28. This question was part of a broader conversation that Freeman and I had at the Australian National University in 1984.

29. One line of evidence comes from an unpublished interview with Fa'apua'a (Unasa, "Research Materials" [1988], 37). In 1988 she was asked if she knew of rape in Manu'a in the early decades of the twentieth century. Having lived most of her life there, she was in a position to know. Fa'apua'a replied that she did not know of any rapes that occurred in Manu'a and then volunteered that she and other young women felt perfectly safe walking unaccompanied near the village. It is difficult to know to what extent this testimony is accurate. Freeman did not include it in his critique of Mead.

30. Gerber, "Cultural Patterning," 135.

31. Tupuola, "Learning Sexuality," 70.

32. Aguilera, Sherry, and Migoya, "Culture."

33. Levine, *Wallowing*, 208–51.

34. Maxwell, "Samoan Temperament," 231. Maxwell emphasized the possibility of bias in the data.

35. Nardi, "Height," 329.

36. Freeman, *Fateful Hoaxing*, 177.

37. Mead, *Coming of Age*, 54–56, 153, 168, 181; see also Orans, *Not Even Wrong*, 61–63.

38. Holmes and Holmes, *Samoan Village*, 90.

39. Mead, *Coming of Age*, 153–54.

40. Mead, *Coming of Age*, 153.

41. Annandale, "Development," 59. Nardi found that mothers worried about the public disgrace of a daughter's pregnancy more than the loss of virginity itself ("Height," 329).

42. This was the title of her article in *Esquire*.

43. Mead, *Coming of Age*, 284–85.

44. Mead, *Coming of Age*, 149, 147–48.

45. In the documentary film *Paradise Bent* the narrator reports that Freeman was asked to comment on the role of *fa'afafine* for the film but declined to do so.

46. Dolgoy, "The Search."

47. O'Meara, *Samoan Planters*, 71–72.

48. Schmidt, "Paradise Lost?"; see also Fraser, "Where Boys."

49. Despite all the survey data on premarital sex in America, there has been relatively little in-depth ethnographic work (see Thompson, *Going All the Way*; and Carpenter, *Virginity Lost*). For Samoa, even less is known on a systematic basis.

50. I have borrowed these metaphors—Dominating Father and Nurturant Mother—from Walter DiMantova, a former undergraduate honors student.

51. Tiffany, "Imagining," 27.

52. Orans's useful synthesis is very brief and to the point ("Hoaxing," 616). Some families are quite restrictive concerning heterosexual relationships by their adolescent daughters; other families range from less restrictive to far less restrictive. The church, church schools, and secular schools are similarly restrictive of heterosexual relationships. If asked, adolescent girls would say that affairs are wrong. Girls are sometimes severely beaten if they have a heterosexual relationship. Nevertheless, some girls have clandestine affairs, and some mothers may encourage high-ranking or wealthy male marriage prospects to be interested in their daughters. Bragging about male sexual

exploits is common. And, lastly, there is a widespread appreciation of sexual attraction and sexual prowess. For a thoughtful overall synthesis of Mead and Freeman see Feinberg, "Margaret Mead and Samoa."

Chapter 12. Virginity and the History of Sex in Samoa

1. Freeman, *Mead and Samoa*, 227, 253, 232, 236.
2. This portrait of the *taupou* is drawn from Freeman, *Mead and Samoa*.
3. Freeman, *Mead and Samoa*, 230–31.
4. Freeman, *Mead and Samoa*, 236; Mead, *Coming of Age*, 275, 98.
5. Freeman, *Mead and Samoa*, 350, 239.
6. Mead, *Coming of Age*, 274.
7. Freeman, *Mead and Samoa*, 350.
8. Mead, "The Adolescent Girl."
9. Mead, *Coming of Age*, 266–77, app. 3.
10. Mead, *Coming of Age*, 259.
11. Mead, *Coming of Age*, 98.
12. Mead, *Coming of Age*, 100–101.
13. Mead, *Coming of Age*, 273–74.
14. See Goldman, *Ancient Polynesian Society*, chap. 11, for a general outline of Samoan social and political structure.
15. Freeman, *Mead and Samoa*, 229–30.
16. Freeman, *Mead and Samoa*, 236.
17. Williams, *Samoan Journals*, 233.
18. Williams, *Samoan Journals*, 233.
19. Williams, *Samoan Journals*, 247–48.
20. Tcherkézoff details these possible misunderstandings in *"First Contacts."* See also Schoeffel, "Sexual Morality."
21. Gilson, *Samoa 1830–1900*, 96; Davidson, *Samoa mo Samoa*, 35.
22. Schoeffel, "The Samoan Concept," 103.
23. Williams, *Samoan Journals*, 283.
24. Daws, "Great Samoan Awakening"; Tiffany, "Politics."
25. Freeman, *Mead and Samoa*, 239.
26. Turner, *Nineteen Years*, 184.
27. Murray, *Forty Years' Missionary Work*, 41.
28. Shankman, "Interethnic Unions."
29. Stevenson, *A Footnote to History*, 26.
30. Gilson, *Samoa 1830–1900*, 179, 180.
31. Meleise'a, *The Making*, 157.
32. Krämer, *Die Samoa-inseln*, 36 (*The Samoa Islands*, 47n88).
33. Krämer, *Die Samoa-inseln*, 36 (47n87).
34. Krämer, *Die Samoa-inseln*, 36 (47n87).
35. Keesing, "The Taupo System," 7.
36. Keesing, "The Taupo System," 5.
37. Freeman's 1948 thesis ("Social Structure of a Samoan Village Community") makes this clear.
38. Freeman, "Social Structure of a Samoan Village," 108.

39. Freeman, "Reply to Ember's Reflections," 914.
40. Stanner, *South Seas,* 325–26.
41. Boyd, "The Record," 185.
42. Stanner, *South Seas,* 326, 327–28.
43. Stanner, *South Seas,* 327.
44. Michener, *World Is My Home,* 38–40. On wartime interethnic unions in American Samoa see Mageo, "Spirit Girls."
45. Freeman, *Mead and Samoa,* 250.
46. Freeman, *Mead and Samoa,* xiv.
47. Shankman, "History of Samoan Sexual."
48. Freeman, personal communication, 1998.
49. Freeman, "Social Structure of a Samoan Village," 245, my emphasis.
50. Freeman, "Social Structure of a Samoan Village," 245, 108.
51. Freeman, "In Praise," 87.
52. Freeman, *Mead and Samoa,* xiv.
53. Freeman "Inductivism," 112.
54. Freeman, "Reply to Ember's Reflections," 915, 911.

Chapter 13. The Many Versions of the Hoaxing Hypothesis

1. Freeman, *Mead and Samoa,* 289–90; Freeman, "Paradigms in Collision: Margaret Mead's Mistake," 68.
2. Freeman, *Fateful Hoaxing,* 138–39, 146.
3. Freeman, *Dilthey's Dream,* 110.
4. Mead, *Letters,* 51.
5. Mead, *Letters,* 55.
6. Freeman, "Fa'apua'a Fa'amū."
7. Freeman, *Fateful Hoaxing,* 3.
8. Freeman, *Fateful Hoaxing,* 3. Other segments of the documentary reinforce the hoaxing argument. In an interview, anthropologist Lola Romanucci-Ross, who worked closely with Mead in New Guinea in the 1960s, recalled Mead's reaction to Freeman's critique after their only personal meeting in 1964. Mead was reportedly distraught, according to Romanucci-Ross, because she thought Freeman had proved her wrong. This segment of the documentary is sometimes used as independent evidence that Mead had been hoaxed but did not realize it until her personal encounter with Freeman. Yet this segment does not include Romanucci-Ross's doubts about hoaxing, which can be found in the original transcript of the interview. Romanucci-Ross was asked directly if she thought that Mead was hoaxed in Samoa; she replied that she did not think so. But this segment is not part of the documentary.
9. Côté, "Implausibility" and "Much Ado"; Orans, *Not Even Wrong.*
10. Freeman, *Fateful Hoaxing,* 134.
11. See Mead, *Coming of Age,* 52, on Pana. Freeman identified Fa'apua'a as Pana (*Fateful Hoaxing,* 117).
12. Orans, *Not Even Wrong,* 99.
13. Orans, *Not Even Wrong,* 90, 97, 92.
14. Orans, *Not Even Wrong,* 91.
15. Orans, *Not Even Wrong,* 73; Freeman, *Fateful Hoaxing,* 125.

16. Unasa, "Research Materials" (1988, 1993).
17. Freeman, *Fateful Hoaxing*, 6–13.
18. Unasa, "Research Materials" (1988), 33b, B.
19. Freeman, *Fateful Hoaxing*, 13.
20. Freeman, *Fateful Hoaxing*, 12, 13.
21. Unasa, "Research Materials" (1993), 6.
22. Unasa, "Research Materials" (1993), 1.
23. Unasa, "Research Materials" (1988), 25, 67, 68.
24. Gartenstein, "Sex, Lies," 23.
25. Unasa, "Research Materials" (1993), 44.
26. Unasa, "Research Materials" (1993), 43, 42.
27. Unasa, "Research Materials" (1988), 29, 88.
28. Unasa, "Research Materials" (1993), 42; Freeman, *Fateful Hoaxing*, 138.
29. Freeman, *Fateful Hoaxing*, 123–28; see also Tcherkézoff, "Is Anthropology?"
30. Freeman, *Fateful Hoaxing*, 14.
31. Côté, *Adolescent Storm*, 25–29; Orans, *Not Even Wrong*, 90–100.
32. Freeman, "There's Tricks," 115–16.
33. Unasa, "Research Materials" (1993), 46.
34. Freeman, "There's Tricks," 115–16, my emphasis.
35. Unasa, "Research Materials" (1993), 67.
36. Freeman, "Inductivism," 179; Freeman, "There's Tricks," 123.
37. Owen, "Samoa," 36. Unasa L. F. Va'a knew Napoleon personally, and he could not confirm the affair (Unasa, e-mail to ASAONET@listserv.uic.edu, March 1, 2008).
38. Mead, *Blackberry*, 167–68.
39. Caffrey and Francis, *To Cherish*, 203.
40. Freeman, *Fateful Hoaxing*, 141, 142.
41. Orans, "Mead Misrepresented."
42. Freeman, *Fateful Hoaxing*, 142.
43. See Orans, "Mead Misrepresented."
44. Freeman, *Fateful Hoaxing*, 231. Nardi made this same point about Samoan girls secretly subverting the wishes of their parents ("Height," 329).
45. Caffrey and Francis, *To Cherish*, 139–40.
46. Freeman, "21st Century Boasian Culturalism."
47. Mead, "Life," 94.
48. Freeman, "21st Century Boasian Culturalism," 4.
49. Shankman, "Requiem," 51–52.
50. Shankman, "Requiem," 52; Shankman, "Culture," 5.
51. Mead, "Life," 94.
52. Freeman, *Fateful Hoaxing*, 212.
53. Freeman, "There's Tricks," 117.
54. Freeman, "Paradigms in Collision: Margaret Mead's Mistake," 68.

Chapter 14. The Nature-Nurture Debate and the Appeal of Freeman's Argument

1. Freeman, "Paradigms in Collision: Margaret Mead's Mistake," 66; see also Freeman, "The Debate."

2. Pinker, *How the Mind Works,* 56.
3. Pinker, *Blank Slate,* 14.
4. Buss, "Human Nature," 963, 961.
5. Ridley, *Nature via Nurture,* 205.
6. Ridley, *Origins of Virtue,* 256, 258–59.
7. Ridley, *Origins of Virtue,* 257.
8. On Mead's role in World War II see Price, *Anthropological Intelligence.*
9. Harris and Mead, "A Conversation," 76.
10. Ghiglieri, *Dark Side,* 28.
11. Ghiglieri, *Dark Side,* 28.
12. Daly and Wilson, *Homicide,* 150.
13. Sulloway, *Born to Rebel,* 159–62; Wright, *Moral Animal,* 75–77.
14. Sommers, *BookTV* presentation.
15. Gardner, *New Age,* 19–24.
16. Freeman, *Mead and Samoa,* 295.
17. Freeman, *Fateful Hoaxing,* 217.
18. Freeman, "Paradigms in Collision: Margaret Mead's Mistake," 66–68.
19. Freeman, *Mead and Samoa,* xvi, 292, 295.
20. Freeman, *Fateful Hoaxing,* 212.
21. Freeman, *Mead and Samoa,* xvi, 281.
22. Mosse, *Nazi Culture,* 57–92.
23. Lewis, "Boas, Darwin."
24. Boas, "Race and Progress," 4.
25. Francis, "Something to Think With," 14.
26. Mead, *Blackberry,* 122.
27. Freeman, *Fateful Hoaxing,* 31.
28. Freeman, "Paradigms in Collision: Margaret Mead's Mistake," 68–69.
29. Freeman, *Mead and Samoa,* 77–78.
30. Rappaport, letter to the editors, 6–7.
31. Mead, *Coming of Age,* 197–98.
32. Rappaport, letter to the editors, 7.
33. Bennett, "Classic Anthropology."
34. Boas, foreword to *Coming of Age,* n.p.
35. Freeman, *Fateful Hoaxing,* 200–201.
36. Mead, *Blackberry,* 240–41, 243.
37. Mead, *Male and Female,* 113.
38. Mead, *Sex and Temperament,* 7.
39. Mead, *Continuities,* 10–11.
40. Mead, *Continuities,* vii.
41. Mead, *Continuities,* vii.
42. Mead, "Anthropology," 480–81.
43. Mead, "Anthropology," 481.
44. Freeman, *Fateful Hoaxing,* 182.
45. Mead, *Blackberry,* 249.
46. Caffrey and Francis, *To Cherish,* 393.
47. Hulbert, *Raising America,* 223.
48. Freeman, "Sociobiology"; Sahlins, *Use and Abuse.*

49. Wilson, *Naturalist*, 331.
50. Wilson, *Naturalist*, 348.
51. Freeman, "Sociobiology," 215, 209, my emphasis.
52. Freeman, "Sociobiology," 215.
53. Freeman, "Anthropology," 99–100.
54. Freeman, "Sociobiology."
55. Mead, *Continuities*, 31.
56. Mead, *Continuities*, 25.
57. Freeman, "Paradigms in Collision: Margaret Mead's Mistake," 70.
58. Mead, "Cultural Determinants," 496.
59. Schlegel and Barry, *Adolescence*, 41–42.
60. Schlegel, "Status, Property"; see also J. Whiting et al., "Duration."
61. Examples of more permissive societies include Mangaia (Marshall, "Sexual Behavior"), Tahiti (Levy, *Tahitians*), the Trobriands (Malinowski, *Sexual Life*), Vanatinai (Lepowsky, *Fruit*), and the Na (Hua, *A Society*). More restrictive societies include a number of societies in southern Europe, the Middle East, and Asia where honor deaths are found.
62. Sanday, "The Sociocultural Context"; Otterbein, "A Cross-Cultural Study."
63. Freeman, *Mead and Samoa*, 128.
64. Freeman, *Mead and Samoa*, 247, 250, 249, my emphasis.
65. Freeman, *Mead and Samoa*, 248, 249–50, my emphasis.
66. A final example of limitations has to do with puberty itself, a biological process. Freeman argued that a fundamental feature of puberty was that hormonal developments within the body triggered the onset of puberty, demonstrating the importance of biology in understanding human development. This is undoubtedly true. But it is also true that the age of the onset of puberty has dropped by a full four years over the last century in industrialized societies, and there is wide variation in the age of the beginning of puberty, ranging from over 18 in the New Guinea Highlands to 12.7 for the New Zealand Maori (Worthman, "Adolescence," 35). Although a precise explanation is still being developed, a probable explanation for this variability seems to be that factors such as nutrition, health, and environment may be influencing hormonal triggers (Worthman, "Adolescence," 36).

Conclusion

1. McDowell, "New Samoa Book," 213.
2. Freeman, "Fa'apua'a Fa'amū," 170.
3. Freeman, *Mead and Samoa*, xvi.
4. Freeman, "In Praise of Heresy," 88.
5. Freeman, "Paradigms in Collision: Margaret Mead's Mistake," 68–70.
6. Murray and Darnell, "Margaret Mead," 570.
7. Murray and Darnell, "Margaret Mead," 570.
8. Caton, "Talking to a Heretic."
9. Ellison, review of *Margaret Mead and Samoa*; Konner, "Bursting."
10. Heimans, "Recorded Interview," 91, 53.
11. Freeman, "Human Nature and Culture," 17.
12. For a summary of the divisions within anthropology see Morell, "Anthropology." See also Ehrenreich and McIntosh, "The New Creationism." For recent

anthropological research on questions about nature and nurture, see the essays in McKinnon and Silverman, *Complexities*.

13. American Anthropological Association, *Program*.

14. Gordan, *Margaret Mead*.

15. There was only one panel where Samoa was discussed, and only four of the fifteen panelists discussed it.

16. There has been abundant criticism of Mead's other ethnographic work, but see Molloy's assessment in *On Creating a Usable Culture*, 142.

17. The *Diane Rehm Show*.

18. Dillon, "Margaret Mead," 327–28.

19. Dillon, "Margaret Mead," 322.

20. For additional assessments and critiques of Mead's work, see di Leonardo (*Exotics*), Foerstel and Gilliam (*Confronting*), Lutkehaus ("Margaret Mead"), Yans ("On the Political Anatomy"), and Molloy (*On Creating*).

21. Cassidy, *Margaret Mead*, 13.

22. Mead, *Blackberry*, 242–43. On Mead as a popularizer, see Mitchell ("Communicating Culture").

23. Chassler, "Afterword," 280–81.

24. Friedan, *Feminine Mystique*, 126–27.

25. Bennett, *Classic Anthropology*, 367.

26. See Vogt, "Anthropology," for a review of the many anthropologists who made anthropology available to the public in the period immediately after World War II.

27. Buikstra, "Anthropology's Image."

28. Tierney, *Darkness*; Borofsky, *Yanomami*.

29. Simonelli and Pressman, "Presenting Anthropological Perspectives," 3.

30. For a recent discussion of the relevance of anthropology see the exchange between Bunzl ("The Quest" and "A Reply to Besteman and Gusterson") and Besteman and Gusterson ("A Response to Matti Bunzl").

31. Handler, *Critics*, 5.

32. Maureen Molloy's book on Mead and the public (*On Creating*) is particularly insightful. See also Lutkehaus, "Margaret Mead."

33. Tiffany has made this point in "Narrative, Voice."

34. Mead, "The Need," 467–68.

Appendix

1. Freeman to Shankman, January 6, 1999, 1.

2. Freeman to Shankman, January 6, 1999, 1–2.

3. Mead, review of *On Becoming a Kwoma*.

4. B. Whiting, *Six Cultures*.

5. Mead, review of *Six Cultures*.

6. From the dust jacket cover of Wallace's *The Three Sirens*.

7. See Kernahan, *White Savages*; and Curtis, "Tiki," for a description of these tiki bars.

8. An earlier undated and unpublished version of Goodman's monograph, *Mead's "Coming of Age in Samoa": A Dissenting View*, preceded the 1983 published version.

9. Freeman, "Inductivism," 157.

10. This conference was sponsored by the Department of Anthropology and the University of Colorado.

11. Shankman, "Fear and Loathing" and "Samoan Conundrum."

12. Caton, "Talking to a Heretic," 129.

13. Shankman, "Sex, Lies."

14. Shankman, "History of Samoan," "Requiem," and "Virginity and Veracity."

15. In his obituary for Freeman anthropologist Donald Tuzin described Freeman as a reluctant respondent to criticism during the controversy rather than an eager participant. Tuzin wrote that the initial recognition that Freeman received after the publication of his first book on Mead was

> [E]xhilarating for him, but it quickly became onerous and severely taxing of his energy and attention. Others would have walked away or stood aloof, but Freeman was devoted to [Sir Karl] Popper's dictum that the method of science is criticism; for the sake of scientific progress, then, no published criticism should go unanswered. Accordingly, with increasing weariness and frustration, Freeman continued to respond to critics until eight days before finally surrendering to congestive heart failure. ("Derek Freeman," 1013)

Although this is a fine tribute to Freeman, it should be noted that his responses to criticism often had little to do with science. He was quick to condemn *ad hominem* attacks on himself but equally quick to use them on others. For example, in one of his very last publications Freeman concluded that my critique of his hoaxing hypothesis was not the result of simple disagreement about the interpretation of Mead's writing but rather a consequence of the grand but misguided legacy of Boas and Mead:

> Consider then the sad predicament of the 57 year old Paul Shankman, who, having based his anthropological career on Boasian culturalism and Margaret Mead, finds his world falling apart, and so much so that in a state of intellectual panic he resorts to outright obfuscation in a vain attempt to prop up what is beyond question an entirely antiquated belief system. He is, it seems to me, deserving of our sympathy. (Freeman, "Controversy," 3)

BIBLIOGRAPHY

Audiovisual Materials

Diane Rehm Show. "To Cherish the Life of the World: 100 Years of Margaret Mead." National Public Radio, 2001.

Donahue. CBS, March 18, 1983.

Margaret Mead and Samoa. Documentary directed by Frank Heimans, 1988.

Margaret Mead: A Portrait by a Friend. Documentary directed by Jean Rouch, American Museum of Natural History, 1977.

Margaret Mead: Taking Note. Documentary directed by Ann Peck, PBS Odyssey series, 1981.

Moana. Documentary directed by Robert J. Flaherty, Paramount Pictures, 1925.

Paradise Bent: Boys Will Be Girls in Samoa. Documentary directed by Heather Croall and written by Karin Altmann, Torrensville, South Australia, Re Angle Pictures, 1999.

Return to Paradise. Feature film directed by Mark Robson and based on James Michener's short story "Mr. Morgan," Aspen Productions, 1953.

Sommers, Christina Hoff. *BookTV* presentation, C-SPAN 2, Independent Women's Forum, Washington, DC, January 8, 2005.

Tales from the Jungle: Margaret Mead. Documentary directed by Peter Oxley, BBC, 2006.

White Shadows in the South Seas. Feature film directed by W. S. Van Dyke, MGM, 1928.

Print Materials

Adickes, Sandra. *To Be Young Was Very Heaven: Women in New York before the First World War.* New York: St. Martin's Press, 1997.

Aguilera, Elizabeth, Allison Sherry, and David Migoya, "A Culture of Hostility." *Sunday Denver Post,* August 17, 2003, 1A, 20A, 21A.

Altman, Lawrence K. "Study Finds That Teenage Virginity Pledges Are Rarely Kept." *New York Times,* March 10, 2004, A20.

American Anthropological Association. *Program: 100th Annual Meeting.* Washington, DC: American Anthropological Association, November 28–December 2, 2001.

Anderson, Nels. "In the Light of Samoa." *Survey,* January 15, 1929, 513–14.

Angier, Natalie. "Coming of Age in Anthropology." *Discover,* April 1983, 26–30.

Annandale, Viopapa. "The Development of Family Planning Activities in Western Samoa." Postgraduate diploma thesis in public health, University of London, 1976.

Appell, G. N., and T. N. Madan. "Derek Freeman: Notes toward an Intellectual Biography." In *Choice and Morality in Anthropological Perspective,* edited by G. N. Appell and T. N. Madan, 3–30. Albany: State University of New York Press, 1988.

Bailey, Beth L. *From Front Porch to Back Seat: Courtship in Twentieth-Century America.* Baltimore, MD: Johns Hopkins University Press, 1988.

Banner, Lois W. "The Bo-Cu Plant: Ruth Benedict and Gender." In Janiewski and Banner, *Reading Benedict/Reading Mead,* 16–32.

———. *Intertwined Lives: Margaret Mead, Ruth Benedict, and Their Circle.* New York: Knopf, 2003.

Barley, Nigel. *Adventures in a Mud Hut: An Innocent Anthropologist Abroad.* New York: Vanguard, 1984.

Barrowclough, Nikki. "Sex, Lies, and Anthropology." *Sydney Morning Herald Magazine,* March 9, 1996, 31–39.

Bateson, Mary Catherine. Letter to the *New York Times,* February 13, 1983, section 4, page 16.

———. *With a Daughter's Eye: A Memoir of Margaret Mead and Gregory Bateson.* New York: William Morrow, 1984.

Beard, Charles A. *An Economic Interpretation of the Constitution of the United States.* New York: Macmillan, 1941.

Bennett, John W. "Classic Anthropology." *American Anthropologist* 100, no. 4 (1998): 951–56.

———. *Classic Anthropology.* New Brunswick, NJ: Transaction Publishers, 1998.

Bernal, Martin. *Black Athena: The Afroasiatic Roots of Classical Civilization.* 3 vols. New Brunswick, NJ: Rutgers University Press, 1987.

Besteman, Catherine, and Hugh Gusterson. "A Response to Matti Bunzl: Public Anthropology, Pragmatism, and Pundits." *American Anthropologist* 110, no. 1 (2008): 61–63.

Blanton, Casey. *Picturing Paradise: Colonial Photography of Samoa, 1875–1925.* Daytona, FL: Daytona Beach Community College, 1995.

Boas, Franz. "Race and Progress." *Science,* July 3, 1931, 1–8.

Borofsky, Robert, ed. *Remembrance of Pacific Pasts: An Invitation to Remake History.* Honolulu: University of Hawai'i Press, 2000.

Borofsky, Robert, with Bruce Albert and others. *Yanomami: The Fierce Controversy and What We Can Learn from It.* Berkeley: University of California Press, 2005.

Boyd, Mary. "The Record in Western Samoa to 1945." In *New Zealand's Record in the Pacific Islands in the Twentieth Century,* edited by A. Ross, 115–88. London: Longman Paul, 1969.

Brady, Ivan. Introduction to the section "Speaking in the Name of the Real: Freeman and Mead on Samoa." *American Anthropologist* 85, no. 4 (1983): 908–9.

Brown, Donald E. *Human Universals.* Philadelphia: Temple University Press, 1991.

Brown, Robert E. *Charles Beard and the Constitution: A Critical Analysis of "An Economic Interpretation of the Constitution."* Princeton, NJ: Princeton University Press, 1956.

Buikstra, Jane. "Anthropology's Image: Our Challenge in the '90s." *Anthropology Newsletter* 31, 89th annual meeting edition (1990): 1.

Bunzl, Matti. "The Quest for Anthropological Relevance: Borgesian Maps and Epistemological Pitfalls." *American Anthropologist* 110, no. 1 (2008): 53–60.

————. "A Reply to Besteman and Gusterson: Swinging the Pendulum." *American Anthropologist* 110, no. 1 (2008): 64–65.

Buss, David. "Human Nature and Culture: An Evolutionary Psychological Perspective." *Journal of Personality* 69 (2001): 955–78.

Caffrey, Margaret M., and Patricia A. Francis, eds. *To Cherish the Life of the World: Selected Letters of Margaret Mead.* New York: Basic Books, 2006.

Calkins, Fay. *My Samoan Chief.* Honolulu: University of Hawai'i Press, 1962.

Carpenter, Laura M. *Virginity Lost: An Intimate Portrait of First Sexual Experiences.* New York: New York University Press, 2005.

Cassidy, Robert. *Margaret Mead: A Voice for the Century.* New York: Universe Books, 1982.

Caton, Hiram. "Conversion in Sarawak: Derek Freeman's Awakening to a New Anthropology." *GlobalAnthro Journal,* January 19, 2006. http://www.anthroglobe.info/docs/conversion_sarawak.htm.

————. "The Exalted Self: Derek Freeman's Quest for the Perfect Identity." *Identity: An International Journal of Theory and Research* 5, no. 4 (2005): 359–83.

————. "The Mead/Freeman Controversy Is Over: A Retrospect." In Côté, "The Mead-Freeman Controversy in Review," 587–606.

————, ed. *The Samoa Reader: Anthropologists Take Stock.* Lanham, MD: University Press of America, 1990.

————, ed. "Talking to a Heretic: Interviews with John Derek Freeman," 2002. Unpublished manuscript, School of the Humanities, Griffith University, Brisbane, Australia.

————. "What the Fighting Was About." In Caton, *Samoa Reader,* 208.

Chappell, David A. "The Forgotten *Mau:* Anti-Navy Protest in American Samoa, 1920–1935." *Pacific Historical Review* 69, no. 2 (2000): 217–60.

Chassler, Sey. "Afterword: Margaret Mead 1901–1978." In *Margaret Mead: Some Personal Views,* edited by Rhoda Metraux, 279–82. New York: Walker, 1979.

Clifford, James. "On Ethnographic Allegory." In *Writing Culture: The Poetics and Politics of Ethnography,* edited by J. Clifford and G. E. Marcus, 98–121. Berkeley: University of California Press, 1986.

Côté, James E. *Adolescent Storm and Stress: An Evaluation of the Mead-Freeman Controversy.* Hillsdale, NJ: Lawrence Erlbaum Associates, 1994.

————. "The Correspondence Associated with Margaret Mead's Samoa Research: What Does It Really Tell Us?" *Pacific Studies* 28, nos. 3–4 (2005): 60–73.

————. "The Implausibility of Freeman's Hoaxing Hypothesis: An Update." *Journal of Youth and Adolescence* 29, no. 5 (2000): 575–85.

————, ed. "The Mead-Freeman Controversy in Review." Special issue, *Journal of Youth and Adolescence* 29, no. 5 (2000).

————. "Much Ado about Nothing: The 'Fateful Hoaxing' of Margaret Mead." *Skeptical Inquirer* 22, no. 6 (1998): 29–34.

————. "Some Tempest! Some Teapot!" *Academic Questions* 8, no. 1 (1995): 5–6.

————. "Was *Coming of Age in Samoa* Based on a 'Fateful Hoaxing'? A Close Look at Freeman's Claim Based on the Mead-Boas Correspondence." *Current Anthropology* 41, no. 4 (2000): 617–20.

————. "Was Mead Wrong about Coming of Age in Samoa? An Analysis of the Mead/Freeman Controversy for Scholars of Adolescence and Human Development." *Journal of Youth and Adolescence* 21, no. 5 (1992): 499–527.

Cox, Paul Alan. *Nafanua: Saving the Samoan Rainforest*. New York: W. H. Freeman, 1997.

———. Review of *Margaret Mead and Samoa: The Making and Unmaking of an Anthropological Myth*. *American Scientist* 71, no. 4 (1983): 407.

Cressman, Luther Sheeleigh. *A Golden Journey: Memoirs of an Archaeologist*. Salt Lake City: University of Utah Press, 1988.

Critchfield, Richard. *Villages*. Garden City, NY: Anchor Press/Doubleday, 1981.

Curtis, Wayne. "Tiki." *American Heritage*, August–September 2006, 38–46.

Daly, Martin, and Margo Wilson. *Homicide*. Hawthorne, NY: Aldine, 1988.

Davidson, James W. *Samoa mo Samoa: The Emergence of the Independent State of Western Samoa*. Melbourne: Oxford University Press, 1967.

Daws, A. Gavan. "The Great Samoan Awakening of 1839." *Journal of the Polynesian Society* 70 (1961): 326–37.

Degler, Carl N. *In Search of Human Nature: The Decline and Revival of Darwinism in American Social Thought*. New York: Oxford University Press, 1991.

Dembart, Lee. "Attack on Anthropologist Mead Affords Insight into Science." *Los Angeles Times*, February 24, 1983, 26.

Diamond, Jared. *Collapse: How Societies Choose to Fail or Succeed*. New York: Viking, 2005.

———. *Guns, Germs, and Steel: The Fates of Human Societies*. New York. W. W. Norton, 1997.

di Leonardo, Micaela. *Exotics at Home: Anthropologies, Others, American Modernity*. Chicago: University of Chicago Press, 1998.

———. "Margaret Mead vs. Tony Soprano: Feminist Anthropology Fights for Public Voice in the New Millennium." *Nation* 272, no.20 (May 21, 2000): 26–32.

Dillon, Wilton. "Margaret Mead and Government." *American Anthropologist* 82, no. 2 (1980): 319–39.

Dolgoy, Reevan. "The Search for Recognition and Social Movement Emergence: Towards an Understanding of the Transformation of the Fa'afafine of Samoa." Ph.D. dissertation, University of Alberta, 2000.

Donahue, Phil. *The Human Animal*. New York: Simon and Schuster, 1985.

Editors of Time-Life Books. *This Fabulous Century: 1920–1930*. New York: Time-Life Books, 1969.

EDK Associates. Telephone survey. *Redbook*, November 1994, 36.

Ehrenreich, B., and J. McIntosh. "The New Creationism: Biology under Attack." *Nation* 264, no. 22 (June 9, 1997): 11–16.

Ellison, Peter T. Review of *Margaret Mead and Samoa: The Making and Unmaking of an Anthropological Myth*. *Ethology and Sociobiology* 5 (1984): 69–70.

Feinberg, Richard. "Margaret Mead and Samoa: *Coming of Age* in Fact and Fiction." *American Anthropologist* 90, no. 3 (1988): 656–63.

Field, Michael J. *Mau: Samoa's Struggle against New Zealand Oppression*. Wellington, New Zealand: A. H. and A. W. Reed, 1984.

Fields, Cheryl M. "Controversial Book Spurs Scholars' Defense of the Legacy of Margaret Mead." *Chronicle of Higher Education*, May 11, 1983, 27–28.

Figiel, Sia. *Where We Once Belonged*. Auckland: Pasifika Press, 1996.

Firth, Raymond. "Social Organization and Social Change." In *Essays on Social Organization and Values*, edited by R. Firth, 30–58. London: Athlone Press, 1964.

———. *We the Tikopia: A Sociological Study of Kinship in Primitive Polynesia*. London: George Allen & Unwin, 1936.

Firth, Rosemary. Review of *Margaret Mead and Samoa: The Making and Unmaking of an Anthropological Myth. RAIN*, no. 57 (August 1983): 11–12.

Flaherty, Frances Hubbard. "Behind the Scenes with Our Samoan Stars: The Trials and Tribulations of Casting a Typical Samoan Family." *Asia* 25 (September 1925): 746–53, 795–96.

———. "Setting Up House and Shop in Samoa: The Struggle to Find Screen Material in the Lyric Beauty of Polynesian Life." *Asia* 25 (August 1925): 638–51, 709–11.

Foerstel, Lenora, and Angela Gilliam, eds. *Confronting the Margaret Mead Legacy: Scholarship, Empire, and the South Pacific.* Philadelphia: Temple University Press, 1992.

Folsom, Joseph Kirk. *The Family: Its Sociology and Social Psychiatry.* New York: Wiley, 1934.

Fox, Robin. "A Life in Anthropology." *Anthropology News* 46, no. 1 (2005): 7.

———. *Participant Observer: Memoir of a Transatlantic Life.* New Brunswick, NJ: Transaction Publishers, 2004.

Francis, Patricia A. "Margaret Mead and Psychology: The Education of an Anthropologist." *Pacific Studies* 28, no.3/4 (2005): 74–90.

———. "'Something to Think With': Mead, Psychology, and the Road to Samoa." Paper prepared for the Annual Meeting of the Association for Social Anthropology in Oceania, Miami, February 16, 2001.

Fraser, Laura. "Where Boys Grow Up to Be Girls." *Marie Claire* 12, no. 12 (December 2002): 72–80.

Freeman, Derek. "All Made of Fantasy: A Rejoinder to Paul Shankman." *American Anthropologist* 100, no. 4 (1988): 972–77.

———. "The Anthropology of Choice: An ANZAAS Presidential Address given in Auckland, New Zealand, on 24 January, 1979." *Canberra Anthropology* 4, no. 1 (1981): 82–100. Reprinted in Freeman, *Dilthey's Dream*, 21–39.

———. "Aztec Abomination at the ANU." *Canberra Times*, September 21, 1979, 2.

———. "The Case against Margaret Mead." *Discover*, April 1983, 33–37.

———. "Controversy: Derek Freeman Replies to Paul Shankman." *Skeptic* 21, no. 1 (2001): 64–66.

———. "Culture and Human Nature: The Analysis of an Anthropological Myth." Unpublished manuscript, 1971. Mandeville Special Collections Library, Geisel Library, University of California, San Diego. http://orpheus.ucsd.edu/speccoll/testing/html/mss0522a.html.

———. "The Debate, at Heart, Is about Evolution." In *The Certainty of Doubt: Tributes to Peter Munz,* edited by Miles Fairburn, 180–202. Wellington, New Zealand: Victoria University Press, 1996.

———. Derek Freeman Papers, 1940–2001. Mandeville Special Collections Library, Geisel Library, University of California, San Diego. http://orpheus.ucsd.edu/speccoll/testing/html/mss0522a.html.

———. *Dilthey's Dream: Essays on Human Nature and Culture.* Canberra: Pandanus Books, 2001.

———. "Everything's Got a Moral . . ." *Pacific Islands Monthly,* July 1983, 7.

———. "Fa'apua'a Fa'amū and Margaret Mead." *American Anthropologist* 91, no. 4 (1989): 1017–22.

———. *The Fateful Hoaxing of Margaret Mead: A Historical Analysis of Her Samoan Research.* Boulder: Westview Press, 1999.

———. "Human Nature and Culture." In Freeman, *Dilthey's Dream,* 1–19.

———. "Inductivism and the Test of Truth: A Rejoinder to Lowell D. Holmes and Others." *Canberra Anthropology* 6, no. 2 (1983): 101–92.

———. "In Praise of Heresy." In Freeman, *Dilthey's Dream,* 79–92.

———. "Letters: Margaret Mead in Samoa." *Science,* July 2, 1999, 47.

———. *Margaret Mead and the Heretic: The Making and Unmaking of an Anthropological Myth.* Ringwood, Australia: Penguin Books, 1996. Australian republication of *Margaret Mead and Samoa.*

———. *Margaret Mead and Samoa: The Making and Unmaking of an Anthropological Myth.* Cambridge, MA: Harvard University Press, 1983.

———. "Margaret Mead's *Coming of Age in Samoa* and Boasian Culturalism: An Historical Analysis." In Freeman, *Dilthey's Dream,* 93–112.

———. "Mead/Freeman Debate Continues." *Pacific Islands Monthly,* July 1987, 43–44.

———. "On Believing as Many as Six Impossible Things before Breakfast." Unpublished manuscript, 1968. Mandeville Special Collections Library, Geisel Library, University of California, San Diego. http://orpheus.ucsd.edu/speccoll/testing/html/msso522a.html.

———. *On the Concept of the Kindred: Curl Bequest Prize Essay, 1960.* Indianapolis: Bobbs-Merrill, 1961.

———. "On the Ethics of Skeptical Inquiry." *Skeptical Inquirer* 23, no. 3 (1999): 60–61.

———. "On Franz Boas and the Samoan Researches of Margaret Mead." *Current Anthropology* 32, no. 3 (1991): 322–29.

———. "Open Letter to the President and Board of the American Anthropological Association." *Anthropology Newsletter,* no. 2 (February 1985): 2, 7.

———. "'O Rose Thou Art Sick!' A Rejoinder to Weiner, Schwartz, Holmes, Shore, and Silverman." *American Anthropologist* 86, no. 2 (1984): 400–405.

———. "Paradigms in Collision: The Far-Reaching Controversy over the Samoan Researches of Margaret Mead and Its Significance for the Human Sciences." *Academic Questions* 5, no. 3 (1992): 23–33.

———. "Paradigms in Collision: Margaret Mead's Mistake and What It Has Done to Anthropology." *Skeptic* 5, no. 3 (1997): 66–73.

———. "Professor Freeman Responds." *Academic Questions* 8, no. 1 (1994–95): 6–7.

———. "The Question of Questions: T. H. Huxley, Evolution by Natural Selection, and Buddhism." Lecture given under the auspices of the Institute for the Humanities at Simon Frazer University, British Columbia, Canada, March 19, 1990. In Freeman, *Dilthey's Dream,* 61–78.

———. "Rejoinder to Patience and Smith." *American Anthropologist* 88, no. 1 (1986): 162–67.

———. "Reply." *Current Anthropology* 41, no. 4 (2000): 620–22.

———. "A Reply to Ember's Reflections on the Freeman-Mead Controversy." *American Anthropologist* 87, no. 4 (1985): 910–17.

———. "Response to Reyman and Hammond." *American Anthropologist* 87, no. 3 (1985): 394–95.

———. Review of *Quest for the Real Samoa: The Mead/Freeman Controversy and Beyond,* by Lowell D. Holmes. *Journal of the Polynesian Society* 96 (1987): 392–95.

———. "Samoa and Margaret Mead: A Rejoinder to Paula Brown Glick and Rosemary Firth." *RAIN* 60 (February 1984): 6–8.

————. "*Social Organization of Manu'a* by Margaret Mead: Some *Errata.*" *Journal of the Polynesian Society* 81 (1972): 70–78.

————. "The Social Structure of a Samoan Village Community." Postgraduate diploma thesis in anthropology, London School of Economics, 1948. Mandeville Special Collections Library, Geisel Library, University of California, San Diego. Reprinted as *The Social Structure of a Samoan Village Community,* edited and introduced by Peter Hempenstall. Canberra: Target Oceania, 2006.

————. "Sociobiology: The 'Antidiscipline' of Anthropology." In *Sociobiology Examined,* edited by A. Montagu, 198–219. New York: Oxford University Press, 1980.

————. "Some Observations on Kinship and Political Organization in Samoa." *American Anthropologist* 66, no. 3 (1964): 553–68.

————. "There's Tricks i' th' World: An Historical Analysis of the Samoan Researches of Margaret Mead." *Visual Anthropology Review* 7, no. 1 (1991): 103–28.

————. "21st Century Boasian Culturalism." *Anthropology News,* May 2000, 4.

————. "Was Margaret Mead Misled or Did She Mislead on Samoa?" *Current Anthropology* 41, no. 4 (2000): 609–14.

Freking, Kevin. "2003 Study: Abstinence Students No More Likely to Abstain." *Boulder Daily Camera,* April 14, 2007, 12A.

Friedan, Betty. *The Feminine Mystique.* New York: Dell, 1963.

Furnas, J. C. *Anatomy of Paradise.* New York: William Sloane Associates, 1937.

Gardner, Martin. "Margaret Mead's Great Samoan Hoax." In *Weird Water and Fuzzy Logic: More Notes of a Fringe Watcher,* 38–50. Amherst, NY: Prometheus Books, 1996.

————. *The New Age: Notes of a Fringe Watcher.* Buffalo, NY: Prometheus Books, 1988.

Gartenstein, Larry. "Sex, Lies, Margaret Mead, and Samoa." *Geo* 13, no. 2 (1991): 16–23.

Gerber, Eleanor. "The Cultural Patterning of Emotions in Samoa." Ph.D. dissertation, University of California, San Diego, 1975.

Ghiglieri, Michael P. *The Dark Side of Man: Tracing the Origins of Male Violence.* Reading, MA: Perseus Books, 1999.

Gilson, Richard Phillip. *Samoa 1830–1900: The Politics of a Multi-Cultural Community.* Melbourne: Oxford University Press, 1970.

Goldie, Peter. "Presentation of Aztec Stone Proceeds Peacefully." *Canberra Times,* September 22, 1979, 2.

Goldman, Irving. *Ancient Polynesian Society.* Chicago: University of Chicago Press, 1970.

Goldstein, Donna M. *Laughter out of Place: Race, Class, Violence, and Sexuality in a Rio Shantytown.* Berkeley: University of California Press, 2003.

Goodenough, Ward. "Margaret Mead and Cultural Anthropology." *Science,* May 27, 1983, 906–8.

Goodman, Ellen. "Muckraking the Mead Legend." *Boston Globe,* May 26, 1983, op-ed page.

Goodman, Richard. *Mead's "Coming of Age in Samoa": A Dissenting View.* Oakland, CA: Pipperine Press, 1983.

————. "Something's Rotten in Anthropology." In Caton, *Samoa Reader,* 274.

Gordan, Joan, ed. *Margaret Mead: The Complete Bibliography 1925–1975.* The Hague: Mouton, 1976.

Grant, Nicole J. "From Margaret Mead's Field Notes: What Counted as 'Sex' in Samoa?" *American Anthropologist* 97, no. 4 (1995): 678–82.

Grosskurth, Phyllis. *Margaret Mead: A Life of Controversy.* London: Penguin Books, 1988.

Handler, Richard. *Critics against Culture: Anthropological Observers of Mass Society.* Madison: University of Wisconsin Press, 2005.

Harris, Marvin. "Margaret and the Giant-Killer." *Sciences* 23, no. 4 (1983): 18–21.

——. *The Rise of Anthropological Theory.* New York: Crowell, 1968.

——. "The Sleep-Crawling Question." *Psychology Today* (May 1983): 24–27.

Harris, T. George, and Margaret Mead. "A Conversation with Margaret Mead and T. George Harris on the Anthropological Age." *Psychology Today* 4, no. 2 (July 1970): 59–76.

Hays, T. E. "Sacred Texts and Introductory Texts: The Case of Mead's Samoa." *Pacific Studies* 20 (1997): 81–103.

Heimann, Judith M. *The Most Offending Soul Alive: Tom Harrisson and His Remarkable Life.* Honolulu: University of Hawai'i Press, 1998.

Heimans, Frank. "Recorded Interview with Derek Freeman, February 12, 2001." Transcript, Oral History Section, National Library of Australia.

Hellman, Hal. *Great Feuds in Science: Ten of the Liveliest Disputes Ever.* New York: Wiley, 1998.

Hempenstall, Peter. Introduction to *The Social Structure of a Samoan Village Community,* by Derek Freeman, xi–xxv. Canberra: Target Oceania, 2006.

Henrie, Marc C., Winfield J. C. Myers, and Jeffrey O. Nelson, eds. "The Fifty Worst (and Best) Books of the Century." *Intercollegiate Review,* Fall 1999, 3–13.

Hereniko, Vilsoni. "Indigenous Knowledge and Academic Imperialism." In *Remembrance of Pacific Pasts: An Invitation to Remake History,* edited by Robert Borofsky, 78–91. Honolulu: University of Hawai'i Press, 2000.

Herzog, Dagmar. *Sex in Crisis: The New Sexual Revolution and the Future of American Politics.* New York: Basic Books, 2008.

Hofferth, Sandra L., Joan R. Kahn, and Wendy Baldwin. "Premarital Sexual Activity among U.S. Teenage Women over the Past Three Decades." *Family Planning Perspectives* 19, no. 2 (1987): 46–53.

Holmes, Lowell D. *Quest for the Real Samoa: The Mead/Freeman Controversy and Beyond.* South Hadley, MA: Bergin and Garvey, 1987.

——. "The Restudy of Manu'an Culture: A Problem in Methodology." Ph.D. dissertation, Northwestern University, Evanston, IL, 1957.

——. Review of *Moana,* directed by Robert Flaherty. *American Anthropologist* 81, no. 3 (1979): 734–36.

——. *Samoan Village.* New York: Holt, Rinehart and Winston, 1974.

——. "A Tale of Two Studies." *American Anthropologist* 85, no. 4 (1983): 929–35.

——. *Ta'ū: Stability and Change in a Samoan Village.* Wellington, New Zealand: Polynesia Society, 1958.

Holmes, Lowell D., and Derek Freeman. "From the Holmes-Freeman Correspondence." In Caton, *Samoa Reader,* 315–22.

Holmes, Lowell D., and Ellen Rhoads Holmes. *Samoan Village Then and Now.* 2nd ed. Fort Worth: Harcourt Brace Jovanovich, 1992.

Horwitz, Tony. *Blue Latitudes.* New York: Picador, 2002.

Howard, Jane. "Angry Storm over the South Seas of Margaret Mead." *Smithsonian* 14, no. 1 (1983): 66–75.

——. *Margaret Mead: A Life.* New York: Fawcett Crest, 1984.

Hsu, F. L. K. "Margaret Mead and Psychological Anthropology." *American Anthropologist* 82, no. 2 (1980): 349–53.

Hua, Cai. *A Society without Husbands or Fathers: The Na of China.* Translated by Asti Hustvedt. New York: Zone Books.

Hulbert, Ann. *Raising America: Experts, Parents, and a Century of Advice about Children.* New York: Alfred A. Knopf, 2003.

Human Events.com. "Ten Most Harmful Books of the 19th and 20th Centuries." Posted May 31, 2005, and updated June 15, 2005. http://www.humanevents.com/article.php?print=yes&id=7591.

Huntsman, Judith. "A Myth Dismissed." *New Zealand Listener* (Wellington), August 20, 1983, 83–84.

"I Let These Words Guide Me." *Parade,* June 18, 2003, 17–18.

Janes, Craig. *Migration, Social Change, and Health: A Samoan Community in Urban California.* Stanford, CA: Stanford University Press, 1990.

Janiewski, Dolores, and Lois W. Banner, eds. *Reading Benedict/Reading Mead: Feminism, Race, and Imperial Visions.* Baltimore, MD: Johns Hopkins University Press, 2004.

Jaroff, Leon. "Margaret Mead." *Time,* March 29, 1999, 183.

Johnson, Mary Elizabeth. "Polynesian Culture." *Saturday Review of Literature,* March 16, 1929, 778.

Kaiser Family Foundation and *Seventeen* magazine. "*SexSmarts* Survey: Virginity and the First Time." Survey released October 9, 2003. http://www.kff.org/entpartnerships/3368-index.cfm.

Keesing, Felix M. "The Taupo System of Samoa: A Study of Institutional Change." *Oceania* 8, no. 1 (1937): 1–14.

Kernahan, Mel. *White Savages in the South Seas.* New York: Verso, 1995.

Klassen, Albert D., Colin J. Williams, and Eugene E. Levitt. *Sex and Morality in the U.S.: An Empirical Enquiry under the Auspices of the Kinsey Institute.* Middletown, CT: Wesleyan University Press, 1989.

Konner, Melvin. "Bursting a South-Sea Bubble." *Nature* 398 (1999): 117–18.

Krämer, Augustin. *Hawaii, Ostmikronesien und Samoa.* Stuttgart: Strecker & Shroeder, 1972.

———. *Die Samoa-inseln.* Stuttgart: E. Schweizerbart, 1902. Translated by Theodore Verhaaren as *The Samoa Islands: An Outline of a Monograph with Particular Consideration of German Samoa,* vol. 1, *Constitution, Pedigrees and Traditions* (Honolulu: University of Hawai'i Press, 1994).

Kristof, Nicholas D. "The Texas Governor: Ally of an Older Generation Embraced Trusted Values amid the Tumult of the 60's." *New York Times,* June 19, 2000, 1, 14.

Kroeber, Alfred. Review of *Growing Up in New Guinea. American Anthropologist* 33, no. 2 (1931): 248–50.

Lapsley, Hilary. *Margaret Mead and Ruth Benedict: The Kinship of Women.* Amherst: University of Massachusetts Press, 1999.

Lefkowitz, Mary R. *History Lesson: A Race Odyssey.* New Haven, CT: Yale University Press, 2008.

———. *Not out of Africa: How Afrocentrism Became an Excuse to Teach Myth as History.* New York: Basic Books, 1996.

Lelalu, Lelei. Letter to the editor in section titled "The Real Samoa." *Newsweek,* February 28, 1983, 8.

Leo, John. "The Revolution Is Over." *Time,* April 9, 1984.

Lepowsky, Maria. *Fruit of the Motherland: Gender in an Egalitarian Society.* New York: Columbia University Press, 1994.

Levine, Elana. *Wallowing in Sex: The New Sexual Culture of 1970s American Television.* Durham, NC: Duke University Press, 2007.

LeVine, Robert A. *Culture, Behavior, and Personality.* Chicago: Aldine, 1973.

Levy, Robert I. *Tahitians: Mind and Experience in the Society Islands.* Chicago: University of Chicago Press, 1973.

Lewis, Herbert. "Boas, Darwin, Science, and Anthropology." *Current Anthropology* 42, no. 3 (2001): 381–406.

Linton, Ralph. Review of *Social Organization of Manu'a. American Anthropologist* 34, no. 1 (1932): 155–58.

Lowie, Robert. Review of *Coming of Age in Samoa. American Anthropologist* 31, no. 3 (1929): 532–34.

Lutkehaus, Nancy C. "American Icon." *Natural History* 110, no. 10 (2001–2): 14–17.

———. *Margaret Mead: The Making of an American Icon.* Princeton, NJ: Princeton University Press, 2008.

———. "Margaret Mead and the 'Rustling-of-the-Wind-in-the-Palm Trees School' of Ethnographic Writing." In *Women Writing Culture,* edited by R. Behar and D. A. Gordon, 186–206. Berkeley: University of California Press, 1995.

Lynd, Robert Staughton, and Helen Merrell Lynd. *Middletown: A Study in American Culture.* New York: Harcourt, Brace, 1929.

———. *Middletown in Transition: A Study in Cultural Conflicts.* New York: Harcourt, Brace, 1937.

Macpherson, Cluny, and La'avasa Macpherson. "The Ifoga: Valuing Social Honour in Contemporary Samoa." *Journal of the Polynesian Society* 114, no. 2 (2005): 109–34.

———. "Towards an Explanation of Recent Trends in Suicide in Western Samoa." *Man* 22 (1987): 305–27.

Mageo, Jeannette. "Male Transvestism and Cultural Change in Samoa." *American Ethnologist* 19, no. 3 (1992): 443–59.

———. "Spirit Girls and Marines: Possession and Ethnopsychiatry as Historical Discourse in Samoa." *American Ethnologist* 23, no. 1 (1996): 61–82.

Maines, Rachel. *The Technology of Orgasm: "Hysteria," the Vibrator, and Women's Sexual Satisfaction.* Baltimore, MD: Johns Hopkins University Press, 1999.

Malinowski, Bronisław. *Argonauts of the Western Pacific.* London: Routledge, 1922.

———. *The Sexual Life of Savages in North-Western Melanesia: An Ethnographic Account of Courtship, Marriage and Family Life among the Natives of the Trobriand Islands, British New Guinea.* London: Routledge, 1929.

Malopa'upo, Isaia. *Coming of Age in American Anthropology: Margaret Mead and Paradise.* Internet book, Upublish.com, 1999. http://www.universal-publishers.com/book.php?method=ISBN&book=1581128452.

Manchester, William. *Goodbye, Darkness: A Memoir of the Pacific War.* Boston: Little, Brown, 1980.

Marcus, George. "One Man's Mead." *New York Times Book Review,* March 27, 1983, 3.

———, and Michael M. J. Fischer. *Anthropology as Cultural Critique: An Experimental Moment in the Human Sciences.* Berkeley: University of California Press, 1986.

"Margaret Mead Today: Mother to the World." *Time,* March 21, 1969. http://www.time.com/time/magazine/article/0,9171,839916-1,00.html.

Marshall, Donald. "Sexual Behavior on Mangaia." In *Human Sexual Behavior,* edited by Robert Suggs and Donald Marshall, 103–62. New York: Basic Books, 1971.

Marshall, Mac. "The Wizard of Oz Meets the Wicked Witch of the East: Mead, Freeman, and Ethnographic Authority." *American Ethnologist* 20, no. 3 (1993): 604–17.

Mataʻafa, Fetaui. Letter to the editor in the section titled "The Real Samoa." *Newsweek*, February 28, 1983, 7–8.

Maxwell, Robert. "A Comparison of Field Research in Canada and Polynesia." In *Marginal Natives: Anthropologists at Work*, edited by M. Freilich, 441–84. New York: Harper & Row, 1970.

———. "Samoan Temperament." Thesis, Cornell University, 1969.

McCabe, Mary Margaret. "Grey Matter: Doing Good and Telling the Truth; How Ancient Africa Exposed the Illusions of Black and White." Review of *History Lesson: A Race Odyssey*, by Mary Lefkowitz. *Times Literary Supplement*, July 18, 2008, 3–4.

McDonald, Forrest. *We the People: The Economic Origins of the Constitution*. Chicago: University of Chicago Press, 1958.

McDowell, Edwin. "New Samoa Book Challenges Margaret Mead's Conclusions." In Caton, *Samoa Reader*, 211–16.

McDowell, Nancy. "The Oceanic Ethnography of Margaret Mead." *American Anthropologist* 82 (1980): 278–302.

———. Review of *Margaret Mead and Samoa*. *Pacific Studies* 4 (1984): 99–140.

McKinnon, Susan, and Sydel Silverman, eds. *Complexities: Beyond Nature and Nurture*. Chicago: University of Chicago Press, 2005.

Mead, Margaret. "The Adolescent Girl in Samoa." Report to the National Research Council, 1927. Unpublished manuscript, Library of Congress.

———. "Anthropological Data on the Problem of Instinct." *Psychosomatic Medicine* 4 (1942): 396–97.

———. *Anthropologists and What They Do*. New York: Franklin Watts, 1965.

———. "Anthropology among the Sciences." *American Anthropologist* 63, no. 3 (1961): 475–82.

———. "Apprenticeship under Boas." In *The Anthropology of Franz Boas*, edited by Walter Goldschmidt, 29–45. *American Anthropologist* 61, no. 5, pt. 2. Menasha, WI: American Anthropological Association, 1959.

———. "The Arts in Bali." *Yale Review* 30, no. 2 (1940): 335–47.

———. *Blackberry Winter: My Earlier Years*. New York: Pocket Books, 1975.

———. "*Coming of Age* Defended." In Caton, *Samoa Reader*, 113–18.

———. *Coming of Age in Samoa: A Psychological Study of Primitive Youth for Western Civilisation*. New York: William Morrow & Company, 1928. Reprint, New York: William Morrow & Company, 1973. Facsimile of the 1928 edition with a new author's preface and a foreword by Franz Boas. Page references are to the 1973 edition.

———. *Continuities in Cultural Evolution*. New Haven, CT: Yale University Press, 1964.

———. "Cultural Determinants of Behavior." In *Behavior and Evolution*, edited by Anne Roe and George Gaylord Simpson, 480–503. New Haven, CT: Yale University Press, 1958.

———. *Growing Up in New Guinea: A Comparative Study of Primitive Education*. New York: Morrow, 1930.

———. *An Inquiry into the Question of Cultural Stability in Polynesia*. 1928. Columbia University Contributions to Anthropology, 9. Reprint, New York: AMS Press, 1969.

———. *Letters from the Field, 1925–1975*. New York: Harper & Row, 1977.

———. "Life as a Samoan Girl." In *All True! The Record of Actual Adventures That Have*

Happened to Ten Women of Today, 94–118. New York: Brewer, Warren and Putnam, 1931.

———. *Male and Female: A Study of the Sexes in a Changing World*. New York: William Morrow, 1949.

———. "The Need for Teaching Anthropology in Normal Schools and Teachers' Colleges." *School and Society* 26, no. 667 (1927): 466–69.

———. *New Lives for Old: Cultural Transformation—Manus, 1928–1953*. New York: Morrow, 1956.

———. "On the Implications for Anthropology of the Gesell-Ilg Approach to Maturation." *American Anthropologist* 49, no. 1 (1947): 69–77.

———. "'Progress' Hits Samoa." *Nation* 133, no. 3448 (August 5, 1931): 138–39.

———. "Return to Samoa." *Redbook* 139, no. 3 (July 1972): 29–34.

———. Review of *On Becoming a Kwoma: Teaching and Learning in a New Guinea Tribe*, by John W. H. Whiting. *American Journal of Sociology* 48, no. 6 (1943): 773–74.

———. Review of *Six Cultures: Studies in Child Rearing*, edited by Beatrice Whiting. *American Anthropologist* 66, no. 3, pt. 1 (1964): 658–60.

———. *Sex and Temperament in Three Primitive Societies*. New York: William Morrow, 1935.

———. *Social Organization of Manuʻa*. Bulletin 76. Honolulu: Bernice P. Bishop Museum, 1930.

———. "Towards a Human Science." *Science*, March 5, 1976, 903–9.

Meleiseʻa, Malama. *Lagaga: A Short History of Samoa*. Suva, Fiji: Institute of Pacific Studies, 1987.

———. *The Making of Modern Samoa*. Suva, Fiji: Institute of Pacific Studies, 1987.

———. "The Postmodern Legacy of a Premodern Warrior Goddess in Modern Samoa." In *Voyages and Beaches: Pacific Encounters, 1769–1840*, edited by Alex Calder, Jonathan Lamb, and Bridget Orr, 55–60. Honolulu: University of Hawaiʻi Press, 2000.

Michener, James. *The World Is My Home: A Memoir*. New York: Random House, 1991.

Millay, Edna St. Vincent. *A Few Figs from Thistles: Poems and Sonnets*. New York: Harper, 1922.

Milner, George B. *Samoan Dictionary: Samoan-English, English-Samoan*. London: Oxford University Press, 1966.

Mitchell, W. E. "Communicating Culture: Margaret Mend and the Practice of Popular Anthropology." In *Popularizing Anthropology*, edited by J. MacClancy and C. McDonaugh, 122–35. New York: Routledge, 1996.

Modell, John. *Into One's Own: From Youth to Adulthood in the United States, 1920–1975*. Berkeley: University of California Press, 1989.

Molloy, Maureen. "Margaret Mead, the Samoan Girl and the Flapper." In Janiewski and Banner, *Reading Benedict/Reading Mead*, 33–47.

———. *On Creating a Usable Culture: Margaret Mead and the Emergence of American Cosmopolitanism*. Honolulu: University of Hawaiʻi Press, 2007.

Monaghan, Peter. "Archival Analysis: An Australian Historian Puts Margaret Mead's Biggest Critic on the Psychoanalytic Sofa." *Chronicle of Higher Education*, January 13, 2006, A14.

———. "Fantasy Island." *Lingua Franca*, July–August 1996, 7–8.

Morell, Virginia. "Anthropology: Nature-Nurture Battleground." *Science*, September 24, 1993, 1798–1802.

Moriarty, Florence, ed. *True Confessions: Sixty Years of Sin, Suffering and Sorrow.* New York: Fireside, 1979.

Mosse, George L. *Nazi Culture: A Documentary History.* New York: Pantheon Books, 1966.

Moyle, Richard. "Sexuality in Samoan Art Forms." *Archives of Sexual Behavior* 4, no. 3 (1975): 227–47.

Murray, Rev. A. W. *Forty Years' Missionary Work in Polynesia and New Guinea from 1835 to 1875.* London: James Nisbet, 1876.

Murray, Stephen O. "On Boasians and Margaret Mead: Reply to Freeman." *Current Anthropology* 32, no. 4 (1991): 448–52.

Murray, Stephen O., and Regna Darnell. "Margaret Mead and Paradigm Shifts within Anthropology during the 1920s." In Côté, "The Mead-Freeman Controversy in Review," 557–73.

Nardi, Bonnie. "The Height of Her Powers: Margaret Mead's Samoa." *Feminist Studies* 10, no. 2 (1984): 323–37.

Newton, Esther. *Margaret Mead Made Me Gay: Personal Essays, Public Ideas.* Durham, NC: Duke University Press, 2000.

Nordström, Alison Devine. "Early Photography in Samoa: Marketing Stereotypes of Paradise." *History of Photography* 15, no. 4 (1991): 272–86.

———. "Paradise Recycled: Photographs of Samoa in Changing Contexts." *Exposure* 28, no. 3 (1991–92): 8–15.

———. "Wood Nymphs and Patriots: Depictions of Samoans in the *National Geographic* Magazine." *Visual Sociology* 7, no. 2 (1992): 49–59.

O'Brien, Frederick. *Atolls of the Sun.* New York: Century, 1922.

———. "The Lure of the South Seas." *Mentor,* February 1, 1922, 7–16.

———. *Mystic Isles of the South Seas.* New York: Century, 1921.

———. *White Shadows in the South Seas.* New York: Century, 1919.

O'Brien, Patty. *The Pacific Muse: Exotic Femininity and the Colonial Pacific.* Seattle: University of Washington Press, 2006.

O'Meara, J. Tim. *Samoan Planters: Tradition and Economic Development in Polynesia.* Fort Worth: Holt, Rinehart and Winston, 1990.

Orans, Martin. "Hoaxing, Polemics, and Science." *Current Anthropology* 41, no. 4 (2000): 615–16.

———. "Mead Misrepresented." *Science,* March 12, 1999, 1649–50.

———. *Not Even Wrong: Margaret Mead, Derek Freeman, and the Samoans.* Novato, CA: Chandler and Sharp, 1996.

———. "Who's Talking about Intercourse?" *Anthropology Newsletter,* March 1996, 2, 4.

Ortner, Sherry B. "Gender and Sexuality in Hierarchical Societies: The Case of Polynesia and Some Comparative Implications." In *Sexual Meanings: The Cultural Construction of Gender and Sexuality,* edited by Sherry B. Ortner and Harriet Whitehead, 359–409. New York: Cambridge University Press, 1982.

Otterbein, Keith. "A Cross-Cultural Study of Rape." *Aggressive Behavior* 5, no. 4 (1979): 425–35.

Owen, Elizabeth. "Samoa: An Uproar over Sex and Violence in Margaret Mead's Idyllic Isles." *Life,* May 1983, 32–40.

Peiss, Kathy. "'Charity Girls' and City Pleasures: Historical Notes on Working-Class Sexuality, 1880–1920." In *Powers of Desire: The Politics of Sexuality,* edited by Ann

Snitow, Christine Stansell, and Sharon Thompson, 74–87. New York: Monthly Review Press, 1983.

Petersen, James R. *The Century of Sex: Playboy's History of the Sexual Revolution: 1900–1999.* New York: Grove Press, 1999.

Pinker, Steven. *The Blank Slate: The Modern Denial of Human Nature.* New York: Viking, 2002.

———. *How the Mind Works.* New York: Norton, 1997.

Poignant, Robin. *Professional Savages: Captive Lives and Western Spectacle.* New Haven, CT: Yale University Press, 2004.

Price, David Andrew. "Coming a Cropper in Samoa." *Wall Street Journal,* March 3, 1999, A17.

Price, David H. *Anthropological Intelligence: The Deployment and Neglect of American Anthropology in the Second World War.* Durham, NC: Duke University Press, 2008.

Pritchard, William T. *Polynesian Reminiscences.* London: Chapman and Hall, 1866.

Rappaport, Roy. Letter to the editors. *Scientific American* 256 (1987): 6–7.

Raybeck, Douglas. *Mad Dogs, Englishmen, and the Errant Anthropologist: Fieldwork in Malaysia.* Prospect Heights, IL: Waveland Press, 1996.

Redfield, Robert. Review of *Coming of Age in Samoa. American Journal of Sociology* 34, no. 4 (1929): 728–30.

———. Review of *Social Organization of Manu'a. American Journal of Sociology* 37, no. 3 (1931): 511–12.

Ridley, Matt. *Genome: The Autobiography of a Species in 23 Chapters.* New York: HarperCollins, 1999.

———. *Nature via Nurture: Genes, Experience, and What Makes Us Human.* New York: HarperCollins, 2003.

———. *The Origins of Virtue: Human Instincts and the Evolution of Cooperation.* New York: Penguin, 1996.

———. *The Red Queen: Sex and the Evolution of Human Nature.* New York: Maxwell Macmillan International, 1994.

Robin, Ron. *Scandals and Scoundrels: Seven Cases That Shook the Academy.* Berkeley: University of California Press, 2004.

Romanucci-Ross, Lola. "Mead Recognizes Her Error." In Caton, *Samoa Reader,* 323.

Rosenblatt, P. "Grief and Mourning." In *Encyclopedia of Cultural Anthropology,* edited by Daniel Levinson and Melvin Ember, 548–49. New York: Henry Holt, 1996.

Rubin, Lillian. *Erotic Wars: What Happened to the Sexual Revolution?* New York: Farrar, Straus & Giroux, 1990.

Rusher, William. "Margaret Mead: Her Facts are Suspect." *Rocky Mountain News,* February 16, 1983, 49.

Sahlins, Marshall. "Cannibalism: An Exchange." *New York Review of Books,* March 22, 1979, 46–47.

———. *The Use and Abuse of Biology: An Anthropological Critique of Sociobiology.* Ann Arbor: University of Michigan Press, 1976.

Sanday, P. "The Sociocultural Context of Rape: A Cross-Cultural Study." *Journal of Social Issues* 37, no. 4 (1981): 5–27.

Sapir, Edward. "The Discipline of Sex." *American Mercury* 16 (1929): 413–20.

———. "Franz Boas." *New Republic,* January 23, 1929, 278–79.

Schama, Simon. *Dead Certainties: Unwarranted Speculations.* New York: Knopf, 1991.

Scheper-Hughes, Nancy. "The Margaret Mead Controversy: Culture, Biology and Anthropological Inquiry." *Human Organization* 43, no. 1 (1984): 85–93.

Schlegel, Alice. "The Cultural Management of Adolescent Sexuality." In *Sexual Nature/Sexual Culture,* edited by P. R. Abramson and S. D. Pinkerton, 177–94. Chicago: University of Chicago Press, 1995.

———. "Status, Property, and the Value on Virginity." *American Ethnologist* 18, no. 4 (1991): 719–34.

Schlegel, Alice, and Herbert Barry III. *Adolescence: An Anthropological Inquiry.* New York: Free Press, 1991.

Schmidt, Johanna. "Paradise Lost? Social Change and Fa'afafine in Samoa." *Current Sociology* 51, nos. 3–4 (2003): 417–32.

Schneider, David M. "The Coming of a Sage to Samoa." *Natural History* 92, no. 6 (1983): 4–10.

Schoeffel, Penelope. "The Samoan Concept of *Feagaiga* and Its Transformation." In *Tonga and Samoa: Images of Gender and Polity,* edited by J. Huntsman, 85–106. Christchurch, New Zealand: Macmillan Brown Centre for Pacific Studies, 1995.

———. "Sexual Morality in Samoa and Its Historical Transformations." In *A Polymath Anthropologist: Essays in Honour of Ann Chowning,* edited by C. Gross, H. D. Lyons, and D. A. Counts, 63–69. Auckland: Dept. of Anthropology, University of Auckland, 2005.

Schoeffel, Penelope, and Malama Meleise'a. "Margaret Mead, Derek Freeman, and Samoa: The Making, Unmaking, and Remaking of an Anthropological Myth." *Canberra Anthropology* 6, no. 1 (1983): 58–69.

Seidman, Steven. *Romantic Longings: Love in America, 1830–1980.* New York: Routledge, 1991.

Shankman, Paul. "All Things Considered: A Reply to Derek Freeman." *American Anthropologist* 100, no. 4 (1998): 977–79.

———. "Culture, Biology, and Evolution: The Mead-Freeman Controversy Revisited." In Côté, "The Mead-Freeman Controversy in Review," 539–56.

———. "Fear and Loathing in Samoa." *Global Reporter* 1, no. 2 (1983): 12.

———. "The History of Samoan Sexual Conduct and the Mead-Freeman Controversy." *American Anthropologist* 98, no. 3 (1996): 555–67.

———. "Interethnic Unions and the Regulation of Sex in Colonial Samoa, 1830–1945." *Journal of the Polynesian Society* 110, no. 2 (2001): 119–47.

———. "Margaret Mead, Derek Freeman, and the Issue of Evolution." *Skeptical Inquirer* 22, no. 6 (1998): 35–39.

———. "Margaret Mead's Other Samoa: Rereading *Social Organization of Manu'a.*" *Pacific Studies* 28, nos. 3–4 (2005): 46–59.

———. "Requiem for a Controversy: Whatever Happened to Margaret Mead?" *Skeptic* 9, no. 1 (2001): 48–53.

———. "The Samoan Conundrum." *Canberra Anthropology* 6, no. 1 (1983): 38–57.

———. "Sex, Lies, and Anthropologists: Margaret Mead, Derek Freeman, and Samoa." In *Research Frontiers in Anthropology,* vol. 4, *Ethnology, Linguistic Anthropology, the Study of Social Problems,* edited by Carol R. Ember and Melvin Ember, 221–38. Englewood Cliffs, NJ: Prentice Hall, 1994.

———. "Virginity and Veracity: Rereading Historical Sources in the Mead-Freeman Controversy." *Ethnohistory* 53, no. 3 (2006): 479–505.

Shore, Bradd. "Evaluations of *Margaret Mead and Samoa*." In Caton, *Samoa Reader,* 282–85.

———. "Paradox Regained: Freeman's Margaret Mead and Samoa." *American Anthropologist* 85, no. 4 (1983): 935–44.

———. *Sala'ilua: A Samoan Mystery.* New York: Columbia University Press, 1982.

———. "A Samoan Theory of Action: Social Control and Social Order in a Polynesian Paradox." Ph. D. dissertation, University of Chicago, 1977.

———. "Sexuality and Gender in Samoa: Conceptions and Missed Conceptions." In *Sexual Meanings: The Cultural Construction of Gender and Sexuality,* edited by Sherry B. Ortner and Harriet Whitehead, 192–215. New York: Cambridge University Press, 1981.

Shweder, Richard. "Storytelling among the Anthropologists." *New York Times Book Review,* September 21, 1986, 39.

Silverstein, Michael. "Boasian Cosmographic Anthropology and the Sociocentric Component of Mind." In *Significant Others: Interpersonal and Professional Commitments in Anthropology,* edited by Richard Handler, 131–59. Madison: University of Wisconsin Press, 2004.

Simonelli, J., and C. S. Pressman. "Presenting Anthropological Perspectives." *Anthropology Newsletter* 33, no. 3 (1992): 3.

Sinclair, Keith. *Halfway round the Harbour: An Autobiography.* Auckland: Penguin Books, 1993.

Sommers, Christina Hoff. *The War against Boys: How Misguided Feminism Is Harming Our Young Men.* New York: Simon and Schuster, 2000.

Spindler, G. D., ed. *The Making of Psychological Anthropology.* Berkeley: University of California Press, 1978.

Stanner, W. E. H. *The South Seas in Transition.* Sydney: Australian Publishing Company, 1953.

Steinem, Gloria. "The Moral Disarmament of Betty Co-Ed." *Esquire* 58, no. 3 (September 1962): 153–57.

Stevenson, Robert Louis. *A Footnote to History: Eight Years of Trouble in Samoa.* London: Cassell, 1892.

Stocking, George W. "The Ethnographer's Magic: Fieldwork in British Anthropology from Tylor to Malinowski." In *Observers Observed: Essays on Ethnographic Fieldwork,* edited by George W. Stocking, 70–120. Madison: University of Wisconsin Press, 1983.

Stopes, Marie Carmichael. *Married Love: A New Contribution to the Solution of Sex Difficulties.* London: Putnam, 1918.

Stover, Merrily. "Samoan Responses to Margaret Mead." Paper presented at the annual meeting of the Association for Social Anthropology in Oceania, Kauai, Hawai'i, February 2–5, 2005. Unpublished manuscript in author's possession.

Sturma, Michael. *South Sea Maidens: Western Fantasy and Sexual Politics in the South Pacific.* Westport, CT: Greenwood Press, 2002.

Sullivan, Tim. "The Gangs of Zion." *High Country News* 37, no. 14 (2005): 9–17.

Sulloway, Frank J. *Born to Rebel: Birth Order, Family Dynamics, and Creative Lives.* New York: Pantheon, 1996.

Tamasese, Tuiatua Tupua. "The Riddle of Samoan History: The Relevance of Language, Names, Honorifics, Genealogy, Ritual and Chant to Historical Analysis." *Journal of Pacific History* 29, no. 1 (1994): 66–79.

Tcherkézoff, Serge. *"First Contacts" in Polynesia, the Samoan Case (1722–1848): Western Misunderstandings about Sexuality and Divinity.* Jointly published by the Journal of Pacific

History (Canberra, Australia) and the Macmillan Brown Centre for Pacific Studies, Canterbury University, New Zealand, 2004.

———. "Is Anthropology about Individual Agency or Culture? Or Why 'Old Derek' Is Doubly Wrong." *Journal of the Polynesian Society* 110, no. 1 (2001): 59–78.

Theroux, Joseph. "'Coming of Age' at the Eye of a New Scholarly Storm." *Pacific Islands Monthly*, March 1983, 11–16.

Thompson, Sharon. *Going All the Way: Teenage Girls' Tales of Sex, Romance, and Pregnancy.* New York: Hill and Wang, 1995.

Thornhill, R., and C. Palmer. *A Natural History of Rape: The Biological Bases of Sexual Coercion.* Cambridge, MA: MIT Press, 1999.

Tierney, Patrick. *Darkness in El Dorado.* New York: W. W. Norton, 2000.

Tiffany, Sharon W. "Imagining the South Seas: Thoughts on the Sexual Politics of Paradise in Samoa." *Pacific Studies* 24, nos. 3–4 (2001): 19–49.

———. "Narrative, Voice, and Genre in Margaret Mead's *Coming of Age in Samoa.*" Paper presented at the annual meeting of the Association for Social Anthropology in Oceania, Kauai, Hawai'i, February 2–5, 2005.

———. "The Politics of Denominational Organization in Samoa." In *Mission, Church and Sect in Oceania,* edited by J. Boutilier, D. R. Hughes, and S. W. Tiffany, 423–56. ASAO Monograph, 6. Lanham, MD: University Press of America, 1978.

Trumbull, Robert. "Samoan Leader Declares: 'Both Anthropologists Are Wrong.'" *New York Times,* May 24, 1983, 18.

Tupuola, AnnaMarie. "Learning Sexuality: Young Samoan Women." In *Bitter Sweet: Indigenous Women in the Pacific,* edited by Allison Jones, Phyllis Herda, and Tamasailau M. Suaalii, 61–72. Dunedin, NZ: University of Otago Press, 2000.

Turner, Rev. George. *Nineteen Years in Polynesia.* London: John Snow, Paternoster Row, 1888.

Tuzin, Donald. "Derek Freeman (1916–2001)." *American Anthropologist* 104, no. 3 (2002): 1013–15.

———. "Discourse, Intercourse, and the Excluded Middle: Anthropology and the Problem of Sexual Experience." In *Sexual Nature / Sexual Culture,* edited by P. R. Abramson and S. D. Pinkerton, 257–75. Chicago: University of Chicago Press, 1995.

Unasa, L. F. Va'a. "The Mead-Freeman Debate in Retrospect." 2001. Unpublished manuscript in author's possession.

———. "Research Materials: Fa'apua'a Fa'amu Questions and Answers." Derek Freeman Papers, box 146, folder 7, 72 pp., 1988. Mandeville Special Collections Library, Geisel Library, University of California, San Diego.

———. "Research Materials: Fa'apua'a Fa'amu Questions and Answers." Derek Freeman Papers, box 146, folder 9, 75 pp., 1993. Mandeville Special Collections Library, Geisel Library, University of California, San Diego.

Vogt, Evon Z. "Anthropology in the Public Consciousness." In *Yearbook of Anthropology 1955,* edited by William L. Thomas Jr., 357–74. New York: Wenner-Gren Foundation for Anthropological Research, 1955.

von Hoffman, Nicholas, and Garry B. Trudeau. *Tales from the Margaret Mead Taproom.* Kansas City: Sheed and Ward, 1976.

Wallace, Irving. *The Three Sirens: A Novel.* New York: Simon and Schuster, 1963.

Watson, James D. *The Double Helix: A Personal Account of the Discovery of the Structure of DNA.* New York: Atheneum, 1968.

Wedgwood, Camilla H. Review of *Coming of Age in Samoa. Oceania* 1 (1930): 123–25.

Weiner, Annette B. "Ethnographic Determinism: Samoa and the Margaret Mead Controversy." *American Anthropologist* 85, no. 4 (1983): 909–19.

Wendt, Albert. "Three Faces of Samoa: Mead's, Freeman's, and Wendt's." *Pacific Islands Monthly,* April 1983, 10–14, 69.

Wendt, Tuaopepe, and Felix S., with Fay Ala'ilima and Nancy McDowell. Untitled, in Book Review Forum. *Pacific Studies* 7, no. 2 (1984): 91–140.

Wetzsteon, Ross. *Republic of Dreams: Greenwich Village, the American Bohemia, 1910–1960.* New York: Simon and Schuster, 2002.

Whiting, Beatrice, ed. *Six Cultures: Studies in Child Rearing.* New York: Wiley, 1963.

Whiting, John W. M., with V. K. Burbank and M. S. Ratner. "The Duration of Maidenhood across Cultures." In *Culture and Human Development: The Selected Papers of John Whiting,* edited by Eleanor Hollenberg Chasdi, 282–305. Cambridge: Cambridge University Press, 1994.

Wiker, Benjamin. *10 Books That Screwed Up the World: And Five Others That Didn't Help.* Washington, DC: Regnery Publishing, 2008.

Williams, John. *The Samoan Journals of John Williams: 1830 and 1832.* Edited by R. Moyle. Canberra: Australian National University Press, 1984.

Williamson, David. *The Heretic.* Melbourne: Penguin Books, 1996.

Wilson, E. O. *Naturalist.* Washington, DC: Island Press, 1994.

Worthman, Carol M. "Adolescence in the Pacific: A Biosocial View." In *Adolescence in Pacific Island Societies,* edited by G. Herdt and S. C. Leavitt, 27–52. Pittsburgh: University of Pittsburgh Press, 1998.

Wright, Robert. "Feminists, Meet Mr. Darwin." *New Republic,* November 28, 1984, 34–46.

———. *The Moral Animal: The New Science of Evolutionary Psychology.* New York: Pantheon, 1994.

Yans, Virginia. "On the Political Anatomy of Mead-Bashing, or Re-thinking Margaret Mead." In Janiewski and Banner, *Reading Benedict/Reading Mead,* 229–48.

Young, Michael W. *Malinowski: Odyssey of an Anthropologist 1884–1920.* New Haven, CT: Yale University Press, 2004.

INDEX

<Index to come in proof>

The Presidents We Imagine:
Two Centuries of White House Fictions on the Page,
on the Stage, Onscreen, and Online
Jeff Smith

Unsafe for Democracy:
World War I and the U.S. Justice Department's Covert Campaign
to Suppress Dissent
William H. Thomas Jr.